# The Headstones of St. Mary's Abbey The Old Graveyard Duleek, County Meath

Duleek Heritage Group

Copyright © Duleek Heritage Group

First Published in Ireland, in 2013, in co-operation with
Choice Publishing, Drogheda, County Louth, Republic of Ireland
www.choicepublishing.ie

ISBN: 978-1-909154-54-4

All rights reserved. No part of this publication may be reproduced, stored in a retrieval system, transmitted in any form, or by any means, electronic, mechanical, photocopying, recording or otherwise, without the prior permission of the copyright holder.

Printed in Ireland by SPRINT-print Ltd

*Duleek Heritage Group*
*Record, Update and Digitise Headstones in*
*St. Mary's Abbey Duleek*

## Introduction

From 2005 until early 2013 Duleek Heritage Group took on the project of St. Mary's Abbey. The object of this project was to photograph, do some rubbings, code and number headstones, measure the height and width of headstones, transcribe as much of each inscription that was legible at the time of recording from each headstone, digitise this information and make it available on the internet. Our plan was to have all the information transcribed with photographs available on the internet to assist ancestral and genealogy researchers and for the past, present and future people of Duleek.

A local historian, the late Enda O'Boyle, had recorded the inscriptions of St. Mary's Abbey and the plaques in St. Kienan's Church of Ireland church for an issue of Riocht Na Midhe in 2000. Enda had started his project in 1975 and had completed it by 2000. The Duleek Heritage Graveyard Committee are very respectful and in awe of the amount of time and effort that Enda put into his recordings and it is at this point that we would like to extend our gratitude to Enda for his preservation, works and recordings of the old churchyard and of the history of Duleek.

It is one of the aims of Duleek Heritage Group and part of our constitution to preserve historical sites and buildings, to raise awareness and stress the importance of maintaining our local heritage and to promote the diverse rich history of Duleek and to uphold and defend these ideals.

## History of St. Mary's Abbey Duleek

Duleek takes its name from the Irish *daimh liag*, a house of stones, probably referring to Saint Cianán's church, said to have been the first stone-built church in Ireland. It is said Saint Patrick established a bishopric in Duleek circa 450 AD, and Saint Cianán became the first bishop in 489 of St. Patrick. A monastery was built on the site, but it was sacked several times by the Vikings between 830 and 1149. In between those raids, the bodies of Brian Ború and his son Morough lay in state in Duleek in April 1014, on their way from the Battle of Clontarf to their burial place. It is stated that Armagh Cathedral is built upon that burial site.

Duleek was pillaged once again by the Normans in 1171. Soon after, however, in 1182, Lord Hugh de Lacy donated land to the Augustians who founded an abbey here and dedicated it to the Blessed Virgin Mary. The same grounds are shared by the St. Kienan's Church of Ireland which was built in 1816 but is now disused.

The abbey site has two high crosses, the oldest of which is the short High Cross, known as the North Cross and probably dating from the 9th century. The North Cross includes elements of many different Celtic themes, such as knots, spirals and mazes. The west face features a number of figure sculptures, including a crucifixion scene and scenes depicting the early life of the Virgin Mary. Another scene may represent the Holy Family, perhaps the Presentation of Christ in the Temple. On the same face, the top panel depicts an event from the history of the monastery. Adamnan, a monk, visited the tomb of Saint Cianán, and despite warnings touched the saint's body, and subsequently lost an eye. Adamnan fasted in penance and miraculously his eye was restored. The south side of the cross contains a winged creature, while the east face and the sides of the cross have some interesting geometrical designs. The centre of the cross has seven raised spirals believed to represent the dance of heavenly bodies around the sun, centuries before Copernicus developed his theory of the earth revolving around the sun.

A portion of the South Cross can be seen inside the ruins of the abbey church. This sandstone cross head is mounted on a base – not the original – it is 90 cm high x 1.05 m arms span x 20 cm thick. There is roll moulding at the edges, a flat cross panel at the centre of the cross head, and four flat bosses at the ends of the arms.

Two tombs inside the abbey church commemorate the Bellew family, who gave their name to neighbouring Bellewstown. One is a mensa-slab, supported by tomb-surrounds, bearing the arms of the Bellew (Bellewstown), Plunkett, Preston (Gormanston) and St Lawrence (Howth) families. The other is the tomb of Lord John Bellew, who was wounded at the Battle of Aughrim on 01 of July 1691. He travelled to London to his wife where he died the 12 of January 1692. He was laid to rest in a vault in Westminster. The following April his body was brought here to this tomb.

A stone within the abbey bears the image of Dr. James Cusack, Bishop of Meath 1679 – 1688.

A massive square tower, towering above the 13th century church, was built beside the earlier round tower in the 16th century. Although the round tower no longer stands, the scar where the towers were joined can be seen clearly visible on the northern face of the square tower.

The remains that can now be seen of St. Mary's Abbey are the South Aisle and the Belfry Tower, built in the 13th century The North Aisle occupied the site of the present disused St. Kienan's Church of Ireland church. The outline of the centre aisle can be seen against the Belfry Tower. St. Kienan's Church was built in 1820 and was closed in 1967 when the Church of Ireland parish of Duleek was amalgamated with St. Mary's of Drogheda.

Duleek's heritage is our legacy from the past, what we live with today, and what we pass on to future generations. Our cultural and natural heritage is an irreplaceable source of life and an inspiration. It is something that is passed down from former generations, a tradition, a rich inheritance of storytelling and legacy of philosophical thought.

Some members of Duleek Heritage Graveyard Group are pictured here recording and processing headstones in June 2005. Ben Ryan, Phyllis Noonan and Helen Fullam are recording a headstone in St. Mary's Abbey. Ben is measuring and Phyllis and Helen are reading the inscription from a rubbing taken using cobblers wax crayon. Pictured also is Liz Lynch and Phyllis rubbing The Bellew Tomb.

St. Mary's Abbey has three entrances the Main Gate – the Church of Ireland entrance the Presbyterian Lane entrance, which is reached from Main Street beside the Credit Union and the Catholic Gate which is on a lane from the Navan Road.

The entrance to the old graveyard known as the Catholic Gate was where Catholic funerals entered. The gateway is a high arched gate just wide enough for four men to carry a coffin on their shoulders. Until the late 1940s a charge was made for every funeral that passed through this gate.

The Catholic Gate entrance to
St. Mary's Abbey

The Presbyterian Lane entrance to
St. Mary's Abbey

The Church of Ireland Entrance Gate

**HEADSTONE PHOTOGRAPHS CODED MAP FOR REFERENCE.**

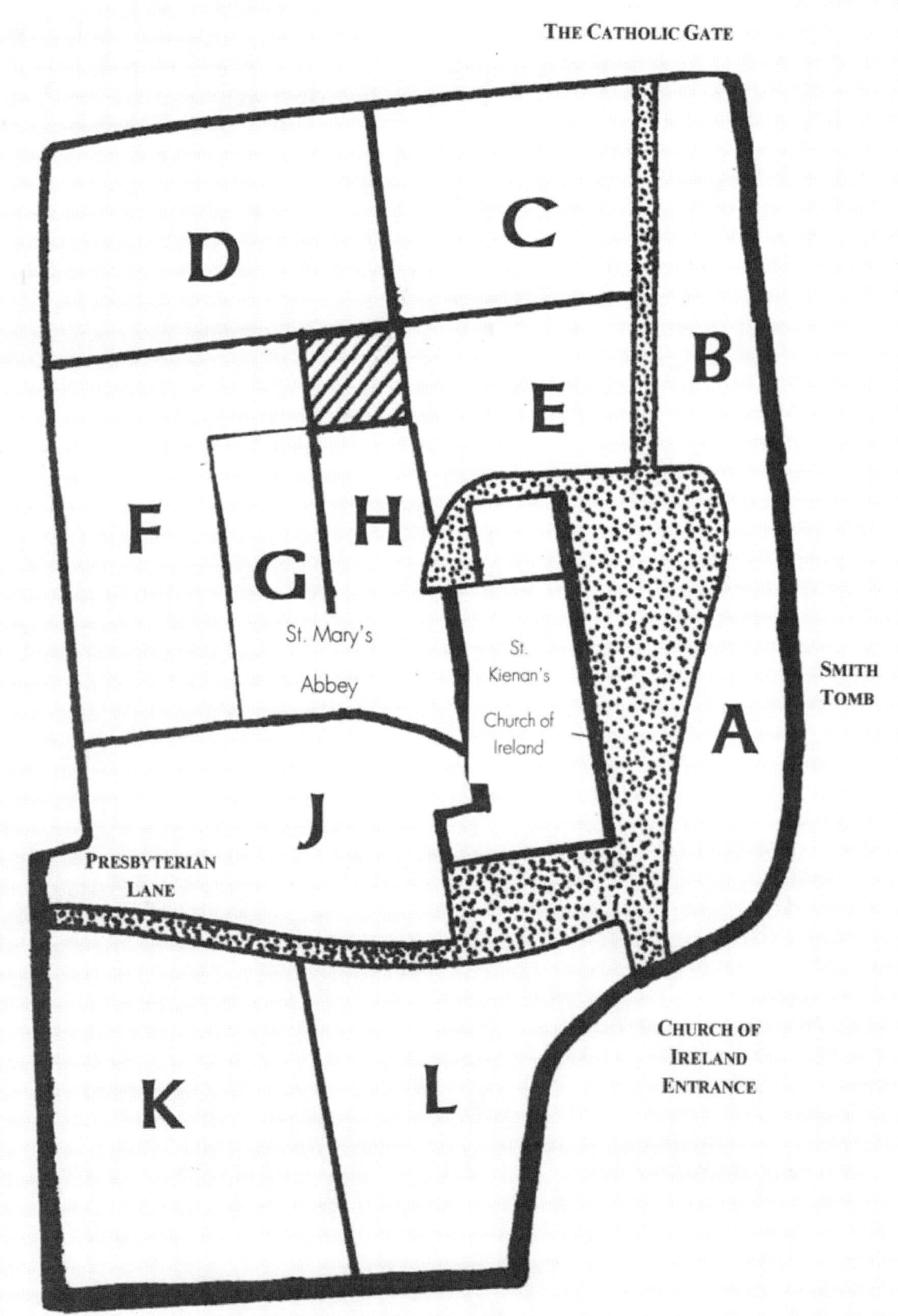

# Acknowledgements

Duleek Heritage Group wish to acknowledge their gratitude to the Duleek Heritage Graveyard Group who started this project in 2005 and tirelessly completed all recording sheets by October 2008. These sheets included all details of each headstone namely memorial number, memorial type, inscriptions, conditions of inscriptions, technique of inscription, list of people interred as per the inscription, measurements, photographs, symbols, ornaments on headstones, photo reference and location references.

In 2012 the Duleek Graveyard Group set about sorting through the photocopies of the recording sheets and the photographs to enable us to complete our records and prepare to print them in book form. It was also decided to share this information on the internet through Facebook and through other channels.

Duleek Heritage Group wishes to acknowledge the enormous amount of work carried out by the Graveyard Group who compiled the recordings in 2005. The Graveyard recorders were:

Ben Ryan, Duleek

Alfie Woods, Duleek

Shaun Lynch, Duleek

Jim Orten, Duleek

Catriona Dillon, Duleek

Liz Lynch, Duleek

Helen Fullam, Donore

Sinéad Fullam, Duleek

Phyllis Noonan Duleek

Janet Leigh, Duleek

Duleek Heritage Group wishes to sincerely thank the Graveyard Team of 2012 – 2013 for all the re-checks of the information gathered and the transfer of the original recording sheets to book form. They were:

Jim Orten, Duleek

Joe Doyle, Duleek

Ben Ryan, Duleek

Liz Lynch, Duleek

Phyllis Noonan, Duleek

Janet Leigh, Duleek

Finally a heartfelt and sincere thanks to Phyllis Noonan who spent hours checking and re-checking the recording sheets while we brought this project to its completion. Phyllis's knowledge of the graveyard and its occupants is outstanding. Her memory is immense.

My thanks to my family who understood my passion and desire to complete this project for Duleek Heritage Group. Thank you. Janet Leigh 2013.

*All photography and headstone coding carried out by Janet Leigh*

| | |
|---|---|
| GRAVEYARD NAME: | **ST. MARY'S ABBEY OLD GRAVEYARD** |
| GRAVEYARD CODE: | D1 |
| COUNTY: | MEATH |
| MEMORIAL NUMBER: | E12 |
| ERECTED BY: | |
| ORIENTATION: | EAST |
| NUMBER OF COMPONENTS: | 3 |
| NUMBER OF INSCRIBED FACES: | 3 |
| NUMBER OF PEOPLE COMMEMORATED: | 9 |
| MEMORIAL TYPE: | GRANITE CELTIC CROSS ON PEDESTAL |
| CONDITION OF MEMORIAL: | SOUND IN PLACE |
| CONDITION OF INSCRIPTION: | CLEAR |
| STONEMASON NAME: | D. SCALLY & SONS GLASNEVIN |
| TECHNIQUE OF INSCRIPTION: | FRONT INCISED ON MARBLE RELIEF SOUTH NORTH INCISED |
| UNDERTAKER: | |
| STONE TOP: | CELTIC CROSS |
| GRAVE TYPE: | TREBLE |
| HEIGHT: | 295CM |
| WIDTH: | 86CM |
| THICKNESS: | 58CM |

| SURNAME: | CHRISTIAN | ADDRESS | DEATH | AGE |
|---|---|---|---|---|
| ARNOLD | WILLIAM | GORMANSTOWN | 26 SEPT 1874 | 63 |
| | MARY THOMASINA | | 15 APR 1901 | 72 |
| | CATHERINE | | 11 AUG 1885 | 19 |
| | MARY | | 06 JAN 1917 | 50 |
| | PATRICK | | 06 APR 1932 | 72 |
| | CHRISTINA | | 11 APR 1940 | 69 |
| BYRNE | JAMES FRANCIS | GORMANSTOWN | 11 OCT 1929 | 37 |
| | THOMASINA | | 22 FEB 1944 | |
| | NORAH CATHERINE(NOONIE) | | 14 MAY 1986 | |

**EAST INSCRIPTION:**
IN AFFECTIONATE REMEMBRANCE
OF
WILLIAM ARNOLD
WHO DIED AT GORMANSTOWN
ON THE 26TH SEPTEMBER 1874
IN THE 63RD YEAR OF HIS AGE
ETERNAL REST GRANT ONTO HIM O LORD
AND HIS WIFE MARY THOMASINA
WHO DIED 15TH APRIL 1901 AGED 72 YEARS

**NORTH INSCRIPTION:**
AND THEIR DAUGHTER
CATHERINE
DIED 11 AUG 1895 AGED 19 YEARS
MARY DIED 6 JAN 1917 AGED 50
THEIR GRANDSON

**SOUTH INSCRIPTION:**
IN LOVING MEMORY OF
NORAH CATHERINE (NONNIE)
BYRNE
GORMANSTOWN
DIED 14TH MAY 1986

JAMES FRANCIS BYRNE
DIED 11 OCT 1929 AGED 37
AND THEIR SON PATRICK
DIED 6 APRIL 1932 AGED 72 YEARS
ALSO THEIR DAUGHTERS CHRISTINA
DIED 11 APRIL 1940 AGED 69
THOMASINA BYRNE
DIED 22ND FEB 1944

| | |
|---|---|
| NAME OF RECORDER: | SHAUN LYNCH AND PHYLLIS NOONAN |
| DATE: | 29 JUNE 2005 |
| PHOTO REFERENCE: | E12 |
| LOCATION/MAP REF: | D1 E12 |

| | |
|---|---|
| GRAVEYARD NAME: | **ST. MARY'S ABBEY OLD GRAVEYARD** |
| GRAVEYARD CODE: | D1 |
| COUNTY: | MEATH |
| MEMORIAL NUMBER: | F6 A |
| ERECTED BY: | |
| ORIENTATION: | EAST |
| NUMBER OF COMPONENTS: | 1 |
| NUMBER OF INSCRIBED FACES: | 1 |
| NUMBER OF PEOPLE COMMEMORATED: | 2 |
| MEMORIAL TYPE: | HEADSTONE |
| CONDITION OF MEMORIAL: | SOUND IN PLACE |
| CONDITION OF INSCRIPTION: | MAINLY DECIPHERABLE |
| STONEMASON NAME: | |
| TECHNIQUE OF INSCRIPTION: | INCISED |
| UNDERTAKER: | |
| STONE TOP: | DISC TOP |
| GRAVE TYPE: | TREBLE |
| HEIGHT: | 116CM |
| WIDTH: | 82CM |
| THICKNESS: | 19CM |

| SURNAME: | CHRISTIAN | ADDRESS | DEATH | AGE |
|---|---|---|---|---|
| ARNOLD | PATRICK | | 23 JUN 1812 | 18 |
| | JAMES | | MAR 1835 | 75 |

**INSCRIPTION:** ERECTED BY JAMES ARNOLD IN MEMORY OF HIS SON PATRICK ARNOLD WHO DEPARTED THIS LIFE 23RD JUNE 1812 AGED 18 YEARS ALSO THE ABOVE JAMES ARNOLD WHO DIED IN MARCH 1835 AGED 75

**ORNAMENTS:**
CROSS ON ALTAR WITH 2 CANDLES WITH CHERUBS EACH SIDE SCROLLED EACH SIDE OF HEADSTONE

| | |
|---|---|
| NAME OF RECORDER: | PHYLLIS NOONAN |
| DATE: | 18 JULY 2005 |
| PHOTO REFERENCE: | F6A |
| LOCATION/MAP REF: | D1 F6A |

| | |
|---|---|
| GRAVEYARD NAME: | **ST. MARY'S ABBEY OLD GRAVEYARD** |
| GRAVEYARD CODE: | D1 |
| COUNTY: | MEATH |
| MEMORIAL NUMBER: | F6B |
| ERECTED BY: | |
| ORIENTATION: | EAST |
| NUMBER OF COMPONENTS: | 3 |
| NUMBER OF INSCRIBED FACES: | 1 |
| NUMBER OF PEOPLE COMMEMORATED: | 9 |
| MEMORIAL TYPE: | CELTIC CROSS ON PEDESTAL |
| CONDITION OF MEMORIAL: | SOUND IN PLACE |
| CONDITION OF INSCRIPTION: | CLEAR |
| STONEMASON NAME: | MOSS JAMES'S STREET DROGHEDA |
| TECHNIQUE OF INSCRIPTION: | INCISED ON MARBLE RELIEF |
| UNDERTAKER: | |
| STONE TOP: | CELTIC CROSS |
| GRAVE TYPE: | TREBLE |
| HEIGHT: | 267CM |
| WIDTH: | 65CM |
| THICKNESS: | 42CM |

| SURNAME: | CHRISTIAN | ADDRESS | DEATH | AGE |
|---|---|---|---|---|
| ARNOLD | RICHARD | HARBOURSTOWN STAMULLEN | 28 DEC 1887 | |
| | PATRICK | | 31 JAN 1926 | |
| | MARGARET | | 05 DEC 1919 | |
| | RICHARD | | 15 FEB 1906 | |
| | PATRICK | | 16 DEC 1906 | |
| | LUCY | | 03 APR 1931 | |
| | PETER | | 26 AUG 1936 | |
| | JOHN | | 04 FEB 1947 | |
| | ELIZABETH | | 02 JULY 1970 | |

**INSCRIPTION:**
IN LOVING MEMORY OF
RICHARD ARNOLD
DIED 28 DEC 1887
PATRICK AND MARGARET ARNOLD
HARBOURSTOWN STAMULLEN
DIED 31ST JAN 1926 ~ 5TH DEC 1919
THEIR FAMILY
RICHARD DIED 15TH FEB 1906
PATRICK DIED 16TH DEC 1929
LUCY DIED 3RD APRIL 1931
PETER DIED 26TH AUG 1936
JOHN DIED 4TH FEB 1947
ELIZABETH DIED 2ND JULY 1970
RIP

**SYMBOLS:**
CELTIC CROSS ON PEDESTAL

| | |
|---|---|
| NAME OF RECORDER: | PHYLLIS NOONAN |
| DATE: | 19 JULY 2006 |
| PHOTO REFERENCE: | F6 |
| LOCATION/MAP REF: | D1 F6 |

| | |
|---|---|
| GRAVEYARD NAME: | **ST. MARY'S ABBEY OLD GRAVEYARD** |
| GRAVEYARD CODE: | D1 |
| COUNTY: | MEATH |
| MEMORIAL NUMBER: | F9 |
| ERECTED BY: | PETER ARNOLD |
| ORIENTATION: | EAST |
| NUMBER OF COMPONENTS: | 1 |
| NUMBER OF INSCRIBED FACES: | 1 |
| NUMBER OF PEOPLE COMMEMORATED: | 6 |
| MEMORIAL TYPE: | LOW MONUMENT |
| CONDITION OF MEMORIAL: | SOUND IN PLACE |
| CONDITION OF INSCRIPTION: | MAINLY DECIPHERABLE |
| STONEMASON NAME: | |
| TECHNIQUE OF INSCRIPTION: | INCISED |
| UNDERTAKER: | |
| STONE TOP: | LOW MONUMENT |
| GRAVE TYPE: | DOUBLE |
| HEIGHT: | |
| WIDTH: | |
| THICKNESS: | |

| SURNAME: | CHRISTIAN | ADDRESS | DEATH | AGE |
|---|---|---|---|---|
| ARNOLD | PATRICK | | 22 JUNE 1811 | |
| | MARY | | 25 DEC 1823 | |
| | GRANDFATHER | | 1797 | |
| | GRANDMOTHER | | 1814 | |
| | CHRISTOPHER | | | |
| | NICHOLAS | REVEREND | 19 OCT 1831 | |

**INSCRIPTION:**
THIS TOMB WAS PLACED HERE BY
PETER ARNOLD OF GLINTSTOWN IN MEMORY
OF HIS FATHER PATRICK WHO DIED 22ND JUNE
1811 AND OF HIS MOTHER MARY WHO DIED
25TH DECEMBER 1823 HERE ALSO LIES THE
REMAINS OF HIS GRANDFATHER AND GRAND
MOTHER THE FORMER DIED IN 1797 THE
LATTER IN 1814 AND UNCLE
CHRISTR
*(END OF SLAB)* TO THE MEMORY OF THE REVD
NICH. ARNOLD UNCLE OF PETER ARNOLD O F GLINTSTOWN WHO
DIED 19TH OCT 1831

**SYMBOL:**
CROSS IHS

| | |
|---|---|
| NAME OF RECORDER: | PHYLLIS NOONAN |
| DATE: | 19 JULY 2005 |
| PHOTO REFERENCE: | F9 |
| LOCATION/MAP REF: | D1 F9 |

| | |
|---|---|
| GRAVEYARD NAME: | **ST. MARY'S ABBEY OLD GRAVEYARD** |
| GRAVEYARD CODE: | D1 |
| COUNTY: | MEATH |
| MEMORIAL NUMBER: | F10 |
| ERECTED BY: | REV NICH ARNOLD |
| ORIENTATION: | EAST |
| NUMBER OF COMPONENTS: | 1 |
| NUMBER OF INSCRIBED FACES: | 1 |
| NUMBER OF PEOPLE COMMEMORATED: | 3 |
| MEMORIAL TYPE: | LOW MONUMENT |
| CONDITION OF MEMORIAL: | SOUND IN PLACE |
| CONDITION OF INSCRIPTION: | MAINLY DECIPHERABLE |
| STONEMASON NAME: | |
| TECHNIQUE OF INSCRIPTION: | INCISED |
| UNDERTAKER: | |
| STONE TOP: | LOW MONUMENT |
| GRAVE TYPE: | SINGLE |
| HEIGHT: | 113CM |
| WIDTH: | 73CM |
| THICKNESS: | |

| SURNAME: | CHRISTIAN | ADDRESS | DEATH | AGE |
|---|---|---|---|---|
| ARNOLD | PETER | GLINTSTOWN | 01 Nov 1797 | |
| | CHRISTOPHER | | 19 Nov 1793 | |
| | PATRICK | | 22 JUNE 1811 | |

**INSCRIPTION:**
THIS STONE WAS PLACED HERE
BY THE REV. NICH ARNOLD OF
GLINTSTOWN IN MEMORY OF HIS FATHER
PETER WHO DIED ON THE 1ST NOV 1797 AND HIS
TWO BROTHERS CHRISTOPHER AND PATRICK
THE FORMER WAS INTERRED ON
THE 19TH NOV 1793 THE LATTER
ON THE 22ND OF JUNE 1811

| | |
|---|---|
| NAME OF RECORDER: | PHYLLIS NOONAN |
| DATE: | 18 JULY 2005 |
| PHOTO REFERENCE: | F10 |
| LOCATION/MAP REF: | D1 F10 |

| | |
|---|---|
| GRAVEYARD NAME: | **ST. MARY'S ABBEY OLD GRAVEYARD** |
| GRAVEYARD CODE: | D1 |
| COUNTY: | MEATH |
| MEMORIAL NUMBER: | B3 A |
| ERECTED BY: | |
| ORIENTATION: | EAST |
| NUMBER OF COMPONENTS: | 3 |
| NUMBER OF INSCRIBED FACES: | 1 |
| NUMBER OF PEOPLE COMMEMORATED: | 1 |
| MEMORIAL TYPE: | CROSS ON PEDESTAL |
| CONDITION OF MEMORIAL: | SOUND IN PLACE |
| CONDITION OF INSCRIPTION: | MAINLY DECIPHERABLE |
| STONEMASON NAME: | |
| TECHNIQUE OF INSCRIPTION: | INCISED |
| UNDERTAKER: | |
| STONE TOP: | CROSS |
| GRAVE TYPE: | DOUBLE |
| HEIGHT: | 150CM |
| WIDTH: | 60CM |
| THICKNESS: | 35CM |

| SURNAME: | CHRISTIAN | ADDRESS | OCCUPATION | DEATH | AGE |
|---|---|---|---|---|---|
| ASHE | HENRY | | RECTOR OF DULEEK 1875 TO 1906 | 11 FEB 1917 | 81 |

**INSCRIPTION:**
IN LOVING MEMORY
OF
REV. HENRY ASHE
RECTOR OF DULEEK FROM 1878 TO 1906
WHO ENTERED INTO REST
11 FEB 1917
AGED 81

"SO HE GIVETH HIS BELOVED SLEEP"
PS: 127.12

| | |
|---|---|
| NAME OF RECORDER: | JANET LEIGH AND PHYLLIS NOONAN |
| DATE: | 25 JUNE 2005 |
| PHOTO REFERENCE: | B3 A |
| LOCATION/MAP REF: | D1 B3 A |

| | |
|---|---|
| GRAVEYARD NAME: | **ST. MARY'S ABBEY OLD GRAVEYARD** |
| GRAVEYARD CODE: | D1 |
| COUNTY: | MEATH |
| MEMORIAL NUMBER: | B3 B |
| ERECTED BY: | |
| ORIENTATION: | EAST |
| NUMBER OF COMPONENTS: | 2 |
| NUMBER OF INSCRIBED FACES: | 1 |
| NUMBER OF PEOPLE COMMEMORATED: | 2 |
| MEMORIAL TYPE: | HEADSTONE |
| CONDITION OF MEMORIAL: | SOUND IN PLACE |
| CONDITION OF INSCRIPTION: | MAINLY DECIPHERABLE |
| STONEMASON NAME: | |
| TECHNIQUE OF INSCRIPTION: | INCISED LEAD FILLED LETTERS |
| UNDERTAKER: | |
| STONE TOP: | ARCH |
| GRAVE TYPE: | DOUBLE |
| HEIGHT: | 120CM |
| WIDTH: | 60CM |
| THICKNESS: | 8CM |

| SURNAME: | CHRISTIAN | ADDRESS | DEATH | AGE |
|---|---|---|---|---|
| ASHE | NORMAN D'ACOURT | | 17 AUG 1886 | 7 |
| ASHE | WELLESLEY ST. GEORGE | | 21 JUNE 1958 | 77 |

**INSCRIPTION:**
IN
LOVING MEMORY
OF
NORMAN D'ACOURT ASHE
DIED 17TH AUG 1886
AGED 7 YEARS
"SAFE"
PS: 119.117
WELLESLEY ST. GEORGE ASHE
DIED 21 JUNE 1958
AGED 77 YEARS
SONS OF THE REV. HENRY ASHE
"SAFE"

**ORNAMENTS:**
SMALL SIDE PILLARS

| | |
|---|---|
| NAME OF RECORDER: | PHYLLIS NOONAN |
| DATE: | 25 JUNE 2005 |
| PHOTO REFERENCE: | B3 B |
| LOCATION/MAP REF: | D1 B3B |

| | |
|---|---|
| GRAVEYARD NAME: | **ST. MARY'S ABBEY OLD GRAVEYARD** |
| GRAVEYARD CODE: | D1 |
| COUNTY: | MEATH |
| MEMORIAL NUMBER: | L34 |
| ERECTED BY: | PETER BANNON |
| ORIENTATION: | EAST |
| NUMBER OF COMPONENTS: | 1 |
| NUMBER OF INSCRIBED FACES: | 1 |
| NUMBER OF PEOPLE COMMEMORATED: | 9 |
| MEMORIAL TYPE: | HEADSTONE |
| CONDITION OF MEMORIAL: | SOUND IN PLACE |
| CONDITION OF INSCRIPTION: | MAINLY DECIPHERABLE |
| STONEMASON NAME: | |
| TECHNIQUE OF INSCRIPTION: | INCISED |
| UNDERTAKER: | |
| STONE TOP: | ARCH |
| GRAVE TYPE: | SINGLE |
| HEIGHT: | 179CM |
| WIDTH: | 79CM |
| THICKNESS: | 16 CM |

| SURNAME: | CHRISTIAN | ADDRESS | DEATH | AGE |
|---|---|---|---|---|
| BANNON | WILLIAM | | | |
| | MARY | | | |
| | 4 CHILDREN | | DIED YOUNG | |
| | MARYANNE | | 19 FEB 1867 | 33 |
| | PETER | WEST ST. DROGHEDA | 13 MAR 1878 | 70 |
| | JANE | | 6 NOV 1893 | 84 |

**INSCRIPTION:**
BY MR PETER BANNON WEST ST
DROGHEDA IN MEMORY OF HIS
FATHER WM BANNON AND OF
HIS MOTHER MARY BANNON AND
4 OF HIS CHILDREN WHO DIED YOUNG
ALSO HIS DAUGHTER MARYANNE
WHO DIED FEBRY 19 1867
AGED 33 YEARS
HERE ALSO LIES THE ABOVE NAMED
PETER BANNON WHO DIED MARCH 13 1878
AGED 70 YEARS
ALSO JANE WIFE OF THE ABOVE PETER
BANNON WHO DIED 6TH NOV 1893 AGED
84 YEARS
MAY THEY REST IN PEACE

**SYMBOLS:**
IHS DISK GLORIA IN EXCELSIS DEO AT BOTTOM
OF DISK
TWO ANGEL FACES FLANK DISK

| | |
|---|---|
| NAME OF RECORDER: | JANET LEIGH |
| DATE: | 31 MAY 2006 |
| PHOTO REFERENCE: | L34 |
| LOCATION/MAP REF: | D1 L34 |

| | |
|---|---|
| GRAVEYARD NAME: | **ST. MARY'S ABBEY OLD GRAVEYARD** |
| GRAVEYARD CODE: | D1 |
| COUNTY: | MEATH |
| MEMORIAL NUMBER: | J22 |
| ERECTED BY: | MARY BARRY |
| ORIENTATION: | EAST |
| NUMBER OF COMPONENTS: | 1 |
| NUMBER OF INSCRIBED FACES: | 1 |
| NUMBER OF PEOPLE COMMEMORATED: | 1 |
| MEMORIAL TYPE: | HEADSTONE |
| CONDITION OF MEMORIAL: | SOUND IN PLACE |
| CONDITION OF INSCRIPTION: | MAINLY DECIPHERABLE |
| STONEMASON NAME: | |
| TECHNIQUE OF INSCRIPTION: | INCISED |
| UNDERTAKER: | |
| STONE TOP: | ROUND |
| GRAVE TYPE: | SINGLE |
| HEIGHT: | 121CM |
| WIDTH: | 73CM |
| THICKNESS: | 10CM |

| SURNAME: | CHRISTIAN | ADDRESS | DEATH | AGE |
|---|---|---|---|---|
| BARRY | THOMAS | | 5 APR 1785 | 51 |
| | | | | |

**INSCRIPTION:**
THIS STONE WAS ERECTED BY MARY BARRY OF THE CITY OF DUBLIN IN MEMORY OF HER UNCLE THOMAS BARRY WHO DEPARTED THIS LIFE THE 5TH APRIL 1785 AGED 51 YEARS ~~

**SYMBOLS:**
CROSS OVER IHS WITH HEART

| | |
|---|---|
| NAME OF RECORDER: | LIZ LYNCH AND PHYLLIS NOONAN |
| DATE: | 16 AUG 2005 |
| PHOTO REFERENCE: | J22 |
| LOCATION/MAP REF: | D1 J22 |

| | |
|---|---|
| GRAVEYARD NAME: | **ST. MARY'S ABBEY OLD GRAVEYARD** |
| GRAVEYARD CODE: | D1 |
| COUNTY: | MEATH |
| MEMORIAL NUMBER: | G5 |
| ERECTED BY: | DAME MARY BERMINGHAM |
| ORIENTATION: | EAST |
| NUMBER OF COMPONENTS: | 1 |
| NUMBER OF INSCRIBED FACES: | 1 |
| NUMBER OF PEOPLE COMMEMORATED: | 9 |
| MEMORIAL TYPE: | TOMB MENSA LAB |
| CONDITION OF MEMORIAL: | SOUND IN PLACE |
| CONDITION OF INSCRIPTION: | MAINLY DECIPHERABLE |
| STONEMASON NAME: | |
| TECHNIQUE OF INSCRIPTION: | INCISED |
| UNDERTAKER: | |
| STONE TOP: | TOMB WITH MENSA SLAB |
| GRAVE TYPE: | TOMB |
| HEIGHT: | 218CM |
| WIDTH: | 133CM |
| THICKNESS: | 132CM |

| SURNAME: | CHRISTIAN | | DEATH | AGE |
|---|---|---|---|---|
| BELLEW | JOHN | LORD | 12 JAN 1692 | |
| KELLY | RICHARD | MDTCD | 14 SEPT 1868 | 59 |
| NANGLE KELLY | DORTHEA | | JAN 1878 | 63 |
| NANGLE | THOMAS | | | |
| NANGLE | REBECCA | | | |
| PENTLAND | REBECCA | | | |
| KELLY | CHARLOTTE-ELIZABETH | | 21 FEB 1886 | 42 |
| | SECOND CHILD | | 13 MAY 1886 | 9 |
| BELLEW-KELLY | JOHN | JPFRCSI | 28 FEB 1901 | 58 |

**SYMBOLS:** COAT OF ARMS TO THE RIGHT OF INSCRIPTION-CROWN ON THE TOP FLANKED BY TWO STAGS/LIONS FAMILY MOTTO SCROLLED ON BOTTOM OF COAT OF ARMS

**INSCRIPTION:**
THIS TOMB HATH REPAIRED
AND THE VAULT MADE BY DAME MARY BERMINGHAM
OF DUNFERT WIFE OF JOHN BELLEW
WHO WAS SHOT IN THE BELLY IN AUGHRIM
FIGHT THE FIRST OF JULY 1691 AS SOONE
AS HE WAS ABLE TO UNDERTAKE
A JOURNEY HE WENT TO HIS LADY IN LONDON
WHERE HE DIED THE 12 OF JAN 1692
HE WAS LAID IN A VAULT IN WESTMINSTER
THE APRIL FOLLOWING HIS CORPSE WAS
BROUGHT HITHER
HERE ALSO LIES THE REMAINS OF
RICHARD KELLY MDTCD OF DROGHEDA
DIED SEPTEMBER 14TH 1868 AGED 59 YEARS
AND HIS WIFE DORTHEA NANGLE-KELLY
DIED JANUARY 1878 AGED 63YEARS
AND SEVERAL OF THEIR CHILDREN WHO DIED IN INFANCY
VIZ. THOMAS, REBECCA NANGLE AND REBECCA PENTLAND
CHARLOTTE ELIZABETH KELLY WIFE OF
JOHN BELLEW F.R.C.S.I. OF DROGHEDA
WHO DIED FEB.21ST 1886 AGED 42 YEARS
AND THEIR SECOND CHILD WHO DIED MAY 3TH 1886 AGED 9 YEARS
ALSO JOHN BELLEW KELLY JPFRCSI OF DROGHEDA
WHO DIED FEB.28TH 1901 AGED 58 YEARS

| | |
|---|---|
| NAME OF RECORDER: | JANET LEIGH, PHYLLIS NOONAN AND LIZ LYNCH |
| DATE: | 5 MAY 2006 |
| PHOTO REFERENCE: | G5 |
| LOCATION/MAP REF: | D1 G5 |

| | |
|---|---|
| GRAVEYARD NAME: | **ST. MARY'S ABBEY OLD GRAVEYARD** |
| GRAVEYARD CODE: | D1 |
| COUNTY: | MEATH |
| MEMORIAL NUMBER: | K27 |
| ERECTED BY: | WIDOW BERREL OF FREELONE |
| ORIENTATION: | EAST |
| NUMBER OF COMPONENTS: | 1 |
| NUMBER OF INSCRIBED FACES: | 1 |
| NUMBER OF PEOPLE COMMEMORATED: | 1 |
| MEMORIAL TYPE: | HEADSTONE |
| CONDITION OF MEMORIAL: | SOUND IN PLACE |
| CONDITION OF INSCRIPTION: | CLEAR |
| STONEMASON NAME: | |
| TECHNIQUE OF INSCRIPTION: | INCISED |
| UNDERTAKER: | |
| STONE TOP: | ROUND |
| GRAVE TYPE: | SINGLE |
| HEIGHT: | 111CM |
| WIDTH: | 75CM |
| THICKNESS: | 12CM |

| SURNAME: | CHRISTIAN | ADDRESS | DEATH | AGE |
|---|---|---|---|---|
| BERREL | PATRICK | | 4 MAR 1837 | 79 |
| | | | | |

**INSCRIPTION:**
ERECTED BY THE WIDOW
BERREL OF FREELONE IN
MEMORY OF HER HUSBAND
PATRICK BERREL WHO DEPARTED
THIS LIFE ON THE 4 DAY
MARCH 1837 AGED 79 YEARS
ALSO FOR HIS AND HER POSTERITY

**SYMBOLS:**
CROSS IHS HEART SCROLLING SURROUND
ROUND STONE EACH BOTTOM WITH FLOWER IN
SUNBURST

| | |
|---|---|
| NAME OF RECORDER: | LIZ LYNCH AND PHYLLIS NOONAN |
| DATE: | 20 APRIL 2008 |
| PHOTO REFERENCE: | K27 |
| LOCATION/MAP REF: | D1 K27 |

| | |
|---|---|
| GRAVEYARD NAME: | **ST. MARY'S ABBEY OLD GRAVEYARD** |
| GRAVEYARD CODE: | D1 |
| COUNTY: | MEATH |
| MEMORIAL NUMBER: | C7 |
| ERECTED BY: | P&W BRIEN |
| ORIENTATION: | EAST |
| NUMBER OF COMPONENTS: | 1 |
| NUMBER OF INSCRIBED FACES: | 1 |
| NUMBER OF PEOPLE COMMEMORATED: | 2 |
| MEMORIAL TYPE: | SMALL STONE |
| CONDITION OF MEMORIAL: | SOUND IN PLACE |
| CONDITION OF INSCRIPTION: | MAINLY DECIPHERABLE |
| STONEMASON NAME: | |
| TECHNIQUE OF INSCRIPTION: | INCISED |
| UNDERTAKER: | |
| STONE TOP: | ROUND |
| GRAVE TYPE: | TREBLE |
| HEIGHT: | 52CM |
| WIDTH: | 32CM |
| THICKNESS: | 12CM |

| SURNAME: | CHRISTIAN | ADDRESS | DEATH | AGE |
|---|---|---|---|---|
| BRIEN | | | | |
| | | | | |

**INSCRIPTION:**
ERECTED
BY P & W BRIEN
DULEEK
IN MEMORY OF THEIR
PARENTS

*Additional information received from Family*
*Erected by Patrick and William Brien*
*Their Parents are:*
*Patrick Bryan b. 1812 d. 1898*
*Sarah Eagar (Egar/Agar) Bryan b. 1848 d. 1904*
*Also buried here is Sarah O'Brien – Patrick and Sarah's*
*Great Grand Daughter who died shortly after birth circa 1944.*

| | |
|---|---|
| NAME OF RECORDER: | PHYLLIS NOONAN AND JIM ORTEN |
| DATE: | 2 JULY 2005 |
| PHOTO REFERENCE: | C7 |
| LOCATION/MAP REF: | D1 C7 |

| | |
|---|---|
| GRAVEYARD NAME: | **ST. MARY'S ABBEY OLD GRAVEYARD** |
| GRAVEYARD CODE: | D1 |
| COUNTY: | MEATH |
| MEMORIAL NUMBER: | L43 |
| ERECTED BY: | |
| ORIENTATION: | EAST |
| NUMBER OF COMPONENTS: | 1 |
| NUMBER OF INSCRIBED FACES: | 1 |
| NUMBER OF PEOPLE COMMEMORATED: | 14 |
| MEMORIAL TYPE: | HEADSTONE |
| CONDITION OF MEMORIAL: | SOUND IN PLACE |
| CONDITION OF INSCRIPTION: | CLEAR |
| STONEMASON NAME: | R. REID |
| TECHNIQUE OF INSCRIPTION: | INCISED AND PAINTED |
| UNDERTAKER: | |
| STONE TOP: | ARCH |
| GRAVE TYPE: | SINGLE |
| HEIGHT: | 113CM |
| WIDTH: | 70CM |
| THICKNESS: | 10CM |

| SURNAME: | CHRISTIAN | ADDRESS | DEATH | AGE |
|---|---|---|---|---|
| BRIEN | JAMES | STATION ROAD DULEEK | 14 JULY 1902 | 75 |
| | JANE | | 02 JUNE 1909 | 73 |
| | MICHAEL | | 06 SEPT 1929 | 47 |
| | JANE | | 18 APRIL 1962 | 81 |
| | PATRICK | | 14 DEC 1911 | 2 |
| | MICHAEL | | 16 MAR 1924 | 12 |
| | JAMES | | 21 APR 1925 | 19 |
| | MARGARET MARY | | INFANT | |
| | EMILY | | 25 OCT 1982 | 78 |
| | KATHLEEN | | 10 JUNE 1935 | 21 |
| | DOMINIC | | 22 SEPT 1946 | 11 |
| INTERRED IN | TOMMY | | | |
| THE NEW | JULIA | | | |
| CEMETERY | CEPTA | | | |

**INSCRIPTION:**
IN LOVING MEMORY OF
JAMES BRIEN STATION ROAD DULEEK
DIED 14-7-1902 AGED 75
HIS WIFE JANE
DIED 2-6-1909 AGED 73
THEIR SON MICHAEL
DIED 6-9-1929 AGED 47
HIS WIFE JANE
DIED 18-4-1962 AGED 81
THEIR SONS DIED
PATRICK 14-12-1911 AGED 2
MICHAEL 16-3-1924 AGED 12
JAMES 21-4-1925 AGED 19
THEIR DAUGHTERS DIED:
MARGARET MARY AN INFANT
EMILY 25-10-1982 AGED 78
KATHLEEN 10-6-1935 AGED 21
AND HER SON DOMINIC
DIED 22-9-1946 AGED 11
THEIR OTHER SON AND DAUGHTERS
TOMMY JULIA AND CEPTA
INTERRED IN NEW CEMETERY
MAY THEY REST IN PEACE

| | |
|---|---|
| NAME OF RECORDER: | BEN RYAN, HELEN FULLAM AND JANET LEIGH |
| DATE: | 27 MAY 2006 |
| PHOTO REF: | L43 |
| LOCATION MAP/REF: | D1 L43 |

| | |
|---|---|
| GRAVEYARD NAME: | **ST. MARY'S ABBEY OLD GRAVEYARD** |
| GRAVEYARD CODE: | D1 |
| COUNTY: | MEATH |
| MEMORIAL NUMBER: | K26 |
| ERECTED BY: | THOMAS BROWN KNOCKISLAND |
| ORIENTATION: | EAST |
| NUMBER OF COMPONENTS: | 1 |
| NUMBER OF INSCRIBED FACES: | 1 |
| NUMBER OF PEOPLE COMMEMORATED: | 2 |
| MEMORIAL TYPE: | HEADSTONE |
| CONDITION OF MEMORIAL: | SOUND IN PLACE |
| CONDITION OF INSCRIPTION: | LEGIBLE |
| STONEMASON NAME: | |
| TECHNIQUE OF INSCRIPTION: | INCISED |
| UNDERTAKER: | |
| STONE TOP: | ROUND |
| GRAVE TYPE: | SINGLE |
| HEIGHT: | 148CM |
| WIDTH: | 75CM |
| THICKNESS: | 12CM |

| SURNAME: | CHRISTIAN | ADDRESS | DEATH | AGE |
|---|---|---|---|---|
| BROWN | MATTHEW | KNOCKISLAND | 29 MAY 1865 | |
| | JOHN | | 08 FEB 1866 | |
| | | | | |

**INSCRIPTION:**
ERECTED BY
THOMAS BROWN OF KNOCKISLAND
IN MEMORY OF HIS BROTHER MATTHEW
BROWN WHO DIED 29TH MAY 1865
ALSO HIS BROTHER JOHN BROWN WHO
DIED 8TH FEB 1866

**SYMBOLS:**
ROUND DISK CROSS IHS AND WINGED
CHERUBS

| | |
|---|---|
| NAME OF RECORDER: | LIZ LYNCH AND PHYLLIS NOONAN |
| DATE: | 20 APRIL 2008 |
| PHOTO REFERENCE: | K26 |
| LOCATION/MAP REF: | D1 K26 |

| | |
|---|---|
| GRAVEYARD NAME: | **ST. MARY'S ABBEY OLD GRAVEYARD** |
| GRAVEYARD CODE: | D1 |
| COUNTY: | MEATH |
| MEMORIAL NUMBER: | A5 |
| ERECTED BY: | |
| ORIENTATION: | EAST |
| NUMBER OF COMPONENTS: | 1 |
| NUMBER OF INSCRIBED FACES: | 1 |
| NUMBER OF PEOPLE COMMEMORATED: | 2 |
| MEMORIAL TYPE: | HEADSTONE |
| CONDITION OF MEMORIAL: | SOUND IN PLACE |
| CONDITION OF INSCRIPTION: | POOR BARELY LEGIBLE |
| STONEMASON NAME: | |
| TECHNIQUE OF INSCRIPTION: | INCISED |
| UNDERTAKER: | |
| STONE TOP: | ROUND |
| GRAVE TYPE: | SINGLE |
| HEIGHT: | 120CM |
| WIDTH: | 16CM |
| THICKNESS: | 8CM |

| SURNAME: | CHRISTIAN | | DEATH | AGE |
|---|---|---|---|---|
| BRUNKER | ELIZABETH | | 18 AUG 1872 | 37 |
| BRUNKER | BW REVD. | | 20 NOV 1877 | 60 |
| | | | | |

**INSCRIPTION:**
SACRED TO THE MEMORY OF
ELIZABETH THE BELOVED WIFE
OF THE REVD BW BRUNKER
INCUMBENT OF THIS PARISH
WHO DEPARTED THIS LIFE
THE 18TH OF AUGUST 1872 AGED
37 YEARS
1ST THESSALONIANS
IV CH 13 & 18 VS
HERE ALSO ARE INTERRED THE
MORTAL REMAINS OF THE
REVD. BW BRUNKER
WHO DIED ON 20TH OF NOVEMBER
1877 AGED 60 YEARS
2ND TIMOTHY CH 4 7 & 8 VS

| | |
|---|---|
| NAME OF RECORDER: | JANET LEIGH AND SINEAD FULLAM |
| DATE: | 18 JUNE 2005 |
| PHOTO REFERENCE: | A5 |
| LOCATION/MAP REF: | D1 A5 |

| | |
|---|---|
| GRAVEYARD NAME: | **ST. MARY'S ABBEY OLD GRAVEYARD** |
| GRAVEYARD CODE: | D1 |
| COUNTY: | MEATH |
| MEMORIAL NUMBER: | G14 |
| ERECTED BY: | JAMES CAFFERY |
| ORIENTATION: | EAST |
| NUMBER OF COMPONENTS: | 1 |
| NUMBER OF INSCRIBED FACES: | 1 |
| NUMBER OF PEOPLE COMMEMORATED: | 4 |
| MEMORIAL TYPE: | HEADSTONE ON GROUND |
| CONDITION OF MEMORIAL: | SOUND IN PLACE ON THE FLOOR OF ABBEY |
| CONDITION OF INSCRIPTION: | MAINLY DECIPHERABLE |
| STONEMASON NAME: | |
| TECHNIQUE OF INSCRIPTION: | INCISED |
| UNDERTAKER: | |
| STONE TOP: | ROUND |
| GRAVE TYPE: | SINGLE |
| HEIGHT: | 150CM |
| WIDTH: | 71CM |
| THICKNESS: | NOT ACCESSIBLE |

| SURNAME: | CHRISTIAN | DEATH | AGE |
|---|---|---|---|
| CAFFERY | THOMAS | 04 MAR 1777 | 70 |
| OSBURN | ALLICE | 04 MAY 1718 | 70 |
| COLLIER | MARY | 04 MAY 1751 | 60 |
| CAFFERY | RICHARD | 1751 | |

**INSCRIPTION:**
IHS
THERE LIETH YE BODY
OF THOMAS CAFFERY WHO DEPD
YE LIFE MARCH YE 4 1717 AGED 70 YEARS
ALSO HIS WIFE ALLICE OSBURN
WHO DIED MAY YE 4 1718 AGD
70 YEARS ALSO YE BODY OF MARY
COLLIER DIED MAY YE 4 1751
AGED 60 YEARS & RICHARD
CAFFERY DIED 1751 ERECTED
BY JAMES CAFFREY

**SYMBOLS:**
IHS IN SUNBURST OLD CROSS ABOVE H
IHS EACH OF CENTRE

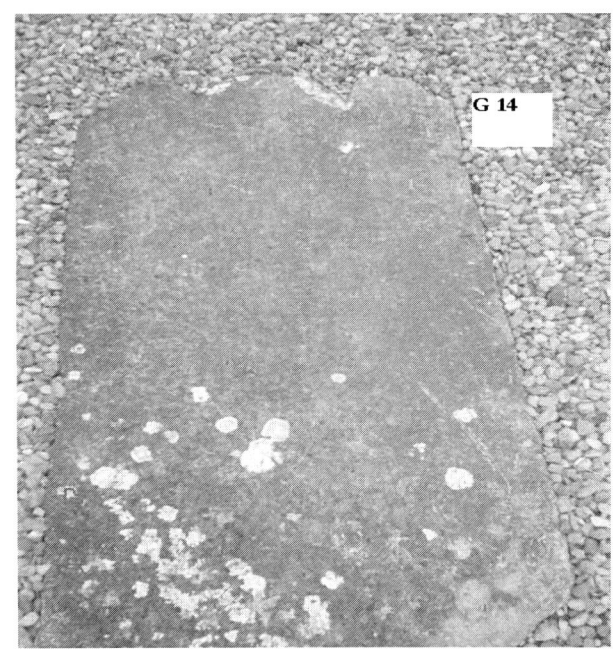

| | |
|---|---|
| NAME OF RECORDER: | JANET LEIGH |
| DATE: | 28 JUNE 2006 |
| PHOTO REFERENCE: | G14 |
| LOCATION/MAP REF: | D1 G14 |

| | |
|---|---|
| GRAVEYARD NAME: | **ST. MARY'S ABBEY OLD GRAVEYARD** |
| GRAVEYARD CODE: | D1 |
| COUNTY: | MEATH |
| MEMORIAL NUMBER: | A9 |
| ERECTED BY: | |
| ORIENTATION: | EAST |
| NUMBER OF COMPONENTS: | 2 |
| NUMBER OF INSCRIBED FACES: | 1 |
| NUMBER OF PEOPLE COMMEMORATED: | 2 |
| MEMORIAL TYPE: | HEADSTONE |
| CONDITION OF MEMORIAL: | GOOD |
| CONDITION OF INSCRIPTION: | GOOD |
| STONEMASON NAME: | T. REID |
| TECHNIQUE OF INSCRIPTION: | INCISED AND PAINTED |
| UNDERTAKER: | |
| STONE TOP: | ROUND |
| GRAVE TYPE: | TREBLE |
| HEIGHT: | 100CM |
| WIDTH: | 70CM |
| THICKNESS: | 15CM |

| SURNAME: | CHRISTIAN | ADDRESS | DEATH | AGE |
|---|---|---|---|---|
| CAFFREY | OLIVER | KINGSGATE | 13 JAN 1977 | 56 |
| CAFFREY | MARGARET | KINGSGATE | 27 JUNE 1999 | 77 |
| | | | | |

**INSCRIPTION:**

IN LOVING MEMORY
OF
OLIVER CAFFREY
KINGSGATE
WHO DIED 13TH JAN 1977
AGED 56 YRS
HIS BELOVED WIFE
MARGARET (PEGGY)
DIED 27TH JUNE 1999
AGED 77 YRS

R.I.P.

**SYMBOLS:**
INCISED CROSSES

| | |
|---|---|
| NAME OF RECORDER: | PHYLLIS NOONAN AND JIM ORTEN |
| DATE: | 25 JUNE 2005 |
| PHOTO REFERENCE: | A9 |
| LOCATION/MAP REF: | D1 A9 |

| | |
|---|---|
| GRAVEYARD NAME: | **ST. MARY'S ABBEY OLD GRAVEYARD** |
| GRAVEYARD CODE: | D1 |
| COUNTY: | MEATH |
| MEMORIAL NUMBER: | G15 |
| ERECTED BY: | THOMAS CAFFREY |
| ORIENTATION: | EAST |
| NUMBER OF COMPONENTS: | 1 |
| NUMBER OF INSCRIBED FACES: | 1 |
| NUMBER OF PEOPLE COMMEMORATED: | 3 |
| MEMORIAL TYPE: | HEADSTONE |
| CONDITION OF MEMORIAL: | SOUND IN PLACE ON FLOOR OF ABBEY |
| CONDITION OF INSCRIPTION: | CLEAR |
| STONEMASON NAME: | |
| TECHNIQUE OF INSCRIPTION: | INCISED |
| UNDERTAKER: | |
| STONE TOP: | ROUND |
| GRAVE TYPE: | SINGLE |
| HEIGHT: | 168CM |
| WIDTH: | 78CM |
| THICKNESS: | NOT ACCESSIBLE LAID ON GROUND OF ABBEY |

| SURNAME: | CHRISTIAN | ADDRESS | DEATH | AGE |
|---|---|---|---|---|
| CAFFREY | CATHERINE | DULEEK | 16 JAN 1812 | 48 |
| OWENS | THOMAS | | 06 JUNE 1804 | 9 |
| CAFFREY | THOMAS | DULEEK | 02 JUNE 1814 | 46 |

**INSCRIPTION:**
ERECTED BY
THOMAS CAFFREY OF DULEEK
IN MEMORY OF HIS WIFE
CATHERINE WHO DEPARTED
THIS LIFE 16TH JANY 1812 AGED
48 YRS. ALSO OF HER SON
THOS. OWENS DIED 6TH
JUNE 1804 AGED 9 YEARS
ALSO THE REMAINS OF THE ABOVE THOS
CAFFREY DIED JUNE 2 1814 AGED 46 YRS
*AS A PARTNER PARENT & CHILD OR FRIEND*
*THEIR DUTY AFFECTION AND VIRTUE BLEND*
*REQUIESCANT IN PACE AMEN*

**SYMBOLS:**
JESUS ON CROSS OF FIRE PILLARS EACH SIDE
OF CROSS FLANKED BY ANGEL FACES WITH WINGS

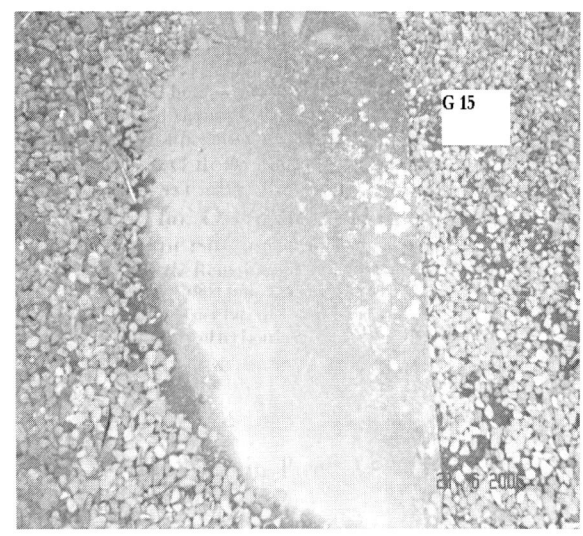

**ORNAMENTS:**
SCROLLED AROUND INSCRIPTION ON EACH SIDE
OF HEADSTONE

| | |
|---|---|
| NAME OF RECORDER: | JANET LEIGH |
| DATE: | 01 JULY 2006 |
| PHOTO REFERENCE: | G15 |
| LOCATION/MAP REF: | D1-G15 |

| | |
|---|---|
| GRAVEYARD NAME: | **ST. MARY'S ABBEY OLD GRAVEYARD** |
| GRAVEYARD CODE: | D1 |
| COUNTY: | MEATH |
| MEMORIAL NUMBER: | G16 |
| ERECTED BY: | PETER CAFFREY |
| ORIENTATION: | EAST |
| NUMBER OF COMPONENTS: | 1 |
| NUMBER OF INSCRIBED FACES: | 1 |
| NUMBER OF PEOPLE COMMEMORATED: | 7 |
| MEMORIAL TYPE: | LOW MONUMENT |
| CONDITION OF MEMORIAL: | POOR |
| CONDITION OF INSCRIPTION: | LEGIBLE |
| STONEMASON NAME: | |
| TECHNIQUE OF INSCRIPTION: | INCISED |
| UNDERTAKER: | |
| STONE TOP: | LOW MONUMENT ON GROUND |
| GRAVE TYPE: | SINGLE |
| HEIGHT: | 163CM |
| WIDTH: | 75CM |
| THICKNESS: | |

| SURNAME: | CHRISTIAN | ADDRESS | DEATH | AGE |
|---|---|---|---|---|
| CAFFREY | JAMES | | 25 JUNE 1792 | 25 |
| CAFFREY | CATHERINE | | JAN 1872 | 69 |
| CAFFREY | JOHN | | AUG 1867 | 64 |

**INSCRIPTION:**

ERECTED
BY PETER CAFFREY OF DULEEK
IN THIS HIS FAMILY BURIAL PLACE
LIETH THE REMAINS OF HIS SON
JAMES CAFFREY WHO DIED THE
25TH DAY OF JUNE 1792 AGED
25 YEARS.= JAMES CAFFREY
LATE BALBRIGGAN DIED JUNE
1866 AGED 68 YEARS AND HIS
WIFE CATHERINE DIED JANUARY
1872 AGED 69 YEARS AND 2 OF
THEIR CHILDREN AND GRAND
SON DIED YOUNG
JOHN CAFFREY DIED AUGUST
1867 AGED 64 YEARS

*REQUIESCANT IN PACE AMEN*

**SYMBOLS:**
I.H.S CROSS AND ANGEL IN SUNBURST
LEAVES TRAILING FROM SUNBURST

| | |
|---|---|
| NAME OF RECORDER: | PHYLLIS NOONAN AND SINEAD FULLAM |
| DATE: | 1 JULY 2006 |
| PHOTO REFERENCE: | G16 |
| LOCATION/MAP REF: | D1 G16 |

| | |
|---|---|
| GRAVEYARD NAME: | **ST. MARY'S ABBEY OLD GRAVEYARD** |
| GRAVEYARD CODE: | D1 |
| COUNTY: | MEATH |
| MEMORIAL NUMBER: | H11 |
| ERECTED BY: | JOHN CALLAGHAN |
| ORIENTATION: | EAST |
| NUMBER OF COMPONENTS: | 1 |
| NUMBER OF INSCRIBED FACES: | 1 |
| NUMBER OF PEOPLE COMMEMORATED: | 8 |
| MEMORIAL TYPE: | HEADSTONE |
| CONDITION OF MEMORIAL: | SOUND IN PLACE |
| CONDITION OF INSCRIPTION: | CLEAR |
| STONEMASON NAME: | |
| TECHNIQUE OF INSCRIPTION: | INCISED |
| UNDERTAKER: | |
| STONE TOP: | SUNBURST DISK |
| GRAVE TYPE: | TREBLE |
| HEIGHT: | 142CM |
| WIDTH: | 74CM |
| THICKNESS: | 15CM |

| SURNAME: | CHRISTIAN | ADDRESS | DEATH | AGE |
|---|---|---|---|---|
| CALLAGHAN | ANDREW | BELLEWSTOWN | 12 SEPT 1808 | 65 |
| | ANDREW | | NOV 1887 | |
| | MARIA | | 28 DEC 1883 | |
| | JAMES | | 16 FEB 1911 | |
| | KATIE | | 01 FEB 1893 | |
| | MARY | | 07 MAY 1919 | |
| | JAMES | | 27 MAY 1907 | |
| | THOMAS | | 23 NOV 1936 | |

**INSCRIPTION:**
ERECTED BY JOHN CALLAGHAN
IN MEMORY OF HIS FATHER
ANDREW CALLAGHAN LATE OF
BELLEWSTOWN WHO DEPARTED
THIS LIFE THE 12TH OF SEPTEMBER
1808 AGED 65 YEARS
ALSO HAVE MERCY ON THE SOUL OF
ANDREW CALLAGHAN DIED NOV.1887
ALSO HIS WIFE MARIA DIED DEC.28TH 1883
HIS BROTHER JAMES DIED FEB.16TH 1911
HIS DAUGHTER KATIE DIED FEB.1ST 1893
HIS DAUGHTER MARY DIED MAY 7TH 1919
HIS SON JAMES DIED MAY 27TH 1909
HIS SON THOMAS DIED
NOV 23RD 1936

*REQUIESCANT IN PACE AMEN*

**SYMBOLS:**
IHS CROSS AND HEART IN SUNBURST DISK

| | |
|---|---|
| NAME OF RECORDER: | LIZ LYNCH AND JANET LEIGH |
| DATE: | 14 JUNE 2006 |
| PHOTO REFERENCE: | H11 |
| LOCATION/MAP REF: | D1 H11 |

| | |
|---|---|
| GRAVEYARD NAME: | **ST. MARY'S ABBEY OLD GRAVEYARD** |
| GRAVEYARD CODE: | D1 |
| COUNTY: | MEATH |
| MEMORIAL NUMBER: | J1 |
| ERECTED BY: | PETER AND PATRICK CALLAGHAN |
| ORIENTATION: | EAST |
| NUMBER OF COMPONENTS: | 1 |
| NUMBER OF INSCRIBED FACES: | 1 |
| NUMBER OF PEOPLE COMMEMORATED: | 5 |
| MEMORIAL TYPE: | HEADSTONE |
| CONDITION OF MEMORIAL: | SOUND IN PLACE |
| CONDITION OF INSCRIPTION: | MAINLY DECIPHERABLE |
| STONEMASON NAME: | |
| TECHNIQUE OF INSCRIPTION: | INCISED |
| UNDERTAKER: | |
| STONE TOP: | SUNBURST DISK |
| GRAVE TYPE: | SINGLE |
| HEIGHT: | 180CM |
| WIDTH: | 85CM |
| THICKNESS: | 10CM |

| SURNAME | CHRISTIAN | ADDRESS | DEATH | AGE |
|---|---|---|---|---|
| CALLAGHAN | PETER | LUNDERSTOWN | 05 FEB 1837 | 84 |
| GRENDIN | MARGARET | DULEEK | 30 MAY 1825 | 22 |
| CALLAGHAN | MARY | | 16 DEC 1870 | 55 |
| | PATRICK | | 12 MAR 1868 | 65 |
| | PETER | | 29 MAR 1866 | 58 |

**INSCRIPTION:**
AD 1841
THIS TESTIMONIAL OF AFFECTION WAS
ERECTD BY PAT AND PETER CALLAGHAN OF
LUNDERSTOWN IN MEMORY OF THEIR BELOVED
FATHER PETER CALLAGHAN LATE OF LUNDERSTOWN
WHO DEPARTED THIS LIFE 5 FEBY 1837 AGED 84
YEARS ~ ALSO IN MEMORY OF THEIR
BELOVED SISTER MARGRET GRENDIN
LATE OF DULEEK WHO EXCHANGED TIME
FOR ETERNITY 30TH MAY 1825 AGED 22 YRS
THE ABOVE NAMED PATRICK CALLAGHAN
DIED 12TH MARCH 1868 AGED 65 YEARS
AND PETER DIED 29TH MARCH 1866 AGED
58 YEARS – MARY WIFE OF
PATRICK CALLAGHAN DIED 16TH DEC 1870
AGED 55 YEARS
*REQUIESCANT IN PACE AMEN*

**ORNAMENTS:** IHS ON CROSS
IN HEART ON SUNBURST
HALF WAY DOWN TWO ROSETTES
MALTESE CROSSES ANGEL
WINGS WITH STARS AND ROSETTES

| | |
|---|---|
| NAME OF RECORDER: | PHYLLIS NOONAN AND JANET LEIGH AND LIZ LYNCH |
| DATE: | 03 AUG 2005 |
| PHOTO REFERENCE: | J1 |
| LOCATION/MAP REF: | D1 J1 |

| | |
|---|---|
| GRAVEYARD NAME: | **ST. MARY'S ABBEY OLD GRAVEYARD** |
| GRAVEYARD CODE: | D1 |
| COUNTY: | MEATH |
| MEMORIAL NUMBER: | J16 |
| ERECTED BY: | |
| ORIENTATION: | EAST |
| NUMBER OF COMPONENTS: | 1 |
| NUMBER OF INSCRIBED FACES: | 1 |
| NUMBER OF PEOPLE COMMEMORATED: | 2 |
| MEMORIAL TYPE: | HEADSTONE |
| CONDITION OF MEMORIAL: | SOUND IN PLACE |
| CONDITION OF INSCRIPTION: | DECIPHERABLE |
| STONEMASON NAME: | |
| TECHNIQUE OF INSCRIPTION: | INCISED |
| UNDERTAKER: | |
| STONE TOP: | SUNBURST DISK ROUND |
| GRAVE TYPE: | SINGLE |
| HEIGHT: | 105CM |
| WIDTH: | 73CM |
| THICKNESS: | 4CM |

| SURNAME: | CHRISTIAN | ADDRESS | DEATH | AGE |
|---|---|---|---|---|
| CALLAGHAN | JOHN | KILSHARVAN | 6 MAY 1774 | 58 |
| | PATRICK | | 6 OCT 1772 | 24 |
| | | | | |

**INSCRIPTION:**
HERE LIETH THE BODY OF JOHN CALLAGHAN OF KILSHARVAN WHO DEPARTED THIS LIFE THE SIXTH DAY OF MAY IN THE YEAR OF OUR LORD 1774 AGED 58 YEARS ALSO HIS SON PATRICK CALLAGHAN WHO DEPARTED THIS LIFE THE 6TH DAY OF OCTOBER 1772 AGED 24 YEARS

*REQUIESCANT IN PACE*

| | |
|---|---|
| NAME OF RECORDER: | HELEN FULLAM AND JANET LEIGH |
| DATE: | 13 AUG 2005 |
| PHOTO REFERENCE: | J16 |
| LOCATION/MAP REF: | D1 J16 |

| | |
|---|---|
| GRAVEYARD NAME: | **ST. MARY'S ABBEY OLD GRAVEYARD** |
| GRAVEYARD CODE: | D1 |
| COUNTY: | MEATH |
| MEMORIAL NUMBER: | J17 |
| ERECTED BY: | CALLAGHAN |
| ORIENTATION: | EAST |
| NUMBER OF COMPONENTS: | 1 |
| NUMBER OF INSCRIBED FACES: | 1 |
| NUMBER OF PEOPLE COMMEMORATED: | 2 |
| MEMORIAL TYPE: | HEADSTONE |
| CONDITION OF MEMORIAL: | SOUND IN PLACE |
| CONDITION OF INSCRIPTION: | MAINLY DECIPHERABLE |
| STONEMASON NAME: | |
| TECHNIQUE OF INSCRIPTION: | INCISED |
| UNDERTAKER: | |
| STONE TOP: | FLAT |
| GRAVE TYPE: | SINGLE |
| HEIGHT: | 56CM |
| WIDTH: | 50CM |
| THICKNESS: | 10CM |

| SURNAME: | CHRISTIAN | ADDRESS | DEATH | AGE |
|---|---|---|---|---|
| CALLAGHAN | PATRICK | | 1704 | |
| FLEICER | CATRIN | | | 46 |

**INSCRIPTION:**
HERE LIETH THE BODY
OF PATRICK CALLAGHAN
WHO DEPARTED THIS LIFE
1704 CATRIN FLEICER
WHO DEPARTED THIS LIFE
…… AGED 46 ERECTED BY …. CALLAGHAN

**SYMBOLS:**
IHS WITH CROSS
SOME INSCRIPTION MISSING

| | |
|---|---|
| NAME OF RECORDER: | HELEN FULLAM, JIM ORTEN AND JANET LEIGH |
| DATE: | 13 AUG 2005 |
| PHOTO REFERENCE: | J17 |
| LOCATION/MAP REF: | D1 J17 |

| | |
|---|---|
| GRAVEYARD NAME: | **ST. MARY'S ABBEY OLD GRAVEYARD** |
| GRAVEYARD CODE: | D1 |
| COUNTY: | MEATH |
| MEMORIAL NUMBER: | H14 |
| ERECTED BY: | |
| ORIENTATION: | EAST |
| NUMBER OF COMPONENTS: | 1 |
| NUMBER OF INSCRIBED FACES: | 1 |
| NUMBER OF PEOPLE COMMEMORATED: | 1 |
| MEMORIAL TYPE: | LOW MONUMENT |
| CONDITION OF MEMORIAL: | SOUND |
| CONDITION OF INSCRIPTION: | CLEAR |
| STONEMASON NAME: | |
| TECHNIQUE OF INSCRIPTION: | INCISED |
| UNDERTAKER: | |
| STONE TOP: | LOW MONUMENT |
| GRAVE TYPE: | SINGLE |
| HEIGHT: | 210CM |
| WIDTH: | 105CM |
| THICKNESS: | 10CM |

| SURNAME: | CHRISTIAN | ADDRESS | DEATH | AGE |
|---|---|---|---|---|
| CAMAC | PATRICK | TOWNSEND STREET CITY OF DUBLIN | 01 JUNE 1808 | 32 |

**INSCRIPTION:**
HERE RESTS THE MORTAL REMAINS
OF MR. PATK CAMAC LATE OF TOWNSEND
STREET IN THE CITY OF DUBLIN WHO
DEPARTED THIS LIFE THE 1ST OF JUNE
1808 IN THE 32ND YEAR OF HIS AGE.
DEEPLY & MOST DESERVEDLY REGRETTED
BY EVERY PERSON WHO HAD FELICITY
OF BEING ACQUAINTED WITH HIM &
MORE DUTIFUL SON LOVING HUSBAND
TENDER FATHER AFFECTIONATE BROTHER
MORE SINCERE FRIEND NEVER EXISTED
MAY THE ALMIGHTY GOD OF GREAT
AND INFINITE MERCY RECEIVE HIS SOUL
INTO EVERLASTING GLORY AMEN

| | |
|---|---|
| NAME OF RECORDER: | JANET LEIGH AND LIZ LYNCH |
| DATE: | 14 JUNE 2006 |
| PHOTO REFERENCE: | H14 |
| LOCATION/MAP REF: | D1 H14 |

| | |
|---|---|
| GRAVEYARD NAME: | **ST. MARY'S ABBEY OLD GRAVEYARD** |
| GRAVEYARD CODE: | D1 |
| COUNTY: | MEATH |
| MEMORIAL NUMBER: | K29A |
| ERECTED BY: | MARY CAMPBELL |
| ORIENTATION: | EAST |
| NUMBER OF COMPONENTS: | 5 |
| NUMBER OF INSCRIBED FACES: | 1 |
| NUMBER OF PEOPLE COMMEMORATED: | 5 |
| MEMORIAL TYPE: | ELABORATE CROSS ON PEDESTAL |
| CONDITION OF MEMORIAL: | SOUND IN PLACE |
| CONDITION OF INSCRIPTION: | CLEAR |
| STONEMASON NAME: | F. WHITE CHORD ROAD DROGHEDA |
| TECHNIQUE OF INSCRIPTION: | INCISED |
| UNDERTAKER: | |
| STONE TOP: | CELTIC CROSS |
| GRAVE TYPE: | DOUBLE |
| HEIGHT: | 250CM |
| WIDTH: | 89CM |
| THICKNESS: | 55CM |

| SURNAME: | CHRISTIAN | ADDRESS | DEATH | AGE |
|---|---|---|---|---|
| CAMPBELL | PATRICK | CARNTOWN | 06 JUNE 1901 | |
| | JANE | | 14 MAR 1908 | |
| | MARY | | 23 JAN 1941 | |
| | PATRICK BENEDICT | | 21 JUNE 1992 | 93 |
| | CATHERINE MARY | | 17 JUNE 2004 | 87 |

**INSCRIPTION:**
ERECTED BY
MARY CAMPBELL
CARNTOWN
IN LOVING MEMORY OF HER HUSBAND
PATRICK
WHO DIED 6TH JUNE 1901
AND HER SISTER-IN-LAW
JANE
WHO DIED 14TH MARCH 1908
ALSO THE ABOVE NAMED MARY
WHO DIED 23RD JAN 1941
AND HER SON PATRICK BENEDICT
WHO DIED 21ST DEC 1992 IN HIS 93RD YEAR
HIS BELOVED WIFE
AND OUR DEAR MOTHER
CATHERINE MARY CAMPBELL
WHO DIED 17TH JUNE 2004 AGED 87 YRS

| | |
|---|---|
| NAME OF RECORDER: | BEN RYAN AND PHYLLIS NOONAN |
| DATE: | 8 OCT 2005 |
| PHOTO REFERENCE: | K29 |
| LOCATION/MAP REF: | D1 K29 |

| | |
|---|---|
| GRAVEYARD NAME: | **ST. MARY'S ABBEY OLD GRAVEYARD** |
| GRAVEYARD CODE: | D1 |
| COUNTY: | MEATH |
| MEMORIAL NUMBER: | K29B |
| ERECTED BY: | JOHN CAMPBELL |
| ORIENTATION: | EAST |
| NUMBER OF COMPONENTS: | 1 |
| NUMBER OF INSCRIBED FACES: | 1 |
| NUMBER OF PEOPLE COMMEMORATED: | 8 |
| MEMORIAL TYPE: | HEADSTONE |
| CONDITION OF MEMORIAL: | SOUND IN PLACE |
| CONDITION OF INSCRIPTION: | CLEAR |
| STONEMASON NAME: | |
| TECHNIQUE OF INSCRIPTION: | INCISED |
| UNDERTAKER: | |
| STONE TOP: | DISK |
| GRAVE TYPE: | DOUBLE |
| HEIGHT: | 155CM |
| WIDTH: | 79CM |
| THICKNESS: | 17CM |

| SURNAME: | CHRISTIAN | ADDRESS | DEATH | AGE |
|---|---|---|---|---|
| CAMPBELL | JANE | | 05 AUG 1812 | 67 |
| | JAMES | | 06 JUNE 1822 | 78 |
| | WILLIAM | | 16 MAR 1833 | 21 |
| | ANNE | | 21 MAY 1834 | 48 |
| | JOHN | | 26 DEC 1838 | 83 |
| | WILLIAM | | 15 NOV 1876 | 13 |
| | MARY | | 16 MAY 1883 | 64 |
| | PATRICK | | 24 APRIL 1901 | 83 |

**INSCRIPTION:**
ERECTED
BY JOHN CAMPBELL OF CARNTOWN
PARISH OF DULEEK IN MEMORY OF HIS
MOTHER JANE CAMPBELL WHO DIED 5TH
AUGST 1812 AGED 67 YEARS
ALSO OF HIS FATHER JAMES
CAMPBELL WHO DIED 6TH JUNE 1822 AGED
78 YEARS ~ AND ALSO OF HIS
SON WILLIAM WHO DIED 16TH MARCH
1833 AGED 21 YEARS AND LIKEWISE
OF HIS BELOVED WIFE ANNE CAMP
BELL WHO DIED 21ST MAY 1834 AGED 48
YEARS
HERE ALSO LIE THE
REMAINS OF THE ABOVE NAMED
JOHN CAMPBELL WHO DEPARTED
THIS LIFE 26TH DECR 1838 AGED 68 YEARS
AND OF HIS GRANDSON WILLIAM CAMPBELL
WHO DEPARTED THIS LIFE 15TH NOVEMBER
1876 AGED 13 YEARS ALSO OF HIS DAUGHTER
IN LAW MRS. MARY CAMPBELL WHO DEPARTED
THIS LIFE THE 16TH MAY 1883 AGED 64 YEARS
ALSO HIS SON PATRICK CAMPBELL WHO DIED
24TH APRIL 1901 AGED 83 YEARS

**SYMBOLS:**
SUNBURST DISK IHS WITH CROSS IN HEART
CHERUBS SCROLLED WORK SURROUND

| | |
|---|---|
| NAME OF RECORDER: | PHYLLIS NOONAN |
| DATE: | 8 OCT 2005 |
| PHOTO REFERENCE: | K29 |
| LOCATION/MAP REF: | D1 K29 |

| | |
|---|---|
| GRAVEYARD NAME: | **ST. MARY'S ABBEY OLD GRAVEYARD** |
| GRAVEYARD CODE: | D1 |
| COUNTY: | MEATH |
| MEMORIAL NUMBER: | D 21 |
| ERECTED BY: | |
| ORIENTATION: | EAST |
| NUMBER OF COMPONENTS: | 2 |
| NUMBER OF INSCRIBED FACES: | 1 |
| NUMBER OF PEOPLE COMMEMORATED: | 5 |
| MEMORIAL TYPE: | HEADSTONE |
| CONDITION OF MEMORIAL: | SOUND IN PLACE |
| CONDITION OF INSCRIPTION: | MAINLY DECIPHERABLE |
| STONEMASON NAME: | REID PLATTEN |
| TECHNIQUE OF INSCRIPTION: | INCISED |
| UNDERTAKER: | |
| STONE TOP: | ROUND |
| GRAVE TYPE: | DOUBLE |
| HEIGHT: | 110CM |
| WIDTH: | 72CM |
| THICKNESS: | 10CM |

| SURNAME: | CHRISTIAN | ADDRESS | DEATH | AGE |
|---|---|---|---|---|
| CAREY | ROBERT | DULEEK | 22 FEB 1877 | |
| | ANNE | | 03 FEB 1897 | |
| | ELLEN | | 11 FEB 1904 | |
| | ANNIE | | 18 JAN 1931 | |
| | FRANCIS | | 26 FEB 1938 | |

**INSCRIPTION:**
IN LOVING MEMORY OF
ROBERT CAREY DULEEK
WHO DIED FEB 22ND 1877
OF ANNE
WHO DIED FEB 3RD 1897
OF ELLEN
WHO DIED FEB 11TH 1904
OF ANNIE
WHO DIED JAN 18TH 1931
OF FRANCIS
WHO DIED FEB 26TH 1938
*THY WILL BE DONE*
*I AM THE RESURRECTION AND THE LIFE*
*JOHN 11 CHAP 25 VERSE*

**ORNAMENTS:**
CROSS IN TREE OF LIFE
WITH HALF SUNBURST

| | |
|---|---|
| NAME OF RECORDER: | PHYLLIS NOONAN |
| DATE: | 15 JULY 2005 |
| PHOTO REFERENCE: | D21 |
| LOCATION/MAP REF: | D1 D21 |

| | |
|---|---|
| GRAVEYARD NAME: | **ST. MARY'S ABBEY OLD GRAVEYARD** |
| GRAVEYARD CODE: | D1 |
| COUNTY: | MEATH |
| MEMORIAL NUMBER: | H5 |
| ERECTED BY: | |
| ORIENTATION: | EAST |
| NUMBER OF COMPONENTS: | 1 |
| NUMBER OF INSCRIBED FACES: | 1 |
| NUMBER OF PEOPLE COMMEMORATED: | 6 |
| MEMORIAL TYPE: | HEADSTONE |
| CONDITION OF MEMORIAL: | SOUND IN PLACE |
| CONDITION OF INSCRIPTION: | CLEAR |
| STONEMASON NAME: | |
| TECHNIQUE OF INSCRIPTION: | INCISED AND PAINTED |
| UNDERTAKER: | |
| STONE TOP: | ROUND |
| GRAVE TYPE: | TRIPLE |
| HEIGHT: | 68CM |
| WIDTH: | 218CM |
| THICKNESS: | 14CM |

| SURNAME: | CHRISTIAN | ADDRESS | DEATH | AGE |
|---|---|---|---|---|
| CARNEY | MARY | LARRIX ST DULEEK | 14 JAN 1977 | 73 |
| | JOHN (JACK) | | 24 JUNE 1978 | 78 |
| | PEADAR | | 29 OCT 1978 | 48 |
| ELLARD | WILLIAM (BILL) | LARRIX ST DULEEK | 03 FEB 2005 | 63 |
| CARNEY | JOHN | | APRIL 1947 | 98 |
| | ELLEN | | 1944 | 84 |

**INSCRIPTION:**
IN LOVING MEMORY OF
OUR MOTHER AND FATHER
MARY CARNEY
LARRIX ST DULEEK
DIED 14TH JAN 1977 AGED 73
HER HUSBAND JOHN (JACK)
DIED 24TH JUNE 1978 AGED 78
THEIR SON PEADAR
DIED 29TH OCT. 1978 AGED 48

WILLIAM (BILL) ELLARD
LARRIX ST., DULEEK
DIED 3RD FEBRUARY 2005
LOVING HUSBAND, DAD AND GRANDDAD
AND BELOVED SON IN LAW OF THE LATE
JACK AND MARY CARNEY
SADLY MISSED AND FOREVER IN OUR THOUGHTS
AGED 63 YEARS

JOHN CARNEY
FATHER OF JACK
DIED APRIL 1947 AGED 98
HIS WIFE ELLEN
DIED 1944 AGED 84
*MAY THEY REST IN PEACE*

| | |
|---|---|
| NAME OF RECORDER: | JANET LEIGH AND LIZ LYNCH |
| DATE: | 7 JUNE 2006 |
| PHOTO REFERENCE: | H5 |
| LOCATION/MAP REF: | D1 H5 |

| | |
|---|---|
| GRAVEYARD NAME: | **ST. MARY'S ABBEY OLD GRAVEYARD** |
| GRAVEYARD CODE: | D1 |
| COUNTY: | MEATH |
| MEMORIAL NUMBER: | B11 |
| ERECTED BY: | |
| ORIENTATION: | EAST |
| NUMBER OF COMPONENTS: | 3 |
| NUMBER OF INSCRIBED FACES: | 1 |
| NUMBER OF PEOPLE COMMEMORATED: | 5 |
| MEMORIAL TYPE: | HEADSTONE |
| CONDITION OF MEMORIAL: | SOUND IN PLACE |
| CONDITION OF INSCRIPTION: | MINT |
| STONEMASON NAME: | |
| TECHNIQUE OF INSCRIPTION: | INCISED AND PAINTED |
| UNDERTAKER: | |
| STONE TOP: | ARCH |
| GRAVE TYPE: | DOUBLE |
| HEIGHT: | 160CM |
| WIDTH: | 66CM |
| THICKNESS: | 8CM |

| SURNAME: | CHRISTIAN | ADDRESS | DEATH | AGE |
|---|---|---|---|---|
| CARRAGHER | JULIA | | 11 MAR 1906 | |
| | JOHN | | 25 MAR 1939 | |
| | GERTRUDE | | 25 FEB 1940 | |
| | PATRICK | | 11 FEB 1944 | |
| | JULIA | | 01 AUG 1958 | |

**INSCRIPTION:**
IN LOVING MEMORY
OF
JULIA CARRAGHER
WHO DIED MARCH 11TH 1906
AND HER BROTHER
JOHN CARRAGHER
DIED MARCH 25TH 1939
AND HIS WIFE
GERTRUDE
DIED FEB 25TH 1940
AND HER FATHER
PATRICK CARRAGHER
DIED FEB 11TH 1944
HIS WIFE JULIA
DIED AUG 1ST 1958
R.I.P.

**SYMBOLS:**
HEART WITH CROSS
THORNS AND FLAMES
SACRED TREE WITH FLOWERS

| | |
|---|---|
| NAME OF RECORDER: | PHYLLIS NOONAN AND BEN RYAN |
| DATE: | 2 JULY 2005 |
| PHOTO REFERENCE: | B11 |
| LOCATION/MAP REF: | D1 B11 |

| | |
|---|---|
| GRAVEYARD NAME: | **ST. MARY'S ABBEY OLD GRAVEYARD** |
| GRAVEYARD CODE: | D1 |
| COUNTY: | MEATH |
| MEMORIAL NUMBER: | H7 |
| ERECTED BY: | RICHARD CAVANAGH |
| ORIENTATION: | EAST |
| NUMBER OF COMPONENTS: | 1 |
| NUMBER OF INSCRIBED FACES: | 1 |
| NUMBER OF PEOPLE COMMEMORATED: | 5 |
| MEMORIAL TYPE: | HEADSTONE SUNBURST DISK |
| CONDITION OF MEMORIAL: | SOUND IN PLACE |
| CONDITION OF INSCRIPTION: | CLEAR |
| STONEMASON NAME: | |
| TECHNIQUE OF INSCRIPTION: | INCISED |
| UNDERTAKER: | |
| STONE TOP: | SUNBURST DISK |
| GRAVE TYPE: | SINGLE |
| HEIGHT: | 180CM |
| WIDTH: | 83CM |
| THICKNESS: | 17CM |

| SURNAME: | CHRISTIAN | ADDRESS | DEATH | AGE |
|---|---|---|---|---|
| CAVANAGH | CATHERINE | DROGHEDA | 03 SEPT 1837 | 16 YRS |
| CAVANAGH | CATHERINE | | 21 AUG 1812 | 55 YRS |
| WALL | CHRISTINE | | 16 APR 1935 | 65 YRS |
| WALL | MICHAEL | | 22 APR 1951 | 81 YRS |
| KENNEDY | ELIZABETH KATHRYN | | 08 NOV 1972 | INFANT |

**INSCRIPTION:**
ERECTED BY RICHARD CAVANAGH OF
DROGHEDA IN MEMORY OF HIS DAUGHTER
CATHERINE WHO DIED 3RD SEPT 1837
AGED 16YEARS ALSO OF HIS MOTHER
CATHERINE CAVANAGH ALIAS PURFIELD
WHO DEPARTED THIS LIFE 21ST AUGUST
1812 AGED 55 YEARS
CHRISTINE WALL DULEEK, DIED 16 APRIL 1935
AGED 65. HER HUSBAND MICHAEL DIED APRIL
22 1951 AGED 81
ELIZABETH KATHRYN KENNEDY
BORN AN ANGEL WRAPPED IN WINGS
8TH NOVEMBER 1972
GREAT GRANDDAUGHTER OF
MICHAEL AND CATHERINE
*REQUIESCANT IN PACE*

**SYMBOLS:**
IHS IN SUNBURST FLANKED BY CHERUBS
CROSS OVER H

| | |
|---|---|
| NAME OF RECORDER: | PHYLLIS NOONAN |
| DATE: | 10 JUNE 2006 |
| PHOTO REFERENCE: | H7 |
| LOCATION/MAP REF: | D1 H7 |

| | |
|---|---|
| GRAVEYARD NAME: | **ST. MARY'S ABBEY OLD GRAVEYARD** |
| GRAVEYARD CODE: | D1 |
| COUNTY: | MEATH |
| MEMORIAL NUMBER: | D19 |
| ERECTED BY: | |
| ORIENTATION: | EAST |
| NUMBER OF COMPONENTS: | 2 |
| NUMBER OF INSCRIBED FACES: | 1 |
| NUMBER OF PEOPLE COMMEMORATED: | 4 |
| MEMORIAL TYPE: | HEADSTONE |
| CONDITION OF MEMORIAL: | SOUND IN PLACE |
| CONDITION OF INSCRIPTION: | CLEAR |
| STONEMASON NAME: | A. WHYTE CHORD ROAD DROGHEDA |
| TECHNIQUE OF INSCRIPTION: | INCISED |
| UNDERTAKER: | |
| STONE TOP: | CELTIC CROSS |
| GRAVE TYPE: | TREBLE |
| HEIGHT: | 178CM |
| WIDTH: | 76CM |
| THICKNESS: | 10CM |

| SURNAME: | CHRISTIAN | ADDRESS | DEATH | AGE |
|---|---|---|---|---|
| CLARKE | THOMAS | DULEEK | 23 JAN 1877 | 45 |
| | BRIDGET | | 25 JAN 1882 | 44 |
| | PATRICK | | 04 JULY 1894 | 29 |
| | RICHARD | | 25 JULY 1937 | 72 |

**INSCRIPTION:**
ERECTED
BY
THE CHILDREN OF
THOMAS AND BRIDGET CLARKE
OF DULEEK
IN LOVING MEMORY OF THEIR FATHER WHO DIED
23 JANUARY 1877 AGED 45 YEARS
AND THEIR MOTHER
WHO DIED 25 JANUARY 1882 AGED 44 YEARS
ALSO THEIR BROTHERS
PATRICK
WHO DIED 4 JULY 1894 AGED 29 YEARS
AND RICHARD
WHO DIED 25 JULY 1937 AGED 72 YEARS
MAY THEY REST IN PEACE

**ORNAMENTS:**
LAMB IN CELTIC CROSS
WITH CHERUB THISTLE HEADSTONE FLANKED
BY 2 STONE BOLLARDS EACH SIDE OF
HEADSTONE

| | |
|---|---|
| NAME OF RECORDER: | LIZ LYNCH AND PHYLLIS NOONAN |
| DATE: | 13 JULY 2005 |
| PHOTO REFERENCE: | D 19 |
| LOCATION/MAP REF: | D1 D19 |

| | |
|---|---|
| GRAVEYARD NAME: | **ST. MARY'S ABBEY OLD GRAVEYARD** |
| GRAVEYARD CODE: | D1 |
| COUNTY: | MEATH |
| MEMORIAL NUMBER: | F21 |
| ERECTED BY: | PETER CLARKE |
| ORIENTATION: | EAST |
| NUMBER OF COMPONENTS: | 1 |
| NUMBER OF INSCRIBED FACES: | 1 |
| NUMBER OF PEOPLE COMMEMORATED: | 5 |
| MEMORIAL TYPE: | CROSS ON PEDESTAL |
| CONDITION OF MEMORIAL: | SOUND |
| CONDITION OF INSCRIPTION: | DECIPHERABLE |
| STONEMASON NAME: | |
| TECHNIQUE OF INSCRIPTION: | INCISED |
| UNDERTAKER: | |
| STONE TOP: | CROSS |
| GRAVE TYPE: | DOUBLE |
| HEIGHT: | 148CM |
| WIDTH: | 45CM |
| THICKNESS: | 25CM |

| SURNAME: | CHRISTIAN | ADDRESS | DEATH | AGE |
|---|---|---|---|---|
| CLARKE | MICHAEL | | 23 MAY 1896 | |
| | MARY CORNELIUS | | DIED YOUNG | |
| | CHRISDINA | | DIED YOUNG | |
| | ELIZABETH | | 24 MAY 1930 | |
| | PETER | DOWNSTOWN | 19 DEC 1974 | |

**INSCRIPTION:**
ERECTED
BY PETER CLARKE IN
LOVING MEMORY OF HIS SON
MICHAEL
WHO DIED MAY 23RD 1896
ALSO MARY CORNELIUS
AND CHRISDINA WHO DIED
YOUNG
AND HIS WIFE ELIZABETH
DIED MAY 24TH 1930
THEIR SON PETER DOWNSTOWN
DIED 19 DEC 1974 AGED 84
RIP

**SYMBOLS:**
FLEUR DE LIS CROSS
WITH ENTWINED IHS ON
PEDESTAL

| | |
|---|---|
| NAME OF RECORDER: | LIZ LYNCH AND PHYLLIS NOONAN |
| DATE: | 19 JULY 2005 |
| PHOTO REFERENCE: | F21 |
| LOCATION/MAP REF: | D1 F21 |

| | |
|---|---|
| GRAVEYARD NAME: | **ST. MARY'S ABBEY OLD GRAVEYARD** |
| GRAVEYARD CODE: | D1 |
| COUNTY: | MEATH |
| MEMORIAL NUMBER: | K40 |
| ERECTED BY: | EDWARD CLINTON |
| ORIENTATION: | EAST |
| NUMBER OF COMPONENTS: | 2 |
| NUMBER OF INSCRIBED FACES: | 1 |
| NUMBER OF PEOPLE COMMEMORATED: | 4 |
| MEMORIAL TYPE: | HEADSTONE |
| CONDITION OF MEMORIAL: | SOUND IN PLACE |
| CONDITION OF INSCRIPTION: | CLEAR |
| STONEMASON NAME: | TOMMY COONEY PLATTIN |
| TECHNIQUE OF INSCRIPTION: | INCISED AND PAINTED |
| UNDERTAKER: | MICHAEL DUIGNAN DULEEK |
| STONE TOP: | ROUND |
| GRAVE TYPE: | DOUBLE |
| HEIGHT: | 117CM |
| WIDTH: | 69CM |
| THICKNESS: | 08 CM |

| SURNAME: | CHRISTIAN | ADDRESS | DEATH | AGE |
|---|---|---|---|---|
| CLINTON | ROSE | GARBALLAGH | 06 OCT 1934 | |
| | MARIE INFANT DAUGHTER | | 06 MAY 1938 | |
| | ROSE | | 20 JAN 1987 | 73 |
| | EDWARD | | 20 APRIL 1996 | 87 |

**INSCRIPTION:**
CLINTON
ERECTED BY EDWARD
IN
LOVING MEMORY OF HIS BELOVED WIFE
ROSE CLINTON
GARBALLAGH
DIED 20TH JAN 1987 AGED 73 YRS
HIS DAUGHTER MARIE
DIED 6TH MAY 1938
AND HIS MOTHER ROSE DIED 6TH OCT 1934
AND THE ABOVE EDWARD (NED)
DIED 20TH APRIL 1996 AGED 87 YRS
*REST IN PEACE*

**SYMBOLS:**
ROSE EACH SIDE OF CLINTON NAME

| | |
|---|---|
| NAME OF RECORDER: | PHYLLIS NOONAN (NEE CLINTON) |
| DATE: | 22 APRIL 2006 |
| PHOTO REFERENCE: | K40 |
| LOCATION/MAP REF: | D1 K40 |

| | |
|---|---|
| GRAVEYARD NAME: | **ST. MARY'S ABBEY OLD GRAVEYARD** |
| GRAVEYARD CODE: | D1 |
| COUNTY: | MEATH |
| MEMORIAL NUMBER: | J19 |
| ERECTED BY: | |
| ORIENTATION: | EAST |
| NUMBER OF COMPONENTS: | 1 |
| NUMBER OF INSCRIBED FACES: | 1 |
| NUMBER OF PEOPLE COMMEMORATED: | 1 |
| MEMORIAL TYPE: | HEADSTONE |
| CONDITION OF MEMORIAL: | SOUND IN PLACE |
| CONDITION OF INSCRIPTION: | MAINLY DECIPHERABLE |
| STONEMASON NAME: | |
| TECHNIQUE OF INSCRIPTION: | INCISED |
| UNDERTAKER: | |
| STONE TOP: | ROUND |
| GRAVE TYPE: | SINGLE |
| HEIGHT: | 84CM |
| WIDTH: | 61CM |
| THICKNESS: | 8CM |

| SURNAME: | CHRISTIAN | ADDRESS | DEATH | AGE |
|---|---|---|---|---|
| CLOSKEY | PATRICK | | 10 DEC 1734 | 52 |

**INSCRIPTION:**
HERE LIES THE BODY OF
PATRICK CLOSKEY DEPED.
THIS LIFE 10TH DESEMBER
IN THE YEAR OF OUER LORD
GOD 1734 AGED 52 YEARS
BEING A REMARK FOR HIS
POSTERITY

**SYMBOLS:**
SPIRALS ON TOP OF
INSCRIPTION

| | |
|---|---|
| NAME OF RECORDER: | HELEN FULLAM, JIM ORTEN AND JANET LEIGH |
| DATE: | 13 AUG 2005 |
| PHOTO REFERENCE: | J19 |
| LOCATION/MAP REF: | D1 J19 |

| | |
|---|---|
| GRAVEYARD NAME: | **ST. MARY'S ABBEY OLD GRAVEYARD** |
| GRAVEYARD CODE: | D1 |
| COUNTY: | MEATH |
| MEMORIAL NUMBER: | J18 |
| ERECTED BY: | THOMAS CLUSKEY |
| ORIENTATION: | EAST |
| NUMBER OF COMPONENTS: | 1 |
| NUMBER OF INSCRIBED FACES: | 1 |
| NUMBER OF PEOPLE COMMEMORATED: | 10 |
| MEMORIAL TYPE: | HEADSTONE |
| CONDITION OF MEMORIAL: | SOUND IN PLACE |
| CONDITION OF INSCRIPTION: | MAINLY DECIPHERABLE |
| STONEMASON NAME: | |
| TECHNIQUE OF INSCRIPTION: | INCISED |
| UNDERTAKER: | |
| STONE TOP: | ROUND DISK |
| GRAVE TYPE: | SINGLE |
| HEIGHT: | 172CM |
| WIDTH: | 87CM |
| THICKNESS: | 10CM |

| SURNAME: | CHRISTIAN | ADDRESS | DEATH | AGE |
|---|---|---|---|---|
| CLUSKEY | CHRISTOPHER | | 24 DEC 1859 | |
| | MARGARET | | 30 MAY 1836 | |
| | ANNE | | | |
| | MARG | | | |
| | THOMAS | LADYMOOR | 31 DEC 1888 | |
| | CATHERINE | | 01 APRIL 1894 | |
| | JOSEPH | | 12 MAY 1894 | |
| | MARY | | 28 AUG 1908 | |
| | MARY MARGARET | | | |
| | WILLIAM | | 14 JAN 1939 | |

**INSCRIPTION:**
IHS
ERECTED
BY THOMAS CLUSKEY OF LADYMOOR
IN MEMORY OF HIS BELOVED FATHER
CHRISTOPHER CLUSKEY WHO DIED 24TH
DECR. 1859 ~ AND ALSO HIS
MOTHER MARGARET CLUSKEY WHO
DIED 30TH MAY 1836 ~ ALSO ANNE
AND MARG. ~ ALSO THE ABOVE THOMAS
CLUSKEY
WHO DIED DEC 31ST 1888 ALSO
HIS DAUGHTER CATHERINE
WHO DIED APRIL 1ST 1894 AND ALSO HIS
SON JOSEPH WHO DIED MAY 12TH 1894 ALSO
HIS WIFE MARY WHO DIED AUG 28TH 1908
HIS DAUGHTER MARY MARGARET
HIS SON WILLIAM WHO DIE 14TH JAN 1939
*REQUIESCANT IN PACE AMEN*

NAME OF RECORDER: HELEN FULLAM, JIM ORTEN AND
JANET LEIGH
DATE: 13 AUGUST 2005
PHOTO REFERENCE: J18
LOCATION/MAP REF: D1 J18

**SYMBOLS:**
FLEUR DE LIS CROSS IN A CIRCLE
GLORIA IN EXCELSIS DEO SCROLLED
BOTTOM OF CROSS TWO WINGED
ANGEL HEADS EITHER SIDE

| | |
|---|---|
| GRAVEYARD NAME: | **ST. MARY'S ABBEY OLD GRAVEYARD** |
| GRAVEYARD CODE: | D1 |
| COUNTY: | MEATH |
| MEMORIAL NUMBER: | J20 |
| ERECTED BY: | CATHERINE CLUSKEY |
| ORIENTATION: | EAST |
| NUMBER OF COMPONENTS: | 1 |
| NUMBER OF INSCRIBED FACES: | 1 |
| NUMBER OF PEOPLE COMMEMORATED: | 6 |
| MEMORIAL TYPE: | HEADSTONE |
| CONDITION OF MEMORIAL: | SOUND IN PLACE |
| CONDITION OF INSCRIPTION: | MAINLY DECIPHERABLE |
| STONEMASON NAME: | |
| TECHNIQUE OF INSCRIPTION: | INCISED |
| UNDERTAKER: | |
| STONE TOP: | ROUND |
| GRAVE TYPE: | SINGLE |
| HEIGHT: | 203CM |
| WIDTH: | 79CM |
| THICKNESS: | 18CM |

| SURNAME: | CHRISTIAN | ADDRESS | DEATH | AGE |
|---|---|---|---|---|
| CLUSKEY | JAMES | | 16 AUG 1837 | 67 |
| | CATHERINE | DULEEK | 01 OCT 1850 | 74 |
| | FRANCIS | | 26 NOV 1859 | 25 |

**INSCRIPTION:**
ERECTED
BY CATHERINE CLUSKEY OF DULEEK
IN MEMORY OF HER BELOVED HUSBAND
JAMES CLUSKEY WHO DIED 16TH OF
AUGUST 1837 AGED 67 YRS. AND 3
OF THEIR CHILDREN WHO DIED YOUNG
HERE ALSO ARE INTERRED THE MOR
TAL REMAINS OF THE ABOVE NAMED
CATHERINE CLUSKEY WHO DIED
OCTOBER THE 1ST 1850 AGED 74 YRS
AND ALSO THEIR SON FRANCIS
CLUSKEY WHO DIED 26TH NOVR.
1859 AGED 25 YRS.

*REQUIESCANT IN PACE AMEN*

**SYMBOLS:**
IHS SUNBURST WITH HEART
CHALICE WITH CROSS IN GOTHIC
WINDOW EITHER SIDE OF SUNBURST WITH A
POINTED 12 ROSETTE ON EACH
SIDE OF CHALICES

| | |
|---|---|
| NAME OF RECORDER: | HELEN FULLAM, JIM ORTEN AND JANET LEIGH |
| DATE: | 13 AUG 2005 |
| PHOTO REFERENCE: | J20 |
| LOCATION/MAP REF: | D1 J20 |

| | |
|---|---|
| GRAVEYARD NAME: | **ST. MARY'S ABBEY OLD GRAVEYARD** |
| GRAVEYARD CODE: | D1 |
| COUNTY: | MEATH |
| MEMORIAL NUMBER: | G10 |
| ERECTED BY: | |
| ORIENTATION: | EAST |
| NUMBER OF COMPONENTS: | 1 |
| NUMBER OF INSCRIBED FACES: | 1 |
| NUMBER OF PEOPLE COMMEMORATED: | 4 |
| MEMORIAL TYPE: | HEADSTONE |
| CONDITION OF MEMORIAL: | SOUND IN PLACE IN ABBEY |
| CONDITION OF INSCRIPTION: | GOOD |
| STONEMASON NAME: | |
| TECHNIQUE OF INSCRIPTION: | INCISED |
| UNDERTAKER: | |
| STONE TOP: | GOTHIC |
| GRAVE TYPE: | SINGLE IN ABBEY |

| SURNAME: | CHRISTIAN | ADDRESS | DEATH | AGE |
|---|---|---|---|---|
| COLEMAN | ELIZABETH | BRIDESBUSH | 27 MAY 1841 | |
| COLEMAN | JOHN | | 24 JUNE 1888 | 88 |
| COLEMAN | ANNE | | 05 FEB 1908 | 74 |
| COLEMAN | MATHEW | | 15 MAY 1918 | 80 |

**INSCRIPTION:**
ERECTED TO THE MEMORY OF ELIZABETH THE
BELOVED AND MUCH REVERED WIFE OF JOHN
COLEMAN OF BRIDESBUSH WHO DIED MAY 27TH A.D
1841 ALSO THE ABOVE JOHN COLEMAN WHO DIED
JUNE 24TH 1888 AGED 88 EARS AND THEIR DAUGHTER
ANNE COLEMAN WHO DIED 5TH FEB 1908 AGED
74 YEARS ALSO THEIR SON MATHEW COLEMAN
WHO DIED MAY 15TH 1918 AGED 80 YEARS

| | |
|---|---|
| NAME OF RECORDERS: | JANET LEIGH |
| DATE: | 6 SEPT 2006 |
| PHOTO REFERENCE: | G 10 |
| LOCATION/MAP REF | D1 G10 |

| | |
|---|---|
| GRAVEYARD NAME: | **ST. MARY'S ABBEY OLD GRAVEYARD** |
| GRAVEYARD CODE: | D1 |
| COUNTY: | MEATH |
| MEMORIAL NUMBER: | J31 |
| ERECTED BY: | THOMAS & CHRISTOPHER COLEMAN |
| ORIENTATION: | EAST |
| NUMBER OF COMPONENTS: | 1 |
| NUMBER OF INSCRIBED FACES: | 1 |
| NUMBER OF PEOPLE COMMEMORATED: | 1 |
| MEMORIAL TYPE: | HEADSTONE |
| CONDITION OF MEMORIAL: | SOUND BUT DISPLACED |
| CONDITION OF INSCRIPTION: | CLEAR |
| STONEMASON NAME: | |
| TECHNIQUE OF INSCRIPTION: | INCISED |
| UNDERTAKER: | |
| STONE TOP: | ROUND |
| GRAVE TYPE: | SINGLE |
| HEIGHT: | 155CM |
| WIDTH: | 90CM |
| THICKNESS: | 13CM |

| SURNAME: | CHRISTIAN | ADDRESS | DEATH | AGE |
|---|---|---|---|---|
| COLEMAN | CHRISTOPHER | | 12 DEC 1790 | 52 |
| | | | | |

**INSCRIPTION:**
ERECTED BY THOMAS COLEMAN
OF DAVIDSTOWN AND HIS BROTHER
CHRISTOPHER COLEMAN FOR THEM
AND THEIR POSTERITY AND IN
MEMORY OF THEIR FATHER CHRISTR
COLEMAN WHO DEPARTED THIS LIFE
12 DECEMR 1790 AGED 52 YEARS

**SYMBOLS:**
CRUCIFIXION OVER ALTER
WITH LIGHTED CANDLES
IHS ON ALTER TWO WINGED
CHERUBS WITH CHEVRON INCISIONS
HEADSTONE PARTIALLY SCROLLED

| | |
|---|---|
| NAME OF RECORDER: | PHYLLIS NOONAN AND BEN RYAN |
| DATE: | 20 AUG 2005 |
| PHOTO REFERENCE: | J31 |
| LOCATION/MAP REF: | D1 J31 |

| | |
|---|---|
| GRAVEYARD NAME: | **ST. MARY'S ABBEY OLD GRAVEYARD** |
| GRAVEYARD CODE: | D1 |
| COUNTY: | MEATH |
| MEMORIAL NUMBER: | G7 |
| ERECTED BY: | SIMON COLEMAN |
| ORIENTATION: | EAST |
| NUMBER OF COMPONENTS: | 1 |
| NUMBER OF INSCRIBED FACES: | 1 |
| NUMBER OF PEOPLE COMMEMORATED: | 2 |
| MEMORIAL TYPE: | HEADSTONE |
| CONDITION OF MEMORIAL: | SOUND IN PLACE |
| CONDITION OF INSCRIPTION: | CLEAR |
| STONEMASON NAME: | |
| TECHNIQUE OF INSCRIPTION: | INCISED |
| UNDERTAKER: | |
| STONE TOP: | ROUND |
| GRAVE TYPE: | SINGLE |
| HEIGHT: | 150CM |
| WIDTH: | 62CM |
| THICKNESS: | 4CM |

| SURNAME: | CHRISTIAN | ADDRESS | DEATH | AGE |
|---|---|---|---|---|
| COLEMAN | JOHN | | 1840 | 86 |
| | ELIZABETH | | 1861 | 55 |

**INSCRIPTION:**
ERECTED BY
SIMON COLEMAN OF SMITHSTOWN
CO MEATH IN MEMORY OF HIS
FATHER JOHN COLEMAN WHO DIED
IN 1840 AGED 86 YEARS
ALSO
ELIZABETH HIS BELOVED WIFE
WHO DIED IN 1861 AGED 55 YEARS
R.I.P.

**SYMBOLS:**
IHS

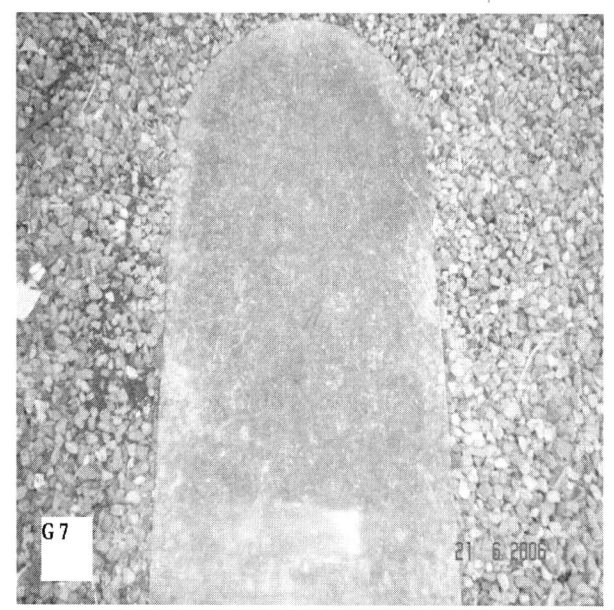

| | |
|---|---|
| NAME OF RECORDER: | LIZ LYNCH AND JANET LEIGH |
| DATE: | 24 JUNE 2006 |
| PHOTO REFERENCE: | G7 |
| LOCATION/MAP REF: | D1 G7 |

| | |
|---|---|
| GRAVEYARD NAME: | **ST. MARY'S ABBEY OLD GRAVEYARD** |
| GRAVEYARD CODE: | D1 |
| COUNTY: | MEATH |
| MEMORIAL NUMBER: | K46 |
| ERECTED BY: | |
| ORIENTATION: | EAST |
| NUMBER OF COMPONENTS: | BROKEN |
| NUMBER OF INSCRIBED FACES: | BROKEN |
| NUMBER OF PEOPLE COMMEMORATED: | 1 |
| MEMORIAL TYPE: | HEADSTONE BROKEN |
| CONDITION OF MEMORIAL: | BROKEN |
| CONDITION OF INSCRIPTION: | MAINLY DECIPHERABLE |
| STONEMASON NAME: | F. WHYTE CHORD DROGHEDA |
| TECHNIQUE OF INSCRIPTION: | INCISED |
| UNDERTAKER: | |
| STONE TOP: | BROKEN |
| GRAVE TYPE: | SINGLE |

| SURNAME: | CHRISTIAN | ADDRESS | DEATH | AGE |
|---|---|---|---|---|
| COLEMAN | CATHERINE | WEST CARN HOUSE DULEEK | 10 JAN 1876 | |

**INSCRIPTION:**
ERECTED
TO THE LOVING MEMORY OF
CATHERINE COLEMAN
WEST CARN HOUSE DULEEK
WHO DEPARTED THIS LIFE
JANUARY 10TH 1876
BY HER FOND CHILDREN
AND GRANDCHILDREN

| | |
|---|---|
| NAME OF RECORDER: | JANET LEIGH AND SINEAD FULLAM |
| DATE: | 6 MAY 2006 |
| PHOTO REFERENCE: | K46 |
| LOCATION/MAP REF: | D1 K46 |

| | |
|---|---|
| GRAVEYARD NAME: | **ST. MARY'S ABBEY OLD GRAVEYARD** |
| GRAVEYARD CODE: | D1 |
| COUNTY: | MEATH |
| MEMORIAL NUMBER: | G8 |
| ERECTED BY: | THOMAS AND JAMES COLEMAN |
| ORIENTATION: | EAST |
| NUMBER OF COMPONENTS: | 1 |
| NUMBER OF INSCRIBED FACES: | 1 |
| NUMBER OF PEOPLE COMMEMORATED: | 3 |
| MEMORIAL TYPE: | HEADSTONE LOW MONUMENT |
| CONDITION OF MEMORIAL: | SOUND IN PLACE IN ABBEY |
| CONDITION OF INSCRIPTION: | CLEAR |
| STONEMASON NAME: | |
| TECHNIQUE OF INSCRIPTION: | INCISED |
| UNDERTAKER: | |
| STONE TOP: | ROUND |
| GRAVE TYPE: | SINGLE |
| HEIGHT: | 159CM |
| WIDTH: | 67CM |
| THICKNESS: | 4CM |

| SURNAME: | CHRISTIAN | ADDRESS | DEATH | AGE |
|---|---|---|---|---|
| COLEMAN | MARGARET | | 24 JULY 1775 | 45 |
| | GEORGE | | 09 AUG 1777 | 22 |
| | PATRICK | | 23 OCT 1777 | 14 |

**INSCRIPTION:**
THIS STONE WAS ERECTED BY
THOMAS AND JAMES COLEMAN
OF DROGHEDA FOR THEM AND THEIR
POSTERITY HERE LIETH THE BODY
OF MARGARET COLEMAN WIFE TO
ABOVE JAMES COLEMAN
WHO DEPARTED THIS LIFE THE 24TH OF
JULY 1775 AGED 45 YEARS
ALSO HERE LIETH THE BODY OF
GEORGE COLEMAN SON TO THE
ABOVE THOMAS COLEMAN
DEPARTED THIS LIFE THE 9 OF
AUGUST 1777 AGED 22 YEARS ALSO
HERE LIETH THE BODY OF HIS
BROTHER PATRICK COLEMAN WHO
DEPARTED THIS LIFE THE 23RD OF
OCTOBER 1777 AGED 14 YEARS

**SYMBOLS:**
IHS

| | |
|---|---|
| NAME OF RECORDER: | LIZ LYNCH, PHYLLIS NOONAN AND JANET LEIGH |
| DATE: | 24 JUNE 2006 |
| PHOTO REFERENCE: | G8 |
| LOCATION/MAP REF: | D1 G8 |

| | |
|---|---|
| GRAVEYARD NAME: | **ST. MARY'S ABBEY OLD GRAVEYARD** |
| GRAVEYARD CODE: | D1 |
| COUNTY: | MEATH |
| MEMORIAL NUMBER: | G9 |
| ERECTED BY: | |
| ORIENTATION: | EAST |
| NUMBER OF COMPONENTS: | 1 |
| NUMBER OF INSCRIBED FACES: | 1 |
| NUMBER OF PEOPLE COMMEMORATED: | 2 |
| MEMORIAL TYPE: | LOW MONUMENT IN ABBEY |
| CONDITION OF MEMORIAL: | SOUND IN PLACE |
| CONDITION OF INSCRIPTION: | CLEAR |
| STONEMASON NAME: | |
| TECHNIQUE OF INSCRIPTION: | INCISED |
| UNDERTAKER: | |
| STONE TOP: | LOW MONUMENT |
| GRAVE TYPE: | SINGLE |

| SURNAME: | CHRISTIAN | ADDRESS | DEATH | AGE |
|---|---|---|---|---|
| COLEMAN | RICHARD | DROGHEDA | 01 DEC 1816 | 30 |
| COLEMAN | JAMES SIMON | DROGHEDA | 18 JUNE 1821 | 30 |

**INSCRIPTION:**
HERE LIETH THE REMAINS OF MR RICHARD COLEMAN OF DROGHEDA WHO DEPARTED THIS LIFE THE 1ST DECEMBER 1816 AGED 30 YEARS DIED ON THE 18TH JUNE 1821 IN THE THIRTIETH YEAR OF HIS AGE JAMES SIMON COLEMAN MERCHANT BROTHER TO RICHARD COLEMAN BOTH OF DROGHEDA

| | |
|---|---|
| NAME OF RECORDER: | JANET LEIGH |
| DATE: | SEPT 2006 |
| PHOTO REFERENCE: | G9 |
| LOCATION/MAP REF: | D1 - G9 |

| | |
|---|---|
| GRAVEYARD NAME: | **ST. MARY'S ABBEY OLD GRAVEYARD** |
| GRAVEYARD CODE: | D1 |
| COUNTY: | MEATH |
| MEMORIAL NUMBER: | G12 |
| ERECTED BY: | RICHARD COLEMAN |
| ORIENTATION: | EAST |
| NUMBER OF COMPONENTS: | 1 |
| NUMBER OF INSCRIBED FACES: | 1 |
| NUMBER OF PEOPLE COMMEMORATED: | 4 |
| MEMORIAL TYPE: | HEADSTONE |
| CONDITION OF MEMORIAL: | SOUND IN PLACE ON ABBEY FLOOR |
| CONDITION OF INSCRIPTION: | CLEAR |
| STONEMASON NAME: | |
| TECHNIQUE OF INSCRIPTION: | INCISED |
| UNDERTAKER: | |
| STONE TOP: | ROUND |
| GRAVE TYPE: | SINGLE |
| HEIGHT: | 158CM |
| WIDTH: | 70CM |
| THICKNESS: | 6CM |

| SURNAME: | CHRISTIAN | ADDRESS | DEATH | AGE |
|---|---|---|---|---|
| COLEMAN | SIMON | | 30 MAR 1800 | 44 |
| | WIFE OF SIMON | | 30 JULY 1803 | 43 |

**INSCRIPTION:**

ERECTED BY RICHD COLEMAN IN MEMORY OF HIS FATHER SIMON COLEMAN WHO DEPARTED THIS LIFE 30TH MARCH 1800 AGED 44 YRS ALSO THE WIFE OF THE ABOVE SIMON COLEMAN WHO DEPARTED THIS LIFE 30TH JULY 1803 AGED 43 YRS: 2 OF THEIR CHILDREN WHO DIED YOUNG

*REQUIESCANT IN PACE AMEN*

**SYMBOLS**
FIGURE OF CHRIST ON CROSS
I.H.S. BELOW FLANKED BY TWO ANGEL HEADS

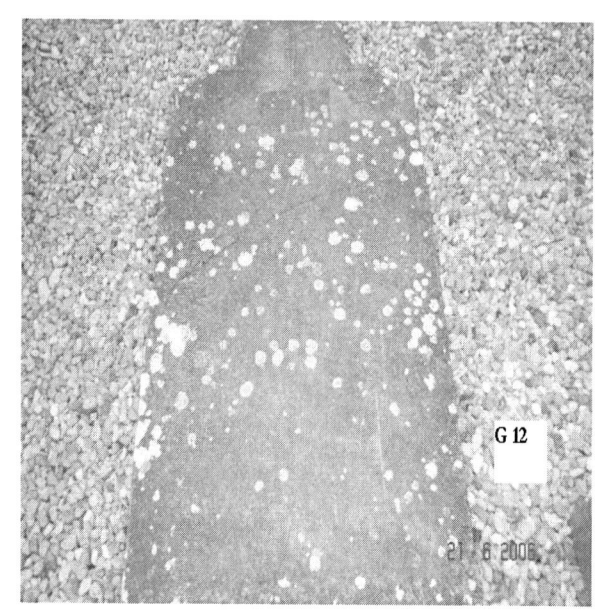

| | |
|---|---|
| NAME OF RECORDER: | JANET LEIGH |
| DATE: | 28 JUNE 2006 |
| PHOTO REFERENCE: | G12 |
| LOCATION/MAP REF: | D1 G12 |

| | |
|---|---|
| GRAVEYARD NAME: | **ST. MARY'S ABBEY OLD GRAVEYARD** |
| GRAVEYARD CODE: | D1 |
| COUNTY: | MEATH |
| MEMORIAL NUMBER: | J6 |
| ERECTED BY: | PATK COLLIER |
| ORIENTATION: | EAST |
| NUMBER OF COMPONENTS: | 1 |
| NUMBER OF INSCRIBED FACES: | 1 |
| NUMBER OF PEOPLE COMMEMORATED: | 3 |
| MEMORIAL TYPE: | HEADSTONE |
| CONDITION OF MEMORIAL: | SOUND IN PLACE |
| CONDITION OF INSCRIPTION: | MAINLY DECIPHERABLE |
| STONEMASON NAME: | |
| TECHNIQUE OF INSCRIPTION: | INCISED |
| UNDERTAKER: | |
| STONE TOP: | ROUND |
| GRAVE TYPE: | SINGLE |
| HEIGHT: | 182CM |
| WIDTH: | 87CM |
| THICKNESS: | 8 CM |

| SURNAME: | CHRISTIAN | ADDRESS | DEATH | AGE |
|---|---|---|---|---|
| COLLIER | WIFE | | 27 APR 1812 | 61 |

**INSCRIPTION:**
THIS STONE WAS ERECTED BY
PATK COLLIER OF BORRANSTOWN
IN MEMORY OF FATHER AND MOTHER AND
HIS BELOVED WIFE WHO DEPARTED THIS LIFE
APRIL 27TH 1812
61 YEARS

**SYMBOLS:**
CROSS ON TOP
IHS IN FULL SUNBURST

| | |
|---|---|
| NAME OF RECORDER: | JANET LEIGH |
| DATE: | 6 AUGUST 2005 |
| PHOTO REFERENCE: | J6 |
| LOCATION/MAP REF: | D1 J6 |

| | |
|---|---|
| GRAVEYARD NAME: | **ST. MARY'S ABBEY OLD GRAVEYARD** |
| GRAVEYARD CODE: | D1 |
| COUNTY: | MEATH |
| MEMORIAL NUMBER: | L45 |
| ERECTED BY: | |
| ORIENTATION: | EAST |
| NUMBER OF COMPONENTS: | 3 |
| NUMBER OF INSCRIBED FACES: | 1 |
| NUMBER OF PEOPLE COMMEMORATED: | 4 |
| MEMORIAL TYPE: | HEADSTONE |
| CONDITION OF MEMORIAL: | SOUND IN PLACE |
| CONDITION OF INSCRIPTION: | CLEAR |
| STONEMASON NAME: | |
| TECHNIQUE OF INSCRIPTION: | INCISED AND PAINTED |
| UNDERTAKER: | |
| STONE TOP: | CROSS |
| GRAVE TYPE: | SINGLE |
| HEIGHT: | 136CM |
| WIDTH: | 59CM |
| THICKNESS: | 7CM |

| SURNAME: | CHRISTIAN | ADDRESS | DEATH | AGE |
|---|---|---|---|---|
| COLLIER | CHRISTOPHER | DULEEK | 25 JUNE 1907 | |
| | MARY | | 24 FEB 1946 | |
| | JACK | | 02 JAN 1981 | |
| | ELSIE | | 02 OCT 1973 | |

**INSCRIPTION:**
IN LOVING MEMORY OF
CHRISTOPHER COLLIER
DULEEK
DIED 25TH JUNE 1907
HIS WIFE MARY
DIED 24TH FEB 1946
THEIR SON JACK DIED 2ND JAN 1981
HIS WIFE ELSIE DIED 2ND OCT 1973
BOTH INTERRED IN HOLY CROSS CEMETERY
REST IN PEACE

**SYMBOLS:**
HEADSTONE CROSS

| | |
|---|---|
| NAME OF RECORDER: | PHYLLIS NOONAN |
| DATE: | 24 JUNE 2013 |
| PHOTO REFERENCE: | L45 |
| LOCATION/MAP REF: | D1 L45 |

| | |
|---|---|
| GRAVEYARD NAME: | **ST. MARY'S ABBEY OLD GRAVEYARD** |
| GRAVEYARD CODE: | D1 |
| COUNTY: | MEATH |
| MEMORIAL NUMBER: | L19 |
| ERECTED BY: | LOVING FAMILY |
| ORIENTATION: | EAST |
| NUMBER OF COMPONENTS: | 1 |
| NUMBER OF INSCRIBED FACES: | 1 |
| NUMBER OF PEOPLE COMMEMORATED: | 7 |
| MEMORIAL TYPE: | HEADSTONE |
| CONDITION OF MEMORIAL: | SOUND IN PLACE |
| CONDITION OF INSCRIPTION: | CLEAR |
| STONEMASON NAME: | |
| TECHNIQUE OF INSCRIPTION: | INCISED AND PAINTED |
| UNDERTAKER: | |
| STONE TOP: | ARCHED WITH CROSS |
| GRAVE TYPE: | TREBLE |
| HEIGHT: | 142CM |
| WIDTH: | 62CM |
| THICKNESS: | 06CM |

| SURNAME: | CHRISTIAN | ADDRESS | DEATH | AGE |
|---|---|---|---|---|
| CONLON | BRIDGET | LARRIX STREET | 24 OCT 1960 | |
| | RICHARD | | 23 SEPT 1937 | |
| | RICHARD | | 17 FEB 1922 | 14 |
| | NORA | | 24 JAN 1989 | |
| | JOSEPH | | 06 APRIL 1989 | |
| | THOMAS | | 04 OCT 1989 | |
| | PETER | | 21 FEB 1999 | |

**INSCRIPTION:**
IN
LOVING MEMORY OF
BRIDGET CONLON
LARRIX STREET
DIED 24TH OCT 1960
HER HUSBAND RICHARD
DIED 23RD SEPT 1937
THEIR SON RICHARD
DIED 17TH FEB 1922 AGED 14 YRS
THEIR DAUGHTER NORA
DIED 24 JAN 1989
THEIR SON'S JOSEPH
DIED 6 APRIL 1989
THOMAS
DIED 4 OCT 1989
PETER
DIED 21 FEB 1999
R.I.P
*ERECTED BY THEIR LOVING FAMILY*

**SYMBOLS:**
CELTIC CROSS SACRED HEART IN CENTRE IVY LEAVES IN ARMS OF CROSS

| | |
|---|---|
| NAME OF RECORDER: | JANET LEIGH AND SINEAD FULLAM |
| DATE: | 20 MAY 2006 |
| PHOTO REFERENCE: | L19 |
| LOCATION/MAP REF: | D1 L19 |

| | |
|---|---|
| GRAVEYARD NAME: | **ST. MARY'S ABBEY OLD GRAVEYARD** |
| GRAVEYARD CODE: | D1 |
| COUNTY: | MEATH |
| MEMORIAL NUMBER: | L18 |
| ERECTED BY: | JAMES CONLON DULEEK |
| ORIENTATION: | EAST |
| NUMBER OF COMPONENTS: | 2 |
| NUMBER OF INSCRIBED FACES: | 1 |
| NUMBER OF PEOPLE COMMEMORATED: | 11 |
| MEMORIAL TYPE: | HEADSTONE CELTIC CROSS |
| CONDITION OF MEMORIAL: | SOUND IN PLACE |
| CONDITION OF INSCRIPTION: | LEGIBLE |
| STONEMASON NAME: | |
| TECHNIQUE OF INSCRIPTION: | INCISED AND PAINTED |
| UNDERTAKER: | |
| STONE TOP: | CROSS |
| GRAVE TYPE: | TREBLE |
| HEIGHT: | 212CM |
| WIDTH: | 67CM |
| THICKNESS: | 14CM |

| SURNAME: | CHRISTIAN | ADDRESS | DEATH | AGE |
|---|---|---|---|---|
| CONLON | MARGARET | | JUNE 1838 | |
| | JAMES | | APRIL 1850 | |
| | HUGH | | APRIL 1879 | |
| | MARY | | FEB 1880 | |
| | JAMES | | APRIL 1880 | |
| | MARGARET | | JAN 1883 | |
| | JANE | | APRIL 1888 | |
| | JAMES | DULEEK | NOV 1903 | |
| | JOHN | | 27 NOV 1940 | 73 |
| | BRIDGET | | 08 DEC 1950 | 78 |
| | BARTHOLOMEW | | 04 FEB 1961 | 86 |

**INSCRIPTION:**
ERECTED
BY
JAMES CONLON DULEEK. IN MEMORY OF
HIS MOTHER MARGARET DIED JUNE 1838
HIS FATHER JAMES DIED APRIL 1850
HIS SON HUGH DIED APRIL 1879
HIS DAUGHTER MARY DIED FEB 1880
HIS SON JAMES DIED APRIL 1880
AND HIS DAUGHTER MARGARET
DIED JAN 1883
ALSO HIS WIFE JANE DIED APRIL 1888
AND THE ABOVE JAMES DIED NOV 1903
ALSO JOHN SON OF THE ABOVE WHO
DIED NOV 27TH 1940 AGED 73 YEARS
BRIDGET CONLON
DIED 8TH DEC 1950 AGED 78 YRS
HER HUSBAND BARTHOLOMEW
DIED 4TH FEB 1961 AGED 86 YRS
R.I.P.

**SYMBOLS:**
CROSS IN CIRCLE CROSS ABOVE IHS

| | |
|---|---|
| NAME OF RECORDER: | BEN RYAN, JANET LEIGH AND HELEN FULLAM |
| DATE: | 20 MAY 2006 |
| PHOTO REFERENCE: | L18 |
| LOCATION/MAP REF: | D1 L18 |

| | |
|---|---|
| GRAVEYARD NAME: | **ST. MARY'S ABBEY OLD GRAVEYARD** |
| GRAVEYARD CODE: | D1 |
| COUNTY: | MEATH |
| MEMORIAL NUMBER: | B6 A |
| ERECTED BY: | MARIE WALL |
| ORIENTATION: | EAST |
| NUMBER OF COMPONENTS: | 2 |
| NUMBER OF INSCRIBED FACES: | 1 |
| NUMBER OF PEOPLE COMMEMORATED: | 1 |
| MEMORIAL TYPE: | HEADSTONE |
| CONDITION OF MEMORIAL: | SOUND IN PLACE |
| CONDITION OF INSCRIPTION: | CLEAR |
| STONEMASON NAME: | |
| TECHNIQUE OF INSCRIPTION: | INCISED |
| UNDERTAKER: | |
| STONE TOP: | ARCH |
| GRAVE TYPE: | SINGLE |
| HEIGHT: | 68CM |
| WIDTH: | 60CM |
| THICKNESS: | 05CM |

| SURNAME: | CHRISTIAN | ADDRESS | DEATH | AGE |
|---|---|---|---|---|
| CONNELL | PAUL | 68 RYAN PARK | 06 DEC 2005 | |

**INSCRIPTION:**
WITH LOVE WE REMEMBER
PAUL CONNELL
68 RYAN PARK
DIED 6TH DECEMBER 2005

REST IN PEACE
ERECTED BY HIS LOVING PARTNER MARIE

| | |
|---|---|
| NAME OF RECORDER: | PHYLLIS NOONAN AND LIZ LYNCH |
| DATE: | 18 APRIL 2008 |
| PHOTO REFERENCE: | B6 A |
| LOCATION/MAP REF: | D1 B6A |

| | |
|---|---|
| GRAVEYARD NAME: | **ST. MARY'S ABBEY OLD GRAVEYARD** |
| GRAVEYARD CODE: | D1 |
| COUNTY: | MEATH |
| MEMORIAL NUMBER: | D16 |
| ERECTED BY: | CHRISTOPHER CONNELL |
| ORIENTATION: | EAST |
| NUMBER OF COMPONENTS: | 1 |
| NUMBER OF INSCRIBED FACES: | 1 |
| NUMBER OF PEOPLE COMMEMORATED: | 3 |
| MEMORIAL TYPE: | LOW MONUMENT |
| CONDITION OF MEMORIAL: | 2 HALVES |
| CONDITION OF INSCRIPTION: | MAINLY DECIPHERABLE |
| STONEMASON NAME: | |
| TECHNIQUE OF INSCRIPTION: | INCISED |
| UNDERTAKER: | |
| STONE TOP: | LOW MONUMENT |
| GRAVE TYPE: | SINGLE LOW MONUMENT |
| HEIGHT: | 261CM |
| WIDTH: | 79CM |
| THICKNESS: | 06CM |

| SURNAME: | CHRISTIAN | ADDRESS | DEATH | AGE |
|---|---|---|---|---|
| CONNELL | RICHARD | SANDY HALL | 26 OCT 1776 | 60 |
| | ALICE | | DEC 1797 | 70 |
| | MARY | | 11 SEPT 1817 | 46 |

**INSCRIPTION:**
ERECTED BY CHRISTOPHER
CONNELL OF SANDY HALL FOR
HIM AND HIS POSTERITY
HERE LIES THE REMAINS OF
HIS FATHER RICHARD CONNELL
WHO DEPARTED THIS LIFE
THE 23TH OF OCTOBER 1776
AGED 60 YEARS ALSO OF HIS
MOTHER ALICE CONNELL DIED
DECEMBER THE 25TH 1797
AGED 70 YEARS HERE ALSO
LIETH THE REMAINS OF HIS
BELOVD WIFE MARY
CONNELL WHO DIED THE
11TH OF SEP 1817 AGED 46
YEARS
*REQUIESCANT IN PACE AMEN*

**SYMBOLS:**
SCROLLED EACH SIDE OF LOW MONUMENT CHRIST ON CROSS ON ALTER WITH TWO CANDLES FLANKED BY WINGED ANGEL HEADS

| | |
|---|---|
| NAME OF RECORDER: | PHYLLIS NOONAN |
| DATE: | 16 JULY 2005 |
| PHOTO REFERENCE: | D16 |
| LOCATION/MAP REF: | D1 D16 |

| | |
|---|---|
| GRAVEYARD NAME: | **ST. MARY'S ABBEY OLD GRAVEYARD** |
| GRAVEYARD CODE: | D1 |
| COUNTY: | MEATH |
| MEMORIAL NUMBER: | F20 |
| ERECTED BY: | NICHOLAS CONNELL |
| ORIENTATION: | EAST |
| NUMBER OF COMPONENTS: | 2 |
| NUMBER OF INSCRIBED FACES: | 1 |
| NUMBER OF PEOPLE COMMEMORATED: | 11 |
| MEMORIAL TYPE: | HEADSTONE |
| CONDITION OF MEMORIAL: | SOUND IN PLACE |
| CONDITION OF INSCRIPTION: | CLEAR |
| STONEMASON NAME: | |
| TECHNIQUE OF INSCRIPTION: | INCISED |
| UNDERTAKER: | |
| STONE TOP: | SUNBURST DISK |
| GRAVE TYPE: | DOUBLE |
| HEIGHT: | 135CM |
| WIDTH: | 75CM |
| THICKNESS: | 10CM |

| SURNAME: | CHRISTIAN | RELATIONSHIP/ADDRESS | DEATH | AGE |
|---|---|---|---|---|
| CONNELL | JOHN | FATHER, LONGFORD | 1ST MAR 1840 | 66 |
| | ANNE | MOTHER | 13TH AUG 1848 | 56 |
| | JOHN | SON | 16TH OCT 1846 | 11 MONTHS |
| | MARY | WIFE | 1ST OCT 1886 | 77 |
| COLLIER | KATE | GRANDDAUGHTER | 30TH APR 1885 | 11 YEARS |
| CONNELL | NICHOLAS | GRANDSON | 7TH AUG 1899 | 16 MONTHS |
| | NICHOLAS | | 18TH NOV 1899 | 86 |
| | WILLIAM | GRANDSON | 23RD NOV 1807 | 28 YEARS |
| | JOHN | SON | 4TH AUG 1923 | 75 |
| | MARGARET | JOHN'S WIFE | 6TH NOV 1927 | 56 |
| | HELEN | | 21ST MARCH 1959 | 7 MONTHS |

**INSCRIPTION:**
ERECTED
BY NICHOLAS CONNELL OF
LONGFORD IN MEMORY OF HIS
FATHER JOHN CONNELL WHO DIED
ON THE 1ST MARCH 1848 AGED 66 YEARS
ALSO HIS MOTHER ANNE CONNELL
WHO DIED 13TH AUGUST 1848 AGED
56 YEARS AND ALSO HIS SON
JOHN CONNELL WHO DIED 16TH OCTOBER
1846 AGED 11 MONTHS AND OF HIS
WIFE MARY CONNELL WHO DIED
OCT 1 1886 AGED 77 YEARS
HIS GRANDDAUGHTER KATE COLLIER WHO DIED
30TH APRIL 1885 AGED 11 YEARS HIS GRANDSON
NICHOLAS CONNELL WHO DIED 7TH AUG 1899
AGED 16 MONTHS ALSO THE ABOVE NAMED
NICHOLAS WHO DIED 18TH NOV 1899 AGED 86 YEARS
HIS GRANDSON WILLIAM DIED 23RD NOV 1907
AGED 28 YEARS
HIS SON JOHN DIED 4TH AUG 1923 AGED
75 YEARS
AND HIS WIFE MARGARET DIED 6TH NOV 1927
AGED 56 YEARS
HELEN CONNELL DIED 21 MARCH 1959

**ORNAMENTS:**
LAMB IN SUNBURST CHALICE MALTESE CROSS

| | |
|---|---|
| NAME OF RECORDER: | PHYLLIS NOONAN |
| DATE: | 13 JULY 2005 |
| PHOTO REFERENCE: | F20 |
| LOCATION/MAP REF: | D1 F20 |

| | |
|---|---|
| GRAVEYARD NAME: | **ST. MARY'S ABBEY OLD GRAVEYARD** |
| GRAVEYARD CODE: | D1 |
| COUNTY: | MEATH |
| MEMORIAL NUMBER: | K19 |
| ERECTED BY: | THOMAS CONNELL DULEEK |
| ORIENTATION: | EAST |
| NUMBER OF COMPONENTS: | 1 |
| NUMBER OF INSCRIBED FACES: | 1 |
| NUMBER OF PEOPLE COMMEMORATED: | 5 AND ANCESTORS |
| MEMORIAL TYPE: | HEADSTONE |
| CONDITION OF MEMORIAL: | COLLAPSED |
| CONDITION OF INSCRIPTION: | DECIPHERABLE |
| STONEMASON NAME: | |
| TECHNIQUE OF INSCRIPTION: | INCISED |
| UNDERTAKER: | |
| STONE TOP: | ROUND TOP COLLAPSED |
| GRAVE TYPE: | SINGLE |
| HEIGHT: | LENGTH 147CM |
| WIDTH: | 73CM |
| THICKNESS: | 09CM |

| SURNAME: | CHRISTIAN | ADDRESS | DEATH | AGE |
|---|---|---|---|---|
| CONNELL | 4 CHILDREN | | | |
| FITZHARRIS | MARY | | 6 JUNE 1795 | 47 |

**INSCRIPTION:**
ERECTED ON THE 6TH FEBRY 1796
BY THOMAS CONNELL OF DULEEK
WHERE RESTS THE REMAINS OF HIS ANCESTORS WITH 4 OF HIS
CHILDREN ALSO HIS WIFE MARY
FITZHARRIS ALIAS CONNELL WHO
DEPARTED THIS LIFE THE 6TH OF JUNE 1795
AGED 47 YEARS TO WHOSE
MEMORY THIS STONE WAS ERECTED
REQUIESCANT IN PACE AMEN

| | |
|---|---|
| NAME OF RECORDER: | HELEN FULLAM AND SINEAD FULLAM |
| DATE: | 24 SEPT 2005 |
| PHOTO REFERENCE: | K19 |
| LOCATION/MAP REF: | D1 K19 |

| | |
|---|---|
| GRAVEYARD NAME: | **ST. MARY'S ABBEY OLD GRAVEYARD** |
| GRAVEYARD CODE: | D1 |
| COUNTY: | MEATH |
| MEMORIAL NUMBER: | H3 |
| ERECTED BY: | ANNE CONNOLLY |
| ORIENTATION: | EAST |
| NUMBER OF COMPONENTS: | 1 |
| NUMBER OF INSCRIBED FACES: | 1 |
| NUMBER OF PEOPLE COMMEMORATED: | 2 |
| MEMORIAL TYPE: | HEADSTONE SUNBURST DISK |
| CONDITION OF MEMORIAL: | SOUND IN PLACE |
| CONDITION OF INSCRIPTION: | CLEAR |
| STONEMASON NAME: | |
| TECHNIQUE OF INSCRIPTION: | INCISED |
| UNDERTAKER: | |
| STONE TOP: | ROUND SUNBURST DISK |
| GRAVE TYPE: | SINGLE |
| HEIGHT: | 153CM |
| WIDTH: | 99CM |
| THICKNESS: | 14CM |

| SURNAME: | CHRISTIAN | ADDRESS | DEATH | AGE |
|---|---|---|---|---|
| CONNOLLY | MICHAEL | PLATTEN | 16 MAR 1946 | 56 |
| | ANNE | | JUNE 1878 | |

**INSCRIPTION:**
ERECTED
BY ANNE CONNOLLY OF PLATTEN IN
MEMORY OF HER BELOVED HUSBAND
MICHAEL CONNOLLY WHO DIED
MARCH 16TH 1846 AGED 56 YEARS
AND HIS WIFE THE ABOVE ANNE CONNOLLY
WHO DIED JUNE …… 1878

**SYMBOLS:**
SUNBURST IHS CROSS AND HEART FLANKED BY
CHERUBS IN THE MIDDLE A ROSETTE WITH A CROSS
ON EITHER SIDE – SCROLLED FROM TOP TO BOTTOM OF
STONE - LOZENGES ABOVE INSCRIPTION

| | |
|---|---|
| NAME OF RECORDER: | JANET LEIGH AND LIZ LYNCH |
| DATE: | 07 JUNE 2006 |
| PHOTO REFERENCE: | H3 |
| LOCATION/MAP REF: | D1 H3 |

| | |
|---|---|
| GRAVEYARD NAME: | **ST. MARY'S ABBEY OLD GRAVEYARD** |
| GRAVEYARD CODE: | D1 |
| COUNTY: | MEATH |
| MEMORIAL NUMBER: | K38 |
| ERECTED BY: | BARTLE CONNOLLY |
| ORIENTATION: | EAST |
| NUMBER OF COMPONENTS: | 4 |
| NUMBER OF INSCRIBED FACES: | 1 |
| NUMBER OF PEOPLE COMMEMORATED: | 2 |
| MEMORIAL TYPE: | CELTIC CROSS |
| CONDITION OF MEMORIAL: | DISPLACED |
| CONDITION OF INSCRIPTION: | MAINLY DECIPHERABLE |
| STONEMASON NAME: | MOSS |
| TECHNIQUE OF INSCRIPTION: | INCISED |
| UNDERTAKER: | |
| STONE TOP: | CELTIC CROSS |
| GRAVE TYPE: | SINGLE |
| HEIGHT: | 275CM |
| WIDTH: | 73CM |
| THICKNESS: | 43CM |

| SURNAME: | CHRISTIAN | ADDRESS | DEATH | AGE |
|---|---|---|---|---|
| CONNOLLY | KATIE | | 25 DEC 1931 | |
| | BARTLE | DULEEK | 22 OCT 1933 | |

**INSCRIPTION:**
ERECTED
BY
BARTLE CONNOLLY
DULEEK
IN MEMORY OF
HIS BELOVED WIFE
KATIE
WHO DEPARTED THIS LIFE
ON CHRISTMAS DAY 1931
AND THE ABOVE NAMED
BARTLE
WHO DIED 22ND OCT 1933
RIP
LORD HAVE MERCY ON THEIR SOULS

**SYMBOLS:**
DISPLACED CELTIC CROSS

| | |
|---|---|
| NAME OF RECORDER: | PHYLLIS NOONAN AND JANET LEIGH |
| DATE: | 22 APRIL 2006 |
| PHOTO REFERENCE: | K38 |
| LOCATION/MAP REF: | D1 K38 |

| | |
|---|---|
| GRAVEYARD NAME: | **ST. MARY'S ABBEY OLD GRAVEYARD** |
| GRAVEYARD CODE: | D1 |
| COUNTY: | MEATH |
| MEMORIAL NUMBER: | J23 |
| ERECTED BY: | |
| ORIENTATION: | EAST |
| NUMBER OF COMPONENTS: | 1 |
| NUMBER OF INSCRIBED FACES: | 1 |
| NUMBER OF PEOPLE COMMEMORATED: | 8 |
| MEMORIAL TYPE: | LOW MONUMENT |
| CONDITION OF MEMORIAL: | SOUND IN PLACE |
| CONDITION OF INSCRIPTION: | MAINLY DECIPHERABLE |
| STONEMASON NAME: | |
| TECHNIQUE OF INSCRIPTION: | INCISED |
| UNDERTAKER: | |
| STONE TOP: | LOW MONUMENT |
| GRAVE TYPE: | DOUBLE |
| HEIGHT: | LENGTH 213CM |
| WIDTH: | 106CM |
| THICKNESS: | LOW MONUMENT |

| SURNAME: | CHRISTIAN | ADDRESS | DEATH | AGE |
|---|---|---|---|---|
| COOKE | BENJM | | 25 JULY 1737 | |
| | MARY | | 15 MAY 1758 | 80 |
| | MARY | | | |
| | WILLIAM | | | |
| | SAMUEL | | | |
| | JOHN | | | |
| WILLCHAGE | ANNE | | 03 DEC 1725 | 28 |
| BERKLEY | ANN | | 25 MAR 1730 | 31 |

**INSCRIPTION:**
HERE LIETH THE BODY OF BENJM
COOKE DECD 25TH JULY 1737 AGED ....
ALSO MARY HIS WIFE DECD 15TH MAY
1758 AGED 80 WITH 4 OF THEIR
CHILDREN MARY WILLIAM SAMUEL
JOHN ALSO ANNE WILLCHAGE ALIAS
COOKE FIRST WIFE TO RICHD COOKE
DECD 3RD DEC 1725 AGED 28
ALSO ANN BERKLEY ALIAS COOKE
DAUGHTER TO CAPTAIN HENRY
BERKLEY OF TULLOW 2D WIFE TO SGT
RICHD COOKE DECD 25 OF
MARCH 1730 AGED 31

| | |
|---|---|
| NAME OF RECORDER: | LIZ LYNCH AND PHYLLIS NOONAN |
| DATE: | 16 AUG 2005 |
| PHOTO REFERENCE: | J23 |
| LOCATION/MAP REF: | D1 J23 |

| | |
|---|---|
| GRAVEYARD NAME: | **ST. MARY'S ABBEY OLD GRAVEYARD** |
| GRAVEYARD CODE: | D1 |
| COUNTY: | MEATH |
| MEMORIAL NUMBER: | F15 |
| ERECTED BY: | JAMES CORCORAN |
| ORIENTATION: | EAST |
| NUMBER OF COMPONENTS: | 1 |
| NUMBER OF INSCRIBED FACES: | 1 |
| NUMBER OF PEOPLE COMMEMORATED: | 2 |
| MEMORIAL TYPE: | HEADSTONE |
| CONDITION OF MEMORIAL: | SOUND IN PLACE |
| CONDITION OF INSCRIPTION: | MAINLY DECIPHERABLE |
| STONEMASON NAME: | |
| TECHNIQUE OF INSCRIPTION: | INCISED |
| UNDERTAKER: | |
| STONE TOP: | ROUND |
| GRAVE TYPE: | SINGLE |
| HEIGHT: | 121CM |
| WIDTH: | 72CM |
| THICKNESS: | 15CM |

| SURNAME: | CHRISTIAN | ADDRESS | DEATH | AGE |
|---|---|---|---|---|
| CORCORAN | ELIZABETH | | 22 SEPT 1779 | 50 |
| | BRIDGET | | 11 OCT 1785 | 23 |

**INSCRIPTION:**
THIS STONE WAS ERECTED
BY JAMES CORCORAN IN
MEMORY OF HIS WIFE
ELIZABETH CORCORAN ALIAS
MADDEN WHO DEPARTED
THIS LIFE SEPTEMBER THE 22
1779 AGED 50 YEARS ~~
ALSO HIS DAUGHTER BRIDGET
CORCORAN WHO DEPARTED
THIS LIFE OCTOBER THE 11TH 1785
AGED 23 YEARS

**SYMBOLS:**
IHS IN SUNBURST

| | |
|---|---|
| NAME OF RECORDER: | PHYLLIS NOONAN |
| DATE: | 19 JULY 2005 |
| PHOTO REFERENCE: | F15 |
| LOCATION/MAP REF: | D1 F15 |

| | |
|---|---|
| GRAVEYARD NAME: | **ST. MARY'S ABBEY OLD GRAVEYARD** |
| GRAVEYARD CODE: | D1 |
| COUNTY: | MEATH |
| MEMORIAL NUMBER: | F2 |
| ERECTED BY: | |
| ORIENTATION: | EAST |
| NUMBER OF COMPONENTS: | 1 |
| NUMBER OF INSCRIBED FACES: | 1 |
| NUMBER OF PEOPLE COMMEMORATED: | 1 AND POSTERITY |
| MEMORIAL TYPE: | HEADSTONE |
| CONDITION OF MEMORIAL: | SOUND IN PLACE |
| CONDITION OF INSCRIPTION: | DECIPHERABLE |
| STONEMASON NAME: | |
| TECHNIQUE OF INSCRIPTION: | INCISED |
| UNDERTAKER: | |
| STONE TOP: | THREE ARCHES |
| GRAVE TYPE: | SINGLE |
| HEIGHT: | 112CM |
| WIDTH: | 80CM |
| THICKNESS: | 11CM |

| SURNAME: | CHRISTIAN | ADDRESS | DEATH | AGE |
|---|---|---|---|---|
| CORRAHAN | RICHARD | THOS. STREET DUBLIN | 17 MAR 1775 | 60 |

**INSCRIPTION:**
THIS STONE AND BURIAL PLACE BELONGETH TO RICHD. CORRAHAN OF THOS. STREET DUBLIN AND HIS POSTERITY HERE LYETH THE BODY OF THE ABOVE WHO DEPARTED THIS LIFE THE 17TH MARCH 1775 AGED 60 YEARS

**SYMBOLS:**
MALTESE CROSS IHS HEART SURROUNDED BY SUNBURST

| | |
|---|---|
| NAME OF RECORDER: | BEN RYAN, SHAUN AND LIZ LYNCH |
| DATE: | 16 JULY 2005 |
| PHOTO REFERENCE: | F2 |
| LOCATION/MAP REF: | D1 F2 |

| | |
|---|---|
| GRAVEYARD NAME: | **ST. MARY'S ABBEY OLD GRAVEYARD** |
| GRAVEYARD CODE: | D1 |
| COUNTY: | MEATH |
| MEMORIAL NUMBER: | H22 |
| ERECTED BY: | THOMAS CORR |
| ORIENTATION: | EAST |
| NUMBER OF COMPONENTS: | 1 |
| NUMBER OF INSCRIBED FACES: | 1 |
| NUMBER OF PEOPLE COMMEMORATED: | 4 |
| MEMORIAL TYPE: | HEADSTONE SET IN ABBEY WALL |
| CONDITION OF MEMORIAL: | SOUND |
| CONDITION OF INSCRIPTION: | MAINLY DECIPHERABLE |
| STONEMASON NAME: | |
| TECHNIQUE OF INSCRIPTION: | INCISED |
| UNDERTAKER: | |
| STONE TOP: | ROUND |
| GRAVE TYPE: | |
| HEIGHT: | 130CM |
| WIDTH: | 17CM |
| THICKNESS: | SET INTO ABBEY WALL |

| SURNAME: | CHRISTIAN | ADDRESS | DEATH | AGE |
|---|---|---|---|---|
| CORR NEE MARREY | CATHERINE | | 1790 | 70 |
| CORR | MARY | | 1798 | 30 |
| CORR | NICHOLAS | | 10 JAN 1799 | 47 |
| CORR NEE RUDDY | MARGARET | | 3 JAN 1798 | 28 |

**INSCRIPTION:**
ERECTED BY THOM
CORR IN MEMORY OF HIS
WIFE CATHERINE ALIAS
MARREY WHO DEP
THIS LIFE ANNO DOM 1790
AGED 70 YEARS ALSO HIS DAUGHTER
MARY WHO DIED ANNO DOM
1798 AGED 30 YEARS ALSO HIS
SON NICHOLAS WHO DIED
THE 10TH JANUARY 1799 AGED
47 Y ALSO MARGARET CORR
ALIAS RUDDY WIFE OF SAID
NICHOLAS WHO DIED 3RD JAN
1798 AGED 28 YEARS

**SYMBOLS:**
SUNBURST HALF LOZENGES CHERUBS WITH WINGS ROSETTES

| | |
|---|---|
| NAME OF RECORDER: | JANET LEIGH AND PHYLLIS NOONAN |
| DATE: | 17 JUNE 2006 |
| PHOTO REFERENCE: | H 22 |
| LOCATION/MAP REF: | D1 H22 |

| | |
|---|---|
| GRAVEYARD NAME: | **ST. MARY'S ABBEY OLD GRAVEYARD** |
| GRAVEYARD CODE: | D1 |
| COUNTY: | MEATH |
| MEMORIAL NUMBER: | C 13 |
| ERECTED BY: | |
| ORIENTATION: | EAST |
| NUMBER OF COMPONENTS: | 2 |
| NUMBER OF INSCRIBED FACES: | 1 |
| NUMBER OF PEOPLE COMMEMORATED: | 3 |
| MEMORIAL TYPE: | GRANITE HEADSTONE |
| CONDITION OF MEMORIAL: | SOUND IN PLACE |
| CONDITION OF INSCRIPTION: | MINT |
| STONEMASON NAME: | |
| TECHNIQUE OF INSCRIPTION: | INCISED |
| UNDERTAKER: | |
| STONE TOP: | ARCH |
| GRAVE TYPE: | TREBLE |
| HEIGHT: | 113CM |
| WIDTH: | 72CM |
| THICKNESS: | 15CM |

| SURNAME: | CHRISTIAN | ADDRESS | DEATH | AGE |
|---|---|---|---|---|
| COX | GUS | REASK DULEEK | 1ST AUG. 1999 | 86 |
| MCKEON | CHRISTOPHER | GASKINSTOWN | | |
| MCKEON | MARY | GASKINSTOWN | | |

**INSCRIPTION:**
IN LOVING MEMORY
OF
GUS COX
REASK DULEEK
DIED 1ST AUGUST 1999
AGE 86 YEARS
ALSO HIS GRANDPARENTS
CHRISTOPHER
AND MARY MCKEON
GASKINSTOWN DULEEK

**SYMBOLS:** CROSS WITH SHEAF OF WHEAT

| | |
|---|---|
| NAME OF RECORDER: | PHYLLIS NOONAN AND JIM ORTEN |
| DATE: | 6 JULY 2002 |
| PHOTO REFERENCE: | C13 |
| LOCATION/MAP REF: | D1 C13 |

| | |
|---|---|
| GRAVEYARD NAME: | **ST. MARY'S ABBEY OLD GRAVEYARD** |
| GRAVEYARD CODE: | D1 |
| COUNTY: | MEATH |
| MEMORIAL NUMBER: | B2 |
| ERECTED BY: | |
| ORIENTATION: | EAST |
| NUMBER OF COMPONENTS: | 2 |
| NUMBER OF INSCRIBED FACES: | 1 |
| NUMBER OF PEOPLE COMMEMORATED: | 2 |
| MEMORIAL TYPE: | HEADSTONE |
| CONDITION OF MEMORIAL: | SOUND IN PLACE |
| CONDITION OF INSCRIPTION: | CLEAR |
| STONEMASON NAME: | MOSS |
| TECHNIQUE OF INSCRIPTION: | INLAID |
| UNDERTAKER: | |
| STONE TOP: | ROUND WITH CROSS |
| GRAVE TYPE: | SINGLE |
| HEIGHT: | 158CM |
| WIDTH: | 63CM |
| THICKNESS: | 07CM |

| SURNAME: | CHRISTIAN | ADDRESS | DEATH | AGE |
|---|---|---|---|---|
| CRINION | MARGARET | CARNTOWN | 11 JUNE 1925 | |
| CRINION | PATRICK | CARNTOWN | 08 FEB 1927 | |

**INSCRIPTION:**
IN LOVING MEMORY
OF
MARGARET CRINION
CARNTOWN
WHO DIED 11 JUNE 1925 HER HUSBAND
PATRICK
WHO DIED 8 FEB 1927

R.I.P.

**SYMBOLS:**
CROSS – HEART CENTRE
FLOWERS – TULIPS -OTHER
PLANTS – HOLLY BERRIES

| | |
|---|---|
| NAME OF RECORDER: | JANET LEIGH AND HELEN FULLAM |
| DATE: | 25 JUNE 2005 |
| PHOTO REFERENCE: | B2 |
| LOCATION/MAP REF: | D1 B2 |

| | |
|---|---|
| GRAVEYARD NAME: | **ST. MARY'S ABBEY OLD GRAVEYARD** |
| GRAVEYARD CODE: | D1 |
| COUNTY: | MEATH |
| MEMORIAL NUMBER: | F27 |
| ERECTED BY: | |
| ORIENTATION: | EAST |
| NUMBER OF COMPONENTS: | 2 |
| NUMBER OF INSCRIBED FACES: | 1 |
| NUMBER OF PEOPLE COMMEMORATED: | 1 |
| MEMORIAL TYPE: | HEADSTONE |
| CONDITION OF MEMORIAL: | SOUND IN PLACE |
| CONDITION OF INSCRIPTION: | MAINLY DECIPHERABLE |
| STONEMASON NAME: | MOSS |
| TECHNIQUE OF INSCRIPTION: | INCISED |
| UNDERTAKER: | |
| STONE TOP: | CELTIC CROSS |
| GRAVE TYPE: | SINGLE |
| HEIGHT: | 196CM |
| WIDTH: | 67CM |
| THICKNESS: | 07CM |

| SURNAME: | CHRISTIAN | ADDRESS | DEATH | AGE |
|---|---|---|---|---|
| CRONIN | PATRICK | DULEEK | 19 OCT 1938 | |

**INSCRIPTION:**
SACRED
TO
THE MEMORY OF
PATRICK CRONIN
DULEEK
WHO DIED 19 OCT 1938

**SYMBOLS:**
CELTIC CROSS WITH
HEART IN FLAMES WITH VINE LEAVES

| | |
|---|---|
| NAME OF RECORDER: | PHYLLIS NOONAN |
| DATE: | 20 JULY 2002 |
| PHOTO REFERENCE: | F27 |
| LOCATION/MAP REF: | D1 F27 |

| | |
|---|---|
| GRAVEYARD NAME: | **ST. MARY'S ABBEY OLD GRAVEYARD** |
| GRAVEYARD CODE: | D1 |
| COUNTY: | MEATH |
| MEMORIAL NUMBER: | K34 |
| ERECTED BY: | |
| ORIENTATION: | EAST |
| NUMBER OF COMPONENTS: | 1 |
| NUMBER OF INSCRIBED FACES: | 1 |
| NUMBER OF PEOPLE COMMEMORATED: | 2 |
| MEMORIAL TYPE: | HEADSTONE |
| CONDITION OF MEMORIAL: | SOUND IN PLACE |
| CONDITION OF INSCRIPTION: | MAINLY DECIPHERABLE |
| STONEMASON NAME: | |
| TECHNIQUE OF INSCRIPTION: | INCISED |
| UNDERTAKER: | |
| STONE TOP: | ROUND |
| GRAVE TYPE: | SINGLE |
| HEIGHT: | 119CM |
| WIDTH: | 78CM |
| THICKNESS: | 13CM |

| SURNAME: | CHRISTIAN | ADDRESS | DEATH | AGE |
|---|---|---|---|---|
| CRUISE | ELIZABETH | | 4 OCT 1793 | 70 |
| | LAURENCE | CITY OF DUBLIN | 2 MAR 1795 | 80 |

**INSCRIPTION:**
GLORIA IN EXCELSIS DEO
BENEATH STONE LIE THE REMAINS OF
MRS ELIZABETH CRUISE WIFE OF MR
LAURENCE CRUISE OF THE CITY OF DUBLIN
WHO DEPARTED THIS LIFE THE 4TH OF
OCTOBER 1793 AGED 70 YEARS
HERE ALSO THE REMAINS OF SAID
MR LAURENCE CRUISE WHO DEPARTED
THIS LIFE THE 2ND DAY OF MARCH 1795
AGED 80 YEARS

**SYMBOLS:**
IHS IN SUNBURST

| | |
|---|---|
| NAME OF RECORDER: | JANET LEIGH AND PHYLLIS NOONAN |
| DATE: | 22ND APRIL 2006 |
| PHOTO REFERENCE: | K34 |
| LOCATION/MAP REF: | D1 K34 |

| | |
|---|---|
| GRAVEYARD NAME: | **ST. MARY'S ABBEY OLD GRAVEYARD** |
| GRAVEYARD CODE: | D1 |
| COUNTY: | MEATH |
| MEMORIAL NUMBER: | K39 |
| ERECTED BY: | JAMES CRUISE OF DROGHEDA |
| ORIENTATION: | EAST |
| NUMBER OF COMPONENTS: | 1 |
| NUMBER OF INSCRIBED FACES: | 1 |
| NUMBER OF PEOPLE COMMEMORATED: | 2 |
| MEMORIAL TYPE: | HEADSTONE |
| CONDITION OF MEMORIAL: | SOUND IN PLACE |
| CONDITION OF INSCRIPTION: | BARELY DECIPHERABLE |
| STONEMASON NAME: | |
| TECHNIQUE OF INSCRIPTION: | INCISED |
| UNDERTAKER: | |
| STONE TOP: | ROUND SUNBURST DISK |
| GRAVE TYPE: | SINGLE |

| SURNAME: | CHRISTIAN | ADDRESS | DEATH | AGE |
|---|---|---|---|---|
| CRUISE | ALICE | | 27 JUNE 1792 | 27 |
| | ALICE | | 07 JAN 1831 ?? | 5 |

**INSCRIPTION:**
ERECTED BY JAMES CRUISE OF DROGHEDA IN MEMORY OF HIS MOTHER ALICE CRUISE WIFE OF PETER CRUISE LATE OF SLANE AND DAUGHTER OF JOHN STRONG ESQ MULLAHFIN WHO DIED 27TH JUNE 1792 AGED 27 YEARS ALSO OF HIS DAUGHTER ALICE CRUISE WHO DEPARTED THIS LIFE 7TH JANUARY 1831 ?? AGED FIVE YEARS

| | |
|---|---|
| NAME OF RECORDER: | PHYLLIS NOONAN AND JANET LEIGH |
| DATE: | 6 JUNE 2006 |
| PHOTO REFERENCE: | K39 |
| LOCATION/MAP REF: | D1 K39 |

| | |
|---|---|
| GRAVEYARD NAME: | **ST. MARY'S ABBEY OLD GRAVEYARD** |
| GRAVEYARD CODE: | D1 |
| COUNTY: | MEATH |
| MEMORIAL NUMBER: | C 10 |
| ERECTED BY: | JAMES CURLEY |
| ORIENTATION: | EAST |
| NUMBER OF COMPONENTS: | 2 |
| NUMBER OF INSCRIBED FACES: | 1 |
| NUMBER OF PEOPLE COMMEMORATED: | 6 |
| MEMORIAL TYPE: | CELTIC CROSS |
| CONDITION OF MEMORIAL: | SOUND IN PLACE |
| CONDITION OF INSCRIPTION: | CLEAR |
| STONEMASON NAME: | |
| TECHNIQUE OF INSCRIPTION: | INCISED |
| UNDERTAKER: | |
| STONE TOP: | CELTIC CROSS |
| GRAVE TYPE: | TREBLE |
| HEIGHT: | 140CM |
| WIDTH: | 62CM |
| THICKNESS: | 07CM |

| SURNAME: | CHRISTIAN | ADDRESS | DEATH | AGE |
|---|---|---|---|---|
| CURLEY | PATRICK | LARRIX ST | DEC 1910 | |
| CURLEY | ELLEN | | JAN 1924 | |
| CURLEY | BRIGID | | DEC 1939 | |
| CURLEY | MARY ANN | | 13 FEB 1959 | |
| CURLEY | PATRICK | | 15 JULY 1964 | |
| CURLEY | BRIGID | | 14 DEC 1965 | |

**INSCRIPTION:**
ERECTED BY
JAMES CURLEY
LARRIX ST
IN MEMORY OF HIS FATHER
PATRICK
WHO DIED DEC 1910, HIS SISTER
ELLEN
WHO DIED JAN 1924, AND HIS MOTHER
BRIGID WHO DIED DEC 1939
ALSO HIS SISTER MARY ANN
DIED 13 FEB 1959
HIS BROTHER PATRICK DIED 15 JULY 1964
HIS SISTER BRIGID DIED 14 OCT 1965

**SYMBOLS:**
HEART SURROUNDED BY
VINE LEAVES ON 4 ARMS OF CELTIC CROSS

| | |
|---|---|
| NAME OF RECORDER: | PHYLLIS NOONAN AND JIM ORTON |
| DATE: | 6 JULY 2005 |
| PHOTO REFERENCE: | C 10 |
| LOCATION/MAP REF: | D1 C10 |

| | |
|---|---|
| GRAVEYARD NAME: | **ST. MARY'S ABBEY OLD GRAVEYARD** |
| GRAVEYARD CODE: | D1 |
| COUNTY: | MEATH |
| MEMORIAL NUMBER: | C11 |
| ERECTED BY: | |
| ORIENTATION: | EAST |
| NUMBER OF COMPONENTS: | 2 |
| NUMBER OF INSCRIBED FACES: | 1 |
| NUMBER OF PEOPLE COMMEMORATED: | 2 |
| MEMORIAL TYPE: | HEADSTONE |
| CONDITION OF MEMORIAL: | SOUND IN PLACE |
| CONDITION OF INSCRIPTION: | CLEAR |
| STONEMASON NAME: | W. GOGARTY |
| TECHNIQUE OF INSCRIPTION: | INCISED AND PAINTED |
| UNDERTAKER: | |
| STONE TOP: | CELTIC CROSS |
| GRAVE TYPE: | TREBLE |
| HEIGHT: | 165CM |
| WIDTH: | 71CM |
| THICKNESS: | 08CM |

| SURNAME: | CHRISTIAN | ADDRESS | DEATH | AGE |
|---|---|---|---|---|
| CURLEY | SARAH ANN | LONGFORD DULEEK | 30 JAN 1931 | |
| CURLEY | PATRICK | LONGFORD DULEEK | 01 JUNE 1941 | |

**INSCRIPTION:**
ERECTED IN LOVING MEMORY
OF SARAH ANN CURLEY
LONGFORD DULEEK
WHO DIED 30TH JAN 1931
AND HER HUSBAND
PATRICK CURLEY
WHO DIED 1ST JUNE 1941
R.I.P

| | |
|---|---|
| NAME OF RECORDER: | PHYLLIS NOONAN AND JIM ORTON |
| DATE: | 6 JULY 2005 |
| PHOTO REFERENCE: | C11 |
| LOCATION/MAP REF: | D1 C11 |

| | |
|---|---|
| GRAVEYARD NAME: | **ST. MARY'S ABBEY OLD GRAVEYARD** |
| GRAVEYARD CODE: | D1 |
| COUNTY: | MEATH |
| MEMORIAL NUMBER: | B14 |
| ERECTED BY: | |
| ORIENTATION: | EAST |
| NUMBER OF COMPONENTS: | 2 |
| NUMBER OF INSCRIBED FACES: | 1 |
| NUMBER OF PEOPLE COMMEMORATED: | 3 |
| MEMORIAL TYPE: | HEADSTONE |
| CONDITION OF MEMORIAL: | GOOD |
| CONDITION OF INSCRIPTION: | VERY GOOD |
| STONEMASON NAME: | T. COONEY |
| TECHNIQUE OF INSCRIPTION: | INCISED AND PAINTED |
| UNDERTAKER: | |
| STONE TOP: | ARCH |
| GRAVE TYPE: | DOUBLE |
| HEIGHT: | 75CM |
| WIDTH: | 52CM |
| THICKNESS: | 04CM |

| SURNAME: | CHRISTIAN | ADDRESS | OCCUPATION | DEATH | AGE |
|---|---|---|---|---|---|
| CURRAN | THOMAS | DOWNSTOWN | | 20 JAN 1918 | |
| | MARGARET | | | 10 OCT 1956 | |
| | JOHN | | SON | 10 FEB 1957 | |

**INSCRIPTION:**
IN MEMORY OF
THOMAS CURRAN
DOWNSTOWN
DIED 20 JAN 1918
HIS WIFE MARGARET
DIED 10 APRIL 1956
THEIR SON JOHN
DIED 10 FEB 1957
R.I.P.

**ORNAMENTS:**
ANGEL ON SMALL PEDESTAL
IN FRONT OF HEADSTONE

| | |
|---|---|
| NAME OF RECORDER: | LIZ LYNCH AND JIM ORTEN |
| DATE: | 2 JULY 2005 |
| PHOTO REFERENCE: | B14 |
| LOCATION/MAP REF: | D1 B14 |

| | |
|---|---|
| GRAVEYARD NAME: | **ST. MARY'S ABBEY OLD GRAVEYARD** |
| GRAVEYARD CODE: | D1 |
| COUNTY: | MEATH |
| MEMORIAL NUMBER: | K49 |
| ERECTED BY: | MARY CURRAN |
| ORIENTATION: | EAST |
| NUMBER OF COMPONENTS: | 1 |
| NUMBER OF INSCRIBED FACES: | 1 |
| NUMBER OF PEOPLE COMMEMORATED: | 5 |
| MEMORIAL TYPE: | HEADSTONE |
| CONDITION OF MEMORIAL: | SOUND IN PLACE |
| CONDITION OF INSCRIPTION: | MAINLY DECIPHERABLE |
| STONEMASON NAME: | |
| TECHNIQUE OF INSCRIPTION: | INCISED |
| UNDERTAKER: | |
| STONE TOP: | ROUND |
| GRAVE TYPE: | SINGLE |
| HEIGHT: | 148CM |
| WIDTH: | 82CM |
| THICKNESS: | 17CM |

| SURNAME: | CHRISTIAN | ADDRESS | DEATH | AGE |
|---|---|---|---|---|
| CURRAN | PATRICK | | | |
| | JUDITH | | | |
| | PAT | | | |
| | HUGH | | | |
| | MARY | | 10 APRIL 1845 | 56 |

**INSCRIPTION:**
ERECTED BY
THE DESIRE OF MARY CURRAN
IN MEMORY OF HER FATHER AND
MOTHER PATKR AND JUDITH CURRAN
ALSO HER BROTHERS PAT AND HUGH
UNDERNEATH DEPOSITED THE REMAINS
OF THE ABOVE MARY CURRAN WHO
DIED THE 10TH APRIL 1845
AGED 56 YEARS

**SYMBOLS:**
IHS IN SUNBURST

| | |
|---|---|
| NAME OF RECORDER: | SHAUN LYNCH, SINEAD FULLAM AND JANET LEIGH |
| DATE: | 6 MAY 2006 |
| PHOTO REFERENCE: | K49 |
| LOCATION/MAP REF: | D1 K49 |

| | |
|---|---|
| GRAVEYARD NAME: | **ST. MARY'S ABBEY OLD GRAVEYARD** |
| GRAVEYARD CODE: | D1 |
| COUNTY: | MEATH |
| MEMORIAL NUMBER: | K51 |
| ERECTED BY: | MICK DALY |
| ORIENTATION: | EAST |
| NUMBER OF COMPONENTS: | 1 |
| NUMBER OF INSCRIBED FACES: | 1 |
| NUMBER OF PEOPLE COMMEMORATED: | 1 |
| MEMORIAL TYPE: | SMALL STONE HEADSTONE |
| CONDITION OF MEMORIAL: | SOUND IN PLACE |
| CONDITION OF INSCRIPTION: | CLEAR |
| STONEMASON NAME: | |
| TECHNIQUE OF INSCRIPTION: | INCISED |
| UNDERTAKER: | |
| STONE TOP: | ROUND |
| GRAVE TYPE: | SINGLE |
| HEIGHT: | 52CM |
| WIDTH: | 40CM |
| THICKNESS: | 18CM |

| SURNAME: | CHRISTIAN | ADDRESS | DEATH | AGE |
|---|---|---|---|---|
| DALY | ALICE | | | |

**INSCRIPTION:**
THIS STONE AND
BURIAL PLACE BE
LONGTH TO MICK
DALY HERE LIETH
THE BODY OF HIS
WIFE ALICE DALY

**SYMBOLS:**
IHS

| | |
|---|---|
| NAME OF RECORDER: | SHAUN LYNCH, SINEAD FULLAM AND JANET LEIGH |
| DATE: | 6 MAY 2006 |
| PHOTO REFERENCE: | K51 |
| LOCATION/MAP REF: | D1 K51 |

| | |
|---|---|
| GRAVEYARD NAME: | **ST. MARY'S ABBEY OLD GRAVEYARD** |
| GRAVEYARD CODE: | D1 |
| COUNTY: | MEATH |
| MEMORIAL NUMBER: | A6 A |
| ERECTED BY: | ALEXANDER DAVIS |
| ORIENTATION: | EAST |
| NUMBER OF COMPONENTS: | 2 |
| NUMBER OF INSCRIBED FACES: | 1 |
| NUMBER OF PEOPLE COMMEMORATED: | 2 |
| MEMORIAL TYPE: | HEADSTONE |
| CONDITION OF MEMORIAL: | SOUND IN PLACE |
| CONDITION OF INSCRIPTION: | MAINLY DECIPHERABLE |
| STONEMASON NAME: | T. GAMBLE SLANE |
| TECHNIQUE OF INSCRIPTION: | INLAID |
| UNDERTAKER: | |
| STONE TOP: | ROUND |
| GRAVE TYPE: | TREBLE |
| HEIGHT: | 154CM |
| WIDTH: | 64CM |
| THICKNESS: | 09CM |

| SURNAME: | CHRISTIAN | ADDRESS | DEATH | AGE |
|---|---|---|---|---|
| DAVIS | MARGARET | CORBALLIS DONORE | 30 DEC 1928 | |
| CARTWRIGHT | SARAH ANN | | 14 JAN 1915 | |

**INSCRIPTION**:
ERECTED BY
ALEXANDER DAVIS
OF CORBALLIS DONORE
IN LOVING MEMORY OF HIS WIFE
MARGARET
WHO DEPARTED THIS LIFE
THE 30TH DEC 1928
ALSO HER MOTHER
SARAH ANN CARTWRIGHT
WHO DEPARTED THIS LIFE
THE 14TH JAN 1915

WITH CHRIST WHICH IS FAR BETTER

| | |
|---|---|
| NAME OF RECORDER: | JANET LEIGH AND HELEN FULLAM |
| DATE: | 18 JUNE 2005 |
| PHOTO REFERENCE: | A6 A |
| LOCATION/MAP REF: | D1 A6A |

| | |
|---|---|
| GRAVEYARD NAME: | **ST. MARY'S ABBEY OLD GRAVEYARD** |
| GRAVEYARD CODE: | D1 |
| COUNTY: | MEATH |
| MEMORIAL NUMBER: | A6 B |
| ERECTED BY: | |
| ORIENTATION: | EAST |
| NUMBER OF COMPONENTS: | 2 |
| NUMBER OF INSCRIBED FACES: | 1 |
| NUMBER OF PEOPLE COMMEMORATED: | 2 |
| MEMORIAL TYPE: | HEADSTONE |
| CONDITION OF MEMORIAL: | UPRIGHT BUT CRACKED |
| CONDITION OF INSCRIPTION: | MAINLY DECIPHERABLE |
| STONEMASON NAME: | |
| TECHNIQUE OF INSCRIPTION: | INLAID |
| UNDERTAKER: | |
| STONE TOP: | ROUND |
| GRAVE TYPE: | TREBLE |
| HEIGHT: | 158CM |
| WIDTH: | 64CM |
| THICKNESS: | 10CM |

| SURNAME: | CHRISTIAN | ADDRESS | DEATH | AGE |
|---|---|---|---|---|
| DAVIS | JOHN | BOYNE VIEW LODGE | 18 JAN 1931 | |
| DAVIS | ANNA MARIA | BOYNE VIEW LODGE | 23 SEPT 1953 | |

**INSCRIPTION:**
COME ONTO ME AND REST
ERECTED
IN LOVING MEMORY OF
JOHN DAVIS
OF BOYNE VIEW LODGE
WHO DIED 18TH JANUARY 1931
ALSO HIS WIFE ANNA MARIA
DIED 23 SEPT 1953

*TO FALL ASLEEP IS NOT TO DIE*
*TO DWELL WITH CHRIST IS BETTER LIFE*
*TILL HE COME*

| | |
|---|---|
| NAME OF RECORDER: | HELEN FULLAM AND JANET LEIGH |
| DATE: | 25 JUNE 2005 |
| PHOTO REFERENCE: | A6 B |
| LOCATION/MAP REF: | D1 A6 B |

| | |
|---|---|
| GRAVEYARD NAME: | **ST. MARY'S ABBEY OLD GRAVEYARD** |
| GRAVEYARD CODE: | D1 |
| COUNTY: | MEATH |
| MEMORIAL NUMBER: | L13 |
| ERECTED BY: | JAMES DAW |
| ORIENTATION: | EAST |
| NUMBER OF COMPONENTS: | 2 |
| NUMBER OF INSCRIBED FACES: | 1 |
| NUMBER OF PEOPLE COMMEMORATED: | 4 |
| MEMORIAL TYPE: | HEADSTONE CELTIC CROSS |
| CONDITION OF MEMORIAL: | SOUND IN PLACE |
| CONDITION OF INSCRIPTION: | CLEAR |
| STONEMASON NAME: | |
| TECHNIQUE OF INSCRIPTION: | INCISED |
| UNDERTAKER: | |
| STONE TOP: | CELTIC CROSS |
| GRAVE TYPE: | SINGLE |
| HEIGHT: | 200CM |
| WIDTH: | 69CM |
| THICKNESS: | 08CM |

| SURNAME: | CHRISTIAN | ADDRESS | DEATH | AGE |
|---|---|---|---|---|
| DAW | MARY | | 05 JUNE 1863 | 52 |
| | LUKE | | 13 MAY 1879 | 79 |
| | MARGARET | | 29 DEC 1917 | 70 |
| | JAMES | | 15 MAR 1923 | 84 |

**INSCRIPTION:**
ERECTED
BY JAMES DAW IN MEMORY OF HIS
MOTHER MARY WHO DIED JUNE 5TH
1863 AGED 52 YEARS ALSO HIS FATHER
LUKE WHO DIED MAY 13TH 1879
AGED 79 YEARS ALSO HIS SISTER
MARGARET WHO DIED 29TH DEC 1917
AGED 70 YEARS
ALSO THE ABOVE JAMES DAW
DIED 15TH MARCH 1923 AGED 84 YEARS

**SYMBOLS:**
CELTIC CROSS WITH SACRED HEART
IN CROSS IHS IN CIRCLE

| | |
|---|---|
| NAME OF RECORDER: | SINEAD FULLAM AND JANET LEIGH |
| DATE: | 6 JUNE 2006 |
| PHOTO REFERENCE: | L13 |
| LOCATION/MAP REF: | D1 L13 |

| | |
|---|---|
| GRAVEYARD NAME: | **ST. MARY'S ABBEY OLD GRAVEYARD** |
| GRAVEYARD CODE: | D1 |
| COUNTY: | MEATH |
| MEMORIAL NUMBER: | J30 |
| ERECTED BY: | |
| ORIENTATION: | EAST |
| NUMBER OF COMPONENTS: | 1 |
| NUMBER OF INSCRIBED FACES: | 1 |
| NUMBER OF PEOPLE COMMEMORATED: | 2 |
| MEMORIAL TYPE: | HEADSTONE |
| CONDITION OF MEMORIAL: | SOUND IN PLACE |
| CONDITION OF INSCRIPTION: | DECIPHERABLE |
| STONEMASON NAME: | |
| TECHNIQUE OF INSCRIPTION: | INCISED |
| UNDERTAKER: | |
| STONE TOP: | ROUND SUNBURST DISK |
| GRAVE TYPE: | SINGLE |
| HEIGHT: | 125CM |
| WIDTH: | 76CM |
| THICKNESS: | 14CM |

| SURNAME: | CHRISTIAN | ADDRESS | DEATH | AGE |
|---|---|---|---|---|
| DAY | PATRICK | BALGEEN | | |
| | CHRISTIAN | | | |

**INSCRIPTION:**

TO THE MEMORY
OF PATK AND CHRISTIAN DAY OF BAL
GEEN WHOSE REMAINS LIE INTERRED
NEAR THIS WITH MANY OF THEIR ANC
ESTORS WAITING FOR A JOYFUL RESUR
RECTION 1826

**SYMBOLS:**

CROSS IHS

| | |
|---|---|
| NAME OF RECORDER: | PHYLLIS NOONAN |
| DATE: | 20 AUGUST 2005 |
| PHOTO REFERENCE: | J30 |
| LOCATION/MAP REF: | D1 J30 |

| | |
|---|---|
| GRAVEYARD NAME: | **ST. MARY'S ABBEY OLD GRAVEYARD** |
| GRAVEYARD CODE: | D1 |
| COUNTY: | MEATH |
| MEMORIAL NUMBER: | K8 |
| ERECTED BY: | THOMAS DOMIGAN |
| ORIENTATION: | EAST |
| NUMBER OF COMPONENTS: | 3 |
| NUMBER OF INSCRIBED FACES: | 1 |
| NUMBER OF PEOPLE COMMEMORATED: | 8 |
| MEMORIAL TYPE: | HEADSTONE |
| CONDITION OF MEMORIAL: | SOUND IN PLACE |
| CONDITION OF INSCRIPTION: | CLEAR |
| STONEMASON NAME: | |
| TECHNIQUE OF INSCRIPTION: | INCISED |
| UNDERTAKER: | |
| STONE TOP: | ROUND |
| GRAVE TYPE: | SINGLE |
| HEIGHT: | 182CM |
| WIDTH: | 76CM |
| THICKNESS: | 10CM |

| SURNAME: | CHRISTIAN | ADDRESS | DEATH | AGE |
|---|---|---|---|---|
| DOMIGAN | MARY | | 11 JAN 1857 | |
| | JOHN | | 02 APR 1859 | |
| | PATRICK | | 03 JULY 1867 | |
| | CHRISTINA | | 23 JULY 1887 | |
| | KATE | | 08 APR 1896 | |
| | ELIZABETH | | 25 MAR 1913 | |
| | WILLIAM | | 26 FEB 1919 | |
| | THOMAS | | 14 MAR 1919 | |

**INSCRIPTION:**
IN MEMORY OF HIS MOTHER
MARY WHO DIED IN JAN 1857
JOHN DIED 2 APRIL 1859
PATRIC DIED 3 JULY 1867
CHRISTINA DIED 23 JULY 1887
ALSO HIS SISTER
KATE DIED 8 APRIL 1896
ALSO HIS DAUGHTER IN LAW
ELIZABETH DIED 25 MARCH 1913
HIS BROTHER
WILLIAM DIED 26 FEB 1919
AND THE ABOVE NAMED
THOMAS DIED 14 MARCH 1919
*R.I.P.*

**SYMBOLS:**
DOVE DESCENDING WITH
BANNER IN BEAK
SURROUNDED BY WILD FLOWERS

| | |
|---|---|
| NAME OF RECORDER: | PHYLLIS NOONAN |
| DATE: | 10 SEPT 2005 |
| PHOTO REFERENCE: | K8 |
| LOCATION/MAP REF: | D1 K8 |

| | | |
|---|---|---|
| GRAVEYARD NAME: | | **ST. MARY'S ABBEY OLD GRAVEYARD** |
| GRAVEYARD CODE: | | D1 |
| COUNTY: | | MEATH |
| MEMORIAL NUMBER: | | K25 |
| ERECTED BY: | | JAMES DORY |
| ORIENTATION: | | EAST |
| NUMBER OF COMPONENTS: | | 1 |
| NUMBER OF INSCRIBED FACES: | | 1 |
| NUMBER OF PEOPLE COMMEMORATED: | | 9 |
| MEMORIAL TYPE: | | HEADSTONE |
| CONDITION OF MEMORIAL: | | SOUND IN PLACE |
| CONDITION OF INSCRIPTION: | | DECIPHERABLE |
| STONEMASON NAME: | | |
| TECHNIQUE OF INSCRIPTION: | | INCISED |
| UNDERTAKER: | | |
| STONE TOP: | | ROUND |
| GRAVE TYPE: | | SINGLE |
| HEIGHT: | | 160CM |
| WIDTH: | | 90CM |
| THICKNESS: | | 16CM |

| SURNAME: | CHRISTIAN | ADDRESS | DEATH | AGE |
|---|---|---|---|---|
| DORY | JOHN | | 21 OCT 1838 | 75 |
| | CATHERINE | | 10 APR 1848 | 63 |
| | PATRICK | | | |
| | THOMAS | | | |
| | JAMES | KNOCKISLAND DULEEK | 06 FEB 1857 | 86 |
| | PATRICK | | 27 AUG 1895 | 84 |
| | JOHN | | 09 FEB 1906 | 21 |
| | ALICIA | | 23 APR 1925 | |
| | GERALD | | 23 AUG 1934 | 3 MONTHS |

**INSCRIPTION:**
AD CROSS 1849
ERECTED BY
JAMES DORY KNOCKISLAND IN
MEMORY OF HIS BROTHER JOHN HE
DEPARTED THIS LIFE 21ST OCT 1838 AGED
75 YEARS ~~ ALSO HIS WIFE CATHERINE
DORY WHO DEPD THIS LIFE APRIL 10TH
1848 AGED 63 YEARS ~~ ALSO HIS 2
BROTHERS PATK AND THOS DORY
THE ABOVE JAMES DORY DIED 6TH FEBY 1857
AGED 86 YEARS. PATRICK DOREY WHO DIES AUG 27TH
1895 AGED 84 YEARS AND JOHN DOREY WHO DIED
FEB 9TH 1906 AGED 21 YEARS.
ALICIA WIFE OF THE ABOVE PATRICK DIED 23RD APRIL
1925 THEIR GRANDSON GERALD DIED 23RD AUG
1934 AGED 3 MONTHS
*REQUIESCANT IN PACE AMEN*

**SYMBOLS:**
HORIZONTAL SUNBURST ROUND CHERUB INCISED
HEARTS TRAILING FOLIAGE

| | |
|---|---|
| NAME OF RECORDER: | PHYLLIS NOONAN AND LIZ LYNCH |
| DATE: | 18 OCT 2005 |
| PHOTO REFERENCE: | K25 |
| LOCATION/MAP REF: | D1 K25 |

| GRAVEYARD NAME: | **ST. MARY'S ABBEY OLD GRAVEYARD** |
|---|---|
| GRAVEYARD CODE: | D1 |
| COUNTY: | MEATH |
| MEMORIAL NUMBER: | C8 |
| ERECTED BY: | |
| ORIENTATION: | EAST |
| NUMBER OF COMPONENTS: | 3 |
| NUMBER OF INSCRIBED FACES: | 1 |
| NUMBER OF PEOPLE COMMEMORATED: | 7 |
| MEMORIAL TYPE: | HEADSTONE WITH CROSS |
| CONDITION OF MEMORIAL: | SOUND IN PLACE |
| CONDITION OF INSCRIPTION: | CLEAR |
| STONEMASON NAME: | |
| TECHNIQUE OF INSCRIPTION: | INCISED PAINTED |
| UNDERTAKER: | |
| STONE TOP: | CROSS |
| GRAVE TYPE: | TREBLE |
| HEIGHT: | 180CM |
| WIDTH: | 58CM |
| THICKNESS: | 10CM |

| SURNAME: | CHRISTIAN | ADDRESS | DEATH | AGE |
|---|---|---|---|---|
| DOWNES | MICHAEL | KELLYSTOWN | 11 AUG 1923 | |
| DOWNES | MARGARET | | 28 JULY 1930 | |
| DOWNES | JAMES | | | |
| DOWNES | ALICE | | | |
| | MICHAEL | | | |
| | PATRICK | | 15 JULY 1971 | |
| | RICHARD | | 17 JULY 1979 | |

**INSCRIPTION:**

IN LOVING MEMORY OF
MICHAEL DOWNES
KELLYSTOWN, WHO DEPARTED
THIS LIFE AUG 11TH 1923
ALSO HIS WIFE
MARGARET
WHO DIED JULY 28TH 1930
AGED 60 YEARS
JAMES DOWNES
HIS WIFE ALICE
SON MICHAEL
PATRICK DOWNES DIED 15-7-71
RICHARD DOWNES DIED 17-11-79
SWEET JESUS MERCY
R.I.P

**SYMBOLS**

CROSS HEART THORNS FLAMES

**ORNAMENTS:** ELABORATE CROSS

| NAME OF RECORDER: | PHYLLIS NOONAN AND JIM ORTON |
|---|---|
| DATE: | 6 JULY 2005 |
| PHOTO REFERENCE: | C8 |
| LOCATION/MAP REFERENCE: | D1 C8 |

| | |
|---|---|
| GRAVEYARD NAME: | **ST. MARY'S ABBEY OLD GRAVEYARD** |
| GRAVEYARD CODE: | D1 |
| COUNTY: | MEATH |
| MEMORIAL NUMBER: | F5 |
| ERECTED BY: | MATHEW DUNN |
| ORIENTATION: | EAST |
| NUMBER OF COMPONENTS: | 1 |
| NUMBER OF INSCRIBED FACES: | 1 |
| NUMBER OF PEOPLE COMMEMORATED: | DUNN FAMILY |
| MEMORIAL TYPE: | HEADSTONE |
| CONDITION OF MEMORIAL: | SOUND IN PLACE |
| CONDITION OF INSCRIPTION: | MAINLY DECIPHERABLE |
| STONEMASON NAME: | |
| TECHNIQUE OF INSCRIPTION: | INCISED |
| UNDERTAKER: | |
| STONE TOP: | LOW HEADSTONE SUNBURST DISK |
| GRAVE TYPE: | SINGLE |
| HEIGHT: | 76CM |
| WIDTH: | 61CM |
| THICKNESS: | 12CM |

| SURNAME: | CHRISTIAN | ADDRESS | DEATH | AGE |
|---|---|---|---|---|
| DUNN | MATHEW | CLATTERSTOWN | | |

**INSCRIPTION:**
THIS STONE WAS ERECTED ANNO DOMINI 1803 BY MATHEW DUNN OF CLATTERSTOWN FOR HIM AND HIS POSTERITY

| | |
|---|---|
| NAME OF RECORDER: | PHYLLIS NOONAN AND BEN RYAN |
| DATE: | 18 JULY 2005 |
| PHOTO REFERENCE: | F5 |
| LOCATION/MAP REF: | D1 F5 |

| | |
|---|---|
| GRAVEYARD NAME: | **ST. MARY'S ABBEY OLD GRAVEYARD** |
| GRAVEYARD CODE: | D1 |
| COUNTY: | MEATH |
| MEMORIAL NUMBER: | B6 |
| ERECTED BY: | THOMAS J. MEKITARIAN |
| ORIENTATION: | EAST |
| NUMBER OF COMPONENTS: | 2 |
| NUMBER OF INSCRIBED FACES: | 1 |
| NUMBER OF PEOPLE COMMEMORATED: | 4 |
| MEMORIAL TYPE: | CELTIC CROSS |
| CONDITION OF MEMORIAL: | SOUND IN PLACE |
| CONDITION OF INSCRIPTION: | CLEAR |
| STONEMASON NAME: | |
| TECHNIQUE OF INSCRIPTION: | INCISED RELIEF |
| UNDERTAKER: | |
| STONE TOP: | CELTIC CROSS |
| GRAVE TYPE: | DOUBLE |
| HEIGHT: | 194CM |
| WIDTH: | 61CM |
| THICKNESS: | 13CM |

| SURNAME: | CHRISTIAN | ADDRESS | DEATH | AGE |
|---|---|---|---|---|
| DUNNE | PATRICK | DULEEK | 19 MAR 1919 | 81 |
| DUNNE | ANNE | DULEEK | 27 MAR 1932 | 87 |
| DUNNE | JULIA | | 23 APR 1944 | |
| DUNNE | PATRICK | | 06 FEB 1970 | |

**INSCRIPTION:**
ERECTED BY
THOMAS J. MEKITARIAN
IN MEMORY OF
HIS GRANDPARENTS
PATRICK AND ANNE DUNNE
DULEEK
WHO DIED 19TH MARCH 1919
AGED 81 YEARS
AND 27TH MARCH 1932
AGED 87 YEARS
R.I.P
ALSO JULIA DUNNE
WHO DIED 23 APRIL 1944
ALSO PATRICK DUNNE
DIED 6 FEB 1970

| | |
|---|---|
| NAME OF RECORDER: | PHYLLIS NOONAN |
| DATE: | 29 JUNE 2005 |
| PHOTO REFERENCE: | B6 |
| LOCATION/MAP REFERENCE: | D1 B6 |

| | |
|---|---|
| GRAVEYARD NAME: | **ST. MARY'S ABBEY OLD GRAVEYARD** |
| GRAVEYARD CODE: | D1 |
| COUNTY: | MEATH |
| MEMORIAL NUMBER: | H2 |
| ERECTED BY: | |
| ORIENTATION: | EAST |
| NUMBER OF COMPONENTS: | 1 |
| NUMBER OF INSCRIBED FACES: | 1 |
| NUMBER OF PEOPLE COMMEMORATED: | 2 |
| MEMORIAL TYPE: | HEADSTONE |
| CONDITION OF MEMORIAL: | SOUND IN PLACE |
| CONDITION OF INSCRIPTION: | MINT |
| STONEMASON NAME: | |
| TECHNIQUE OF INSCRIPTION: | INCISED AND PAINTED |
| UNDERTAKER: | |
| STONE TOP: | SQUARE STONE |
| GRAVE TYPE: | SINGLE |
| HEIGHT: | 36CM |
| WIDTH: | 85CM |
| THICKNESS: | 18CM |

| SURNAME: | CHRISTIAN | ADDRESS | DEATH | AGE |
|---|---|---|---|---|
| DUNNE | MICHAEL | PRIORYLAND | 28/05/1978 | |
| DUNNE | EMMA | | 20/11/1989 | |

**INSCRIPTION:**
IN LOVING MEMORY OF
MICHAEL DUNNE
PRIORYLAND, DULEEK
DIED 28TH MAY 1978
HIS WIFE EMMA
DIED 20TH NOVEMBER 1989
*DEATH IS NOT EXTINGUISHING THE LIGHT*
*IT IS PUTTING OUT THE LAMP BECAUSE*
*THE DAWN HAS COME*

| | |
|---|---|
| NAME OF RECORDER: | JANET LEIGH AND LIZ LYNCH |
| DATE: | 07 JUNE 2006 |
| PHOTO REFERENCE: | H2 |
| LOCATION/MAP REF: | D1-H2 |

| | |
|---|---|
| GRAVEYARD NAME: | **ST. MARY'S ABBEY OLD GRAVEYARD** |
| GRAVEYARD CODE: | D1 |
| COUNTY: | MEATH |
| MEMORIAL NUMBER: | J21 |
| ERECTED BY: | NICHOLAS DWYER |
| ORIENTATION: | EAST |
| NUMBER OF COMPONENTS: | 3 |
| NUMBER OF INSCRIBED FACES: | 1 |
| NUMBER OF PEOPLE COMMEMORATED: | 6 |
| MEMORIAL TYPE: | HEADSTONE |
| CONDITION OF MEMORIAL: | GOOD |
| CONDITION OF INSCRIPTION: | CLEAR |
| STONEMASON NAME: | |
| TECHNIQUE OF INSCRIPTION: | INCISED |
| UNDERTAKER: | |
| STONE TOP: | CROSS |
| GRAVE TYPE: | TREBLE |
| HEIGHT: | 240CM |
| WIDTH: | 68CM |
| THICKNESS: | 12CM |

| SURNAME: | CHRISTIAN | ADDRESS | DEATH | AGE |
|---|---|---|---|---|
| DWYER | ANNIE | | 21 SEPT 1921 | |
| | JOSEPH | | 10 MAY 1934 | 36 |
| | NICHOLAS | DULEEK | 23 FEB 1935 | 67 |
| | ELIZABETH | | 15 SEPT 1937 | |
| | CHRISTOPHER | | 07 DEC 1957 | 63 |
| | KATHERINE | | 08 JAN 1963 | 73 |

**INSCRIPTION:**
ERECTED
BY
NICHOLAS DWYER DULEEK
IN LOVING MEMORY OF HIS WIFE
ANNIE
WHO DIED SEPT 21ST 1921
ALSO HIS SON JOSEPH WHO DIED
MAY 10TH 1934 AGED 36 YEARS
AND THE ABOVE
NICHOLAS DWYER
DIED FEB 23RD 1935 AGED 67 YEARS
ALSO HIS DAUGHTER ELIZABETH
WHO DIED SEPT 15TH 1937
HIS SON CHRISTOPHER
DIED DEC. 7TH 1957 AGED 63 YRS
WHOSE WIFE KATHLEEN
DIED JAN 8TH 1963 AGED 73 YRS.
RIP

**SYMBOLS:**
CROSS SACRED HEART
WITH THORNS

| | |
|---|---|
| NAME OF RECORDER: | JIM ORTEN |
| DATE: | 13 AUG 2005 |
| PHOTO REFERENCE: | J21 |
| LOCATION/MAP REF: | D1 J21 |

| | |
|---|---|
| GRAVEYARD NAME: | **ST. MARY'S ABBEY OLD GRAVEYARD** |
| GRAVEYARD CODE: | D1 |
| COUNTY: | MEATH |
| MEMORIAL NUMBER: | G13 |
| ERECTED BY: | PETER CAFFREY |
| ORIENTATION: | EAST |
| NUMBER OF COMPONENTS: | 1 |
| NUMBER OF INSCRIBED FACES: | 1 |
| NUMBER OF PEOPLE COMMEMORATED: | 5 |
| MEMORIAL TYPE: | HEADSTONE ON GROUND |
| CONDITION OF MEMORIAL: | SOUND IN PLACE ON THE FLOOR OF ABBEY |
| CONDITION OF INSCRIPTION: | CLEAR |
| STONEMASON NAME: | |
| TECHNIQUE OF INSCRIPTION: | INCISED |
| UNDERTAKER: | |
| STONE TOP: | ROUND |
| GRAVE TYPE: | SINGLE |
| HEIGHT: | 177CM |
| WIDTH: | 77CM |
| THICKNESS: | NOT ACCESSIBLE |

| SURNAME: | CHRISTIAN | ADDRESS | DEATH | AGE |
|---|---|---|---|---|
| ELLIOTT | ANN | | 14 FEB 1777 | 26 |

**INSCRIPTION:**
THIS BURIAL PLACE BELONGETH TO
PETER CAFFREY OF DULEEK AND HIS
POSTERITY HERE LIETH FOUR OF HIS
CHILDREN
AND THE BODY OF ANN ELLIOTT FOR
WHOME THIS STONE WAS ERECTED
WHO DEPARTED THIS LIFE THE 14TH OF
FEBRUARY ANNO DOMINI 1777 AGED 26

**SYMBOLS:**
IHS WITH + IN SUNBURST
HEART UNDER THE H
CROSS ABOVE THE H

| | |
|---|---|
| NAME OF RECORDER: | JANET LEIGH |
| DATE: | 28 JUNE 2006 |
| PHOTO REFERENCE | G 13 |
| LOCATION/MAP REF: | D1 G13 |

| | |
|---|---|
| GRAVEYARD NAME: | **ST. MARY'S ABBEY OLD GRAVEYARD** |
| GRAVEYARD CODE: | D1 |
| COUNTY: | MEATH |
| MEMORIAL NUMBER: | J29 |
| ERECTED BY: | JAMES ELLIOTT |
| ORIENTATION: | EAST |
| NUMBER OF COMPONENTS: | 1 |
| NUMBER OF INSCRIBED FACES: | 1 |
| NUMBER OF PEOPLE COMMEMORATED: | 1 |
| MEMORIAL TYPE: | LOW MONUMENT |
| CONDITION OF MEMORIAL: | SOUND IN PLACE |
| CONDITION OF INSCRIPTION: | MAINLY DECIPHERABLE |
| STONEMASON NAME: | |
| TECHNIQUE OF INSCRIPTION: | INCISED |
| UNDERTAKER: | |
| STONE TOP: | LOW MONUMENT |
| GRAVE TYPE: | SINGLE |
| HEIGHT: | LENGTH 184CM |
| WIDTH: | 94CM |
| THICKNESS: | NOT ACCESSIBLE |

| SURNAME: | CHRISTIAN | ADDRESS | DEATH | AGE |
|---|---|---|---|---|
| ELLIOTT | CATHERINE | | 21 SEPT 1787 | 37 |

**INSCRIPTION:**
ERECTED
BY JAMES ELLIOTT QR. MR. SGT 58 REG
IN MEMORY OF HIS BELOVED WIFE
CATHERINE ELLIOTT
WHO DEPARTED THIS LIFE THE 21ST SEPTR
ANNO DOMINO 1787
AGED 37 YEARS
SHE WAS AN AFFECTIONATE WIFE & A TENDER
MOTHER
BELOVED BY ALL WHO KNEW HER
FOR HER MANY VIRTUES
AND DIED REGRETTED
UNDERNEATH ALSO RESTS THE BODIES OF HIS
ANCESTORS

| | |
|---|---|
| NAME OF RECORDER: | PHYLLIS NOONAN AND BEN RYAN |
| DATE: | 20 AUG 2005 |
| PHOTO REFERENCE: | J 29 |
| LOCATION/MAP REF: | D1 J29 |

| | |
|---|---|
| GRAVEYARD NAME: | **ST. MARY'S ABBEY OLD GRAVEYARD** |
| GRAVEYARD CODE: | D1 |
| COUNTY: | MEATH |
| MEMORIAL NUMBER: | J28 |
| ERECTED BY: | MISS STYLES |
| ORIENTATION: | EAST |
| NUMBER OF COMPONENTS: | 5 |
| NUMBER OF INSCRIBED FACES: | 1 |
| NUMBER OF PEOPLE COMMEMORATED: | 8 |
| MEMORIAL TYPE: | TABLE TOMB |
| CONDITION OF MEMORIAL: | SOUND IN PLACE |
| CONDITION OF INSCRIPTION: | MAINLY DECIPHERABLE |
| STONEMASON NAME: | |
| TECHNIQUE OF INSCRIPTION: | INCISED |
| UNDERTAKER: | |
| STONE TOP: | TABLE TOMB |
| GRAVE TYPE: | MULTIPLE |
| HEIGHT: | LENGTH 224CM |
| WIDTH: | 105CM |
| THICKNESS: | 64 CM INCLUDES PEDESTAL PILLARS |

| SURNAME: | CHRISTIAN | ADDRESS | DEATH | AGE |
|---|---|---|---|---|
| ELLIOTT | JOSEPH | KILNEW | 27 FEB 1846 | 27 |
| | WILLIAM | | 16 JUNE 1834 | 15 |
| | ESTER | | 07 FEB 1843 | 54 |
| STYLES | ELINOR | | 04 MAR 1850 | 76 |
| EDWARDS | SUSAN | | 04 DEC 1850 | 78 |
| ELLIOTT | FRANCIS | | 02 SEPT 1851 | 72 |
| ELLIOTT GRIFFIN | FRANCIS | BORN IN NY USA 19 MARCH 1841 | 14 MAR 1860 | 19 |
| ELLIOTT | MARY | | 25TH APRIL 1871 | 50 |

**INSCRIPTION:**
ERECTED
BY MISS STYLES IN MEMORY OF HER
AFFECTIONATE NEPHEW MR. JOSEPH ELLIOTT
OF KILNEW WHO DEPARTED THIS LIFE ON THE
27 DAY OF FEBRUARY 1846 AGED 27 YEARS
MR. WILLIAM ELLIOTT DEPARTED THIS LIFE 16TH
JUNE 1834 AGED 15 YEARS
MRS. ESTER ELLIOTT WHO DEPARTED 7 FEBRUARY
1843 AGED 54 YEARS
ELINOR STYLES DIED 4TH MARCH 1850
AGED 76 YEARS SUSAN EDWARDS DIED 4TH
DECR 1850 AGED 78 YEARS FRANCIS ELLIOTT
DIED 2ND SEPR 1851 AGED 72 YEARS
FRANCIS ELLIOTT GRIFFIN DIED 14TH MARCH
1860 BORN IN NEW YORK AMERICA 19TH
MARCH 1841
MARY DAUGHTER OF THE ABOVE FRANCIS ELLIOTT
DIED APRIL 25TH 1871 AGED 50 YEARS

| | |
|---|---|
| NAME OF RECORDER: | PHYLLIS NOONAN AND BEN RYAN |
| DATE: | 20 AUG 2005 |
| PHOTO REFERENCE: | J28 |
| LOCATION/MAP REF: | D1 J28 |

| | |
|---|---|
| GRAVEYARD NAME: | **ST. MARY'S ABBEY OLD GRAVEYARD** |
| GRAVEYARD CODE: | D1 |
| COUNTY: | MEATH |
| MEMORIAL NUMBER: | B10 |
| ERECTED BY: | |
| ORIENTATION: | EAST |
| NUMBER OF COMPONENTS: | 2 |
| NUMBER OF INSCRIBED FACES: | 1 |
| NUMBER OF PEOPLE COMMEMORATED: | 1 |
| MEMORIAL TYPE: | HEADSTONE |
| CONDITION OF MEMORIAL: | SOUND IN PLACE |
| CONDITION OF INSCRIPTION: | MAINLY DECIPHERABLE |
| STONEMASON NAME: | |
| TECHNIQUE OF INSCRIPTION: | INCISED |
| UNDERTAKER: | |
| STONE TOP: | ROUND |
| GRAVE TYPE: | SINGLE |
| HEIGHT: | 84CM |
| WIDTH: | 44CM |
| THICKNESS: | 5CM |

| SURNAME: | CHRISTIAN | ADDRESS | DEATH | AGE |
|---|---|---|---|---|
| FAY | PATRICK | RAHILL | 13 JUNE 1909 | |

**INSCRIPTION:**
IN LOVING MEMORY
OF
PATRICK FAY
RAHILL
WHO DIED 13 JUNE 1909

**SYMBOLS:**
CROSS

| | |
|---|---|
| NAME OF RECORDER: | HELEN FULLAM AND JANET LEIGH |
| DATE: | 2 JULY 2005 |
| PHOTO REFERENCE: | B10 |
| LOCATION/MAP REF: | D1 B10 |

| | |
|---|---|
| GRAVEYARD NAME: | **ST. MARY'S ABBEY OLD GRAVEYARD** |
| GRAVEYARD CODE: | D1 |
| COUNTY: | MEATH |
| MEMORIAL NUMBER: | K11 |
| ERECTED BY: | |
| ORIENTATION: | EAST |
| NUMBER OF COMPONENTS: | 2 |
| NUMBER OF INSCRIBED FACES: | 1 |
| NUMBER OF PEOPLE COMMEMORATED: | 1 |
| MEMORIAL TYPE: | HEADSTONE |
| CONDITION OF MEMORIAL: | SOUND IN PLACE |
| CONDITION OF INSCRIPTION: | LEGIBLE |
| STONEMASON NAME: | MOSS |
| TECHNIQUE OF INSCRIPTION: | INCISED |
| UNDERTAKER: | |
| STONE TOP: | ROUND |
| GRAVE TYPE: | SINGLE |
| HEIGHT: | 86CM |
| WIDTH: | 48CM |
| THICKNESS: | 05CM |

| SURNAME: | CHRISTIAN | ADDRESS | DEATH | AGE |
|---|---|---|---|---|
| FAY | MARGARET | RAHILL | 6 NOV 1911 | |

**INSCRIPTION:**
IN LOVING MEMORY
OF
MARGARET FAY
RAHILL
WHO DIED 6 NOV 1911
RIP

**SYMBOLS:**
CROSS

| | |
|---|---|
| NAME OF RECORDER: | LIZ LYNCH AND JANET LEIGH |
| DATE: | 27 AUG 2005 |
| PHOTO REFERENCE: | K11 |
| LOCATION/MAP REF: | D1 K11 |

| | |
|---|---|
| GRAVEYARD NAME: | **ST. MARY'S ABBEY OLD GRAVEYARD** |
| GRAVEYARD CODE: | D1 |
| COUNTY: | MEATH |
| MEMORIAL NUMBER: | A7 |
| ERECTED BY: | |
| ORIENTATION: | EAST |
| NUMBER OF COMPONENTS: | 2 BROKEN |
| NUMBER OF INSCRIBED FACES: | 1 |
| NUMBER OF PEOPLE COMMEMORATED: | 4 |
| MEMORIAL TYPE: | ARCHED HEADSTONE |
| CONDITION OF MEMORIAL: | COLLAPSED |
| CONDITION OF INSCRIPTION: | MAINLY DECIPHERABLE |
| STONEMASON NAME: | |
| TECHNIQUE OF INSCRIPTION: | INCISED INLAID LEAD LETTERING |
| UNDERTAKER: | |
| STONE TOP: | ARCHED |
| GRAVE TYPE: | DOUBLE |
| HEIGHT: | 161CM |
| WIDTH: | 77CM |
| THICKNESS: | 9CM |

| SURNAME: | CHRISTIAN | ADDRESS | DEATH | AGE |
|---|---|---|---|---|
| FERGUSON | CATHERINE ANNE | ABBEY LODGE | 12 MAY 1913 | |
| FERGUSON | WILLIAM | | 07 DEC 1913 | |
| FERGUSON | ELIZABETH | | 18 JUNE 1935 | |
| FERGUSON | KATHERINE | | 07 MAR 1949 | |

**INSCRIPTION:**
IN
LOVING MEMORY
OF
OUR DEAR MOTHER
CATHERINE ANNE FERGUSON
ABBEY LODGE
WHO DIED MAY 12TH 1913
AND OUR DEAR FATHER
WILLIAM FERGUSON
WHO DIED DEC 7TH 1913
AND THEIR DAUGHTERS
ELIZABETH
BURIED AT WALTHENS ST. LAWRENCE
18TH JUNE 1935
KATHERINE
WHO DIED MARCH 7TH 1949

**SYMBOLS:**
FOLIAGE AND FLOWERS

| | |
|---|---|
| NAME OF RECORDER: | PHYLLIS NOONAN AND JIM ORTEN |
| DATE: | 18 JUNE 2005 |
| PHOTO REFERENCE: | A7 |
| LOCATION/MAP REF: | D1 A7 |

| | |
|---|---|
| Graveyard Name: | St. Mary's Abbey Old Graveyard |
| Graveyard Code: | D1 |
| County: | Meath |
| Memorial Number: | K37 |
| Erected By: | Theresa Fitzharris |
| Orientation: | East |
| Number of Components: | 2 |
| Number of Inscribed Faces: | 1 |
| Number of People Commemorated: | |
| Memorial Type: | Headstone with top missing iron railings surround |
| Condition of Memorial: | Collapsed |
| Condition of Inscription: | Some missing |
| Stonemason Name: | |
| Technique of Inscription: | Incised |
| Undertaker: | |
| Stone Top: | Missing collapsed |
| Grave Type: | Double |
| Height: | 170 cm |
| Width: | 63 cm |
| Thickness: | 9 cm |

| Surname: | Christian | Address | Birth | Death | Age |
|---|---|---|---|---|---|
| Fitzharris | John | Duleek | 05 Feb 1830 | 27 Feb 1873 | |
| | Margaret | | 05 Feb 1862 | 30 May 1885 | |
| | John | | 14 Mar 18..? | | |
| | | | | | |

**Inscription:**
Erected
By
Theresa Fitzharris
Duleek
In Memory of her Husband
John Fitzharris
Born 5th February 1830
Died 27th Feby 1873
Also her Daughter
Margaret
Born 5th February 1862
Died 30th May 1885
And of her Son
John
Born 14th March 18..?

**Ornaments:**
Single Tulip at top of stone

**Comments:**
Iron Railings Surround Headstone collapsed and cracked

| | |
|---|---|
| Name of Recorder: | Janet Leigh and Phyllis Noonan |
| Date: | 27 April 2006 |
| Photo Reference: | K37 |
| Location/Map Ref: | D1 K37 |

| | |
|---|---|
| GRAVEYARD NAME: | **ST. MARY'S ABBEY OLD GRAVEYARD** |
| GRAVEYARD CODE: | D1 |
| COUNTY: | MEATH |
| MEMORIAL NUMBER: | J15 |
| ERECTED BY: | MICHAEL FLEMING |
| ORIENTATION: | EAST |
| NUMBER OF COMPONENTS: | 1 |
| NUMBER OF INSCRIBED FACES: | 1 |
| NUMBER OF PEOPLE COMMEMORATED: | 11 + |
| MEMORIAL TYPE: | HEADSTONE |
| CONDITION OF MEMORIAL: | SOUND IN PLACE |
| CONDITION OF INSCRIPTION: | DECIPHERABLE |
| STONEMASON NAME: | |
| TECHNIQUE OF INSCRIPTION: | INCISED |
| UNDERTAKER: | |
| STONE TOP: | ROUND |
| GRAVE TYPE: | TREBLE |
| HEIGHT: | 159CM |
| WIDTH: | 64CM |
| THICKNESS: | 10CM |

| SURNAME: | CHRISTIAN | ADDRESS | DEATH | AGE |
|---|---|---|---|---|
| FLEMING | PATRICK | DAW, DULEEK | CHILD | |
| | ROSANA | | CHILD | |
| | MARY | | CHILD | |
| | MARGARET | | CHILD | |
| FLEMING | CHILDREN WHO DIED YOUNG | | | |
| FLEMING | BRIGID | | 29 SEPT 1842 | 55 |
| | MICHAEL | | 17 FEB 1855 | 62 |
| | JOHN | | 13 JUNE 1885 | 75 |
| | MICHAEL | | 22 DEC 1896 | |
| | MARY HELEN | | 26 APR 1899 | |
| | CATHERINE | | 10 OCT 1907 | |
| | MARGARET | | 10 OCT 1926 | |
| | JOHN | | 17 DEC 1933 | 63 |

**INSCRIPTION:**
ERECTED BY
MICHAEL FLEMING
DAW PARISH OF DULEEK
TO THE MEMORY OF FOUR OF HIS BELOVED
CHILDREN PATRICK ROSANA MARY AND
MARGARET ~ THE REMAINDER OF HIS
CHILDREN WHO DIED YOUNG
ALSO BRIGID FLEMING WHO
DEPARTED THIS LIFE 29TH SEPTER
1842 AGED 55 YEARS
ALSO THE ABOVE MICHAEL
FLEMING WHO DEPARTED
THIS LIFE FEBY THE 17TH 1855
AGED 62 YEARS ALSO HIS SON
JOHN FLEMING WHO DIED JUNE
13TH 1885 AGED 75 YEARS
MICHAEL FLEMING DIED DEC 22ND 1896
MARY HELEN FLEMING
DIED 26TH APRIL 1899
CATHERINE FLEMING
DIED OCT 10TH 1907
MARGARET FLEMING DIED OCT 10TH
1926
JOHN FLEMING
DIED SEP 17 1933 AGED 63 YEARS
*REQUICIUM IN PACE*

**SYMBOLS:**
IHS IN SUNBURST CHALICE
AND DOUBLE CROSS EACH SIDE OF THE CROSS

| | |
|---|---|
| NAME OF RECORDER: | LIZ LYNCH |
| DATE: | 6 AUG 2005 |
| PHOTO REFERENCE: | J15 |
| LOCATION/MAP REF: | D1 J15 |

| | |
|---|---|
| GRAVEYARD NAME: | **ST. MARY'S ABBEY OLD GRAVEYARD** |
| GRAVEYARD CODE: | D1 |
| COUNTY: | MEATH |
| MEMORIAL NUMBER: | L2 |
| ERECTED BY: | BERNARD FORD |
| ORIENTATION: | EAST |
| NUMBER OF COMPONENTS: | 2 |
| NUMBER OF INSCRIBED FACES: | 1 |
| NUMBER OF PEOPLE COMMEMORATED: | 4 |
| MEMORIAL TYPE: | CELTIC CROSS |
| CONDITION OF MEMORIAL: | SOUND IN PLACE |
| CONDITION OF INSCRIPTION: | CLEAR |
| STONEMASON NAME: | P. WHYTE DROGHEDA |
| TECHNIQUE OF INSCRIPTION: | INCISED |
| UNDERTAKER: | |
| STONE TOP: | CELTIC CROSS |
| GRAVE TYPE: | SINGLE |
| HEIGHT: | 190CM |
| WIDTH: | 65CM |
| THICKNESS: | 10CM |

| SURNAME: | CHRISTIAN | ADDRESS | DEATH | AGE |
|---|---|---|---|---|
| FORD | ELLEN | | | |
| | MARY ANNE | | | |
| | JULIA | | | |
| | BERNARD | | 12 JULY 1887 | 72 |

**INSCRIPTION:**
ERECTED
BY
BERNARD FORD
IN MEMORY OF HIS BELOVED WIFE
ELLEN FORD
AND HIS TWO SISTERS
MARY ANNE AND JULIA
HERE ALSO LIETH THE REMAINS
OF THE ABOVE NAMED
BERNARD FORD
WHO DIED 12TH JULY 1887 AGED 72 YEARS
*MAY THEY REST IN PEACE*

**SYMBOLS:**
LAMB ON CROSS IN CENTRE OF CROSS
ORNAMENTATION ON CROSS AND ARMS

| | |
|---|---|
| NAME OF RECORDER: | LIZ LYNCH |
| DATE: | 16 MAY 2006 |
| PHOTO REFERENCE: | L2 |
| LOCATION/MAP REF: | D1 L2 |

| | |
|---|---|
| GRAVEYARD NAME: | **ST. MARY'S ABBEY OLD GRAVEYARD** |
| GRAVEYARD CODE: | D1 |
| COUNTY: | MEATH |
| MEMORIAL NUMBER: | K6 |
| ERECTED BY: | FORDE FAMILY |
| ORIENTATION: | EAST |
| NUMBER OF COMPONENTS: | 1 |
| NUMBER OF INSCRIBED FACES: | 1 |
| NUMBER OF PEOPLE COMMEMORATED: | 7 |
| MEMORIAL TYPE: | HEADSTONE |
| CONDITION OF MEMORIAL: | SOUND IN PLACE |
| CONDITION OF INSCRIPTION: | CLEAR |
| STONEMASON NAME: | FITZPATRICK & SONS GLASNEVIN DUBLIN |
| TECHNIQUE OF INSCRIPTION: | INCISED |
| UNDERTAKER: | |
| STONE TOP: | ARCH |
| GRAVE TYPE: | SINGLE |
| HEIGHT: | 150CM |
| WIDTH: | 65CM |
| THICKNESS: | 09CM |

| SURNAME: | CHRISTIAN | ADDRESS | DEATH | AGE |
|---|---|---|---|---|
| FORDE | WILLIAM | NEWLANES | 11 JAN 1889 | 56 |
| | ALICE | | 21 JUNE 1902 | 55 |
| | FELIX | | 1867 | 4 |
| | ALICE | | 12 MAY 1884 | 15 |
| | BERNARD | | 18 JUNE 1939 | 74 |
| | WILLIAM | | 15 SEPT 1950 | 75 |
| COSTER | KATHLEEN | | 31 MAY 1952 | 80 |

**INSCRIPTION:**
ERECTED IN LOVING MEMORY OF
OUR FATHER
WILLIAM FORDE
NEWLANES
WHO DIED 11TH JAN 1889 AGED 56 YEARS
AND OUR MOTHER
ALICE FORDE
WHO DIED 21ST JUNE 1902 AGED 55 YEARS
ALSO OF OUR BROTHER
FELIX
WHO DIED
1867 AGED 4 YEARS
AND OUR SISTER
ALICE
WHO DIED 12TH MAY 1884 AGED 15 YEARS
ALSO OF OUR BROTHERS
LT. COL. BERNARD FORDE
R.A.M.C; M.B:: C.M.C; L.L.B.
WHO DIED
18 JUNE 1939 AGED 74 YEARS
WILLIAM
WHO DIED 15 SEPT. 1950 AGED 75 YEARS
THEIR SISTER KATHLEEN COSTER
WHO DIED 31 MAY 1952 AGED 80 YEARS
R.I.P.

**SYMBOLS:**
CROSS IN CIRCLE FOLIAGE AND FLEUR DE LIS CROSS EACH SIDE

**ORNAMENTS:**
TWO COLUMNS FOLIAGE ON TOP
WRITING IN SCROLL

| | |
|---|---|
| NAME OF RECORDER: | JANET LEIGH |
| DATE: | 10 AUGUST 2005 |
| PHOTO REFERENCE: | K6 |
| LOCATION/MAP REF: | D1 K6 |

| | |
|---|---|
| GRAVEYARD NAME: | **ST. MARY'S ABBEY OLD GRAVEYARD** |
| GRAVEYARD CODE: | D1 |
| COUNTY: | MEATH |
| MEMORIAL NUMBER: | L24 |
| ERECTED BY: | CATHERINE FULLAM DONORE |
| ORIENTATION: | EAST |
| NUMBER OF COMPONENTS: | 4 |
| NUMBER OF INSCRIBED FACES: | 1 |
| NUMBER OF PEOPLE COMMEMORATED: | 3 |
| MEMORIAL TYPE: | ELABORATE HEADSTONE |
| CONDITION OF MEMORIAL: | SOUND IN PLACE |
| CONDITION OF INSCRIPTION: | CLEAR |
| STONEMASON NAME: | |
| TECHNIQUE OF INSCRIPTION: | INCISED |
| UNDERTAKER: | |
| STONE TOP: | APEX WITH CROSS MISSING |
| GRAVE TYPE: | DOUBLE |
| HEIGHT: | 180CM |
| WIDTH: | 57CM |
| THICKNESS: | 28CM |

| SURNAME: | CHRISTIAN | | DEATH | AGE |
|---|---|---|---|---|
| FULLAM | PATRICK | | 12 AUG 1847 | 33 |
| | MARGARET | YOUNG | | |
| | BRIDGET | YOUNG | | |

**INSCRIPTION:**
ERECTED
BY CATHERINE FULLAM
OF DONORE TO THE
MEMORY OF HER BELOVED
HUSBAND PATRICK
FULLAM WHO DEPARTED
THIS LIFE AUGUST THE
12TH 1847 AGED 33 YEARS
ALSO HER TWO CHILDREN
MARGARET AND BRIDGET
WHO DIED YOUNG
MAY THEY REST IN PEACE

**SYMBOLS:**
PEDESTAL IN 4 PARTS CROSS MISSING
SMALL CROSS WITH IHS

| | |
|---|---|
| NAME OF RECORDER: | LIZ LYNCH AND PHYLLIS NOONAN |
| DATE: | 25 JUNE 2006 |
| PHOTO REFERENCE: | L24 |
| LOCATION/MAP REF: | D1 L24 |

| | |
|---|---|
| GRAVEYARD NAME: | **ST. MARY'S ABBEY OLD GRAVEYARD** |
| GRAVEYARD CODE: | D1 |
| COUNTY: | MEATH |
| MEMORIAL NUMBER: | L23 |
| ERECTED BY: | JOHN FULLAM |
| ORIENTATION: | EAST |
| NUMBER OF COMPONENTS: | 1 |
| NUMBER OF INSCRIBED FACES: | 1 |
| NUMBER OF PEOPLE COMMEMORATED: | 2 |
| MEMORIAL TYPE: | HEADSTONE |
| CONDITION OF MEMORIAL: | SOUND IN PLACE |
| CONDITION OF INSCRIPTION: | CLEAR |
| STONEMASON NAME: | |
| TECHNIQUE OF INSCRIPTION: | INCISED |
| UNDERTAKER: | |
| STONE TOP: | ROUND |
| GRAVE TYPE: | SINGLE |
| HEIGHT: | 88CM |
| WIDTH: | 45CM |
| THICKNESS: | 17CM |

| SURNAME: | CHRISTIAN | ADDRESS | DEATH | AGE |
|---|---|---|---|---|
| FULLAM | THOMAS | | 16 MAR 1787 | 10 |
| | JOHN | | 02 APR 1795 | 64 |

INSCRIPTION:
THIS STONE AND BU
RIAL PLACE BELONGETH
TO JOHN FULLAM FOR HIM
AND HIS POSTERITY
ANNO DOMINI 1788
HERE LIETH THE BODY OF HIS
SON THOMAS FULLAM WHO
DEPARTED THIS LIFE THE 16TH OF
MARCH 1797 AGED 10 YEARS
HERE ALSO LIETH THE BODY OF
THE ABOVE JOHN FULLAM WHO
DEPARTED THIS LIFE THE 2ND OF
APRIL 1795 AGED 64 YEARS

| | |
|---|---|
| NAME OF RECORDER: | LIZ LYNCH AND JANET LEIGH |
| DATE: | 7 JUNE 2006 |
| PHOTO REFERENCE: | L23 |
| LOCATION/MAP REF: | D1 L23 |

| | |
|---|---|
| GRAVEYARD NAME: | **ST. MARY'S ABBEY OLD GRAVEYARD** |
| GRAVEYARD CODE: | D1 |
| COUNTY: | MEATH |
| MEMORIAL NUMBER: | B8 |
| ERECTED BY: | JOHN GAFFNEY |
| ORIENTATION: | EAST |
| NUMBER OF COMPONENTS: | 3 |
| NUMBER OF INSCRIBED FACES: | 1 |
| NUMBER OF PEOPLE COMMEMORATED: | 5 |
| MEMORIAL TYPE: | HEADSTONE |
| CONDITION OF MEMORIAL: | GOOD |
| CONDITION OF INSCRIPTION: | MAINLY DECIPHERABLE |
| STONEMASON NAME: | T. REID PLATIN |
| TECHNIQUE OF INSCRIPTION: | INCISED |
| UNDERTAKER: | |
| STONE TOP: | ROUND CELTIC CROSS WITH HEART |
| GRAVE TYPE: | TREBLE |
| HEIGHT: | 216CM |
| WIDTH: | 68CM |
| THICKNESS: | 10CM |

| SURNAME: | CHRISTIAN | ADDRESS | OCCUPATION | DEATH | AGE |
|---|---|---|---|---|---|
| GAFFNEY | MARY | | | 24 FEB 1913 | 74 |
| | JOHN | GASKINSTOWN | | 27 DEC 1933 | 97 |
| | JACK | | GRANDSON | 17 JUL 1943 | 27 |
| | MARY | | | 17 DEC 1954 | |
| | JOHN | | | 27 MAY 1955 | |

**INSCRIPTION:**
ERECTED
BY
JOHN GAFFNEY OF GASKINSTOWN
IN LOVING MEMORY OF HIS WIFE
MARY WHO DIED FEB 24TH 1913
AGED 74 YEARS
ALSO THE ABOVE
JOHN GAFFNEY
WHO DIED 27TH DECEMBER 1933
AGED 97 YEARS
ALSO THEIR GRANDSON JACK
DIED 17 JULY 1943 AGED 27
HIS MOTHER MARY
WHO DIED 17 DEC 1954
AND HER HUSBAND JOHN
DIED 27 MAY 1955
*SACRED HEART OF JESUS HAVE
MERCY ON THEM*
R.I.P

**SYMBOLS:**
IHS ENTWINED CELTIC CROSS
WITH HEART

| | |
|---|---|
| NAME OF RECORDER: | LIZ LYNCH AND JIM ORTEN |
| DATE: | 2 JULY 2005 |
| PHOTO REFERENCE: | B8 |
| LOCATION/MAP REF: | D1 B8 |

| | |
|---|---|
| GRAVEYARD NAME: | **ST. MARY'S ABBEY OLD GRAVEYARD** |
| GRAVEYARD CODE: | D1 |
| COUNTY: | MEATH |
| MEMORIAL NUMBER: | K43 |
| ERECTED BY: | ANDREW GALAGHER |
| ORIENTATION: | EAST |
| NUMBER OF COMPONENTS: | 2 |
| NUMBER OF INSCRIBED FACES: | 1 |
| NUMBER OF PEOPLE COMMEMORATED: | 5 |
| MEMORIAL TYPE: | HEADSTONE |
| CONDITION OF MEMORIAL: | SOUND IN PLACE |
| CONDITION OF INSCRIPTION: | BARELY LEGIBLE |
| STONEMASON NAME: | |
| TECHNIQUE OF INSCRIPTION: | INCISED |
| UNDERTAKER: | |
| STONE TOP: | ROUND |
| GRAVE TYPE: | DOUBLE |
| HEIGHT: | 146CM |
| WIDTH: | 90CM |
| THICKNESS: | 03CM |

| SURNAME: | CHRISTIAN | ADDRESS | DEATH | AGE |
|---|---|---|---|---|
| GALAGHER | WILLIAM | MANANS TOWN | 06 MAY 1805 | |
| | JANE | | 20 JUNE 1819 | |
| GALLAGHER | ANDREW | | 10      1860 | 67 |
| GALLAGHER | MARGARET | | 02 DEC 1870 | 74 |
| GALLAGHER | TERESA | | 25 MAY 1900 | 60 |

**INSCRIPTION:**
ERECTED BY ANDREW GALLAGHER
OF MANANS TOWN IN MEMORY
OF HIS FATHER WILLIAM GALAGHER
WHO DIED MAY 6 1805 ALSO
HIS MOTHER JANE GALAGHER
DIED JUNE 26 1819
ALSO THE ABOVE NAMED ANDREW GALLAGHER
WHO DIED 10TH …… 1860 AGED 67
AND HIS WIFE MARGARET GALLAGHER
WHO DIED 2 DECR 1870 AGED 74 YEARS
ALSO HIS DAUGHTER TERESA GALLAGHER
WHO DIED 25TH MAY 1900 AGED 60 YEARS

| | |
|---|---|
| NAME OF RECORDER: | LIZ LYNCH AND PHYLLIS NOONAN |
| DATE: | 6 MAY 2006 |
| PHOTO REFERENCE: | K43 |
| LOCATION/MAP REF: | D1 K43 |

| | |
|---|---|
| GRAVEYARD NAME: | **ST. MARY'S ABBEY OLD GRAVEYARD** |
| GRAVEYARD CODE: | D1 |
| COUNTY: | MEATH |
| MEMORIAL NUMBER: | K42 |
| ERECTED BY: | THOMAS GALLAGHER |
| ORIENTATION: | EAST |
| NUMBER OF COMPONENTS: | 3 |
| NUMBER OF INSCRIBED FACES: | 1 |
| NUMBER OF PEOPLE COMMEMORATED: | 5 |
| MEMORIAL TYPE: | HEADSTONE CELTIC CROSS |
| CONDITION OF MEMORIAL: | SOUND IN PLACE |
| CONDITION OF INSCRIPTION: | MAINLY DECIPHERABLE |
| STONEMASON NAME: | |
| TECHNIQUE OF INSCRIPTION: | INCISED |
| UNDERTAKER: | |
| STONE TOP: | CELTIC CROSS |
| GRAVE TYPE: | SINGLE |
| HEIGHT: | 190CM |
| WIDTH: | 58CM |
| THICKNESS: | 10CM |

| SURNAME: | CHRISTIAN | ADDRESS | DEATH | AGE |
|---|---|---|---|---|
| GALLAGHER | SIMON | | 24 DEC 1861 | 72 |
| | ALICE | | 13 FEB 1873 | 76 |
| | JULIA | | DIED YOUNG | |
| | THOMAS | | 2 MAR 1876 | 48 |
| | WILLIAM | | 22 OCT 1888 | 64 |

**INSCRIPTION:**
ERECTED BY THOMAS GALLAGHER IN
MEMORY OF HIS BELOVED FATHER
SIMON GALLAGHER
WHO DIED 24TH DECEMBER 1861 AGED 72 YEARS
ALICE GALLAGHER
WHO DIED 13 FEB 1873 AGED 76 YEARS.
ALSO HIS SISTER JULIA WHO DIED YOUNG.
ALSO THE ABOVE NAMED
THOMAS GALLAGHER
WHO DEPARTED THIS LIFE THE 2 OF MARCH 1876
AGED 48 YEARS AND ALSO HIS SON
WILLIAM GALLAGHER
WHO DEPARTED THIS LIFE ON 22ND OCTOBER 1888
AGED 64 YEARS

**SYMBOLS:**
IHS IN CIRCLE IN CENTRE OF CROSS

| | |
|---|---|
| NAME OF RECORDER: | PHYLLIS NOONAN |
| DATE: | 20 MAY 2006 |
| PHOTO REFERENCE: | K42 |
| LOCATION/MAP REF: | D1 K42 |

| | |
|---|---|
| GRAVEYARD NAME: | **ST. MARY'S ABBEY OLD GRAVEYARD** |
| GRAVEYARD CODE: | D1 |
| COUNTY: | MEATH |
| MEMORIAL NUMBER: | L26 |
| ERECTED BY: | CHRISTOPHER AND MARY GARRIGAN DULEEK |
| ORIENTATION: | EAST |
| NUMBER OF COMPONENTS: | 1 |
| NUMBER OF INSCRIBED FACES: | 1 |
| NUMBER OF PEOPLE COMMEMORATED: | 3 |
| MEMORIAL TYPE: | HEADSTONE |
| CONDITION OF MEMORIAL: | SOUND IN PLACE |
| CONDITION OF INSCRIPTION: | MAINLY DECIPHERABLE |
| STONEMASON NAME: | |
| TECHNIQUE OF INSCRIPTION: | INCISED |
| UNDERTAKER: | |
| STONE TOP: | ROUND |
| GRAVE TYPE: | SINGLE |
| HEIGHT: | 103CM |
| WIDTH: | 39CM |
| THICKNESS: | 12CM |

| SURNAME: | CHRISTIAN | | DEATH | AGE |
|---|---|---|---|---|
| GARRIGAN | | FATHER | | |
| | | MOTHER | | |
| | MARGARET | | 11 JAN 1790 | 9 |

**INSCRIPTION:**
ERECTED BY CHRISTO
PHER GARRIGAN OF DU
LEEK AND MARY HIS WIF
IN MEMORY OF HIS FATHER
AND MOTHER. HERE LIETH
THE REMAINS OF THEIR
BELOVED DAUGHTER MAR
GARET GARRIGAN WHO
DEPARTED THIS LIFE THE
11TH OF JANUARY 1790 AGED
9 YEARS. REQUISCANT IN
PACE AMEN. SHE WAS
ENDOWED WITH PERFEC
TIONS OF BODY AND MIND
AND WAS SINCERELY RE
GRETTED BY ALL THAT KNEW
HER

**SYMBOLS:**
IHS SACRED HEART IN SUNBURST
HEART BELOW FLANKED BY TWO ANGELS

| | |
|---|---|
| NAME OF RECORDER: | JANET LEIGH |
| DATE: | 31 MAY 2006 |
| PHOTO REFERENCE: | L26 |
| LOCATION/MAP REF: | D1 L26 |

| | |
|---|---|
| GRAVEYARD NAME: | **ST. MARY'S ABBEY OLD GRAVEYARD** |
| GRAVEYARD CODE: | D1 |
| COUNTY: | MEATH |
| ERECTED BY: | PATRICK GARRITY |
| ORIENTATION: | EAST |
| NUMBER OF COMPONENTS: | 1 |
| NUMBER OF INSCRIBED FACES: | 1 |
| NUMBER OF PEOPLE COMMEMORATED: | 7 |
| MEMORIAL TYPE: | SMALL HEADSTONE |
| CONDITION OF MEMORIAL: | SOUND IN PLACE |
| CONDITION OF INSCRIPTION: | MAINLY DECIPHERABLE |
| STONEMASON NAME: | |
| TECHNIQUE OF INSCRIPTION: | INCISED |
| UNDERTAKER: | |
| STONE TOP: | SUNBURST DISK ROUND |
| GRAVE TYPE: | TREBLE BURIAL PLOT |
| HEIGHT: | 128CM |
| WIDTH: | 72CM |
| THICKNESS: | 11CM |

| SURNAME: | CHRISTIAN | ADDRESS | DEATH | AGE |
|---|---|---|---|---|
| GARRITY | ANNE | DULEEK | 25 MAY 1797 | 52 |
| | ELIZABETH | | 11 MAY 1780 | 40 |
| | THOMAS | | 15 SEPT 1888 | 75 |
| LYNCH | MATHEW | | 09 FEB 1879 | 77 |
| LYNCH | LUKE | | | |
| MCCORMACK | ANNE | | | |
| LYNCH | CATHERINE | | | |

**INSCRIPTION:**
ERECTED BY PATRICK GARRITY
OF DULEEK IN MEMORY OF HIS
WIFE ANNE GARRITY ALIAS
MARTIN WHO DEPARTED THIS LIFE
THE 25TH MAY 1797 AGED 52 YEARS
ALSO HIS SISTER ELIZABETH
GARRITY WHO DIED THE 11TH MAY
1780 AGED 40 YEARS
ALSO THOMAS GARRITY WHO DIED SEP 15TH
1888 AGED 78YRS ALSO MATHEW LYNCH
WHO DIED FEB 9TH 1879 AGED 77 YEARS
ALSO HIS SON LUKE LYNCH ALSO
HIS DAUGHTER ANNE MCCORMACK
ALSO CATHERINE LYNCH

**SYMBOLS:**
SUNBURST WITH CRUCIFIXION IHS
HEART GLORY BE TO GOD ON HIGH
FLANKED BY WINGED CHERUBS

| | |
|---|---|
| NAME OF RECORDER: | PHYLLIS NOONAN |
| DATE: | 6 JULY 2005 |
| PHOTO REFERENCE: | D 12 |
| LOCATION/MAP REF: | D1 D12 |

| | |
|---|---|
| GRAVEYARD NAME: | **ST. MARY'S ABBEY OLD GRAVEYARD** |
| GRAVEYARD CODE: | D1 |
| COUNTY: | MEATH |
| MEMORIAL NUMBER: | F7 |
| ERECTED BY: | |
| ORIENTATION: | EAST |
| NUMBER OF COMPONENTS: | 4 |
| NUMBER OF INSCRIBED FACES: | 1 |
| NUMBER OF PEOPLE COMMEMORATED: | 4 AND POSTERITY |
| MEMORIAL TYPE: | CROSS ON PEDESTAL |
| CONDITION OF MEMORIAL: | SOUND IN PLACE |
| CONDITION OF INSCRIPTION: | GOOD |
| STONEMASON NAME: | |
| TECHNIQUE OF INSCRIPTION: | INCISED |
| UNDERTAKER: | |
| STONE TOP: | CROSS |
| GRAVE TYPE: | DOUBLE |
| HEIGHT: | 201CM |
| WIDTH: | 80CM |
| THICKNESS: | 52CM |

| SURNAME: | CHRISTIAN | ADDRESS | DEATH | AGE |
|---|---|---|---|---|
| GERAGHTY | JOANNA | | 19 FEB 1899 | |
| | PATRICK | | 19 FEB 1899 | |
| | PATRICK | | 3 MAY 1904 | |

**INSCRIPTION:**
JOANNA AND
PATRICK GERAGHTY
ASHBOURNE
DIED THE 19TH FEB 1899

HIS GRANDPARENTS
BROTHERS COUSINS
AND RELATIONS

ALSO HIS FATHER
PATRICK GERAGHTY
DIED 3RD MAY 1904
RIP

ANNIE GERAGHTY ABBEY ROAD
DIED 22 AUG 1961

**ORNAMENTS:**
CROSS ON SCULPTURED PEDESTAL

| | |
|---|---|
| NAME OF RECORDER: | PHYLLIS NOONAN |
| DATE: | 19 JULY 2005 |
| PHOTO REFERENCE: | F7 |
| LOCATION/MAP REF: | D1 F7 |

| | |
|---|---|
| GRAVEYARD NAME: | **ST. MARY'S ABBEY OLD GRAVEYARD** |
| GRAVEYARD CODE: | D1 |
| COUNTY: | MEATH |
| MEMORIAL NUMBER: | L41 |
| ERECTED BY: | |
| ORIENTATION: | EAST |
| NUMBER OF COMPONENTS: | 1 |
| NUMBER OF INSCRIBED FACES: | 1 |
| NUMBER OF PEOPLE COMMEMORATED: | 5 |
| MEMORIAL TYPE: | HEADSTONE |
| CONDITION OF MEMORIAL: | SOUND IN PLACE |
| CONDITION OF INSCRIPTION: | MAINLY DECIPHERABLE |
| STONEMASON NAME: | MOSS P & H |
| TECHNIQUE OF INSCRIPTION: | RAISED LEAD |
| UNDERTAKER: | |
| STONE TOP: | CELTIC CROSS |
| GRAVE TYPE: | DOUBLE |
| HEIGHT: | 193CM |
| WIDTH: | 73CM |
| THICKNESS: | 08CM |

| SURNAME: | CHRISTIAN | ADDRESS | DEATH | AGE |
|---|---|---|---|---|
| GERAGHTY | LUKE | CARNTOWN DULEEK | 19 SEPT 1900 | |
| | ANNE | | OCT 1883 | |
| NORRIS | KATE | | 12 DEC 1898 | |
| GERAGHTY | MATTHEW | | 10 MAR 1903 | |
| | CATHERINE | | 07 FEB 1918 | |

**INSCRIPTION:**
SACRED
TO THE MEMORY OF
LUKE GERAGHTY
CARNTOWN
WHO DIED 19 SEPT 1900
HIS DAUGHTERS ANNE
WHO DIED OCT 1883
AND KATE NORRIS
WHO DIED 12 DEC 1898
ALSO HIS SON
MATTHEW
WHO DIED 10 MARCH 1909
AND ALSO HIS WIFE
CATHERINE
WHO DIED 7 FEB 1918

**SYMBOLS:**
CELTIC CROSS IHS IN CENTRE
EITHER SIDE ANGEL FACE AND WINGS
DOVE ON TOP ARM OF CROSS LAMB ON THE BOTTOM ARM

| | |
|---|---|
| NAME OF RECORDER: | JANET LEIGH |
| DATE: | 27 MAY 2006 |
| PHOTO REFERENCE: | L41 |
| LOCATION/MAP REF: | D1 L41 |

| | |
|---|---|
| GRAVEYARD NAME: | **ST. MARY'S ABBEY OLD GRAVEYARD** |
| GRAVEYARD CODE: | D1 |
| COUNTY: | MEATH |
| MEMORIAL NUMBER: | L42 |
| ERECTED BY: | |
| ORIENTATION: | EAST |
| NUMBER OF COMPONENTS: | 1 |
| NUMBER OF INSCRIBED FACES: | 1 |
| NUMBER OF PEOPLE COMMEMORATED: | 2 |
| MEMORIAL TYPE: | HEADSTONE |
| CONDITION OF MEMORIAL: | SOUND IN PLACE |
| CONDITION OF INSCRIPTION: | MAINLY DECIPHERABLE |
| STONEMASON NAME: | |
| TECHNIQUE OF INSCRIPTION: | INCISED |
| UNDERTAKER: | |
| STONE TOP: | ROUND |
| GRAVE TYPE: | DOUBLE |
| HEIGHT: | 142CM |
| WIDTH: | 76CM |
| THICKNESS: | 14CM |

| SURNAME: | CHRISTIAN | ADDRESS | DEATH | AGE |
|---|---|---|---|---|
| GERATHY | MICHAEL | | 10 FEB 1790 | 42 |
| | CATHERIN | | 08 SEPT 1784 | 71 |
| | | | | |

**INSCRIPTION:**
THIS STONE AND BURIAL PLACE
BELONGETH TO MICHAEL GERATHY
CARPENTER AND HIS POSTERITY HERE
LIETH THE REMAINS OF THE ABOVE
MICHAEL GERATHY WHO DEPARTED
THIS LIFE FEBRUARY THE 10TH 1790
AGED 42 YEARS HERE ALSO LIETH
THE REMAINS OF HIS MOTHER CATHERIN
GERATHY WHO DEPARTED THIS LIFE
SEPTEMBER THE 8TH 1784 AGED 71 YEARS

**SYMBOLS:**
CROSS OVER IHS IN SUNBURST

| | |
|---|---|
| NAME OF RECORDER: | BEN RYAN, HELEN FULLAM AND JANET LEIGH |
| DATE: | 27 MAY 2006 |
| PHOTO REFERENCE: | L42 |
| LOCATION/MAP REF: | D1 L42 |

| | |
|---|---|
| GRAVEYARD NAME: | **ST. MARY'S ABBEY OLD GRAVEYARD** |
| GRAVEYARD CODE: | D1 |
| COUNTY: | MEATH |
| MEMORIAL NUMBER: | L6 |
| ERECTED BY: | MARY ANNE GOGARTY |
| ORIENTATION: | EAST |
| NUMBER OF COMPONENTS: | 3 |
| NUMBER OF INSCRIBED FACES: | 1 |
| NUMBER OF PEOPLE COMMEMORATED: | 10 |
| MEMORIAL TYPE: | HEADSTONE |
| CONDITION OF MEMORIAL: | SOUND IN PLACE |
| CONDITION OF INSCRIPTION: | CLEAR |
| STONEMASON NAME: | F. WHYTE CHORD ROAD |
| TECHNIQUE OF INSCRIPTION: | INCISED |
| UNDERTAKER: | |
| STONE TOP: | ROUND WITH CROSS |
| GRAVE TYPE: | SINGLE |
| HEIGHT: | 290CM |
| WIDTH: | 75CM |
| THICKNESS: | 10CM |

| SURNAME: | CHRISTIAN | ADDRESS | DEATH | AGE |
|---|---|---|---|---|
| GOGARTY | BERNARD | | 24 AUG 1879 | 44 |
| | THOMAS | | 29 NOV 1877 | 2 |
| | MARY | | 12 OCT 1895 | 22 |
| | PETER | | 06 JULY 1905 | 35 |
| | MATTHEW | | 29 FEB 1912 | 45 |
| | MARY ANNE | DULEEK | 05 NOV 1922 | 84 |
| | NICHOLAS | | 24 MAY 1938 | |
| | JAMES | | 15 JUNE 1948 | |
| | BERNARD | COLLON | 14 MAY 1978 | |
| | MARY | | 12 JUNE 1992 | |

INSCRIPTION:
ERECTED
BY
MARY ANNE GOGARTY
DULEEK
IN MEMORY OF HER HUSBAND
BERNARD
WHO DIED 24 AUG 1879 AGED 44 YRS
THEIR SON
THOMAS
WHO DIED 29 NOV 1877 AGED 2 YRS
AND THEIR DAUGHTER
MARY
WHO DIED 12 OCT 1895 AGED 22 YRS
ALSO THEIR SONS
PETER
WHO DIED 6 JULY 1905 AGED 35 YRS
AND MATTHEW
WHO DIED 29 FEB 1912 AGED 45 YRS
THE ABOVE NAMED
MARY ANNE
WHO DIED 5 NOV 1922 AGED 84 YRS
HER SONS
NICHOLAS DIED 24 MAY 1938
JAMES DIED 15 JUNE 1948
BERNARD GOGARTY
COLLON DIED 14 MAY 1978
HIS SISTER MARY
DIED 12 JUNE 1992
QUEEN OF THE MOST HOLY ROSARY
HAVE MERCY ON THEM R.I.P

SYMBOLS:
SACRED HEART IHS ON CROSS WITH IVY LEAVES
ANVIL AND NAILS WITH IVY LEAVES
CROSS ON TOP TWO COLUMNS EACH SIDE

| | |
|---|---|
| NAME OF RECORDER: | JANET LEIGH |
| DATE: | 17 MAY 2006 |
| PHOTO REFERENCE: | L6 |
| LOCATION/MAP REF: | D1 L6 |

| | |
|---|---|
| GRAVEYARD NAME: | **ST. MARY'S ABBEY OLD GRAVEYARD** |
| GRAVEYARD CODE: | D1 |
| COUNTY: | MEATH |
| MEMORIAL NUMBER: | F12 |
| ERECTED BY: | PATRICK GOLDON |
| ORIENTATION: | EAST |
| NUMBER OF COMPONENTS: | 1 |
| NUMBER OF INSCRIBED FACES: | 1 |
| NUMBER OF PEOPLE COMMEMORATED: | 3 |
| MEMORIAL TYPE: | HEADSTONE |
| CONDITION OF MEMORIAL: | SOUND IN PLACE |
| CONDITION OF INSCRIPTION: | MAINLY DECIPHERABLE |
| STONEMASON NAME: | |
| TECHNIQUE OF INSCRIPTION: | INCISED |
| UNDERTAKER: | |
| STONE TOP: | SUNBURST DISK |
| GRAVE TYPE: | TREBLE |
| HEIGHT: | 151CM |
| WIDTH: | 80CM |
| THICKNESS: | 14CM |

| SURNAME: | CHRISTIAN | ADDRESS | DEATH | AGE |
|---|---|---|---|---|
| GOLDON | WILLIAM | | 25 MAR 1728 | 60 |
| | JANE | | 20 NOV 1726 | 54 |
| | THOMAS | | 09 JUNE 1738 | 32 |

**INSCRIPTION:**
MEMENTONORI
THIS STONE AND BURIAL PLACE
BELONGETH TO MR. PATRICK GOLDON
OF THE CITY OF DUBLIN MERCHANT
AND HIS POSTERITY
HERE LYETH THE BODY OF HIS MOTHER
MRS. JANE GOLDON WHO DEPARTED THIS
LIFE NOVR. 20TH 1726 AGED 54 HERE ALSO
LYETH THE BODY OF HIS FATHER MR. WM.
GOLDON WHO DEPARTED THIS LIFE
MARCH 25TH 1728 AGED 60 AND ALSO
HIS BROTHER MR. THOS. GOLDON WHO
DEPARTED THIS LIFE JUN 9TH 1738
AGED 32

*REQUIESCANT IN PACE*

**SYMBOLS:**
CROSS OVER IHS WITH
HEART DISK WITH CHERUBS
EACH SIDE

| | |
|---|---|
| NAME OF RECORDER: | PHYLLIS NOONAN |
| DATE: | 19 JULY 2005 |
| PHOTO REFERENCE: | F12 |
| LOCATION/MAP REF: | D1 F12 |

| | |
|---|---|
| GRAVEYARD NAME: | **ST. MARY'S ABBEY OLD GRAVEYARD** |
| GRAVEYARD CODE: | D1 |
| COUNTY: | MEATH |
| MEMORIAL NUMBER: | D18 |
| ERECTED BY: | |
| ORIENTATION: | EAST |
| NUMBER OF COMPONENTS: | 2 |
| NUMBER OF INSCRIBED FACES: | 1 |
| NUMBER OF PEOPLE COMMEMORATED: | 6 |
| MEMORIAL TYPE: | HEADSTONE SURROUND |
| CONDITION OF MEMORIAL: | VERY GOOD |
| CONDITION OF INSCRIPTION: | PARTIALLY FADED |
| STONEMASON NAME: | F. GOGARTY |
| TECHNIQUE OF INSCRIPTION: | INCISED |
| UNDERTAKER: | |
| STONE TOP: | TAPERED STONE ON BASE |
| GRAVE TYPE: | TRIPLE GRAVE PLOT |
| HEIGHT: | 69CM |
| WIDTH: | 56CM |
| THICKNESS: | 16CM |

| SURNAME: | CHRISTIAN | ADDRESS | DEATH | AGE |
|---|---|---|---|---|
| GORMAN | THOMAS | LOUGHER DULEEK | 20 OCT 1979 | 66 |
| | PATRICK | LOUGHER DULEEK | 30 AUG 1981 | 65 |
| | CHRISTOPHER | LOUGHER DULEEK | 25 NOV 1933 | |
| | ANNIE | LOUGHER DULEEK | 11 NOV 1994 | 78 |

**INSCRIPTION:**
IN LOVING MEMORY OF
THOMAS GORMAN
LOUGHER
DIED 20TH OCT. 1978 AGED 66
HIS BROTHER PATRICK
DIED 30TH AUG. 1981 AGED 65
HIS FATHER CHRISTOPHER
DIED 25TH NOV 1933
ALSO THEIR GRANDPARENTS
HIS WIFE ANNIE
DIED 11TH NOV 1994 AGED 78
R.I.P

| | |
|---|---|
| NAME OF RECORDER: | SHAUN LYNCH |
| DATE: | 13 JULY 2005 |
| PHOTO REFERENCE: | D18 |
| LOCATION/MAP REF: | D1 D18 |

| | |
|---|---|
| GRAVEYARD NAME: | **ST. MARY'S ABBEY OLD GRAVEYARD** |
| GRAVEYARD CODE: | D1 |
| COUNTY: | MEATH |
| MEMORIAL NUMBER: | E13 |
| ERECTED BY: | |
| ORIENTATION: | EAST |
| NUMBER OF COMPONENTS: | 2 |
| NUMBER OF INSCRIBED FACES: | 1 |
| NUMBER OF PEOPLE COMMEMORATED: | 7 |
| MEMORIAL TYPE: | HEADSTONE |
| CONDITION OF MEMORIAL: | SOUND IN PLACE |
| CONDITION OF INSCRIPTION: | CLEAR |
| STONEMASON NAME: | |
| TECHNIQUE OF INSCRIPTION: | INCISED AND PAINTED |
| UNDERTAKER: | |
| STONE TOP: | ROUND |
| GRAVE TYPE: | SINGLE |
| HEIGHT: | 90CM |
| WIDTH: | 49CM |
| THICKNESS: | 12CM |

| SURNAME: | CHRISTIAN | ADDRESS | DEATH | AGE |
|---|---|---|---|---|
| GORMAN | BRIDGET | | 02 DEC 1904 | |
| | JANE | | 04 MAR 1925 | |
| | WILLIAM | | 01 NOV 1935 | |
| | MARY | | 27 MAR 1957 | |
| | CHRISTINA | | 20 MAY 1961 | |
| | WILLIAM | | 25 FEB 1954 | |
| | JOSEPHINE | | 10 DEC 1976 | |

**INSCRIPTION:**
IN LOVING MEMORY OF
BRIDGET GORMAN
WHO DIED DEC 2ND 1904
ALSO HER MOTHER JANE
DIED MARCH 4TH 1925
AND HER FATHER WILLIAM
DIED NOV 1ST 1935
HER SISTERS
MARY DIED MARCH 27TH 1957
CHRISTINA DIED MAY 20TH 1961
HER BROTHER WILLIAM GORMAN
DIED 25TH FEB 1954
HIS SISTER JOSEPHINE
DIED 10TH DEC 1976
*SWEET JESUS MERCY*
RIP

**SYMBOLS:**
IHS WITH CROSS

| | |
|---|---|
| NAME OF RECORDER: | LIZ LYNCH |
| DATE: | 16 JULY 2005 |
| PHOTO REFERENCE: | E13 |
| LOCATION/MAP REF: | D1 E13 |

| | |
|---|---|
| GRAVEYARD NAME: | **ST. MARY'S ABBEY OLD GRAVEYARD** |
| GRAVEYARD CODE: | D1 |
| COUNTY: | MEATH |
| MEMORIAL NUMBER: | J14 |
| ERECTED BY: | |
| ORIENTATION: | EAST |
| NUMBER OF COMPONENTS: | 1 |
| NUMBER OF INSCRIBED FACES: | 1 |
| NUMBER OF PEOPLE COMMEMORATED: | 2 |
| MEMORIAL TYPE: | HEADSTONE |
| CONDITION OF MEMORIAL: | SOUND IN PLACE |
| CONDITION OF INSCRIPTION: | DECIPHERABLE |
| STONEMASON NAME: | |
| TECHNIQUE OF INSCRIPTION: | INCISED |
| UNDERTAKER: | |
| STONE TOP: | ROUND |
| GRAVE TYPE: | SINGLE |
| HEIGHT: | 145CM |
| WIDTH: | 71CM |
| THICKNESS: | 19CM |

| SURNAME: | CHRISTIAN | ADDRESS | DEATH | AGE |
|---|---|---|---|---|
| GRAHAM | MARY | | 19 SEPT 1861 | 80 |
| | PATRICK | | 16 OCT 1864 | 45 |

**INSCRIPTION:**

A.D. ERECTED 1868
BY WILLIAM GRAHAM DULEEK
IN MEMORY OF MARY GRAHAM
WHO DIED 19TH SEPR 1861 AGED 80
YRS ALSO PATRICK GRAHAM WHO
DIED 16TH OCT 1864 AGED 45 YRS.
*RESQUISCANT IN PACE AMEN*

| | |
|---|---|
| NAME OF RECORDER: | LIZ LYNCH |
| DATE: | 6 AUG 2005 |
| PHOTO REFERENCE: | J14 |
| LOCATION/MAP REF: | D1 J14 |

| | |
|---|---|
| GRAVEYARD NAME: | **ST. MARY'S ABBEY OLD GRAVEYARD** |
| GRAVEYARD CODE: | D1 |
| COUNTY: | MEATH |
| MEMORIAL NUMBER: | C4 |
| ERECTED BY: | |
| ORIENTATION: | EAST |
| NUMBER OF COMPONENTS: | 2 |
| NUMBER OF INSCRIBED FACES: | 1 |
| NUMBER OF PEOPLE COMMEMORATED: | 3 |
| MEMORIAL TYPE: | HEADSTONE |
| CONDITION OF MEMORIAL: | SOUND IN PLACE |
| CONDITION OF INSCRIPTION: | MINT |
| STONEMASON NAME: | MOSS. DROGHEDA |
| TECHNIQUE OF INSCRIPTION: | INCISED |
| UNDERTAKER: | |
| STONE TOP: | ARCHED |
| GRAVE TYPE: | SINGLE |
| HEIGHT: | 162CM |
| WIDTH: | 69CM |
| THICKNESS: | 9CM |

| SURNAME: | CHRISTIAN | ADDRESS | DEATH | AGE |
|---|---|---|---|---|
| HACKETT | ROBERT | | 11 NOV 1908 | |
| | MARY ANNE | | 22 FEB 1908 | |
| | ROBERT JOHN | | 25 APR 1896 | |

**INSCRIPTION:**
ERECTED
IN LOVING MEMORY OF
ROBERT HACKETT
WHO DIED AT KELLS 11 NOV 1908
HIS DAUGHTER
MARY ANNE
WHO DIED 22 FEB 1908
AND HIS SON
ROBERT JOHN
WHO DIED 25 APRIL 1896

R.I.P

**SYMBOLS:**
CROSS

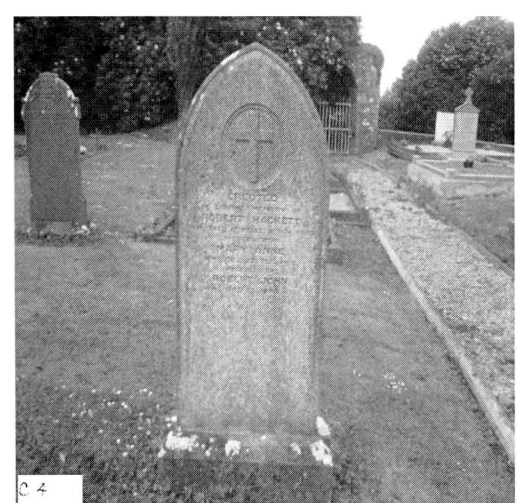

**ORNAMENTS:**
FOLIAGE

| | |
|---|---|
| NAME OF RECORDER: | JANET LEIGH AND HELEN FULLAM |
| DATE: | 02 JULY 2005 |
| PHOTO REFERENCE: | C4 |
| LOCATION/MAP REF | D1 C4 |

| | |
|---|---|
| GRAVEYARD NAME: | **ST. MARY'S ABBEY OLD GRAVEYARD** |
| GRAVEYARD CODE: | D1 |
| COUNTY: | MEATH |
| MEMORIAL NUMBER: | L5 |
| ERECTED BY: | |
| ORIENTATION: | EAST |
| NUMBER OF COMPONENTS: | 2 |
| NUMBER OF INSCRIBED FACES: | 1 |
| NUMBER OF PEOPLE COMMEMORATED: | 1 |
| MEMORIAL TYPE: | HEADSTONE |
| CONDITION OF MEMORIAL: | SOUND IN PLACE |
| CONDITION OF INSCRIPTION: | LEGIBLE |
| STONEMASON NAME: | |
| TECHNIQUE OF INSCRIPTION: | INCISED |
| UNDERTAKER: | |
| STONE TOP: | ROUND |
| GRAVE TYPE: | SINGLE |
| HEIGHT: | 94CM |
| WIDTH: | 54CM |
| THICKNESS: | 8.5CM |

| SURNAME: | CHRISTIAN | ADDRESS | DEATH | AGE |
|---|---|---|---|---|
| HALPIN | JOHN | | 02 FEB 1923 | |

**INSCRIPTION:**
IN MEMORY OF
JOHN HALPIN
TOWNRATH
WHO DIED 2 FEB 1923
R.I.P.

**SYMBOLS:**
INCISED CROSS ON TOP OF INSCRIPTION

| | |
|---|---|
| NAME OF RECORDER: | LIZ LYNCH |
| DATE: | 16 MAY 2006 |
| PHOTO REFERENCE: | L5 |
| LOCATION/MAP REF: | D1 L5 |

| | |
|---|---|
| GRAVEYARD NAME: | **ST. MARY'S ABBEY OLD GRAVEYARD** |
| GRAVEYARD CODE: | D1 |
| COUNTY: | MEATH |
| MEMORIAL NUMBER: | H8 |
| ERECTED BY: | |
| ORIENTATION: | EAST |
| NUMBER OF COMPONENTS: | 3 - CROSS DISPLACED |
| NUMBER OF INSCRIBED FACES: | 1 |
| NUMBER OF PEOPLE COMMEMORATED: | 1 |
| MEMORIAL TYPE: | CROSS AND PEDESTAL |
| CONDITION OF MEMORIAL: | IN PLACE |
| CONDITION OF INSCRIPTION: | MAINLY DECIPHERABLE |
| STONEMASON NAME: | |
| TECHNIQUE OF INSCRIPTION: | INCISED |
| UNDERTAKER: | |
| STONE TOP: | PEDESTAL CROSS DISPLACED |
| GRAVE TYPE: | SINGLE |
| HEIGHT: | 58CM |
| WIDTH: | 59CM |
| THICKNESS: | 34CM |

| SURNAME: | CHRISTIAN | ADDRESS | DEATH | AGE |
|---|---|---|---|---|
| HATCH | MABEL | LONGFORD DULEEK | 16 JULY 1937 | |

**INSCRIPTION:**
IN LOVING MEMORY
OF
MABEL HATCH
LONGFORD DULEEK
WHO DEPARTED THIS LIFE
JULY 16TH 1937

TILL HE COME

**COMMENT:**
CROSS DISPLACED LYING ON THE GRAVE

| | |
|---|---|
| NAME OF RECORDER: | SINEAD FULLAM AND JANET LEIGH |
| DATE: | 10 JUNE 06 |
| PHOTO REFERENCE: | H8 |
| LOCATION/MAP REF: | D1 H8 |

| | |
|---|---|
| GRAVEYARD NAME: | **ST. MARY'S ABBEY OLD GRAVEYARD** |
| GRAVEYARD CODE: | D1 |
| COUNTY: | MEATH |
| MEMORIAL NUMBER: | H12 |
| ERECTED BY: | |
| ORIENTATION: | EAST |
| NUMBER OF COMPONENTS: | 1 |
| NUMBER OF INSCRIBED FACES: | 2 |
| NUMBER OF PEOPLE COMMEMORATED: | 6 |
| MEMORIAL TYPE: | PEDESTAL CROSS MISSING |
| CONDITION OF MEMORIAL: | SOUND IN PLACE |
| CONDITION OF INSCRIPTION: | CLEAR |
| STONEMASON NAME: | |
| TECHNIQUE OF INSCRIPTION: | INCISED |
| UNDERTAKER: | |
| STONE TOP: | CROSS MISSING |
| GRAVE TYPE: | MULTIPLE |
| HEIGHT: | 58CM |
| WIDTH: | 72CM |
| THICKNESS: | 39CM |

| SURNAME: | CHRISTIAN | ADDRESS | DEATH | AGE |
|---|---|---|---|---|
| HATCH | MARK | DULEEK | 27 JUN 1927 | |
| | RICHARD CHARLES | | 13 MAR 1891 | |
| | NICHOLS STEPHEN | | 01 JUL 1916 | |
| | MINNIE | | 20 JUL 1919 | |
| | MARK PENDRY | | 30 DEC 1922 | |
| | JEMIMA | | 13 OCT 1937 | |

**INSCRIPTION:**
*EAST FACE*
TO THE
DEAR MEMORY OF
MARK HATCH DULEEK
DIED JUNE 27TH 1927
BELOVED HUSBAND OF JEMIMA HATCH
AND THEIR CHILDREN
RICHARD CHARLES DIED MARCH 13TH 1891
NICHOLAS STEPHEN
KILLED IN FRANCE JULY 1ST 1916
MINNIE DIED JULY 20TH 1919
MARK PENDREY (CAPTAIN A.V.C.)
DIED DEC30TH 1922

*NORTH FACE.*
HERE ALSO LIETH
JEMIMA THE
BELOVED WIFE OF
MARK HATCH
DIED OCT.13TH 1937

AT REST

| | |
|---|---|
| NAME OF RECORDER: | JANET LEIGH |
| DATE: | 14 JUNE 2006 |
| PHOTO REFERENCE: | H12 |
| LOCATION/MAP REF: | D1 H12 |

| | |
|---|---|
| GRAVEYARD NAME: | **ST. MARY'S ABBEY OLD GRAVEYARD** |
| GRAVEYARD CODE: | D1 |
| COUNTY: | MEATH |
| MEMORIAL NUMBER: | H13 |
| ERECTED BY: | WILLIAM HATCH |
| ORIENTATION: | EAST |
| NUMBER OF COMPONENTS: | 1 |
| NUMBER OF INSCRIBED FACES: | 1 |
| NUMBER OF PEOPLE COMMEMORATED: | 6 |
| MEMORIAL TYPE: | HEADSTONE |
| CONDITION OF MEMORIAL: | SOUND IN PLACE |
| CONDITION OF INSCRIPTION: | CLEAR |
| STONEMASON NAME: | |
| TECHNIQUE OF INSCRIPTION: | INCISED |
| UNDERTAKER: | |
| STONE TOP: | ROUND |
| GRAVE TYPE: | MULTIPLE |
| HEIGHT: | 166CM |
| WIDTH: | 66CM |
| THICKNESS: | 17CM |

| SURNAME: | CHRISTIAN | ADDRESS | DEATH | AGE |
|---|---|---|---|---|
| HATCH | JOHN | | 08 DEC 1876 | 82 |
| HATCH | NICHOLAS | | 18 MAY 1863 | 70 |
| HATCH | CHARLES | | 10 DEC 1860 | 50 |
| HATCH | ELIZABETH | | 05 FEB 1883 | 58 |
| HATCH | NICHOLAS | | 14 MAR 1901 | 54 |
| HATCH | WILLIAM | | 18 NOV 1912 | 63 |

**INSCRIPTION:**
ERECTED
BY
WILLIAM HATCH
DULEEK
TO THE MEMORY OF HIS FATHER
JOHN HATCH WHO DEPARTED
THIS LIFE DECEMBER 8TH 1876 AGED
82 YEARS
HIS UNCLE NICHOLAS HATCH
DIED MAY 18TH 1863 AGED 70
YEARS
AND OF HIS UNCLE CHARLES HATCH
DIED DECEMBER 10TH 1860 AGED 50
YEARS
ALSO OF HIS MOTHER
ELIZABETH HATCH
WHO DIED MARCH 14TH 1901 AGED 54 YEARS
WILLIAM HATCH
BORN 22ND JUNE 1849
DIED 18TH NOV.1913

SEVERED ONLY TILL HE COME
I KNOW THAT MY REDEEMER LIVETH
JOB.13-25VS

| | |
|---|---|
| NAME OF RECORDER: | JANET LEIGH |
| DATE: | 14 JUNE 2006 |
| PHOTO REFERENCE: | H13 |
| LOCATION/MAP REF: | D1 H13 |

| | |
|---|---|
| GRAVEYARD NAME: | **ST. MARY'S ABBEY OLD GRAVEYARD** |
| GRAVEYARD CODE: | D1 |
| COUNTY: | MEATH |
| MEMORIAL NUMBER: | L22 |
| ERECTED BY: | |
| ORIENTATION: | EAST |
| NUMBER OF COMPONENTS: | 1 |
| NUMBER OF INSCRIBED FACES: | 1 |
| NUMBER OF PEOPLE COMMEMORATED: | 2 |
| MEMORIAL TYPE: | HEADSTONE |
| CONDITION OF MEMORIAL: | SOUND |
| CONDITION OF INSCRIPTION: | MAINLY DECIPHERABLE |
| STONEMASON NAME: | |
| TECHNIQUE OF INSCRIPTION: | INCISED |
| UNDERTAKER: | |
| STONE TOP: | ROUND |
| GRAVE TYPE: | SINGLE |
| HEIGHT: | 100CM |
| WIDTH: | 59CM |
| THICKNESS: | 09CM |

| SURNAME: | CHRISTIAN | ADDRESS | DEATH | AGE |
|---|---|---|---|---|
| HATCH | CHARLIS | | 16 DEC 1738 | 68 |
| | RICHARD | | 13 MAY 1920 | |
| | | | | |

**INSCRIPTION:**
HERE LIETH YE BODY
OF CHARLIS HATCH
WHO DEPARTED THIS LIFE
DISBR YE 16TH 1738
AGED 68 YEARS
RICHARD HATCH – L.P.C.S.I.:L.R.O.C.P.I.
-DIED MAY 31ST 1920
I HAVE FINISHED THE WORK
THOU GAVEST ME TO DO

| | |
|---|---|
| NAME OF RECORDER: | JANET LEIGH AND SINEAD FULLAM |
| DATE: | 20 MAY 2006 |
| PHOTO REFERENCE: | L22 |
| LOCATION/MAP REF: | D1 L22 |

| | |
|---|---|
| GRAVEYARD NAME: | **ST. MARY'S ABBEY OLD GRAVEYARD** |
| GRAVEYARD CODE: | D1 |
| COUNTY: | MEATH |
| MEMORIAL NUMBER: | L20 |
| ERECTED BY: | MARION HEADE |
| ORIENTATION: | EAST |
| NUMBER OF COMPONENTS: | 2 |
| NUMBER OF INSCRIBED FACES: | 1 |
| NUMBER OF PEOPLE COMMEMORATED: | 3 |
| MEMORIAL TYPE: | HEADSTONE |
| CONDITION OF MEMORIAL: | SOUND |
| CONDITION OF INSCRIPTION: | CLEAR |
| STONEMASON NAME: | |
| TECHNIQUE OF INSCRIPTION: | INCISED |
| UNDERTAKER: | |
| STONE TOP: | CROSS |
| GRAVE TYPE: | SINGLE |
| HEIGHT: | 172CM |
| WIDTH: | 73CM |
| THICKNESS: | 13CM |

| SURNAME: | CHRISTIAN | ADDRESS | DEATH | AGE |
|---|---|---|---|---|
| HEADE | JOHN | DULEEK | 04 JAN 1912 | |
| | NICHOLAS | | 02 MAY 1884 | |
| | MARY | | 04 APR 1905 | |

**INSCRIPTION:**
SACRED
TO THE MEMORY OF
JOHN HEADE
DULEEK
WHO DIED 4 JAN 1912
HIS FATHER NICHOLAS WHO DIED 2 MAY 1884
AND HIS MOTHER MARY WHO DIED 4 APRIL 1905
R.I.P.
*ERECTED BY HIS WIFE MARION*

**SYMBOLS:**
CROSS IN A CIRCLE ANGEL ON TOP AND SIDES OF CROSS HORIZONTAL CROSS WITH LAMB IN CENTRE IHS

| | |
|---|---|
| NAME OF RECORDER: | BEN RYAN AND HELEN FULLAM |
| DATE: | 20 MAY 2006 |
| PHOTO REFERENCE: | L20 |
| LOCATION/MAP REF: | D1 L20 |

| | |
|---|---|
| GRAVEYARD NAME: | **ST. MARY'S ABBEY OLD GRAVEYARD** |
| GRAVEYARD CODE: | D1 |
| COUNTY: | MEATH |
| MEMORIAL NUMBER: | L21 |
| ERECTED BY: | |
| ORIENTATION: | EAST |
| NUMBER OF COMPONENTS: | 1 |
| NUMBER OF INSCRIBED FACES: | 1 |
| NUMBER OF PEOPLE COMMEMORATED: | 8 |
| MEMORIAL TYPE: | HEADSTONE |
| CONDITION OF MEMORIAL: | SOUND IN PLACE |
| CONDITION OF INSCRIPTION: | EXCELLENT |
| STONEMASON NAME: | T. COONEY |
| TECHNIQUE OF INSCRIPTION: | INCISED AND PAINTED |
| UNDERTAKER: | |
| STONE TOP: | FLAT |
| GRAVE TYPE: | SINGLE |
| HEIGHT: | 96CM |
| WIDTH: | 69CM |
| THICKNESS: | 05CM |

| SURNAME: | CHRISTIAN | ADDRESS | DEATH | AGE |
|---|---|---|---|---|
| HEARTY NEE DUNNE | CATHERINE | | 29 MAY 1923 | 33 |
| HEARTY | OWEN | INTERRED IN MANCHESTER | 04 NOV 1940 | 60 |
| HEARTY | CLEMENT | INFANT | | |
| HEARTY | MICHAEL | | 23 MAY 1949 | 28 |
| DUNNE | JOHN | | 25 JUN 1932 | 80 |
| DUNNE | CATHERINE | | 29 JUL 1935 | 74 |
| DUNNE | MICHAEL | | 09 OCT 1950 | 63 |
| DUNNE | JOHN (JACK) | | 01 AUG 1980 | 85 |

**INSCRIPTION:**
IN LOVING MEMORY
OF CATHERINE HEARTY (NEE DUNNE)
DIED 29TH MAY 1923 AGED 33
HER HUSBAND OWEN
DIED 4TH NOV 1940 AGED 60
INTERRED IN MANCHESTER
THEIR SONS
CLEMENT DIED IN INFANCY
MICHAEL
DIED 23RD MAY 1948 AGED 28
HER PARENTS JOHN DUNNE
DIED 25TH JUNE 1932 AGED 80
CATHERINE
DIED 29TH JULY 1935 AGED 74
THEIR SONS
MICHAEL DIED 9TH OCT 1950 AGED 63
JOHN (JACK) DIED 1ST AUG 1980 AGED 85
R.I.P.

**SYMBOLS:**
CROSS AT LEFT HAND SIDE LENGTH OF HEADSTONE

| | |
|---|---|
| NAME OF RECORDER: | BEN RYAN AND HELEN FULLAM |
| DATE: | 20 MAY 2006 |
| PHOTO REFERENCE: | L21 |
| LOCATION/MAP REF: | D1 L21 |

| | |
|---|---|
| GRAVEYARD NAME: | **ST. MARY'S ABBEY OLD GRAVEYARD** |
| GRAVEYARD CODE: | D1 |
| COUNTY: | MEATH |
| MEMORIAL NUMBER: | E10 |
| ERECTED BY: | PATRICK HEENEY |
| ORIENTATION: | EAST |
| NUMBER OF COMPONENTS: | 3 |
| NUMBER OF INSCRIBED FACES: | 1 |
| NUMBER OF PEOPLE COMMEMORATED: | 3 |
| MEMORIAL TYPE: | HEADSTONE WITH FLEUR DE LIS CROSS |
| CONDITION OF MEMORIAL: | SOUND IN PLACE |
| CONDITION OF INSCRIPTION: | CLEAR |
| STONEMASON NAME: | T. REID PLATTEN |
| TECHNIQUE OF INSCRIPTION: | INCISED |
| UNDERTAKER: | |
| STONE TOP: | CROSS |
| GRAVE TYPE: | SINGLE |
| HEIGHT: | 156CM |
| WIDTH: | 45CM |
| THICKNESS: | 11CM |

| SURNAME: | CHRISTIAN | ADDRESS | DEATH | AGE |
|---|---|---|---|---|
| HEENEY | MARGARET | | 23 APR 1902 | 38 YEARS |
| | PATRICK | | 28 FEB 1931 | |
| | ROBERT | | 28 MAR 1941 | |

**INSCRIPTION:**
ERECTED
BY PATRICK HEENEY
IN MEMORY OF HIS WIFE
MARGARET
WHO DIED APRIL 23RD 1902
AGED 38 YEARS
HER HUSBAND PATRICK
WHO DIED 28TH FEB 1931
AND THEIR SON ROBERT
WHO DIED 28TH MARCH 1941
R.I.P

**SYMBOLS:**
ENTWINED IHS ON
FLEUR DE LIS CROSS

| | |
|---|---|
| NAME OF RECORDER: | SHAUN LYNCH |
| DATE: | 16 JULY 2005 |
| PHOTO REFERENCE: | E10 |
| LOCATION/MAP REF: | D1 E10 |

| | |
|---|---|
| GRAVEYARD NAME: | **ST. MARY'S ABBEY OLD GRAVEYARD** |
| GRAVEYARD CODE: | D1 |
| COUNTY: | MEATH |
| MEMORIAL NUMBER: | J13 |
| ERECTED BY: | MRS. HICKEY |
| ORIENTATION: | EAST |
| NUMBER OF COMPONENTS: | 1 |
| NUMBER OF INSCRIBED FACES: | 1 |
| NUMBER OF PEOPLE COMMEMORATED: | 6 |
| MEMORIAL TYPE: | HEADSTONE FIXED IN WALL |
| CONDITION OF MEMORIAL: | SOUND IN WALL |
| CONDITION OF INSCRIPTION: | MAINLY DECIPHERABLE |
| STONEMASON NAME: | |
| TECHNIQUE OF INSCRIPTION: | INCISED |
| UNDERTAKER: | |
| STONE TOP: | CELTIC CROSS IN DISK |
| GRAVE TYPE: | SINGLE |
| HEIGHT: | 197CM |
| WIDTH: | 61CM |
| THICKNESS: | 12CM |

| SURNAME: | CHRISTIAN | ADDRESS | DEATH | AGE |
|---|---|---|---|---|
| HOEY | JANE | | 01 MAY 1851 | 60 |
| HOEY | ANDREW | | 23 FEB 1874 | 94 |
| HICKEY | MRS | DULEEK | 22 JULY 1900 | 72 |
| HICKEY | JAMES | | 08 DEC 1900 | 34 |
| HICKEY | ALICE | | 02 AUG 1901 | 31 |
| ANDREWS | MARGARET | | 22 MAR 1903 | |

**INSCRIPTION:**
ERECTED
BY
MRS HICKEY
DULEEK
IN MEMORY OF HER DEAR MOTHER
JANE HOEY
WHO DIED 1 MAY 1851 AGED 60 YRS
ALSO HER DEAR FATHER
ANDREW HOEY
WHO DIED 23 FEB 1874 AGED 94 YRS
THE LORD HAVE MERCY ON THEIR SOULS
AND THE ABOVE MRS. HICKEY
WHO DIED JULY 22ND 1900
AGED 72 YEARS
AND HER SON JAMES HICKEY
WHO DIED DEC 8TH 1900
AGED 34 YEARS
ALSO HIS WIFE
ALICE HICKEY
WHO DIED 2ND AUG 1901 AGED 31 YRS
AND MARGARET ANDREWS
DAUGHTER OF THE ABOVE MRS. HICKEY
WHO DIED 22ND MARCH 1903      RIP

**SYMBOLS:**
LAMB IN CENTRE OF CELTIC CROSS
FLOWER

| | |
|---|---|
| NAME OF RECORDER: | JANET LEIGH AND SINEAD FULLAM |
| DATE: | 6 AUG 2005 |
| PHOTO REF: | J13 |
| LOCATION/MAP REF: | D1 J13 |

| | |
|---|---|
| GRAVEYARD NAME: | **ST. MARY'S ABBEY OLD GRAVEYARD** |
| GRAVEYARD CODE: | D1 |
| COUNTY: | MEATH |
| MEMORIAL NUMBER: | J25 |
| ERECTED BY: | THOMAS HOEY |
| ORIENTATION: | EAST |
| NUMBER OF COMPONENTS: | 1 |
| NUMBER OF INSCRIBED FACES: | 1 |
| NUMBER OF PEOPLE COMMEMORATED: | 4 |
| MEMORIAL TYPE: | HEADSTONE |
| CONDITION OF MEMORIAL: | SOUND IN PLACE |
| CONDITION OF INSCRIPTION: | MAINLY DECIPHERABLE |
| STONEMASON NAME: | |
| TECHNIQUE OF INSCRIPTION: | INCISED |
| UNDERTAKER: | |
| STONE TOP: | STEPPED DISK SUNBURST |
| GRAVE TYPE: | DOUBLE |
| HEIGHT: | 121CM |
| WIDTH: | 81CM |
| THICKNESS: | 13CM |

| SURNAME: | CHRISTIAN | ADDRESS | DEATH | AGE |
|---|---|---|---|---|
| HOEY | THOMAS | GAFNEY | | |
| | | | | |

**INSCRIPTION:**
ERECTED AD 1817 BY THOMAS
HOEY OF GAFNEY FOR HIM & HIS POSTERITY
HERE LIETH THE REMAINS OF HIS WIFE
AND HIS FATHER AND MOTHER

**SYMBOLS:**
CROSS OVER IHS IN
SUNBURST DISK

| | |
|---|---|
| NAME OF RECORDER: | LIZ LYNCH AND PHYLLIS NOONAN |
| DATE: | 16 AUGUST 2005 |
| PHOTO REFERENCE: | J25 |
| LOCATION/MAP REF: | D1 J25 |

| | |
|---|---|
| GRAVEYARD NAME: | **ST. MARY'S ABBEY OLD GRAVEYARD** |
| GRAVEYARD CODE: | D1 |
| COUNTY: | MEATH |
| MEMORIAL NUMBER: | D8 |
| ERECTED BY: | NICHOLAS CARILLON |
| ORIENTATION: | EAST |
| NUMBER OF COMPONENTS: | 1 |
| NUMBER OF INSCRIBED FACES: | 1 |
| NUMBER OF PEOPLE COMMEMORATED: | 1 |
| MEMORIAL TYPE: | HEADSTONE |
| CONDITION OF MEMORIAL: | SOUND IN PLACE |
| CONDITION OF INSCRIPTION: | CLEAR |
| STONEMASON NAME: | |
| TECHNIQUE OF INSCRIPTION: | INCISED |
| UNDERTAKER: | |
| STONE TOP: | SUNBURST DISK ROUND |
| GRAVE TYPE: | SINGLE |
| HEIGHT: | 91CM |
| WIDTH: | 64CM |
| THICKNESS: | 17CM |

| SURNAME: | CHRISTIAN | ADDRESS | DEATH | AGE |
|---|---|---|---|---|
| HOLGAN | PATRICK | LITTLEHILLTOWN | 01 JAN 1758 | 63 YRS |

**INSCRIPTION:**
I.H.S
HERE LIETH THE BODY OF
PATRICK HOLGAN WHO
DEPARTED THIS LIFE
JANUARY THE 1ST 1758 AGED
63 YEARS ERECTED BY
NICHOLAS CARRILLAN IN
LITTLEHILLTOWN
ANNO DOMINI 1764

**SYMBOLS:**
IHS WITH CROSS

| | |
|---|---|
| NAME OF RECORDER: | PHYLLIS NOONAN AND LIZ LYNCH |
| DATE: | 6 JUNE 2006 |
| PHOTO REFERENCE: | D8 |
| LOCATION/MAP REF: | D1 D8 |

| | |
|---|---|
| GRAVEYARD NAME: | **ST. MARY'S ABBEY OLD GRAVEYARD** |
| GRAVEYARD CODE: | D1 |
| COUNTY: | MEATH |
| MEMORIAL NUMBER: | E8 |
| ERECTED BY: | MARY HOLT |
| ORIENTATION: | EAST |
| NUMBER OF COMPONENTS: | 2 |
| NUMBER OF INSCRIBED FACES: | 1 |
| NUMBER OF PEOPLE COMMEMORATED: | 3 |
| MEMORIAL TYPE: | HEADSTONE |
| CONDITION OF MEMORIAL: | SOUND IN PLACE |
| CONDITION OF INSCRIPTION: | CLEAR |
| STONEMASON NAME: | MOSS |
| TECHNIQUE OF INSCRIPTION: | INCISED |
| UNDERTAKER: | |
| STONE TOP: | ROUND |
| GRAVE TYPE: | SINGLE |
| HEIGHT: | 178CM |
| WIDTH: | 70CM |
| THICKNESS: | 8CM |

| SURNAME: | CHRISTIAN | ADDRESS | DEATH | AGE |
|---|---|---|---|---|
| HOLT | HUGH | | 12 JUN 1922 | |
| | ELIZABETH | | 12 JUL 1924 | |
| MOORE | MARIA | | 27 AUG 1899 | |

**INSCRIPTION:**
ERECTED
BY
MARY HOLT
DROGHEDA
IN MEMORY OF HER FATHER
HUGH WHO DIED 12TH JUNE 1922
AND HER MOTHER
ELIZABETH
WHO DIED 12TH JULY 1924
ALSO HER GRANDMOTHER
MARIA MOORE
WHO DIED 27TH AUG 1899
R.I.P.

| | |
|---|---|
| NAME OF RECORDER: | LIZ LYNCH |
| DATE: | 16 JULY 2005 |
| PHOTO REFERENCE: | E8 |
| LOCATION/MAP REF: | D1 E8 |

| | |
|---|---|
| GRAVEYARD NAME: | **ST. MARY'S ABBEY OLD GRAVEYARD** |
| GRAVEYARD CODE: | D1 |
| COUNTY: | MEATH |
| MEMORIAL NUMBER: | F3 |
| ERECTED BY: | MRS. HUSSY |
| ORIENTATION: | EAST |
| NUMBER OF COMPONENTS: | 1 |
| NUMBER OF INSCRIBED FACES: | 1 |
| NUMBER OF PEOPLE COMMEMORATED: | 1 |
| MEMORIAL TYPE: | LOW MONUMENT |
| CONDITION OF MEMORIAL: | SOUND IN PLACE |
| CONDITION OF INSCRIPTION: | MAINLY DECIPHERABLE |
| STONEMASON NAME: | |
| TECHNIQUE OF INSCRIPTION: | INCISED |
| UNDERTAKER: | |
| STONE TOP: | LOW MONUMENT |
| GRAVE TYPE: | SINGLE |
| HEIGHT: | 192CM |
| WIDTH: | 99CM |
| THICKNESS: | 10CM |

| SURNAME: | CHRISTIAN | ADRESS | DEATH | AGE |
|---|---|---|---|---|
| HUSSY | PETER | DULEEK SOLDIER | 13 DEC 1755 | |

**INSCRIPTION:**
HERE LIES THE REMAINS OF MR PETER HUSSY OF DULEEK WHO SERVED FOR 15 YEARS IN HER MAJESTY'S REGIMENT OF FOOT RESPECTED BY HIS OFFICERS AND BELOVED BY HIS COMRADES WHO DEPARTED THIS LIFE ON THE 13TH DEC 1755 DEEPLY REGRETTED BY HIS AFFLICTED WIDOW WHO HAS ERECTED THIS STONE TO HIS MEMORY

*REQUIESCANT IN PACE AMEN*

| | |
|---|---|
| NAME OF RECORDER: | PHYLLIS NOONAN AND BEN RYAN |
| DATE: | 18 JULY 2005 |
| PHOTO REFERENCE: | F3 |
| LOCATION/MAP REF: | D1 F3 |

| | |
|---|---|
| GRAVEYARD NAME: | **ST. MARY'S ABBEY OLD GRAVEYARD** |
| GRAVEYARD CODE: | D1 |
| COUNTY: | MEATH |
| MEMORIAL NUMBER: | A1 |
| ERECTED BY: | THEIR LOVING CHILDREN |
| ORIENTATION: | EAST |
| NUMBER OF COMPONENTS: | 3 |
| NUMBER OF INSCRIBED FACES: | 1 |
| NUMBER OF PEOPLE COMMEMORATED: | 8 |
| MEMORIAL TYPE: | HEADSTONE |
| CONDITION OF MEMORIAL: | SOUND IN PLACE |
| CONDITION OF INSCRIPTION: | LEGIBLE |
| STONEMASON NAME: | |
| TECHNIQUE OF INSCRIPTION: | INCISED PAINTED |
| UNDERTAKER: | |
| STONE TOP: | CROSS |
| GRAVE TYPE: | TREBLE |
| HEIGHT: | 190CM |
| WIDTH: | 82CM |
| THICKNESS: | 10CM |
| PEOPLE RECORDED: | |

| SURNAME: | CHRISTIAN | ADDRESS | DEATH | AGE |
|---|---|---|---|---|
| KEELAN | ALICIA | CORBALLIS | 09 APR 1934 | |
| KEELAN | JOHN | CORBALLIS | 31 MAR 1938 | |
| MULDOON | ANNIE | | 02 FEB 1958 | 53 |
| KEELAN | PETER | | 07 APR 1961 | 59 |
| KEELAN | ALICE | | 05 FEB 1996 | 87 |
| KEELAN | WILLIAM | | 25 DEC 1947 | 10 WEEKS |
| KEELAN | PATRICK | | 10 JAN 1966 | 16 |
| KEELAN | RICHARD | | 06 OCT 2003 | 61 |

**INSCRIPTION:**
IN LOVING MEMORY
OF ALICIA KEELAN
CORBALLIS
DIED THE 9TH APRIL 1934
HER HUSBAND JOHN
DIED THE 31ST MARCH 1938
THEIR DAUGHTER
ANNIE MULDOON
DIED 2ND FEB 1958 AGED 53
THEIR SON PETER
DIED THE 7TH APRIL 1961
HIS WIFE ALICE
DIED THE 5TH FEB 1996
THEIR SONS
WILLIAM DIED THE 25TH DEC 1947 AGED 10 WEEKS
PATRICK DIED THE 10TH JAN 1966 AGED 16
RICHARD DIED THE 6TH OCT 2003 AGED 61
SACRED HEART OF JESUS
HAVE MERCY ON THEM

ERECTED BY THEIR LOVING CHILDREN

**SYMBOLS:**
HEART WITH CROSS THORNS AND FLAMES

**ORNAMENT:**
ELABORATE CROSS WITH FLEUR DE LIS

| | |
|---|---|
| NAME OF RECORDER: | PHYLLIS NOONAN AND SINEAD FULLAM |
| DATE: | 18 JUNE 2005 |
| PHOTO REFERENCE: | A1 |
| LOCATION/MAP REF: | D1 A1 |

| | |
|---|---|
| GRAVEYARD NAME: | **ST. MARY'S ABBEY OLD GRAVEYARD** |
| GRAVEYARD CODE: | D1 |
| COUNTY: | MEATH |
| MEMORIAL NUMBER: | C12 |
| ERECTED BY: | |
| ORIENTATION: | EAST |
| NUMBER OF COMPONENTS: | 2 |
| NUMBER OF INSCRIBED FACES: | 1 |
| NUMBER OF PEOPLE COMMEMORATED: | 6 |
| MEMORIAL TYPE: | HEADSTONE |
| CONDITION OF MEMORIAL: | SOUND IN PLACE |
| CONDITION OF INSCRIPTION: | CLEAR |
| STONEMASON NAME: | |
| TECHNIQUE OF INSCRIPTION: | INCISED AND PAINTED |
| UNDERTAKER: | |
| STONE TOP: | ROUND |
| GRAVE TYPE: | TREBLE |
| HEIGHT: | 205CM |
| WIDTH: | 76CM |
| THICKNESS: | 10CM |

| SURNAME: | CHRISTIAN | ADDRESS | DEATH | AGE |
|---|---|---|---|---|
| KELLY | JAMES | DULEEK | 1920 | 77 |
| KELLY | JANE | DULEEK | 1916 | |
| KELLY | ALPHONSUS | DULEEK | 1915 | |
| KELLY | JOHN | DULEEK | 1966 | |
| KELLY | MARY | DULEEK | 1969 | |
| KELLY | MICHAEL | DULEEK | 1975 | 77 |

**INSCRIPTION:**
IN MEMORY OF
JAMES KELLY DULEEK
DIED 1920 AGED 77
HIS WIFE JANE DIED 1916
THEIR SON P ALPHONSUS DIED 1915
THEIR SON JOHN DIED 1966
THEIR DAUGHTER MARY DIED 1969
THEIR SON MICHAEL J
DIED 9.FEB 1975 AGED 77

R.I.P.

| | |
|---|---|
| NAME OF RECORDER: | PHYLLIS NOONAN AND JIM ORTON |
| DATE: | 6 JULY 2002 |
| PHOTO REFERENCE: | C12 |
| LOCATION/MAP REF: | D1 C12 |

| | |
|---|---|
| GRAVEYARD NAME: | **ST. MARY'S ABBEY OLD GRAVEYARD** |
| GRAVEYARD CODE: | D1 |
| COUNTY: | MEATH |
| MEMORIAL NUMBER: | D2 |
| ERECTED BY: | THOMAS KELLY |
| ORIENTATION: | EAST |
| NUMBER OF COMPONENTS: | 1 |
| NUMBER OF INSCRIBED FACES: | 1 |
| NUMBER OF PEOPLE COMMEMORATED: | 3 |
| MEMORIAL TYPE: | ELABORATE HEADSTONE |
| CONDITION OF MEMORIAL: | SOUND DISPLACED |
| CONDITION OF INSCRIPTION: | MAINLY DECIPHERABLE |
| STONEMASON NAME: | |
| TECHNIQUE OF INSCRIPTION: | INCISED |
| UNDERTAKER: | |
| STONE TOP: | COLLAPSED |
| GRAVE TYPE: | DOUBLE |
| HEIGHT: | 191CM |
| WIDTH: | 86CM |
| THICKNESS: | 13CM |

| SURNAME: | CHRISTIAN | ADDRESS | DEATH | AGE |
|---|---|---|---|---|
| KELLY | PATRICK | DULEEK GATE, DROGHEDA | 07 NOV 1788 | 70 |
| KELLY | CHILD | | | |
| KELLY | CHILD | | | |

**INSCRIPTION:**
ERECTED ANNO DOMINE 1793
BY THOMAS KELLY OF RATHMULLAN FARMER
IN MEMORY OF HIS
FATHER PATRICK KELLY LATE OF
DULEEK GATE DROGHEDA WHO
DEPARTED THIS LIFE THE 7TH DAY
OF NOVEMBER 1788 AGED 70
YEARS, ALSO THE REMAINS OF 2 OF HIS CHILDREN

*REQUISCANT IN PACE AMEN*

**SYMBOLS.**
CRUCIFIXION FLANKED BY 2 ANGELS

**ORNAMENTS:**
SCROLLED AROUND EDGES

| | |
|---|---|
| NAME OF RECORDER: | PHYLLIS NOONAN |
| DATE: | 11 JULY 2005 |
| PHOTO REFERENCE: | D2 |
| LOCATION/MAP REF: | D1 D2 |

| | |
|---|---|
| GRAVEYARD NAME: | **ST. MARY'S ABBEY OLD GRAVEYARD** |
| GRAVEYARD CODE: | D1 |
| COUNTY: | MEATH |
| MEMORIAL NUMBER: | D22 |
| ERECTED BY: | JOHN KELLY |
| ORIENTATION: | EAST |
| NUMBER OF COMPONENTS: | 1 |
| NUMBER OF INSCRIBED FACES: | 1 |
| NUMBER OF PEOPLE COMMEMORATED: | 3 |
| MEMORIAL TYPE: | HEADSTONE |
| CONDITION OF MEMORIAL: | SOUND |
| CONDITION OF INSCRIPTION: | CLEAR |
| STONEMASON NAME: | |
| TECHNIQUE OF INSCRIPTION: | INCISED |
| UNDERTAKER: | |
| STONE TOP: | MISSING |
| GRAVE TYPE: | SINGLE |
| HEIGHT: | 122CM |
| WIDTH: | 66CM |
| THICKNESS: | 11CM |

| SURNAME: | CHRISTIAN | ADDRESS | DEATH | AGE |
|---|---|---|---|---|
| KELLY | JOHN | DULEEK N.T. | 05 MAY 1923 | |
| | ELEANOR | | 08 APR 1887 | |
| | ELEANORA | | 11 OCT 1921 | |

**INSCRIPTION:**
ERECTED BY
JOHN KELLY NT DULEEK
IN LOVING MEMORY OF HIS DAUGHTER ELEANOR
WHO DIED APRIL 8TH 1887
AND OF HIS WIFE ELEANORA
WHO DIED OCT.11TH 1921
THE ABOVE JOHN KELLY
DIED MAY 5TH 1923

*SWEET JESUS MERCY*

**SYMBOLS:**
ELABORATE INTERWOVEN
I.H.S. TWO FLOWERS EITHER SIDE

| | |
|---|---|
| NAME OF RECORDER: | PHYLLIS NOONAN |
| DATE: | 14 JULY 2005 |
| PHOTO REFERENCE: | D22 |
| LOCATION/MAP REF: | D1 D22 |

| | |
|---|---|
| GRAVEYARD NAME: | **ST. MARY'S ABBEY OLD GRAVEYARD** |
| GRAVEYARD CODE: | D1 |
| COUNTY: | MEATH |
| MEMORIAL NUMBER: | K32 |
| ERECTED BY: | PATRICK KELLY |
| ORIENTATION: | EAST |
| NUMBER OF COMPONENTS: | 1 |
| NUMBER OF INSCRIBED FACES: | 1 |
| NUMBER OF PEOPLE COMMEMORATED: | 6 |
| MEMORIAL TYPE: | HEADSTONE |
| CONDITION OF MEMORIAL: | SOUND IN PLACE |
| CONDITION OF INSCRIPTION: | MAINLY DECIPHERABLE |
| STONEMASON NAME: | |
| TECHNIQUE OF INSCRIPTION: | INCISED |
| UNDERTAKER: | |
| STONE TOP: | ROUND STEPPED |
| GRAVE TYPE: | SINGLE |
| HEIGHT: | 128CM |
| WIDTH: | 75CM |
| THICKNESS: | 13CM |

| SURNAME: | CHRISTIAN | ADDRESS | DEATH | AGE |
|---|---|---|---|---|
| KELLY | FATHER | WINDY | | |
| | MOTHER | | | |
| | JAMES | | 08 SEPT 1840 | 27 |
| | THOMAS | | 29 JULY 1865 | 75 |
| | MATHEW | | 08 FEB 1857 | 40 |
| | MARY | | 25 DEC 1857 | 65 |

**INSCRIPTION:**
ERECTED ANNO DOMINI 1809
BY PATRICK KELLY OF WINDY
IN MEMORY OF HIS FATHER
AND MOTHER ALSO OF HIS
POSTERITY
RENEWED BY THOS KELLY
WINDY IN MEMORY OF HIS SON
JAMES KELLY HE DIED THE 8TH
SEPR 1840 AGED 27 YEARS
ALSO THE ABOVE THOS KELLY WHO
DIED 29 JULY 1865 AGED 75 YEARS ALSO
HIS SON MATW KELLY DIED FEB 8TH
1857 AGED 40 YEARS ALSO MRS MARY
KELLY WIFE OF THE ABOVE THOMAS
KELLY WHO DIED DECR 25TH 1857
AGED 65 YEARS

**SYMBOLS:**
IHS IN SUNBURST DISK

| | |
|---|---|
| NAME OF RECORDER: | JANET LEIGH AND PHYLLIS NOONAN |
| DATE: | 22 APRIL 2006 |
| PHOTO REFERENCE: | K32 |
| LOCATION/MAP REF: | D1 K32 |

| GRAVEYARD NAME: | **ST. MARY'S ABBEY OLD GRAVEYARD** |
|---|---|
| GRAVEYARD CODE: | D1 |
| COUNTY: | MEATH |
| MEMORIAL NUMBER: | K16 |
| ERECTED BY: | THOS KELLY |
| ORIENTATION: | EAST |
| NUMBER OF COMPONENTS: | 1 |
| NUMBER OF INSCRIBED FACES: | 1 |
| NUMBER OF PEOPLE COMMEMORATED: | 3 |
| MEMORIAL TYPE: | HEADSTONE |
| CONDITION OF MEMORIAL: | SOUND |
| CONDITION OF INSCRIPTION: | LEGIBLE |
| STONEMASON NAME: | |
| TECHNIQUE OF INSCRIPTION: | INCISED |
| UNDERTAKER: | |
| STONE TOP: | ROUND |
| GRAVE TYPE: | SINGLE |
| HEIGHT: | 99CM |
| WIDTH: | 65CM |
| THICKNESS: | 09CM |

| SURNAME: | CHRISTIAN | ADDRESS | DEATH | AGE |
|---|---|---|---|---|
| KELLY | THOMAS | | 11 NOV 18074 | 54 |
| | THOMAS | | 27 MAR 1770 | 56 |
| KELCH | MARGARET | | 11 SEPT 1820 | 79 |

**INSCRIPTION:**
ERECTED AD 1821
BY THOS KELLY OF DROGHEDA
IN MEMORY OF HIS FATHER
THOS KELLY
WHO DIED 11TH NOV 1807 AGED 54 YEARS
ALSO HIS GRANDFATHER
THOS KELLY WHO DIED THE 27TH
MARCH 1770 AGED 56 YEARS
ALSO HIS BELOVED WIFE MARGARET KELCH WHO DIED
11TH SEPT 1820 AGED 79 YRS
ALSO FOR HIM AND HIS POSTERITY
*REQUIESCANT IN PACE*

**SYMBOLS:**
CRUCIFIXION CROSS
SCROLL WORK

| NAME OF RECORDER: | SINEAD FULLAM AND HELEN FULLAM |
|---|---|
| DATE: | 20 SEPT 2005 |
| PHOTO REFERENCE: | K16 |
| LOCATION/MAP REF: | D1 K16 |

| | |
|---|---|
| GRAVEYARD NAME: | **ST. MARY'S ABBEY OLD GRAVEYARD** |
| GRAVEYARD CODE: | D1 |
| COUNTY: | MEATH |
| MEMORIAL NUMBER: | G17 |
| ERECTED BY: | KELLY FAMILY |
| ORIENTATION: | EAST |
| NUMBER OF COMPONENTS: | 1 |
| NUMBER OF INSCRIBED FACES: | 1 |
| NUMBER OF PEOPLE COMMEMORATED: | 3 |
| MEMORIAL TYPE: | LOW MONUMENT |
| CONDITION OF MEMORIAL: | SOUND IN PLACE ON FLOOR OF ABBEY |
| CONDITION OF INSCRIPTION: | CLEAR |
| STONEMASON NAME: | |
| TECHNIQUE OF INSCRIPTION: | INCISED |
| UNDERTAKER: | |
| STONE TOP: | LOW MONUMENT SQUARE |
| GRAVE TYPE: | SINGLE |
| HEIGHT: | 215CM |
| WIDTH: | 106CM |
| THICKNESS: | NOT ACCESSIBLE ON FLOOR OF ABBEY |

| SURNAME: | CHRISTIAN | ADDRESS | DEATH | AGE |
|---|---|---|---|---|
| KELLY | RICHARD | LIEUT COLONEL | 07 JAN 1846 | 68 |
| | ANNE | | 30 SEPT 1861 | 82 |

**INSCRIPTION:**
SACRED
TO THE MEMORY OF RICHARD KELLY
LATE LIEUT COLONEL IN THE 34TH REG. WHO
DEPARTED THIS LIFE ON THE 7TH JANUARY 1846
AT WESTON IN THE COUNTY MEATH IN THE 68TH
YEAR OF HIS AGE
(IN HIS OWN WORDS) TRUSTING IN THE RICH
AND INFINITE MERCIES OF HIS GRACIOUS REDEEMER
HE HUMBLY HOPES AND JOYFULLY EXPECTS
THAT HIS VILE BODY BENEATH THIS STONE MAY
AGAIN BE UNITED TO HIS IMMORTAL SOUL AND
THAT HE MAY HAVE THE GLORIOUS PRIVILEGE
OF JOINING REDEEMED SINNERS IN THE PRAISES
OF HIM WHO HATH "SWALLOWED UP DEATH IN
VICTORY"
THIS STONE WAS PLACED HERE BY HIS
SORROWING FAMILY AS A SMALL TRIBUTE OF
AFFECTION AND TO RECORD THEIR GREAT LOSS
ALSO TO THE MEMORY OF ANNE KELLY
WIDOW OF THE ABOVE NAMED RICHARD KELLY
AND DAUGHTER OF THE LATE FRANCIS THOME
ESQ. WHO DEPARTED THIS LIFE ON THE 30TH
OF SEPTEMBER 1861 AGED 82 YEARS

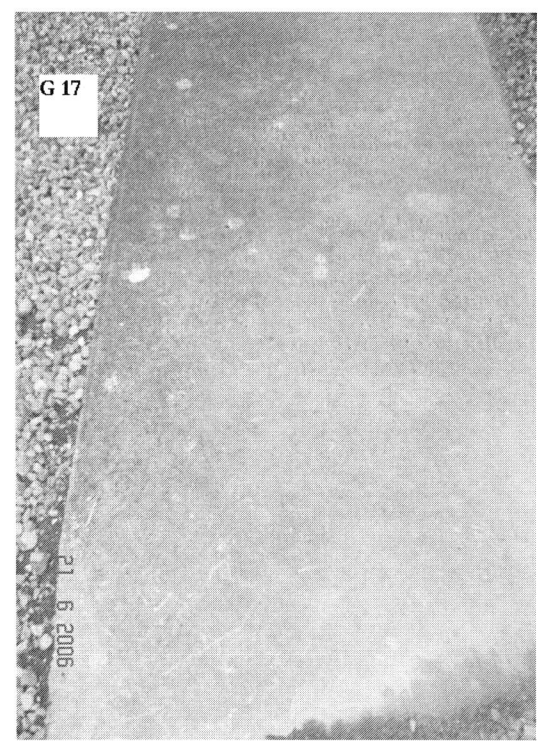

| | |
|---|---|
| NAME OF RECORDER: | JANET LEIGH |
| DATE: | 01 JULY 2006 |
| PHOTO REFERENCE: | G17 |
| LOCATION/MAP REF: | D1-G17 |

| | |
|---|---|
| GRAVEYARD NAME: | **ST. MARY'S ABBEY OLD GRAVEYARD** |
| GRAVEYARD CODE: | D1 |
| COUNTY: | MEATH |
| MEMORIAL NUMBER: | J9 |
| ERECTED BY: | |
| ORIENTATION: | EAST |
| NUMBER OF COMPONENTS: | 1 |
| NUMBER OF INSCRIBED FACES: | 1 |
| NUMBER OF PEOPLE COMMEMORATED: | 1 |
| MEMORIAL TYPE: | HEADSTONE |
| CONDITION OF MEMORIAL: | SOUND N PLACE |
| CONDITION OF INSCRIPTION: | CLEAR |
| STONEMASON NAME: | |
| TECHNIQUE OF INSCRIPTION: | INCISED |
| UNDERTAKER: | |
| STONE TOP: | ROUND |
| GRAVE TYPE: | SINGLE |
| HEIGHT: | 83CM |
| WIDTH: | 43CM |
| THICKNESS: | 04CM |

| SURNAME: | CHRISTIAN | ADDRESS | DEATH | AGE |
|---|---|---|---|---|
| KELLY | SUSAN | DOWNSTOWN | 18 NOV 1951 | 78 |

**INSCRIPTION:**
IN LOVING MEMORY
OF
SUSAN KELLY
DOWNSTOWN
WHO DIED 18 NOV 1951
AGED 78 YRS

RIP

**SYMBOLS:**
CROSS

| | |
|---|---|
| NAME OF RECORDER: | JANET LEIGH AND SINEAD FULLAM |
| DATE: | 6 AUG 2005 |
| PHOTO REFERENCE: | J9 |
| LOCATION/MAP REF: | D1 J9 |

| | |
|---|---|
| GRAVEYARD NAME: | **ST. MARY'S ABBEY OLD GRAVEYARD** |
| GRAVEYARD CODE: | D1 |
| COUNTY: | MEATH |
| MEMORIAL NUMBER: | H9 |
| ERECTED BY: | |
| ORIENTATION: | EAST |
| NUMBER OF COMPONENTS: | 1 |
| NUMBER OF INSCRIBED FACES: | 1 |
| NUMBER OF PEOPLE COMMEMORATED: | 6 |
| MEMORIAL TYPE: | LOW MONUMENT |
| CONDITION OF MEMORIAL: | SOUND IN PLACE– STONE BROKE IN TWO PLACES |
| CONDITION OF INSCRIPTION: | LEGIBLE |
| STONEMASON NAME: | |
| TECHNIQUE OF INSCRIPTION: | INCISED |
| UNDERTAKER: | |
| STONE TOP: | SQUARE LOW MONUMENT |
| GRAVE TYPE: | SINGLE |
| HEIGHT: | 180CM |
| WIDTH: | 103CM |
| THICKNESS: | 04 CM |

| SURNAME: | CHRISTIAN | ADDRESS | DEATH | AGE |
|---|---|---|---|---|
| KETTLEWELL | THOMAS | | 1813 | |
| KETTLEWELL | MARY | | 1827 | |
| KETTLEWELL | WILLIAM | | 20 MAY 1831 | 51 |
| JOHNSTONE | ANNE | | 18 JUN 1838 | |
| KETTLEWELL | THOMAS | | 06 MAR 1837 | 30 |
| KETTLEWELL | EVANS | | 29 AUG 1851 | 69 |

**INSCRIPTION:**
UNDERNEATH LIE THE REMAINS OF THOMAS
KETTLEWELL OF THOMASTOWN IN THE COUNTY
OF MEATH ESQRE WHO DIED IN THE YEAR OF
OUR LORD 1813. MARY HIS WIFE WHO DIED
IN THE YEAR 1827. OF WILLIAM KETTLEWELL
ELDEST SON OF THE ABOVE THOMAS AND
WHO DIED ON THE 20TH MAY
IN THE FIFTY FIRST OF HIS AGE
ALSO OF ANNE JOHNSTONE RELICT OF THE
REVD F JOHNSTONE RECTOR OF DONOUGHMORE
CO DOWN WHO DIED JUNE 18TH
ALSO OF THOMAS KETTLEWELL ESQRE
CAPTAIN OF HID MAJESTY'S SERVICE WHO DIED
MARCH 6TH 1837 AGED 30
ALSO EVANS KETTLEWELL ESQRE WHO
DEPARTED THIS LIFE ON THE 29TH DAY OF
AUGUST 1851 AGED 69YEARS

| | |
|---|---|
| NAME OF RECORDER: | SINEAD AND HELEN FULLAM |
| DATE: | 10 JUNE 2006 |
| PHOTO REFERENCE: | H9 |
| LOCATION/MAP REF: | D1 H9 |

| | |
|---|---|
| GRAVEYARD NAME: | **ST. MARY'S ABBEY OLD GRAVEYARD** |
| GRAVEYARD CODE: | D1 |
| COUNTY: | MEATH |
| MEMORIAL NUMBER: | H10 |
| ERECTED BY: | |
| ORIENTATION: | EAST |
| NUMBER OF COMPONENTS: | 1 |
| NUMBER OF INSCRIBED FACES: | 1 |
| NUMBER OF PEOPLE COMMEMORATED: | 3 |
| MEMORIAL TYPE: | LOW MONUMENT |
| CONDITION OF MEMORIAL: | SOUND IN PLACE |
| CONDITION OF INSCRIPTION: | LEGIBLE |
| STONEMASON NAME: | |
| TECHNIQUE OF INSCRIPTION: | INCISED |
| UNDERTAKER: | |
| STONE TOP: | LOW MONUMENT |
| GRAVE TYPE: | SINGLE |
| HEIGHT: | |
| WIDTH: | |
| THICKNESS: | |

| SURNAME: | CHRISTIAN | ADDRESS | DEATH | AGE |
|---|---|---|---|---|
| KETTLEWELL | JOHN | | | |
| KETTLEWELL | MILADY | | 1809 | |
| KETTLEWELL | EVENA | | 29 AUG 1851 | 69 |

**INSCRIPTION:**
THE BURIAL PLACE OF JOHN KETTLEWELL OF
.....


*(AT THE BOTTOM)*
HERE ALSO LIES THE BODY OF
MILADY KETTLEWELL DAUGHTER OF THOMAS AND
MARY KETTLEWELL WHO DIED IN THE YEAR
1809 ALSO EVENA KETTLEWELL WHO DEPARTED
THIS LIFE THE 29TH DAY OF AUGUST 1851 AGED
69 YRS

| | |
|---|---|
| NAME OF RECORDER: | JANET LEIGH |
| DATE: | 10 OCT 2006 |
| PHOTO REFERENCE: | H10 |
| LOCATION/MAP REF: | D1 H10 |

| | |
|---|---|
| GRAVEYARD NAME: | **ST. MARY'S ABBEY OLD GRAVEYARD** |
| GRAVEYARD CODE: | D1 |
| COUNTY: | MEATH |
| MEMORIAL NUMBER: | K35 |
| ERECTED BY: | CATHERINE LACEY |
| ORIENTATION: | EAST |
| NUMBER OF COMPONENTS: | 2 |
| NUMBER OF INSCRIBED FACES: | 1 |
| NUMBER OF PEOPLE COMMEMORATED: | 7 |
| MEMORIAL TYPE: | HEADSTONE CELTIC CROSS |
| CONDITION OF MEMORIAL: | SOUND IN PLACE |
| CONDITION OF INSCRIPTION: | MAINLY DECIPHERABLE |
| STONEMASON NAME: | MOSS |
| TECHNIQUE OF INSCRIPTION: | INCISED |
| UNDERTAKER: | |
| STONE TOP: | CELTIC CROSS |
| GRAVE TYPE: | TREBLE |
| HEIGHT: | 185CM |
| WIDTH: | 69CM |
| THICKNESS: | 09CM |

| SURNAME: | CHRISTIAN | ADDRESS | DEATH | AGE |
|---|---|---|---|---|
| LACEY | JOHN | | 20 FEB 1925 | 77 YEARS |
| | MARY C | | 13 FEB 1891 | 3 MONTHS |
| | JAMES P. | | 29 JUL 1905 | 16 YEARS |
| | MARGARET M | | 10 DEC 1909 | 27 YEARS |
| | MARY | | 04 JAN 1921 | 27 YEARS |
| O'BAOIGHILL | DEASMUMHAN | | 06 JUL 1919 | 8 YEARS |
| LACEY | CATHERINE | | 23 DEC 1935 | 82 YEARS |

**INSCRIPTION:**
ERECTED
BY
CATHERINE LACEY
DULEEK
IN MEMORY OF HER DEAR HUSBAND
JOHN
WHO DIED 25 FEB 1925 AGED 77 YEARS
AND THEIR CHILDREN
MARY C WHO DIED 13TH FEB 1891
AGED 3 MONTHS
JAMES P WHO DIED 29 JULY 1905
AGED 16 YEARS
MARGARET M WHO DIED 10TH DEC 1909
AGED 27 YEARS
MARY (MYSIE) WHO DIED 4TH JAN 1921
AGED 27 YEARS
ALSO THEIR GRANDSON DEASMUMHAN O'BAOIGHILL
WHO DIED 6TH JULY 1919 IN HIS 8TH YEAR
AND THE ABOVE NAMED
CATHERINE LACEY
WHO DIED 23RD DEC 1935 AGED 82 YEARS

**SYMBOLS:**
SACRED HEART INFLAMES ENTWINED BY THORNS IN CROSS
VINE LEAVES IN CROSS ARMS
BRIAR ROSE IN CROSS ARM
TULIP IN CROSS ARM
SHAMROCK IN CROSS ARM

| | |
|---|---|
| NAME OF RECORDER: | JANET LEIGH AND PYHLLIS NOONAN |
| DATE: | 22 APRIL 2006 |
| PHOTO REFERENCE: | K35 |
| LOCATION/MAP REF: | D1 K35 |

| | |
|---|---|
| GRAVEYARD NAME: | **ST. MARY'S ABBEY OLD GRAVEYARD** |
| GRAVEYARD CODE: | D1 |
| COUNTY: | MEATH |
| MEMORIAL NUMBER: | B1 A |
| ERECTED BY: | |
| ORIENTATION: | EAST |
| NUMBER OF COMPONENTS: | 3 |
| NUMBER OF INSCRIBED FACES: | 1 |
| NUMBER OF PEOPLE COMMEMORATED: | 2 |
| MEMORIAL TYPE: | CROSS ON PEDESTAL |
| CONDITION OF MEMORIAL: | SOUND IN PLACE |
| CONDITION OF INSCRIPTION: | CLEAR |
| STONEMASON NAME: | |
| TECHNIQUE OF INSCRIPTION: | INCISED AND PAINTED BLACK |
| UNDERTAKER: | |
| STONE TOP: | CROSS |
| GRAVE TYPE: | TREBLE |
| HEIGHT: | 200CM |
| WIDTH: | 58CM |
| THICKNESS: | 39CM |

| SURNAME: | CHRISTIAN | ADDRESS | DEATH | AGE |
|---|---|---|---|---|
| LAW | MICHAEL AUGUSTINE FITZGERALD | BEAMOND | 03 OCT 1917 | 56 |
| | MARY MELVILLE | | 15 AUG 1939 | 76 |

**INSCRIPTION:**
IN LOVING MEMORY
OF MICHAEL AUGUSTINE
FITZGERALD LAW JP
OF BEAMOND
WHO DIED ON OCTOBER 3RD 1917 AGED 56
AND OF HIS WIFE
MARY MELVILLE
WHO DIED AUGUST 15 1939 AGED 76

WELL DONE GOOD AND FAITHFUL SERVANT

| | |
|---|---|
| NAME OF RECORDER: | PHYLLIS NOONAN AND JIM ORTEN |
| DATE: | 25 JUNE 2005 |
| PHOTO REFERENCE: | B1A |
| LOCATION/MAP REF: | D1 B1A |

| | |
|---|---|
| GRAVEYARD NAME: | **ST. MARY'S ABBEY OLD GRAVEYARD** |
| GRAVEYARD CODE: | D1 |
| COUNTY: | MEATH |
| MEMORIAL NUMBER: | B1 B |
| ERECTED BY: | |
| ORIENTATION: | EAST |
| NUMBER OF COMPONENTS: | 2 |
| NUMBER OF INSCRIBED FACES: | 1 |
| NUMBER OF PEOPLE COMMEMORATED: | 1 |
| MEMORIAL TYPE: | CROSS ON PEDESTAL |
| CONDITION OF MEMORIAL: | SOUND IN PLACE |
| CONDITION OF INSCRIPTION: | CLEAR |
| STONEMASON NAME: | |
| TECHNIQUE OF INSCRIPTION: | INCISED ON MARBLE |
| UNDERTAKER: | |
| STONE TOP: | CROSS |
| GRAVE TYPE: | TREBLE |
| HEIGHT: | 100CM |
| WIDTH: | 40CM |
| THICKNESS: | 10CM |

| SURNAME: | CHRISTIAN | ADDRESS | DEATH | AGE |
|---|---|---|---|---|
| LAW | OLIVE MARY | | 09 OCT 1892 | 1 YR 10 MTHS |

**INSCRIPTION:**
OLIVE MARY
LAW
DIED OCTOBER 9TH 1892
AGED 1 YEAR & 10 MONTHS

"JESUS CALLED A LITTLE CHILD
UNTO HIM"

| | |
|---|---|
| NAME OF RECORDER: | PHYLLIS NOONAN AND JIM ORTEN |
| DATE: | 25 JUNE 2005 |
| PHOTO REFERENCE: | B1 B |
| LOCATION/MAP REF: | D1 B1B |

| | |
|---|---|
| GRAVEYARD NAME: | **ST. MARY'S ABBEY OLD GRAVEYARD** |
| GRAVEYARD CODE: | D1 |
| COUNTY: | MEATH |
| MEMORIAL NUMBER: | B1 C |
| ERECTED BY: | |
| ORIENTATION: | EAST |
| NUMBER OF COMPONENTS: | 2 |
| NUMBER OF INSCRIBED FACES: | 1 |
| NUMBER OF PEOPLE COMMEMORATED: | 1 |
| MEMORIAL TYPE: | HEADSTONE |
| CONDITION OF MEMORIAL: | SOUND IN PLACE |
| CONDITION OF INSCRIPTION: | CLEAR |
| STONEMASON NAME: | |
| TECHNIQUE OF INSCRIPTION: | INCISED AND PAINTED |
| UNDERTAKER: | |
| STONE TOP: | HEADSTONE |
| GRAVE TYPE: | TREBLE |
| HEIGHT: | 90CM |
| WIDTH: | 54CM |
| THICKNESS: | 5CM |

| SURNAME: | CHRISTIAN | ADDRESS | OCCUPATION | DEATH | AGE |
|---|---|---|---|---|---|
| LAW | FRANCIS CECIL | | MAJ. ROYAL MARINES | 29 JULY 1958 | 67 |

**INSCRIPTION:**
IN LOVING MEMORY OF
MAJOR FRANCIS CECIL LAW
D.S.C. ROYAL MARINES
OF WESTON
WHO DIED 29 JULY 1958 AGED 67

WHERE THERE IS GOD
THERE IS NO NEED

| | |
|---|---|
| NAME OF RECORDER: | PHYLLIS. NOONAN AND JIM ORTON |
| DATE: | 26 JUNE 2005 |
| PHOTO REFERENCE: | B1 C |
| LOCATION/MAP REF: | D1 B1 C |

| | |
|---|---|
| GRAVEYARD NAME: | **ST. MARY'S ABBEY OLD GRAVEYARD** |
| GRAVEYARD CODE: | D1 |
| COUNTY: | MEATH |
| MEMORIAL NUMBER: | H4 |
| ERECTED BY: | |
| ORIENTATION: | EAST |
| NUMBER OF COMPONENTS: | |
| NUMBER OF INSCRIBED FACES: | 1 |
| NUMBER OF PEOPLE COMMEMORATED: | 1 |
| MEMORIAL TYPE: | HEADSTONE |
| CONDITION OF MEMORIAL: | SUNK IN GROUND |
| CONDITION OF INSCRIPTION: | TRACES SUNK IN GROUND |
| STONEMASON NAME: | |
| TECHNIQUE OF INSCRIPTION: | INCISED |
| UNDERTAKER: | |
| STONE TOP: | ROUND |
| GRAVE TYPE: | SINGLE |
| HEIGHT: | 43CM |
| WIDTH: | 62CM |
| THICKNESS: | 11CM |

| SURNAME: | CHRISTIAN | ADDRESS | DEATH | AGE |
|---|---|---|---|---|
| LAWLESS | PETER | | | |

**INSCRIPTION:**

THIS STONE WAS ERECTED
BY PETER LAWLESS IN
MEMORY OF HIS FATHER
R.............

**SYMBOLS:**
I.H.S WITH CROSS

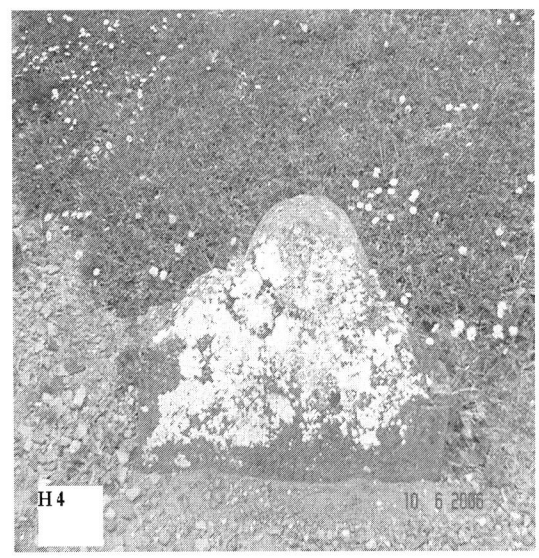

| | |
|---|---|
| NAME OF RECORDER: | LIZ LYNCH AND JANET LEIGH |
| DATE: | 07 JUNE 2006 |
| PHOTO REFERENCE: | H4 |
| LOCATION/MAP REF: | D1 H4 |

| | |
|---|---|
| GRAVEYARD NAME: | **ST. MARY'S ABBEY OLD GRAVEYARD** |
| GRAVEYARD CODE: | D1 |
| COUNTY: | MEATH |
| MEMORIAL NUMBER: | D 4 |
| ERECTED BY: | ELIZABETH LEE |
| ORIENTATION: | EAST |
| NUMBER OF COMPONENTS: | 3 |
| NUMBER OF INSCRIBED FACES: | 1 |
| NUMBER OF PEOPLE COMMEMORATED: | 7 |
| MEMORIAL TYPE: | HEADSTONE |
| CONDITION OF MEMORIAL: | SOUND IN PLACE |
| CONDITION OF INSCRIPTION: | DECIPHERABLE |
| STONEMASON NAME: | REID |
| TECHNIQUE OF INSCRIPTION: | INCISED AND PAINTED |
| UNDERTAKER: | |
| STONE TOP: | MISSING |
| GRAVE TYPE: | TREBLE |
| HEIGHT: | 127CM |
| WIDTH: | 54CM |
| THICKNESS: | 10CM |

| SURNAME: | CHRISTIAN | ADDRESS | DEATH | AGE |
|---|---|---|---|---|
| LEE | PATRICK | | 19 MAY 1932 | 78 YEARS |
| | MAGGIE | | 06 MAR 1899 | 3 YEARS |
| | PETER | | 15 FEB 1937 | 36 YEARS |
| | ELIZABETH | | 29 DEC 1962 | 95 YEARS |
| | JOSEPHINE | | 19 MAY 1963 | |
| | PATRICK | | 19 FEB 1972 | 67 YEARS |
| | JOHN | | 23 DEC 1976 | 79 YEARS |

**INSCRIPTION:**
ERECTED BY
ELIZABETH LEE DULEEK
IN LOVING MEMORY OF HER
HUSBAND PATRICK DIED
MAY 19TH 1932 AGED 78 YEARS
AND HER DAUGHTER MAGGIE DIED
MARCH 6TH 1899 AGED 3 YEARS
ALSO HER SON PETER DIED
FEB 15TH 1937 AGED 36 YEARS
THE ABOVE ELIZABETH DIED
29TH DEC 1962 AGED 95 YEARS
HER DAUGHTER JOSEPHINE
DIED 19TH MAY 1963
HER SON PATRICK
DIED 18TH FEB. 1972 AGED 67
JOHN LEE
DIED 23RD DEC 1976 AGED 79
R.I.P.

| | |
|---|---|
| NAME OF RECORDER: | JANET LEIGH AND PHYLLIS NOONAN |
| DATE: | 16 JULY 2005 |
| PHOTO REFERENCE: | D4 |
| LOCATION/MAP REF: | D1 D4 |

| | |
|---|---|
| GRAVEYARD NAME: | **ST. MARY'S ABBEY OLD GRAVEYARD** |
| GRAVEYARD CODE: | D1 |
| COUNTY: | MEATH |
| MEMORIAL NUMBER: | D3 |
| ERECTED BY: | |
| ORIENTATION: | EAST |
| NUMBER OF COMPONENTS: | 2 |
| NUMBER OF INSCRIBED FACES: | 1 |
| NUMBER OF PEOPLE COMMEMORATED: | |
| MEMORIAL TYPE: | HEADSTONE |
| CONDITION OF MEMORIAL: | SOUND IN PLACE |
| CONDITION OF INSCRIPTION: | CLEAR |
| STONEMASON NAME: | |
| TECHNIQUE OF INSCRIPTION: | INCISED |
| UNDERTAKER: | |
| STONE TOP: | ARCH |
| GRAVE TYPE: | SINGLE |
| HEIGHT: | 74CM |
| WIDTH: | 14.5CM |
| THICKNESS: | 07CM |

| SURNAME: | CHRISTIAN | ADDRESS | DEATH | AGE |
|---|---|---|---|---|
| LEE | FAMILY | NEWLANES | | |

**INSCRIPTION:**
IN LOVING MEMORY
OF
THE LEE FAMILY
NEWLANES

R.I.P.

| | |
|---|---|
| NAME OF RECORDER: | PHYLLIS NOONAN AND LIZ LYNCH |
| DATE: | 11 JULY 2005 |
| PHOTO REFERENCE: | D3 |
| LOCATION/MAP REF: | D1 D3 |

| | |
|---|---|
| GRAVEYARD NAME: | **ST. MARY'S ABBEY OLD GRAVEYARD** |
| GRAVEYARD CODE: | D1 |
| COUNTY: | MEATH |
| MEMORIAL NUMBER: | D11 |
| ERECTED BY: | |
| ORIENTATION: | EAST |
| NUMBER OF COMPONENTS: | 1 |
| NUMBER OF INSCRIBED FACES: | 1 |
| NUMBER OF PEOPLE COMMEMORATED: | 1 |
| MEMORIAL TYPE: | SMALL HEADSTONE |
| CONDITION OF MEMORIAL: | SOUND IN PLACE |
| CONDITION OF INSCRIPTION: | CLEAR IN PLACES |
| STONEMASON NAME: | |
| TECHNIQUE OF INSCRIPTION: | INCISED |
| UNDERTAKER: | |
| STONE TOP: | ARCH |
| GRAVE TYPE: | SINGLE |
| HEIGHT: | 78CM |
| WIDTH: | 48CM |
| THICKNESS: | 14CM |

| SURNAME: | CHRISTIAN | ADDRESS | DEATH | AGE |
|---|---|---|---|---|
| LEE | JOHN | | 1776 | |

**INSCRIPTION:**
THIS BURIAL PLACE
BELONGETH TO JOHN
LEE AND FAMILY
1776

**SYMBOLS:**
CROSS WITH IHS

| | |
|---|---|
| NAME OF RECORDER: | PHYLLIS NOONAN |
| DATE: | 16 JULY 2005 |
| PHOTO REFERENCE: | D 11 |
| LOCATION/MAP REF: | D1 D11 |

| | |
|---|---|
| GRAVEYARD NAME: | **ST. MARY'S ABBEY OLD GRAVEYARD** |
| GRAVEYARD CODE: | D1 |
| COUNTY: | MEATH |
| MEMORIAL NUMBER: | E3 |
| ERECTED BY: | PATRICK |
| ORIENTATION: | EAST |
| NUMBER OF COMPONENTS: | 7 |
| NUMBER OF INSCRIBED FACES: | 1 |
| NUMBER OF PEOPLE COMMEMORATED: | 5 |
| MEMORIAL TYPE: | PEDESTAL |
| CONDITION OF MEMORIAL: | SOUND IN PLACE |
| CONDITION OF INSCRIPTION: | CLEAR |
| STONEMASON NAME: | |
| TECHNIQUE OF INSCRIPTION: | INCISED |
| UNDERTAKER: | |
| STONE TOP: | ELABORATE CROSS FLEUR DE LIS |
| GRAVE TYPE: | TREBLE |
| HEIGHT: | 376CM |
| WIDTH: | 64CM |
| THICKNESS: | 44CM |

| SURNAME: | CHRISTIAN | ADDRESS | DEATH | AGE |
|---|---|---|---|---|
| LENEHAN | BRIDGET | LOUGHER | 02 NOV 1906 | 45 YEARS |
| | JAMES | | 27 JUL 1925 | 35 YEARS |
| | BILLY | | 25 JAN 1929 | 34 YEARS |
| | KATIE | | 27 FEB 1931 | 42 YEARS |
| | PATRICK | | 04 DEC 1937 | 78 YEARS |

**INSCRIPTION:**
ERECTED BY
PATRICK LENEHAN OF LOUGHER
IN MEMORY OF HIS BELOVED WIFE
BRIDGET LENEHAN
WHO DEPARTED THIS LIFE
ON THE 2ND OCT 1906
AGED 45 YEARS
AND THEIR SONS
JAMES
WHO DIED 27 JULY 1925 AGED 35 YEARS
AND BILLY
WHO DIED 25 JAN 1929 AGED 34 YEARS
ALSO THEIR DAUGHTER
KATIE
WHO DIED 27 FEB 1931 AGED 42 YEARS
AND THE ABOVE NAMED
PATRICK
WHO DIED 4 DEC 1937 AGED 78 YEARS

**SYMBOLS:**
ELABORATE CROSS WITH IHS

**ORNAMENTS:**
ROPED CARVING ON
FOUR SIDES OF HEADSTONE

| | |
|---|---|
| NAME OF RECORDER: | LIZ LYNCH AND CATRIONA DILLON |
| DATE: | 16 JULY 2005 |
| PHOTO REFERENCE: | E3 |
| LOCATION/MAP REF: | D1 E3 |

| | |
|---|---|
| GRAVEYARD NAME: | **ST. MARY'S ABBEY OLD GRAVEYARD** |
| GRAVEYARD CODE: | D1 |
| COUNTY: | MEATH |
| MEMORIAL NUMBER: | B4 B |
| ERECTED BY: | |
| ORIENTATION: | EAST |
| NUMBER OF COMPONENTS: | 3 |
| NUMBER OF INSCRIBED FACES: | 1 |
| NUMBER OF PEOPLE COMMEMORATED: | 4 |
| MEMORIAL TYPE: | HEADSTONE |
| CONDITION OF MEMORIAL: | SOUND IN PLACE |
| CONDITION OF INSCRIPTION: | CLEAR |
| STONEMASON NAME: | GOGARTY DONORE |
| TECHNIQUE OF INSCRIPTION: | INCISED AND PAINTED |
| UNDERTAKER: | |
| STONE TOP: | CROSS |
| GRAVE TYPE: | TREBLE |
| HEIGHT: | 199CM |
| WIDTH: | 70CM |
| THICKNESS: | 8CM |

| SURNAME: | CHRISTIAN | ADDRESS | DEATH | AGE |
|---|---|---|---|---|
| LENEHAN | JANE | GILTOWN | 04 SEPT 1924 | |
| LENEHAN | LAURENCE | GILTOWN | 30 AUG 1939 | |
| LENEHAN | PATRICK | GILTOWN | 12 FEB 1939 | |
| MAGUIRE | ELLEN | | 25 MAY 1979 | |

**INSCRIPTION:**
ERECTED
IN LOVING MEMORY OF
JANE LENEHAN GILTOWN
DIED SEP 4TH 1924
HER HUSBAND LAURENCE LENEHAN
DIED AUG 30TH 1939
THEIR SON PATRICK
DIED FEB 12TH 1939
THEIR DAUGHTER
ELLEN MAGUIRE
DIED MAY 25TH 1979
R.I.P

**SYMBOLS:**
CENTRAL HEART CROSSED BY THORNS AND
DROPS OF BLOOD TOPPED BY FLAMES
SURROUNDING CROSS FLANKED BY
HAMMER AND 3 NAILS IN HALF TREFOIL

| | |
|---|---|
| NAME OF RECORDER: | LIZ LYNCH: |
| DATE: | 29 JUNE 2005 |
| PHOTO REFERENCE: | B4 B |
| LOCATION/MAP REF: | D1 B4B |

| | |
|---|---|
| GRAVEYARD NAME: | **ST. MARY'S ABBEY OLD GRAVEYARD** |
| GRAVEYARD CODE: | D1 |
| COUNTY: | MEATH |
| MEMORIAL NUMBER: | F22A |
| ERECTED BY: | CHRISTINA LOUGHRAN |
| ORIENTATION: | EAST |
| NUMBER OF COMPONENTS: | 2 |
| NUMBER OF INSCRIBED FACES: | 1 |
| NUMBER OF PEOPLE COMMEMORATED: | 6 |
| MEMORIAL TYPE: | HEADSTONE |
| CONDITION OF MEMORIAL: | SOUND IN PLACE |
| CONDITION OF INSCRIPTION: | CLEAR |
| STONEMASON NAME: | |
| TECHNIQUE OF INSCRIPTION: | INCISED |
| UNDERTAKER: | |
| STONE TOP: | ARCH TOP |
| GRAVE TYPE: | TREBLE |
| HEIGHT: | 113 |
| WIDTH: | 61 |
| THICKNESS: | 8CM |

| SURNAME: | CHRISTIAN | ADDRESS | DEATH | AGE |
|---|---|---|---|---|
| LOUGHRAN | JAMES | KEENOGUE | 03 JAN 1960 | 83 |
| | MARY ANNE | | 03 MAR 1942 | 60 |
| | CHRISTOPHER | | 08 JAN 1914 | 7 |
| | JOSEPHINE | | 13 APR 1934 | 14 |
| | ELLEN | | 26 JUN 1934 | 24 |
| | ALICE CHRISTINA | | 15 MAY 1989 | 83 |

**INSCRIPTION:**
IN LOVING MEMORY
OF
JAMES LOUGHRAN
KEENOGUE
DIED 3RD JAN 1960 AGED 83
HIS WIFE MARY ANNE
DIED 3RD MARCH 1942 AGED 60
THEIR SON
CHRISTOPHER
DIED 8TH JAN 1914 AGED 7
THEIR DAUGHTERS
JOSEPHINE
DIED 26TH JUNE 1934 AGED 24
ALICE CHRISTINA LOUGHRAN
DIED 15TH MAY 1989 AGED 83
RIP

**SYMBOLS:**
CROSS WITH IHS IN CIRCLE

| | |
|---|---|
| NAME OF RECORDER: | PHYLLIS NOONAN: |
| DATE: | 20 JULY 2005 |
| PHOTO REFERENCE: | F22A |
| LOCATION/MAP REF: | D1 F22A |

| | |
|---|---|
| GRAVEYARD NAME: | **ST. MARY'S ABBEY OLD GRAVEYARD** |
| GRAVEYARD CODE: | D1 |
| COUNTY: | MEATH |
| DENOMINATION: | |
| MEMORIAL NUMBER: | F22B |
| ERECTED BY: | |
| ORIENTATION: | EAST |
| NUMBER OF COMPONENTS: | 1 |
| NUMBER OF INSCRIBED FACES: | 1 |
| NUMBER OF PEOPLE COMMEMORATED: | 1 |
| MEMORIAL TYPE: | LOW MONUMENT |
| CONDITION OF MEMORIAL: | SOUND IN PLACE |
| CONDITION OF INSCRIPTION: | CLEAR |
| STONEMASON NAME: | |
| TECHNIQUE OF INSCRIPTION: | INCISED |
| UNDERTAKER: | |
| STONE TOP: | LOW MONUMENT |
| GRAVE TYPE: | TREBLE |
| HEIGHT: | LENGTH 183CM |
| WIDTH: | 75CM |
| THICKNESS: | |

PEOPLE RECORDED:

| SURNAME: | CHRISTIAN | ADDRESS | DEATH | AGE |
|---|---|---|---|---|
| LOUGHRAN | FRANK | | 13 JUNE 2001 | |

**INSCRIPTION:**
IN LOVING MEMORY
OF
FRANK LOUGHRAN
21 – 8 -1916
13 – 6- 2001

ETERNAL REST GRANT
UNTO HIM O'LORD

**SYMBOLS:**
CROSS

| | |
|---|---|
| NAME OF RECORDER: | PHYLLIS NOONAN |
| DATE: | 19 JULY 2005 |
| PHOTO REFERENCE: | F22B |
| LOCATION/MAP REF: | D1 F22B |

| | |
|---|---|
| GRAVEYARD NAME: | **ST. MARY'S ABBEY OLD GRAVEYARD** |
| GRAVEYARD CODE: | D1 |
| COUNTY: | MEATH |
| MEMORIAL NUMBER: | F22C |
| ERECTED BY: | |
| ORIENTATION: | EAST |
| NUMBER OF COMPONENTS: | 1 |
| NUMBER OF INSCRIBED FACES: | 1 |
| NUMBER OF PEOPLE COMMEMORATED: | 1 |
| MEMORIAL TYPE: | LOW MONUMENT |
| CONDITION OF MEMORIAL: | SOUND IN PLACE |
| CONDITION OF INSCRIPTION: | CLEAR |
| STONEMASON NAME: | |
| TECHNIQUE OF INSCRIPTION: | INCISED |
| UNDERTAKER: | |
| STONE TOP: | LOW MONUMENT |
| GRAVE TYPE: | TREBLE |
| HEIGHT: | LENGTH 183CM |
| WIDTH: | 75CM |

| SURNAME: | CHRISTIAN | ADDRESS | DEATH | AGE |
|---|---|---|---|---|
| LOUGHRAN | EVELYN | | 14 FEB 2006 | |

**INSCRIPTION:**
IN LOVING MEMORY
OF
EVELYN LOUGHRAN
18 -9 -1929
14 -2 -2006

MAY PERPETUAL LIGHT
SHINE UPON HER

**SYMBOLS:**
CROSS

| | |
|---|---|
| NAME OF RECORDER: | PHYLLIS NOONAN AND LIZ LYNCH |
| DATE: | 18 JULY 2006 |
| PHOTO REFERENCE: | F22C |
| LOCATION/MAP REF: | D1 F22C |

| | |
|---|---|
| GRAVEYARD NAME: | **ST. MARY'S ABBEY OLD GRAVEYARD** |
| GRAVEYARD CODE: | D1 |
| COUNTY: | MEATH |
| MEMORIAL NUMBER: | B15 |
| ERECTED BY: | |
| ORIENTATION: | EAST |
| NUMBER OF COMPONENTS: | 3 |
| NUMBER OF INSCRIBED FACES: | 1 |
| NUMBER OF PEOPLE COMMEMORATED: | 4 |
| MEMORIAL TYPE: | HEADSTONE |
| CONDITION OF MEMORIAL: | SOUND IN PLACE |
| CONDITION OF INSCRIPTION: | CLEAR |
| STONEMASON NAME: | T. REID DONORE |
| TECHNIQUE OF INSCRIPTION: | INLAID |
| UNDERTAKER: | |
| STONE TOP: | FLAT |
| GRAVE TYPE: | QUAD FOUR |
| HEIGHT: | 104CM |
| WIDTH: | 71CM |
| THICKNESS: | 5CM |

| SURNAME: | CHRISTIAN | ADDRESS | DEATH | AGE |
|---|---|---|---|---|
| LYNCH | THOMAS | GASKINSTOWN | 08 FEB 1972 | 78 |
| | ELIZABETH | | | |
| | BERNADETTE | | | |
| | TERESA | | 10 NOV 1974 | 81 |

**INSCRIPTION:**

IN LOVING MEMORY
OF
THOMAS LYNCH
GASKINSTOWN
WHO DIED 8TH FEB 1972
AGED 78 YEARS
HIS MOTHER ELIZABETH
HIS DAUGHTER BERNADETTE
HIS WIFE TERESA DIED
10TH NOV 1974 AGED 81 YEARS
R.I.P.

**SYMBOLS:**

CROSS

| | |
|---|---|
| NAME OF RECORDER: | JANET LEIGH AND HELEN FULLAM |
| DATE: | 02 JULY 2005 |
| PHOTO REFERENCE: | B15 |
| LOCATION/MAP REF: | D1 B15 |

| | |
|---|---|
| GRAVEYARD NAME: | **ST. MARY'S ABBEY OLD GRAVEYARD** |
| GRAVEYARD CODE: | D1 |
| COUNTY: | MEATH |
| MEMORIAL NUMBER: | E2 |
| ERECTED BY: | T. LYNCH |
| ORIENTATION: | EAST |
| NUMBER OF COMPONENTS: | COLLAPSED CROSS |
| NUMBER OF INSCRIBED FACES: | 1 |
| NUMBER OF PEOPLE COMMEMORATED: | 2 |
| MEMORIAL TYPE: | HEADSTONE CROSS |
| CONDITION OF MEMORIAL: | COLLAPSED |
| CONDITION OF INSCRIPTION: | MAINLY DECIPHERABLE |
| STONEMASON NAME: | |
| TECHNIQUE OF INSCRIPTION: | INCISED |
| UNDERTAKER: | |
| STONE TOP: | CROSS |
| GRAVE TYPE: | SINGLE |
| HEIGHT: | 128CM |
| WIDTH: | 72CM |
| THICKNESS: | 15CM |

| SURNAME: | CHRISTIAN | ADDRESS | DEATH | AGE |
|---|---|---|---|---|
| LYNCH | BERNADETTE | | | |
| | ELIZABETH | | | |

**INSCRIPTION:**
IN
LOVING
MEMORY
OF
MY DAUGHTER BERNADETTE
AND MY MOTHER ELIZABETH LYNCH

**SYMBOLS:**

| | |
|---|---|
| NAME OF RECORDER: | SINEAD FULLAM AND HELEN FULLAM |
| DATE: | 16 JULY 2005 |
| PHOTO REFERENCE: | E2 |
| LOCATION/MAP REF: | D1 E2 |

| | |
|---|---|
| GRAVEYARD NAME: | **ST. MARY'S ABBEY OLD GRAVEYARD** |
| GRAVEYARD CODE: | D1 |
| COUNTY: | MEATH |
| MEMORIAL NUMBER: | K45 |
| ERECTED BY: | JAMES LYNCH |
| ORIENTATION: | EAST |
| NUMBER OF COMPONENTS: | 1 |
| NUMBER OF INSCRIBED FACES: | 1 |
| NUMBER OF PEOPLE COMMEMORATED: | 11 + |
| MEMORIAL TYPE: | LOW MONUMENT |
| CONDITION OF MEMORIAL: | SOUND IN PLACE |
| CONDITION OF INSCRIPTION: | MAINLY DECIPHERABLE |
| STONEMASON NAME: | |
| TECHNIQUE OF INSCRIPTION: | INCISED |
| UNDERTAKER: | |
| STONE TOP: | LOW MONUMENT |
| GRAVE TYPE: | SINGLE |
| HEIGHT: | 222CM |
| WIDTH: | 98CM |
| THICKNESS: | 08CM |

| SURNAME: | CHRISTIAN | ADDRESS | DEATH | AGE |
|---|---|---|---|---|
| LYNCH | WALTER | NEWLANES | 08 NOV 1810 | |
| | MARGARET | | 15 DEC 1836 | |
| | KATE | | 01 MAR 1862 | |
| | 8 CHILDREN OF WALTER AND MARGARET LYNCH | | | |

**INSCRIPTION:**
+ IHS
THIS TOMB WAS PLACED HERE
BY JAMES LYNCH OF NEWLANES IN
MEMORY OF HIS FATHER WALTER WHO
DIED NOVR 8TH 1810 AND HIS MOTHER
MARGARET WHO DIED DECR 15TH 1836
ALSO 8 OF THEIR CHILDREN
HERE ALSO LIE THE REMAINS OF HIS
ANCESTORS HERE ALSO LIETH THE
REMAINS OF KATE THE BELOVED WIFE
OF THE ABOVE JAMES LYNCH WHO DIED
MARCH 1ST 1862
*MAY THEY REST IN PEACE*

| | |
|---|---|
| NAME OF RECORDER: | SHAUN LYNCH |
| DATE: | 06 MAY 2006 |
| PHOTO REFERENCE: | K45 |
| LOCATION/MAP REF: | D1 K45 |

| | |
|---|---|
| GRAVEYARD NAME: | **ST. MARY'S ABBEY OLD GRAVEYARD** |
| GRAVEYARD CODE: | D1 |
| COUNTY: | MEATH |
| MEMORIAL NUMBER: | K44 |
| ERECTED BY: | |
| ORIENTATION: | EAST |
| NUMBER OF COMPONENTS: | 1 |
| NUMBER OF INSCRIBED FACES: | 1 |
| NUMBER OF PEOPLE COMMEMORATED: | 4 |
| MEMORIAL TYPE: | LOW MONUMENT |
| CONDITION OF MEMORIAL: | SOUND IN PLACE |
| CONDITION OF INSCRIPTION: | MAINLY DECIPHERABLE |
| STONEMASON NAME: | |
| TECHNIQUE OF INSCRIPTION: | INCISED |
| UNDERTAKER: | |
| STONE TOP: | LOW MONUMENT |
| GRAVE TYPE: | SINGLE |
| HEIGHT: | 222CM |
| WIDTH: | 98CM |
| THICKNESS: | 05CM |

| SURNAME: | CHRISTIAN | ADDRESS | DEATH | AGE |
|---|---|---|---|---|
| LYNCH | PATRICK | BALRATH | 12 NOV 1812 | |
| | MARGARET | | 19 DEC 1819 | |
| | HUGH | | 30 AUG 1847 | |
| | MICHAEL | | 14 JUN 1873 | |

**INSCRIPTION:**
+ IHS
THIS TOMB WAS PLACED HERE BY MICHAEL
LYNCH OF BALRATH IN MEMORY OF HIS FATHER
PATRICK LYNCH WHO DIED NOV 12TH 1812
AND OF HIS MOTHER MARGARET LYNCH WHO
DIED DECR 19 1819 ALSO HIS BROTHER HUGH
LYNCH WHO DIED AUG 30TH 1847
THE ABOVE NAMED MICHAEL LYNCH
DEPARTED THIS LIFE 14TH JUNE 1873
*MAY THEY REST IN PEACE*

| | |
|---|---|
| NAME OF RECORDER: | SINEAD FULLAM AND JANET LEIGH |
| DATE: | 06 MAY 2006 |
| PHOTO REFERENCE: | K44 |
| LOCATION/MAP REF: | D1 K44 |

| | |
|---|---|
| GRAVEYARD NAME: | **ST. MARY'S ABBEY OLD GRAVEYARD** |
| GRAVEYARD CODE: | D1 |
| COUNTY: | MEATH |
| MEMORIAL NUMBER: | K47 |
| ERECTED BY: | RICHARD LYNCH |
| ORIENTATION: | EAST |
| NUMBER OF COMPONENTS: | 1 |
| NUMBER OF INSCRIBED FACES: | 1 |
| NUMBER OF PEOPLE COMMEMORATED: | 1 |
| MEMORIAL TYPE: | HEADSTONE |
| CONDITION OF MEMORIAL: | SOUND IN PLACE |
| CONDITION OF INSCRIPTION: | CLEAR |
| STONEMASON NAME: | |
| TECHNIQUE OF INSCRIPTION: | INCISED |
| UNDERTAKER: | |
| STONE TOP: | ROUND |
| GRAVE TYPE: | SINGLE |
| HEIGHT: | 121CM |
| WIDTH: | 60CM |
| THICKNESS: | 13CM |

| SURNAME: | CHRISTIAN | ADRESS | DEATH | AGE |
|---|---|---|---|---|
| LYNCH | MARGRET | | 25 APRIL 1771 | 26 |

**INSCRIPTION:**
THIS STONE AND BURIAL
PLACE BELONGETH TO
RICHARD LYNCH AND
HIS POSTERITY LIKEWISE
HERE LYETH THE BODY
OF HIS DAUGHTER MARGRET
LYNCH WHO DEPARTED
THIS LIFE ON THE 25TH APRIL
AND IN THE YEAR OF OUR LORD
1771 AND IN THE 26TH YEAR OF
HER AGE DIED

**SYMBOLS:**
IHS SUNBURST HEART IN CENTRE
SCALLOP ON EDGE OF STONE

| | |
|---|---|
| NAME OF RECORDER: | SINEAD FULLAM AND JANET LEIGH |
| DATE: | 06 MAY 2006 |
| PHOTO REFERENCE: | K47 |
| LOCATION/MAP REF: | D1 K47 |

| | |
|---|---|
| GRAVEYARD NAME: | **ST. MARY'S ABBEY OLD GRAVEYARD** |
| GRAVEYARD CODE: | D1 |
| COUNTY: | MEATH |
| MEMORIAL NUMBER: | L37 |
| ERECTED BY: | BRYAN LYNCH |
| ORIENTATION: | EAST |
| NUMBER OF COMPONENTS: | 1 |
| NUMBER OF INSCRIBED FACES: | 1 |
| NUMBER OF PEOPLE COMMEMORATED: | 4 |
| MEMORIAL TYPE: | HEADSTONE |
| CONDITION OF MEMORIAL: | SOUND IN PLACE |
| CONDITION OF INSCRIPTION: | MAINLY DECIPHERABLE |
| STONEMASON NAME: | |
| TECHNIQUE OF INSCRIPTION: | INCISED |
| UNDERTAKER: | |
| STONE TOP: | ROUND |
| GRAVE TYPE: | SINGLE |
| HEIGHT: | 127CM |
| WIDTH: | 66CM |
| THICKNESS: | 09CM |

| SURNAME: | CHRISTIAN | ADDRESS | DEATH | AGE |
|---|---|---|---|---|
| LYNCH | ROSE | | 28 DEC 1786 | 55 |
| | PATRICK | | 18 MAR 1775 | 79 |
| MADDEN | JANE | | 20 MAR 1778 | 28 |
| LYNCH | JOHN | | 20 MAR 1778 | 28 |

**INSCRIPTION:**
THIS STONE AND BURIAL PLACE BE
LONG TO BRYAN LYNCH OF LEHORNA
AND COUNTY OF MEATH AND HIS POS
TERITY HERE LIETH THE BODY OF HIS
MOTHER ROSE LYNCH WHO DEPARTED
THIS LIFE THE 28TH OF DECMR 1786 AGED
55 YEARS
HERE ALSO LIETH THE BODY
OF HIS FATHER PATTK LYNCH WHO DEPARTED
THIS LIFE THE 18TH MARCH 1775 AGED
79 YEARS HERE LIKEWISE LIETH THE BODY OF JANE
MADDEN WIFE OF BARTHOLW MADDEN AND
SISTER OF THE ABOVE BRYAN SHE DE
PARTED THIS LIFE THE 20TH MARCH 1778 AGED
28 YEARS AND ALSO THE BODY OF JOHN LYNCH
WHO DEPARTED THIS LIFE THE 20TH MARCH
1778 AGED 28 YEARS MAY THE LORD BE
PROTECTION
UNTO THEM AMEN

**SYMBOLS:**
IHS IN SUNBURST

| | |
|---|---|
| NAME OF RECORDER: | HELEN FULLAM, BEN RYAN AND JANET LEIGH |
| DATE: | 27 MAY 2006 |
| PHOTO REFERENCE: | L37 |
| LOCATION/MAP REF: | D1 L37 |

| | |
|---|---|
| GRAVEYARD NAME: | **ST. MARY'S ABBEY OLD GRAVEYARD** |
| GRAVEYARD CODE: | D1 |
| COUNTY: | MEATH |
| MEMORIAL NUMBER: | D17 |
| ERECTED BY: | JAMES LYNCH |
| ORIENTATION: | EAST |
| NUMBER OF COMPONENTS: | 1 |
| NUMBER OF INSCRIBED FACES: | 1 |
| NUMBER OF PEOPLE COMMEMORATED: | 1 |
| MEMORIAL TYPE: | HEADSTONE |
| CONDITION OF MEMORIAL: | SOUND IN PLACE |
| CONDITION OF INSCRIPTION: | LEGIBLE |
| STONEMASON NAME: | |
| TECHNIQUE OF INSCRIPTION: | INCISED |
| UNDERTAKER: | |
| STONE TOP: | ROUND |
| GRAVE TYPE: | SINGLE |
| HEIGHT: | 57CM |
| WIDTH: | 46CM |
| THICKNESS: | 10CM |

| SURNAME: | CHRISTIAN | ADDRESS | DEATH | AGE |
|---|---|---|---|---|
| LYNCH | MARY | DOWNSTOWN | 31 JAN 1919 | |

**INSCRIPTION:**

ERECTED
JAMES LYNCH
DOWNSTOWN
IN MEMORY OF HIS WIFE MARY
WHO DIED JANUARY 31ST 1919

| | |
|---|---|
| NAME OF RECORDER: | PHYLLIS NOONAN |
| DATE: | 13 JULY 2005 |
| PHOTO REFERENCE: | D17 |
| LOCATION/MAP REF: | D1 D17 |

| | |
|---|---|
| GRAVEYARD NAME: | **ST. MARY'S ABBEY OLD GRAVEYARD** |
| GRAVEYARD CODE: | D1 |
| COUNTY: | MEATH |
| MEMORIAL NUMBER: | D1 |
| ERECTED BY: | |
| ORIENTATION: | EAST |
| NUMBER OF COMPONENTS: | 1 |
| NUMBER OF INSCRIBED FACES: | 1 |
| NUMBER OF PEOPLE COMMEMORATED: | 2 |
| MEMORIAL TYPE: | SMALL HEADSTONE |
| CONDITION OF MEMORIAL: | COLLAPSED IN PLACE |
| CONDITION OF INSCRIPTION: | CLEAR |
| STONEMASON NAME: | |
| TECHNIQUE OF INSCRIPTION: | INCISED |
| UNDERTAKER: | |
| STONE TOP: | ARCH |
| GRAVE TYPE: | SINGLE |
| HEIGHT: | 19CM |
| WIDTH: | 42CM |
| THICKNESS: | 5CM |

| SURNAME: | CHRISTIAN | ADDRESS | DEATH | AGE |
|---|---|---|---|---|
| MACARAW | FRANCIS | | | |
| MACARAW DWYER | MINNIE | | | |

**INSCRIPTION:**
TO THE MEMORY OF
FRANCIS
AND
MINNIE (DWYER) MACARAW

*NO ONE EVER HOPED IN THE LORD AND WAS CONFOUNDED*
*REST IN PEACE*

| | |
|---|---|
| NAME OF RECORDER: | PHYLLIS NOONAN |
| DATE: | 16 JULY 2005 |
| PHOTO REFERENCE: | D1 |
| LOCATION/MAP REF: | D1 D1 |

| | |
|---|---|
| GRAVEYARD NAME: | **ST. MARY'S ABBEY OLD GRAVEYARD** |
| GRAVEYARD CODE: | D1 |
| COUNTY: | MEATH |
| MEMORIAL NUMBER: | B4 A |
| ERECTED BY: | |
| ORIENTATION: | EAST |
| NUMBER OF COMPONENTS: | 3 |
| NUMBER OF INSCRIBED FACES: | 1 |
| NUMBER OF PEOPLE COMMEMORATED: | 2 |
| MEMORIAL TYPE: | HEADSTONE |
| CONDITION OF MEMORIAL: | SOUND IN PLACE |
| CONDITION OF INSCRIPTION: | MINT |
| STONEMASON NAME: | |
| TECHNIQUE OF INSCRIPTION: | INCISED AND PAINTED |
| UNDERTAKER: | |
| STONE TOP: | ELABORATE CROSS |
| GRAVE TYPE: | TREBLE |
| HEIGHT: | 210CM |
| WIDTH: | 69CM |
| THICKNESS: | 10CM |

| SURNAME: | CHRISTIAN | ADDRESS | DEATH | AGE |
|---|---|---|---|---|
| MAGUIRE | ELLEN | GILTOWN | 25 MAY 1979 | |
| MAGUIRE | JOHN | GILTOWN | 01 JUN 2003 | |

**INSCRIPTION:**
JESUS HAVE MERCY
IN
LOVING MEMORY
OF
ELLEN MAGUIRE
GILTOWN
DIED 25TH MAY 1979
HER HUSBAND JOHN
DIED 1ST JUNE 2003

R.I.P.

**SYMBOLS:**
HEART WITH THORNS CROSS AND FLAMES
BLOOD DROPS ON HEART WITH HAMMER
AND 3 NAILS IN HALF TREFOIL ON EACH
SIDE

| | |
|---|---|
| NAME OF RECORDER: | PHYLLIS NOONAN AND LIZ LYNCH |
| DATE: | 29 JUNE 2005 |
| PHOTO REFERENCE: | B4 A |
| LOCATION/MAP REF: | D1 B4A |

| | |
|---|---|
| GRAVEYARD NAME: | **ST. MARY'S ABBEY OLD GRAVEYARD** |
| GRAVEYARD CODE: | D1 |
| COUNTY: | MEATH |
| MEMORIAL NUMBER: | D9 |
| ERECTED BY: | |
| ORIENTATION: | EAST |
| NUMBER OF COMPONENTS: | 1 |
| NUMBER OF INSCRIBED FACES: | 1 |
| NUMBER OF PEOPLE COMMEMORATED: | 5 |
| MEMORIAL TYPE: | HEADSTONE |
| CONDITION OF MEMORIAL: | SOUND IN PLACE |
| CONDITION OF INSCRIPTION: | CLEAR |
| STONEMASON NAME: | |
| TECHNIQUE OF INSCRIPTION: | INCISED |
| UNDERTAKER: | |
| STONE TOP: | WINGED |
| GRAVE TYPE: | SINGLE |
| HEIGHT: | 102CM |
| WIDTH: | 73CM |
| THICKNESS: | 20CM -14CM |

| SURNAME: | CHRISTIAN | ADDRESS | DEATH | AGE |
|---|---|---|---|---|
| MAGUIRE | THOMAS | HILLTOWN | 11 JUN 1784 | 79 |
| MAGUIRE | MARY | | 28 MAR 1778 | 69 |
| | CHILD | | | |
| | CHILD | | | |
| | CHILD | | | |

**INSCRIPTION:**
THIS BURIAL PLACE BELONGETH
TO THOS MAGUIRE OF HILLLTOWN
AND HIS POSTERITY WHERE LIETH
THREE OF HIS CHILDREN 1759
ALSO MARY WIFE OF THE ABOVE
THOMAS WHO DEPARTED THIS
LIFE 28TH MARCH 1778 AGED
69 YEARS ALSO THE SAID THOMAS
WHO DEPARTED THIS LIFE 11TH JUNE
1784 AGED 79 YEARS

**SYMBOLS:**
2 IHS WITH CROSSES

| | |
|---|---|
| NAME OF RECORDER: | PHYLLIS NOONAN AND LIZ LYNCH |
| DATE: | 11 JULY 2005 |
| PHOTO REFERENCE: | D9 |
| LOCATION/MAP REF: | D1 D9 |

| | |
|---|---|
| GRAVEYARD NAME: | **ST. MARY'S ABBEY OLD GRAVEYARD** |
| GRAVEYARD CODE: | D1 |
| COUNTY: | MEATH |
| MEMORIAL NUMBER: | K41 |
| ERECTED BY: | |
| ORIENTATION: | EAST |
| NUMBER OF COMPONENTS: | 1 |
| NUMBER OF INSCRIBED FACES: | 1 |
| NUMBER OF PEOPLE COMMEMORATED: | 4 |
| MEMORIAL TYPE: | HEADSTONE |
| CONDITION OF MEMORIAL: | SOUND |
| CONDITION OF INSCRIPTION: | CLEAR |
| STONEMASON NAME: | |
| TECHNIQUE OF INSCRIPTION: | INCISED |
| UNDERTAKER: | |
| STONE TOP: | POINTED |
| GRAVE TYPE: | DOUBLE |
| HEIGHT: | 86CM |
| WIDTH: | 50CM |
| THICKNESS: | 03CM |

| SURNAME: | CHRISTIAN | ADDRESS | DEATH | AGE |
|---|---|---|---|---|
| MARTIN | WILLIAM | GASKINSTOWN | | |
| | MARGARET | | | |
| | OWEN | | | |
| | PATRICK | | | |

**INSCRIPTION:**

IN LOVING MEMORY OF
WILLIAM MARTIN
GASKINSTOWN
HIS WIFE MARGARET
AND THEIR SONS
OWEN AND PATRICK
R.I.P.

**SYMBOLS:**

SMALL CROSS INCISED AT TOP OF STONE

| | |
|---|---|
| NAME OF RECORDER: | PHYLLIS NOONAN |
| DATE: | 24 APRIL 2006 |
| PHOTO REFERENCE: | K41 |
| LOCATION/MAP REF: | D1 K41 |

| | |
|---|---|
| GRAVEYARD NAME: | **ST. MARY'S ABBEY OLD GRAVEYARD** |
| GRAVEYARD CODE: | D1 |
| COUNTY: | MEATH |
| MEMORIAL NUMBER: | F4 |
| ERECTED BY: | WIFE OF THOMAS MATHEWS |
| ORIENTATION: | EAST |
| NUMBER OF COMPONENTS: | 1 |
| NUMBER OF INSCRIBED FACES: | 1 |
| NUMBER OF PEOPLE COMMEMORATED: | 2 |
| MEMORIAL TYPE: | LOW MONUMENT |
| CONDITION OF MEMORIAL: | BROKEN IN 6 PIECES IN PLACE |
| CONDITION OF INSCRIPTION: | MAINLY DECIPHERABLE |
| STONEMASON NAME: | |
| TECHNIQUE OF INSCRIPTION: | INCISED |
| UNDERTAKER: | |
| STONE TOP: | LOW MONUMENT |
| GRAVE TYPE: | SINGLE |
| HEIGHT: | 207CM |
| WIDTH: | 107CM |
| THICKNESS: | 08CM |

| SURNAME: | CHRISTIAN | ADDRESS | DEATH | AGE |
|---|---|---|---|---|
| MATHEWS | THOMAS | CITY OF DUBLIN IRONMONGER | 25 NOV 1801 | |
| | THOMAS | COUNTY OF DUBLIN | 07 NOV 1817 | |
| | | | | |

**INSCRIPTION:**
GLORIA IN EXCELSIS
HERE LIETH THE REMAINS OF THOMAS
MATHEWS OF THE CITY OF DUBLIN IRONMONGER
WHO DEPARTED THIS LIFE THE 25TH NOVBR.
1801 AGED --? YEARS
ALSO HIS SON THOMAS MATHEWS
OF DUNL—LOW COUNTY DUBLIN
WHO IN THE BLOOM OF YOUTH WAS
BY ACCIDENTAL DEATH CUT OFF
IN HIM SOCIETY HAS LOST A PROUD ADORNMENT
TENDER IN YEARS – SAGE IN OLD - TOLI
THE SUM OF HIS TALENTS
HAD NOT REACHED ITS MERIDIAN WHEN IT
CEASED TO SHINE
DEPARTED THIS LIFE THE 7TH NOV 1811
LEAVING HIS AFFLICTED MOTHER TO DEPLORE HER LOSS
WHO HAS ERECTED THIS TOMB TO THEIR MEMORY
......CANT IN PACE. AMEN

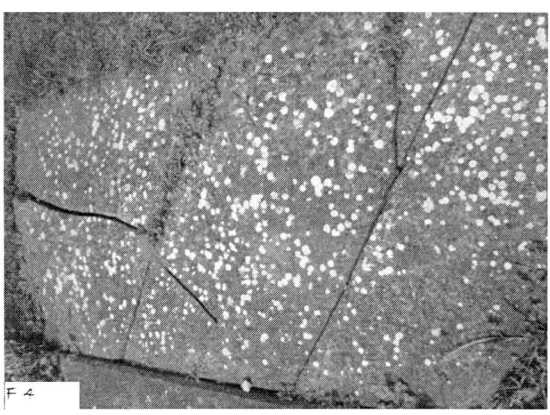

| | |
|---|---|
| NAME OF RECORDER: | PHYLLIS NOONAN AND BEN RYAN |
| DATE: | 18 JULY 2005 |
| PHOTO REFERENCE: | F4 |
| LOCATION/MAP REF: | D1 F4 |

| | |
|---|---|
| GRAVEYARD NAME: | **ST. MARY'S ABBEY OLD GRAVEYARD** |
| GRAVEYARD CODE: | D1 |
| COUNTY: | MEATH |
| MEMORIAL NUMBER: | L7 |
| ERECTED BY: | |
| ORIENTATION: | EAST |
| NUMBER OF COMPONENTS: | 1 |
| NUMBER OF INSCRIBED FACES: | 1 |
| NUMBER OF PEOPLE COMMEMORATED: | 2 |
| MEMORIAL TYPE: | HEADSTONE |
| CONDITION OF MEMORIAL: | SOUND IN PLACE |
| CONDITION OF INSCRIPTION: | CLEAR |
| STONEMASON NAME: | |
| TECHNIQUE OF INSCRIPTION: | INCISED |
| UNDERTAKER: | |
| STONE TOP: | ROUND |
| GRAVE TYPE: | TREBLE |
| HEIGHT: | 97CM |
| WIDTH: | 45CM |
| THICKNESS: | 05CM |

| SURNAME: | CHRISTIAN | ADDRESS | DEATH | AGE |
|---|---|---|---|---|
| MATTHEWS | EILEEN | | 25 OCT 1952 | |
| | MICHAEL | | 16 APR 1957 | |

**INSCRIPTION:**
IN
LOVING MEMORY OF
EILEEN MATTHEWS
DIED 25 OCT 1952
HER HUSBAND MICHAEL
DIED 16 APRIL 1957

R.I.P

**SYMBOLS:**
SACRED HEART IN CIRCLE SURROUNDED
BY IVY LEAVES

| | |
|---|---|
| NAME OF RECORDER: | JANET LEIGH |
| DATE: | 17 MAY 2006 |
| PHOTO REFERENCE: | L7 |
| LOCATION/MAP REF: | D1 L7 |

| | |
|---|---|
| GRAVEYARD NAME: | **ST. MARY'S ABBEY OLD GRAVEYARD** |
| GRAVEYARD CODE: | D1 |
| COUNTY: | MEATH |
| MEMORIAL NUMBER: | K18 |
| ERECTED BY: | JAMES MCCABE DULEEK |
| ORIENTATION: | EAST |
| NUMBER OF COMPONENTS: | 1 |
| NUMBER OF INSCRIBED FACES: | 1 |
| NUMBER OF PEOPLE COMMEMORATED: | 3 |
| MEMORIAL TYPE: | HEADSTONE |
| CONDITION OF MEMORIAL: | SOUND |
| CONDITION OF INSCRIPTION: | CLEAR |
| STONEMASON NAME: | |
| TECHNIQUE OF INSCRIPTION: | INCISED |
| UNDERTAKER: | |
| STONE TOP: | ROUND |
| GRAVE TYPE: | SINGLE |
| HEIGHT: | 91CM |
| WIDTH: | 71CM |
| THICKNESS: | 13CM |

| SURNAME: | CHRISTIAN | ADDRESS | DEATH | AGE |
|---|---|---|---|---|
| MCCABE | FATHER | | 1895 | |
| | MOTHER | | 1893 | |
| | BROTHER | | 1892 | |
| | | | | |

**INSCRIPTION:**
ERECTED
BY JAMES MCCABE DULEEK IN
MEMORY OF HIS FATHER AND MOTHER
WHO DIED 1895 THE LATTER
DIED 1893 AND HIS BROTHER DIED 1892

**SYMBOLS:**
CROSS OVER IHS IN DISK WINGED ANGEL HEADS

| | |
|---|---|
| NAME OF RECORDER: | PHYLLIS NOONAN |
| DATE: | 24 SEPT 2005 |
| PHOTO REFERENCE: | K18 |
| LOCATION/MAP REF: | D1 K18 |

| | |
|---|---|
| GRAVEYARD NAME: | **ST. MARY'S ABBEY OLD GRAVEYARD** |
| GRAVEYARD CODE: | D1 |
| COUNTY: | MEATH |
| MEMORIAL NUMBER: | L38 |
| ERECTED BY: | |
| ORIENTATION: | EAST |
| NUMBER OF COMPONENTS: | 5 |
| NUMBER OF INSCRIBED FACES: | 1 |
| NUMBER OF PEOPLE COMMEMORATED: | 8 |
| MEMORIAL TYPE: | HEADSTONE |
| CONDITION OF MEMORIAL: | SOUND IN PLACE |
| CONDITION OF INSCRIPTION: | MAINLY DECIPHERABLE |
| STONEMASON NAME: | |
| TECHNIQUE OF INSCRIPTION: | INCISED |
| UNDERTAKER: | |
| STONE TOP: | CROSS |
| GRAVE TYPE: | SINGLE |
| HEIGHT: | 256CM |
| WIDTH: | 57CM |
| THICKNESS: | 20CM |

| SURNAME: | CHRISTIAN | ADDRESS | DEATH | AGE |
|---|---|---|---|---|
| MCCABE | THOMAS | | 01 APR 1882 | |
| | BRIDGET | | 04 JUN 1896 | |
| | JOHN | | 28 MAY 1882 | |
| | JAMES | | 04 MAR 1884 | |
| | MARGARET | | 09 MAY 1899 | |
| MURPHY | MARGARET | | 02 SEPT 1902 | |
| MCCABE | MICHAEL | | 25 JAN 1919 | |
| GOGARTY | MARYANNE | | 18 DEC 1927 | |

**INSCRIPTION:**
SACRED
TO THE MEMORY OF
THOMAS MCCABE
DIED 1 APRIL 1882 HIS DAUGHTER
BRIDGET
DIED 4 JUNE 1896 HIS BROTHER
JOHN MCCABE
DIED 28 MAY 1882 AND HIS SON
JAMES
DIED 4 MARCH 1884
ALSO HIS WIFE
MARGARET MCCABE
DIED 9 MAY 1899
AND HIS DAUGHTER
MARGARET MURPHY
DIED 2 SEP 1902
ALSO HIS SON MICHAEL MCCABE
WHO DIED JAN 25TH 1919
AND HIS DAUGHTER
MARYANNE GOGARTY
WHO DIED DEC 18TH 1927
R.I.P.

**SYMBOLS:**
CELTIC CROSS AT TOP OF ARCH HEADSTONE
LAMB LYING ON CROSS

| | |
|---|---|
| NAME OF RECORDER: | BEN RYAN, HELEN FULLAM AND JANET LEIGH |
| DATE: | 27 MAY 2006 |
| PHOTO REFERENCE: | L38 |
| LOCATION/MAP REF: | D1 L38 |

| | |
|---|---|
| GRAVEYARD NAME: | **ST. MARY'S ABBEY OLD GRAVEYARD** |
| GRAVEYARD CODE: | D1 |
| COUNTY: | MEATH |
| MEMORIAL NUMBER: | C5 |
| ERECTED BY: | |
| ORIENTATION: | EAST |
| NUMBER OF COMPONENTS: | 2 |
| NUMBER OF INSCRIBED FACES: | 1 |
| NUMBER OF PEOPLE COMMEMORATED: | 5 |
| MEMORIAL TYPE: | HEADSTONE |
| CONDITION OF MEMORIAL: | SOUND IN PLACE |
| CONDITION OF INSCRIPTION: | CLEAR |
| STONEMASON NAME: | |
| TECHNIQUE OF INSCRIPTION: | INCISED AND PAINTED |
| UNDERTAKER: | |
| STONE TOP: | ARCHED |
| GRAVE TYPE: | TREBLE |
| HEIGHT: | 95CM |
| WIDTH: | 50CM |
| THICKNESS: | 04CM |

| SURNAME: | CHRISTIAN | ADDRESS | DEATH | AGE |
|---|---|---|---|---|
| MCCOURT | JOHN | GARBALLAGH, DULEEK | 18 MAY 1938 | |
| MCCOURT | MARY | | 04 MAY 1947 | |
| | PATRICK | | 12 OCT.1951 | |
| | CONOR | | 12 OCT.1951 | |
| | MARY | | 12 OCT.1951 | |
| | PEGGIE | | | |

**INSCRIPTION:**
IN LOVING MEMORY OF
JOHN MCCOURT
GARBALLAGH, DULEEK
WHO DIED 18 MAY 1938
HIS WIFE MARY DIED
4TH MAY 1947 THEIR SONS
PATRICK AND CONNOR
THEIR DAUGHTER MARY
DIED 12TH OCT.1951 AND
THEIR GRANDCHILD PEGGIE

R.I.P

**SYMBOLS:**
HEART CROSS, FLAMES IN CIRCLE FLANKED BY FLOWERS

| | |
|---|---|
| NAME OF RECORDER: | PHYLLIS NOONAN AND JIM ORTEN |
| DATE: | 06 JULY 2005 |
| PHOTO REFERENCE: | C5 |
| LOCATION/MAP REF: | D1 C5 |

| | |
|---|---|
| GRAVEYARD NAME: | **ST. MARY'S ABBEY OLD GRAVEYARD** |
| GRAVEYARD CODE: | D1 |
| COUNTY: | MEATH |
| MEMORIAL NUMBER: | E 7 |
| ERECTED BY: | JOHN MCCOURT |
| ORIENTATION: | EAST |
| NUMBER OF COMPONENTS: | 2 |
| NUMBER OF INSCRIBED FACES: | 1 |
| NUMBER OF PEOPLE COMMEMORATED: | 9 |
| MEMORIAL TYPE: | HEADSTONE |
| CONDITION OF MEMORIAL: | BROKEN TOP ON GROUND |
| CONDITION OF INSCRIPTION: | DECIPHERABLE |
| STONEMASON NAME: | F. WHYTE |
| TECHNIQUE OF INSCRIPTION: | INCISED |
| UNDERTAKER: | |
| STONE TOP: | BROKEN ON GROUND |
| GRAVE TYPE: | SINGLE |
| HEIGHT: | TOP 68CM - BOTTOM 88CM |
| WIDTH: | TOP 64CM |
| THICKNESS: | 09CM |

| SURNAME: | CHRISTIAN | ADDRESS | DEATH | AGE |
|---|---|---|---|---|
| MCCOURT | PETER | | 03 MAY 1901 | 19 YEARS |
| | MARY | | 28 MAR 1903 | 26 YEARS |
| | LOUISA | | 09 FEB 1901 | |
| | JOSEPH | | 09 JAN 1905 | 16 YEARS |
| | RICHARD | | 04 SEPT 1904 | 26 YEARS |
| | ALICE | | 21 AUG 1906 | 14 YEARS |
| | ALICE | | 19 AUG 1911 | 65 YEARS |
| | BRIDGET | | 31 JAN 1919 | 30 YEARS |
| | JOHN | | 20 FEB 1919 | 85 YEARS |

**INSCRIPTION:**
ERECTED BY
JOHN MCCOURT
IN MEMORY OF HIS SON
PETER
WHO DIED 3 MAY 1901 AGED 19 YEARS
AND HIS DAUGHTER
MARY
WHO DIED 28 MARCH 1903 AGED 26 YEARS
ALSO LOUISA
WIFE OF HIS SON THOMAS
WHO DIED 9 FEB 1901
ALSO HIS SONS JOSEPH
WHO DIED 9 JAN 1905 AGED 16 YEARS AND
RICHARD DIED 4 SEP 1904 AGED 26 YEARS
AND ALSO HIS DAUGHTER ALICE
DIED 21 AUG 1906 AGED 14 YEARS
AND HIS WIFE ALICE DIED 19 AUG 1911 AGED 65 YEARS
ALSO HIS DAUGHTER BRIDGET WHO DIED
JAN 31ST 1919 AGED 30 YEARS
AND THE ABOVE JOHN MCCOURT
WHO DIED FEB 20 1919 AGED 85 YEARS R.I.P

**SYMBOLS:**
SACRED HEART NAILS AND HAMMER

| | |
|---|---|
| NAME OF RECORDER: | LIZ LYNCH |
| DATE: | 16 JULY 2005 |
| PHOTO REFERENCE: | E7 |
| LOCATION/MAP REF: | D1 E7 |

| | |
|---|---|
| GRAVEYARD NAME: | **ST. MARY'S ABBEY OLD GRAVEYARD** |
| GRAVEYARD CODE: | D1 |
| COUNTY: | MEATH |
| MEMORIAL NUMBER: | B7 |
| ERECTED BY: | |
| ORIENTATION: | EAST |
| NUMBER OF COMPONENTS: | 2 |
| NUMBER OF INSCRIBED FACES: | 1 |
| NUMBER OF PEOPLE COMMEMORATED: | 4 |
| MEMORIAL TYPE: | HEADSTONE |
| CONDITION OF MEMORIAL: | SOUND IN PLACE |
| CONDITION OF INSCRIPTION: | MAINLY DECIPHERABLE |
| STONEMASON NAME: | W. GOGARTY |
| TECHNIQUE OF INSCRIPTION: | INCISED AND PAINTED |
| UNDERTAKER: | |
| STONE TOP: | ROUND |
| GRAVE TYPE: | DOUBLE |
| HEIGHT: | 110CM |
| WIDTH: | 43CM |
| THICKNESS: | 8CM |

| SURNAME: | CHRISTIAN | ADDRESS | OCCUPATION | DEATH | AGE |
|---|---|---|---|---|---|
| MCENTEGGART | MICHAEL | KINGSGATE | | 05 MAR 1936 | |
| | MARELLA | | | 22 MAY 1917 | |
| | JOHN | | INFANT | | |
| | JOSEPH | | INFANT | | |

**INSCRIPTION:**
IN LOVING MEMORY
OF
MICHAEL MCENTEGGART
KINGSGATE
DIED 5 MARCH 1936
HIS DAUGHTER MARELLA
DIED 22 MAY 1917
AND HIS INFANT CHILDREN
JOHN AND JOSEPH

R.I.P.

**SYMBOLS:**
CROSS OVER IHS FLANKED
BY TULIPS

| | |
|---|---|
| NAME OF RECORDER: | PHYLLIS NOONAN |
| DATE: | 29 JUNE 2005 |
| PHOTO REFERENCE: | B 7 |
| LOCATION/MAP REF: | D1 B7 |

| | |
|---|---|
| GRAVEYARD NAME: | **ST. MARY'S ABBEY OLD GRAVEYARD** |
| GRAVEYARD CODE: | D1 |
| COUNTY: | MEATH |
| MEMORIAL NUMBER: | C1 |
| ERECTED BY: | JANE CARROLL |
| ORIENTATION: | EAST |
| NUMBER OF COMPONENTS: | 2 |
| NUMBER OF INSCRIBED FACES: | 1 |
| NUMBER OF PEOPLE COMMEMORATED: | 2 |
| MEMORIAL TYPE: | HEADSTONE |
| CONDITION OF MEMORIAL: | REASONABLE, TOP SECTION MISSING |
| CONDITION OF INSCRIPTION: | CLEAR |
| STONEMASON NAME: | |
| TECHNIQUE OF INSCRIPTION: | INCISED |
| UNDERTAKER: | |
| STONE TOP: | MISSING |
| GRAVE TYPE: | SINGLE |
| HEIGHT: | 145CM |
| WIDTH: | 68CM |
| THICKNESS: | 10CM |

| SURNAME: | CHRISTIAN | ADDRESS | DEATH | AGE |
|---|---|---|---|---|
| MCGLUE | JAMES | DULEEK STREET, DROGHEDA | JAN 1874 | |
| | MARY | | AUG 1900 | 104 |

**INSCRIPTION:**
ERECTED
BY
JANE CARROLL
DULEEK ST DROGHEDA IN MEMORY OF
HER GRANDFATHER JAMES MCGLUE
DIED JAN. 1874 AND HIS WIFE
MARY DIED AUG 21ST 1900
AGED 104 YEARS

R.I.P

**SYMBOLS:**
LAMB ON PRONE CROSS

| | |
|---|---|
| NAME OF RECORDER: | LIZ LYNCH |
| DATE: | 2 JULY 2005 |
| PHOTO REFERENCE: | C1 |
| LOCATION/MAP REF: | D1 C1 |

| | |
|---|---|
| GRAVEYARD NAME: | **ST. MARY'S ABBEY OLD GRAVEYARD** |
| GRAVEYARD CODE: | D1 |
| COUNTY: | MEATH |
| MEMORIAL NUMBER: | B 13 |
| ERECTED BY: | |
| ORIENTATION: | EAST |
| NUMBER OF COMPONENTS: | 4 |
| NUMBER OF INSCRIBED FACES: | 1 |
| NUMBER OF PEOPLE COMMEMORATED: | 2 |
| MEMORIAL TYPE: | CROSS |
| CONDITION OF MEMORIAL: | SOUND IN PLACE |
| CONDITION OF INSCRIPTION: | MAINLY DECIPHERABLE |
| STONEMASON NAME: | |
| TECHNIQUE OF INSCRIPTION: | INCISED ON MARBLE RELIEF |
| UNDERTAKER: | |
| STONE TOP: | CROSS |
| GRAVE TYPE: | DOUBLE |
| HEIGHT: | 150CM |
| WIDTH: | 72CM |
| THICKNESS: | 16CM |

| SURNAME: | CHRISTIAN | ADDRESS | DEATH | AGE |
|---|---|---|---|---|
| MCGUINNESS | LIZZIE | | 04 FEB 1907 | 28 |
| MCCABE | JANE | | 22 DEC 1985 | |
| MCGUINNESS | FAMILY | | | |

**INSCRIPTION:**
IN
MEMORY
OF LIZZIE MCGUINNESS WHO DIED ON
THE 4 DAY OF FEBRUARY 1907 AGED 28
R.I.P.
IN LOVING MEMORY OF
JANE MCCABE (NEE MCGUINNESS)
DIED 22ND DEC 1985
ALSO THE MCGUINNESS FAMILY
REST IN PEACE

| | |
|---|---|
| NAME OF RECORDER: | PHYLLIS NOONAN AND BEN RYAN |
| DATE: | 02 JULY 2005 |
| PHOTO REFERENCE: | B13 |
| LOCATION/MAP REF: | D1 B13 |

| | |
|---|---|
| GRAVEYARD NAME: | **ST. MARY'S ABBEY OLD GRAVEYARD** |
| GRAVEYARD CODE: | D1 |
| COUNTY: | MEATH |
| MEMORIAL NUMBER: | C9 |
| ERECTED BY: | ANNIE MCKENNA |
| ORIENTATION: | EAST |
| NUMBER OF COMPONENTS: | 1 |
| NUMBER OF INSCRIBED FACES: | 1 |
| NUMBER OF PEOPLE COMMEMORATED: | 3 |
| MEMORIAL TYPE: | HEADSTONE |
| CONDITION OF MEMORIAL: | SOUND IN PLACE |
| CONDITION OF INSCRIPTION: | MAINLY DECIPHERABLE |
| STONEMASON NAME: | |
| TECHNIQUE OF INSCRIPTION: | INCISED |
| UNDERTAKER: | |
| STONE TOP: | CELTIC CROSS ON DISK |
| GRAVE TYPE: | SINGLE |
| HEIGHT: | 113CM |
| WIDTH: | 61CM |
| THICKNESS: | 8CM |

| SURNAME: | CHRISTIAN | ADDRESS | DEATH | AGE |
|---|---|---|---|---|
| MCINTEGART | PATRICK | | 12 OCT 1890 | |
| | MARY | | 16 SEP 1896 | |
| | JOHN | | INFANT | 2 YEARS |

**INSCRIPTION:**
IN LOVING MEMORY
OF
PATRICK MC INTEGART
WHO DIED 12.OCT.1890
AND HIS WIFE MARY
WHO DIED 16 SEPT 1896
AND THEIR INFANT SON
JOHN
WHO DIED AGED 2 YEARS

ERECTED BY THEIR DAUGHTER
ANNIE MCKENNA

**SYMBOLS**
CELTIC CROSS

| | |
|---|---|
| NAME OF RECORDER: | PHYLLIS NOONAN AND JIM ORTON |
| DATE: | 6 JULY 2005 |
| PHOTO REFERENCE: | C9 |
| LOCATION/MAP REF: | D1 C9 |

| | |
|---|---|
| GRAVEYARD NAME: | **ST. MARY'S ABBEY OLD GRAVEYARD** |
| GRAVEYARD CODE: | D1 |
| COUNTY: | MEATH |
| MEMORIAL NUMBER: | A4 |
| ERECTED BY: | |
| ORIENTATION: | EAST |
| NUMBER OF COMPONENTS: | 2 |
| NUMBER OF INSCRIBED FACES: | 1 |
| NUMBER OF PEOPLE COMMEMORATED: | 3 |
| MEMORIAL TYPE: | HEADSTONE |
| CONDITION OF MEMORIAL: | SOUND IN PLACE |
| CONDITION OF INSCRIPTION: | CLEAR |
| STONEMASON NAME: | MOSS |
| TECHNIQUE OF INSCRIPTION: | INCISED |
| UNDERTAKER: | |
| STONE TOP: | FLAT |
| GRAVE TYPE: | TREBLE |
| HEIGHT: | 126CM |
| WIDTH: | 70CM |
| THICKNESS: | 8CM |

| SURNAME: | CHRISTIAN | ADDRESS | BIRTH | DEATH | AGE |
|---|---|---|---|---|---|
| MCKEEN | WILLIAM DONNAN | ISLANDMAGEE BELLEWSTOWN | 30 AUG 1933 | 07 OCT 1953 | 20 |
| MCKEEN | THOMAS | | 24 DEC 1868 | 03 OCT 1954 | 86 |
| MCKEEN | MARY ANN | | 24 APR 1912 | 02 FEB 1973 | 61 |

**INSCRIPTION:**

WILLIAM DONNAN MCKEEN
ISLANDMAGEE AND BELLEWSTOWN
BORN 30 AUG 1933 DIED 7 OCT 1953
HIS FATHER THOMAS
BORN 24 DEC 1868 DIED 3 OCT 1954
ALSO HIS MOTHER
MARY ANN MCKEEN
BORN 24 APRIL 1912 DIED 2 FEB 1973

| | |
|---|---|
| NAME OF RECORDER: | HELEN FULLAM AND JANET LEIGH |
| DATE: | 18 JUNE 2005 |
| PHOTO REFERENCE: | A4 |
| LOCATION/MAP REF: | D1 A4 |

| | |
|---|---|
| GRAVEYARD NAME: | **ST. MARY'S ABBEY OLD GRAVEYARD** |
| GRAVEYARD CODE: | D1 |
| COUNTY: | MEATH |
| MEMORIAL NUMBER: | F11 |
| ERECTED BY: | |
| ORIENTATION: | EAST |
| NUMBER OF COMPONENTS: | 2 |
| NUMBER OF INSCRIBED FACES: | 1 |
| NUMBER OF PEOPLE COMMEMORATED: | 2 |
| MEMORIAL TYPE: | HEADSTONE |
| CONDITION OF MEMORIAL: | SOUND IN PLACE |
| CONDITION OF INSCRIPTION: | CLEAR |
| STONEMASON NAME: | |
| TECHNIQUE OF INSCRIPTION: | INCISED |
| UNDERTAKER: | |
| STONE TOP: | ARCHED |
| GRAVE TYPE: | SINGLE |
| HEIGHT: | 106CM |
| WIDTH: | 38CM |
| THICKNESS: | 05CM |

| SURNAME: | CHRISTIAN | ADDRESS | DEATH | AGE |
|---|---|---|---|---|
| MCKEEVER | JOHN | DULEEK | 1888 | |
| | ELIZABETH | | 1917 | |

**INSCRIPTION:**
IN
LOVING MEMORY OF
JOHN
AND ELIZABETH MCKEEVER
DULEEK
WHO DIED 1888 AND 1917
RIP

**SYMBOLS:**
CROSS

| | |
|---|---|
| NAME OF RECORDER: | PHYLLIS NOONAN |
| DATE: | 19 JULY 2005 |
| PHOTO REFERENCE: | F11 |
| LOCATION/MAP REF: | D1 F11 |

| | |
|---|---|
| GRAVEYARD NAME: | **ST. MARY'S ABBEY OLD GRAVEYARD** |
| GRAVEYARD CODE: | D1 |
| COUNTY: | MEATH |
| MEMORIAL NUMBER: | F23 |
| ERECTED BY: | |
| ORIENTATION: | EAST |
| NUMBER OF COMPONENTS: | 2 |
| NUMBER OF INSCRIBED FACES: | 1 |
| NUMBER OF PEOPLE COMMEMORATED: | 4 |
| MEMORIAL TYPE: | HEADSTONE |
| CONDITION OF MEMORIAL: | SOUND IN PLACE |
| CONDITION OF INSCRIPTION: | MAINLY DECIPHERABLE |
| STONEMASON NAME: | |
| TECHNIQUE OF INSCRIPTION: | INCISED ON BASE PEDESTAL |
| UNDERTAKER: | |
| STONE TOP: | CROSS |
| GRAVE TYPE: | SINGLE |
| HEIGHT: | 127CM |
| WIDTH: | 46CM |
| THICKNESS: | 10CM |

| SURNAME: | CHRISTIAN | ADDRESS | DEATH | AGE |
|---|---|---|---|---|
| MCKEEVER | MATHEW | DULEEK | 02 MAY 1883 | |
| | JAMES | | 06 OCT 1883 | |
| | CATHERINE | | 09 APR 1905 | |
| | MARY | | 29 FEB 1928 | |

**INSCRIPTION:**
IN LOVING MEMORY OF
MATHEW MCKEEVER DULEEK
WHO DIED MAY 2ND 1883 AND OF
HIS FATHER JAMES WHO DIED
OCT 6TH 1883 ALSO HIS MOTHER
CATHERINE
WHO DIED APRIL 29TH 1905
AND MARY MCKEEVER
WHO DIED FEB 29TH 1928

**SYMBOLS:**
IHS IN CIRCLE OF CROSS
WITH FLEUR DE LIS ARMS

| | |
|---|---|
| NAME OF RECORDER: | SINEAD FULLAM |
| DATE: | 20 JULY 2005 |
| PHOTO REFERENCE: | F23 |
| LOCATION/MAP REF: | D1 F23 |

| | |
|---|---|
| GRAVEYARD NAME: | **ST. MARY'S ABBEY OLD GRAVEYARD** |
| GRAVEYARD CODE: | D1 |
| COUNTY: | MEATH |
| MEMORIAL NUMBER: | D7 |
| ERECTED BY: | |
| ORIENTATION: | EAST |
| NUMBER OF COMPONENTS: | 2 |
| NUMBER OF INSCRIBED FACES: | 1 |
| NUMBER OF PEOPLE COMMEMORATED: | 8 |
| MEMORIAL TYPE: | HEADSTONE |
| CONDITION OF MEMORIAL: | SOUND IN PLACE |
| CONDITION OF INSCRIPTION: | CLEAR |
| STONEMASON NAME: | |
| TECHNIQUE OF INSCRIPTION: | INCISED |
| UNDERTAKER: | |
| STONE TOP: | ARCH |
| GRAVE TYPE: | SINGLE |
| HEIGHT: | 143CM |
| WIDTH: | 56CM |
| THICKNESS: | 6.5CM |

| SURNAME: | CHRISTIAN | ADDRESS | DEATH | AGE |
|---|---|---|---|---|
| MCKENNA | JANE | DROGHEDA ROAD | 09 MAR 1918 | |
| | JOHN | | 13 APR 1918 | |
| | CHRISTOPHER | | NOV 1903 | |
| | THOMAS | | 30 AUG 1920 | |
| | JOHN | | 04 AUG 1951 | |
| | BRIGID | | 01 APR 1954 | |
| | JAMES | | JAN 1951 | |
| | PATRICK | | MAY 1928 | |

**INSCRIPTION:**
IN LOVING MEMORY
OF JANE MCKENNA
DROGHEDA ROAD
DIED 9TH MARCH 1918
HER HUSBAND JOHN DIED
13TH APRIL 1918
THEIR SONS DIED
CHRISTOPHER NOV 1903
THOMAS 30TH AUG 1920
JOHN 4TH AUG 1954
PATRICK AND JAMES
DIED IN CANADA
MAY 1928 AND JAN 1951
THEIR DAUGHTER BRIGID DIED
1 APRIL 1954
R.I.P

**SYMBOLS:**
CROSS IN FLAMES FLANKED BY IVY

| | |
|---|---|
| NAME OF RECORDER: | PHYLLIS NOONAN |
| DATE: | 11 JULY 2005 |
| PHOTO REFERENCE: | D7 |
| LOCATION/MAP REF: | D1 D7 |

| | |
|---|---|
| GRAVEYARD NAME: | **ST. MARY'S ABBEY OLD GRAVEYARD** |
| GRAVEYARD CODE: | D1 |
| COUNTY: | MEATH |
| MEMORIAL NUMBER: | J10 |
| ERECTED BY: | PETER MCKEONE |
| ORIENTATION: | EAST |
| NUMBER OF COMPONENTS: | 1 |
| NUMBER OF INSCRIBED FACES: | 1 |
| NUMBER OF PEOPLE COMMEMORATED: | 5 |
| MEMORIAL TYPE: | HEADSTONE |
| CONDITION OF MEMORIAL: | SOUND IN PLACE |
| CONDITION OF INSCRIPTION: | MAINLY DECIPHERABLE |
| STONEMASON NAME: | |
| TECHNIQUE OF INSCRIPTION: | INCISED |
| UNDERTAKER: | |
| STONE TOP: | ROUND |
| GRAVE TYPE: | SINGLE |
| HEIGHT: | 120CM |
| WIDTH: | 71CM |
| THICKNESS: | 09CM |

| SURNAME: | CHRISTIAN | ADDRESS | DEATH | AGE |
|---|---|---|---|---|
| MCKEONE | FATHER | | | |
| | MOTHER | | | |
| | BROTHERS | | | |
| | SISTERS | | | |
| | CHILD | | | |

**INSCRIPTION:**
ERECTED BY
PETER MCKEONE OF IRISHTOWN IN
MEMORY OF HIS FATHER AND MOTHER
BROTHERS AND SISTERS ALSO ONE OF HIS
CHILDREN WHO DIED YOUNG
RENOVATED BY THEIR
GRANDCHILDREN 1926

+AD 1849 +

**SYMBOLS:**
SUNBURST WITH IHS WITH
CROSS CIRCULAR SCROLL ELOBRATE
CHALICE WITH FLAME AND CROSSES

| | |
|---|---|
| NAME OF RECORDER: | JANET LEIGH AND SINEAD FULLAM |
| DATE: | 6 AUGUST 2005 |
| PHOTO REFERENCE: | J10 |
| LOCATION/MAP REF: | D1 J10 |

| | |
|---|---|
| GRAVEYARD NAME: | **ST. MARY'S ABBEY OLD GRAVEYARD** |
| GRAVEYARD CODE: | D1 |
| COUNTY: | MEATH |
| MEMORIAL NUMBER: | J7 |
| ERECTED BY: | JAMES MCKOWNE |
| ORIENTATION: | EAST |
| NUMBER OF COMPONENTS: | 1 |
| NUMBER OF INSCRIBED FACES: | 1 |
| NUMBER OF PEOPLE COMMEMORATED: | 2 |
| MEMORIAL TYPE: | HEADSTONE |
| CONDITION OF MEMORIAL: | FAIR |
| CONDITION OF INSCRIPTION: | MAINLY DECIPHERABLE |
| STONEMASON NAME: | |
| TECHNIQUE OF INSCRIPTION: | INCISED |
| UNDERTAKER: | |
| STONE TOP: | |
| GRAVE TYPE: | SINGLE |
| HEIGHT: | 69CM |
| WIDTH: | 64CM |
| THICKNESS: | 15CM |

| SURNAME: | CHRISTIAN | ADDRESS | DEATH | AGE |
|---|---|---|---|---|
| MCKOWNE | FATHER | | 1776 | |
| | MOTHER | | | |

**INSCRIPTION:**
THIS BURIAL
STONE BELONGS TO JAMES
MCKOWNE WHEREIN
LIES HIS FATHER AND MOTHER 1776

**SYMBOLS:**
CROSS IHS WITH SMALL
HEART

| | |
|---|---|
| NAME OF RECORDER: | BEN RYAN |
| DATE: | 6 AUGUST 2005 |
| PHOTO REFERENCE: | J7 |
| LOCATION/MAP REF: | D1 J7 |

| | |
|---|---|
| GRAVEYARD NAME: | **ST. MARY'S ABBEY OLD GRAVEYARD** |
| GRAVEYARD CODE: | D1 |
| COUNTY: | MEATH |
| MEMORIAL NUMBER: | K9 |
| ERECTED BY: | PATRICK MCNALLY DULEEK STREET DROGHEDA |
| ORIENTATION: | EAST |
| NUMBER OF COMPONENTS: | 3 |
| NUMBER OF INSCRIBED FACES: | 1 |
| NUMBER OF PEOPLE COMMEMORATED: | 6 |
| MEMORIAL TYPE: | HEADSTONE |
| CONDITION OF MEMORIAL: | SOUND IN PLACE |
| CONDITION OF INSCRIPTION: | LEGIBLE |
| STONEMASON NAME: | |
| TECHNIQUE OF INSCRIPTION: | INCISED |
| UNDERTAKER: | |
| STONE TOP: | DISK INSERTED BETWEEN TWO PILLARS |
| GRAVE TYPE: | SINGLE |
| HEIGHT: | 194CM |
| WIDTH: | 80CM |
| THICKNESS: | 18CM |

| SURNAME: | CHRISTIAN | ADDRESS | DEATH | AGE |
|---|---|---|---|---|
| MCNALLY | ELIZABETH | | 15 JULY 1854 | 64 |
| | 2 CHILDREN | | DIED YOUNG | |
| BAN | PATRICK | | | |
| BAN | ANNE | | | |
| MCNALLY | PATRICK | | 5 NOV 1899 | |

**INSCRIPTION:**
ERECTED
BY
PATK MCNALLY DULEEK STREET
DROGHEDA IN MEMORY OF HIS
BELOVED WIFE ELIZABETH WHO
DEPARTED THIS LIFE THE 15TH JULY
1854 AGED 64 YEARS ALSO 2 OF
THEIR CHILDREN DIED YOUNG AND
ALSO HIS FATHER AND MOTHER IN LAW
PATK AND ANNE BAN WHO LIE BENEATH
AND HIS SON PATRICK DIED 5 NOV 1899
R.I.P
*REQUIESCANT IN PACE*

**SYMBOLS:**
FLOWERS SCROLLS 2 URNS WITH
CROSS ON TOP

**ORNAMENTS:**
ANGEL IN RELIEF WITH HORIZONTAL
CROSS WITH LAMB

| | |
|---|---|
| NAME OF RECORDER: | PHYLLIS NOONAN AND HELEN FULLAM |
| DATE: | 10 SEPT 2005 |
| PHOTO REFERENCE: | K9 |
| LOCATION/MAP REF | D1 K9 |

| | |
|---|---|
| GRAVEYARD NAME: | **ST. MARY'S ABBEY OLD GRAVEYARD** |
| GRAVEYARD CODE: | D1 |
| COUNTY: | MEATH |
| MEMORIAL NUMBER: | J8 |
| ERECTED BY: | |
| ORIENTATION: | EAST |
| NUMBER OF COMPONENTS: | 1 |
| NUMBER OF INSCRIBED FACES: | 1 |
| NUMBER OF PEOPLE COMMEMORATED: | 1 |
| MEMORIAL TYPE: | HEADSTONE |
| CONDITION OF MEMORIAL: | SOUND IN PLACE |
| CONDITION OF INSCRIPTION: | MAINLY DECIPHERABLE |
| STONEMASON NAME: | |
| TECHNIQUE OF INSCRIPTION: | INCISED |
| UNDERTAKER: | |
| STONE TOP: | ROUND |
| GRAVE TYPE: | SINGLE |
| HEIGHT: | 57CM |
| WIDTH: | 40CM |
| THICKNESS: | 07CM |

| SURNAME: | CHRISTIAN | ADDRESS | DEATH | AGE |
|---|---|---|---|---|
| MCOONE | JAMES | | 1757 | |

**INSCRIPTION:**

THE BURIAL PLACE OF
JAMES MCOONE
FOR HIM AND HIS POSTERITY
ANNO DOM 1757

| | |
|---|---|
| NAME OF RECORDER: | JANET LEIGH AND SINEAD FULLAM |
| DATE: | 06 AUGUST 2005 |
| PHOTO REFERENCE: | J8 |
| LOCATION/MAP REF: | D1 J8 |

| | |
|---|---|
| GRAVEYARD NAME: | **ST. MARY'S ABBEY OLD GRAVEYARD** |
| GRAVEYARD CODE: | D1 |
| COUNTY: | MEATH |
| MEMORIAL NUMBER: | K17 |
| ERECTED BY: | JAMES MEADE |
| ORIENTATION: | EAST |
| NUMBER OF COMPONENTS: | 4 |
| NUMBER OF INSCRIBED FACES: | 1 |
| NUMBER OF PEOPLE COMMEMORATED: | 9 |
| MEMORIAL TYPE: | HEADSTONE ELABORATE |
| CONDITION OF MEMORIAL: | SOUND IN PLACE |
| CONDITION OF INSCRIPTION: | CLEAR |
| STONEMASON NAME: | MOSS |
| TECHNIQUE OF INSCRIPTION: | INCISED |
| UNDERTAKER: | |
| STONE TOP: | CELTIC CROSS |
| GRAVE TYPE: | SINGLE |
| HEIGHT: | 278CM |
| WIDTH: | 79CM |
| THICKNESS: | 16CM |

| SURNAME: | CHRISTIAN | ADDRESS | DEATH | AGE |
|---|---|---|---|---|
| MEADE | ELIZABETH | | 10 MAR 1889 | |
| | CHRISTOPHER | | 03 JULY 1906 | |
| | JOHN | | 26 DEC 1910 | |
| | ANNE | | 15 OCT 1937 | |
| | JAMES | MAIN ST. DULEEK | 07 FEB 1951 | |
| | MARY | | 10 OCT 1980 | |
| | ROSEANNE | | 04 FEB 1985 | |
| | EVA | | 09 APR 1994 | |
| | CHRISTOPHER | | 02 NOV 1995 | |

**INSCRIPTION:**
ERECTED
BY
JAMES MEADE
MAIN STREET
IN MEMORY OF HIS MOTHER
ELIZABETH
WHO DIED 10 MARCH 1889
HIS FATHER
CHRISTOPHER
WHO DIED 3 JULY 1906
AND HIS BROTHER
JOHN
WHO DIED 26 DEC 1910
ALSO ANNE MEADE WIFE
OF THE ABOVE NAMED JOHN
WHO DIED 15 OCT 1937
THE ABOVE NAMED JAMES DIED
7 FEB 1951
MARY MEADE DIED 10 OCT 1980
ROSEANNE MEADE DIED 4 FEB 1985
EVA MEADE DIED 9 APRIL 1994
CHRISTOPHER MEADE 2 NOV 1995
R.I.P.

**SYMBOLS:**
CELTIC CROSS VINE AND FLOWER
IHS INTERWOVEN IN CENTRE

**ORNAMENTS:**
SACRED IN FLAMES WITH CROSS
WITH THORNS AND BLOOD DROPS
HAMMER NAIL SPEAR AND SPONGE
TWO PILLARS EACH SIDE WITH FOUR FISH
HEADS AND CORAL

| | |
|---|---|
| NAME OF RECORDER: | BEN RYAN AND JANET LEIGH |
| DATE: | 24 SEPT 2005 |
| PHOTO REFERENCE: | K17 |
| LOCATION/MAP REF: | D1 K17 |

| | |
|---|---|
| GRAVEYARD NAME: | **ST. MARY'S ABBEY OLD GRAVEYARD** |
| GRAVEYARD CODE: | D1 |
| COUNTY: | MEATH |
| MEMORIAL NUMBER: | K13 |
| ERECTED BY: | MARGARET COLEMAN |
| ORIENTATION: | EAST |
| NUMBER OF COMPONENTS: | 2 |
| NUMBER OF INSCRIBED FACES: | 1 |
| NUMBER OF PEOPLE COMMEMORATED: | 1 |
| MEMORIAL TYPE: | HEADSTONE |
| CONDITION OF MEMORIAL: | SOUND IN PLACE |
| CONDITION OF INSCRIPTION: | CLEAR |
| STONEMASON NAME: | |
| TECHNIQUE OF INSCRIPTION: | INCISED AND PAINTED |
| UNDERTAKER: | |
| STONE TOP: | SQUARE LOW |
| GRAVE TYPE: | SINGLE |
| HEIGHT: | 73CM |
| WIDTH: | 58CM |
| THICKNESS: | 05CM |

| SURNAME: | CHRISTIAN | ADDRESS | DEATH | AGE |
|---|---|---|---|---|
| MEADE | LAURENCE | | 31 JAN 1969 | 88 |

**INSCRIPTION:**
ERECTED BY
MARGARET COLEMAN
IN LOVING MEMORY
OF HER BROTHER
LAURENCE MEADE
WHO DIED 31ST JAN 1969
AGED 88 YEARS
RIP

**SYMBOLS:**
INCISED AND PAINTED CROSS IN HEADSTONE

| | |
|---|---|
| NAME OF RECORDER: | PHYLLIS NOONAN AND BEN RYAN |
| DATE: | 10 SEPT 2005 |
| PHOTO REFERENCE: | K13 |
| LOCATION/MAP REF: | D1 K13 |

| | |
|---|---|
| GRAVEYARD NAME: | **ST. MARY'S ABBEY OLD GRAVEYARD** |
| GRAVEYARD CODE: | D1 |
| COUNTY: | MEATH |
| MEMORIAL NUMBER: | J12 |
| ERECTED BY: | MICHAEL BYRNE |
| ORIENTATION: | EAST |
| NUMBER OF COMPONENTS: | 1 |
| NUMBER OF INSCRIBED FACES: | 1 |
| NUMBER OF PEOPLE COMMEMORATED: | 4 |
| MEMORIAL TYPE: | HEADSTONE FIXED TO WALL |
| CONDITION OF MEMORIAL: | SOUND |
| CONDITION OF INSCRIPTION: | MAINLY DECIPHERABLE |
| STONEMASON NAME: | |
| TECHNIQUE OF INSCRIPTION: | INCISED |
| UNDERTAKER: | |
| STONE TOP: | ROUND |
| GRAVE TYPE: | SINGLE |
| HEIGHT: | 168CM |
| WIDTH: | 31CM |
| THICKNESS: | 11CM |

| SURNAME: | CHRISTIAN | ADDRESS | DEATH | AGE |
|---|---|---|---|---|
| MOONEY | JAMES | | 27 OCT 1826 | 70 |
| | JOHN | CORBALLIS | AUG 1823 | 60 |
| BYRNE | BRIDGET | | 06 JAN 1845 | 87 |
| | MICHAEL | SODSTOWN | 30 SEPT 1868 | |

**INSCRIPTION:**
ERECTED BY MICHAEL BYRNE OF SODS
TOWN IN MEMORY OF HIS UNCLE JAMES
MOONEY WHO DEPARTED THIS LIFE 27
OCTR 1836 AGED 70 YEARS ALSO OF
HIS UNCLE JOHN MOONEY LATE OF
CORBALLIS WHO DIED IN AUG 1823
AGED 60 ALSO HIS MOTHER
BRIDGET BYRNE WHO WAS INTERRED HERE
ON 6TH JANRY 1845 AGED 87 YEARS
YOUR PRAYERS ARE REQUESTED ~~
THEREFORE IT IS HOLY AND WHOLESOME
THOUGHT TO PRAY FOR THE DEAD THAT
THEY MAY BE LOOSED FROM SINS
MAC 12 X11 46 ALSO MICHAEL
BYRNE DIED 30TH SEPTR 1868
RESQUISCANT IN PACE

**SYMBOLS:**
SUNBURST IHS WITH CROSS
CIRCULAR SCROLL WITH
GLORIA IN EXCELSIS DEO INSCRIBED
INSIDE SURROUNDED BY TWO WINGED
ANGEL HEADS

| | |
|---|---|
| NAME OF RECORDER: | JANET LEIGH AND SINEAD FULLAM |
| DATE: | 6 AUG 2005 |
| PHOTO REFERENCE: | J12 |
| LOCATION/MAP REF: | D1 J12 |

| | |
|---|---|
| GRAVEYARD NAME: | **ST. MARY'S ABBEY OLD GRAVEYARD** |
| GRAVEYARD CODE: | D1 |
| COUNTY: | MEATH |
| MEMORIAL NUMBER: | E1 |
| ERECTED BY: | JAMES MOONEY |
| ORIENTATION: | EAST |
| NUMBER OF COMPONENTS: | 3 |
| NUMBER OF INSCRIBED FACES: | 1 |
| NUMBER OF PEOPLE COMMEMORATED: | 8 |
| MEMORIAL TYPE: | HEADSTONE |
| CONDITION OF MEMORIAL: | COLLAPSED |
| CONDITION OF INSCRIPTION: | DECIPHERABLE |
| STONEMASON NAME: | WHYTE CHORD ROAD. DROGHEDA |
| TECHNIQUE OF INSCRIPTION: | INCISED |
| UNDERTAKER: | |
| STONE TOP: | COLLAPSED |
| GRAVE TYPE: | TREBLE |
| HEIGHT: | 162CM COLLAPSED |
| WIDTH: | 62CM COLLAPSED |
| THICKNESS: | 7CM COLLAPSED |

| SURNAME: | CHRISTIAN | ADDRESS | OCCUPATION | DEATH | AGE |
|---|---|---|---|---|---|
| MOONEY | ELLEN | DULEEK | WIFE | 18 JUN 1899 | |
| | RICHARD | | SON | 29 SEPT 1900 | 15 MONTHS |
| | ELIZABETH | | WIFE | 23 FEB 1913 | 44 YEARS |
| | JAMES | | | 28 OCT 1927 | |
| | MARY | | SISTER | 06 NOV 1949 | |
| | ROBERT | | SON | 18 OCT 1969 | |
| | CATHERINE | | DAUGHTER | 28 MAR 1971 | |
| | PETER | | SON | 21 APR 1980 | |

**INSCRIPTION:**
ERECTED
BY
JAMES MOONEY
DULEEK
IN MEMORY OF HIS WIFE
ELLEN
WHO DIED 18 JUNE 1899
AND THEIR SON
RICHARD
WHO DIED 29 SEPT 1900 AGED 15 MONTHS
ALSO HIS WIFE
ELIZABETH
WHO DIED 23 FEB 1913 AGED 44 YEARS
AND THE ABOVE JAMES
DIED OCT 28TH 1927
ALSO HIS SISTER
MARY MOONEY
DIED 6 NOV 1949
THEIR SON ROBERT
DIED 18 OCT 1969
THEIR DAUGHTER CATHERINE
DIED 28 MARCH 1971
ALSO PETER DIED 21 APRIL 1980

**SYMBOLS:**
IHS

| | |
|---|---|
| NAME OF RECORDER: | PHYLLIS NOONAN |
| DATE: | 10 APRIL 2006 |
| PHOTO REFERENCE: | E1 |
| LOCATION/MAP REF: | D1 E1 |

| | |
|---|---|
| GRAVEYARD NAME: | **ST. MARY'S ABBEY OLD GRAVEYARD** |
| GRAVEYARD CODE: | D1 |
| COUNTY: | MEATH |
| MEMORIAL NUMBER: | K20 |
| ERECTED BY: | |
| ORIENTATION: | EAST |
| NUMBER OF COMPONENTS: | 1 |
| NUMBER OF INSCRIBED FACES: | 1 |
| NUMBER OF PEOPLE COMMEMORATED: | FAMILY |
| MEMORIAL TYPE: | HEADSTONE |
| CONDITION OF MEMORIAL: | ERODED |
| CONDITION OF INSCRIPTION: | MAINLY DECIPHERABLE |
| STONEMASON NAME: | |
| TECHNIQUE OF INSCRIPTION: | INCISED |
| UNDERTAKER: | |
| STONE TOP: | ROUND ARCH |
| GRAVE TYPE: | SINGLE |
| HEIGHT: | 78CM |
| WIDTH: | 43CM |
| THICKNESS: | 10CM |

| SURNAME: | CHRISTIAN | ADDRESS | DEATH | AGE |
|---|---|---|---|---|
| MOONEY | LAWR | | | |
| | FAMILY | | | |

**INSCRIPTION:**
LAWR MOONEY
AND FAMILY

| | |
|---|---|
| NAME OF RECORDER: | PHYLLIS NOONAN |
| DATE: | 25 SEPT 2005 |
| PHOTO REFERENCE: | K20 |
| LOCATION/MAP REF: | D1 K20 |

| | |
|---|---|
| GRAVEYARD NAME: | **ST. MARY'S ABBEY OLD GRAVEYARD** |
| GRAVEYARD CODE: | D1 |
| COUNTY: | MEATH |
| MEMORIAL NUMBER: | H 19 |
| ERECTED BY: | ROBERT MOONEY |
| ORIENTATION: | EAST |
| NUMBER OF COMPONENTS: | 1 |
| NUMBER OF INSCRIBED FACES: | 1 |
| NUMBER OF PEOPLE COMMEMORATED: | 10 |
| MEMORIAL TYPE: | HEADSTONE |
| CONDITION OF MEMORIAL: | EXCELLENT |
| CONDITION OF INSCRIPTION: | EXCELLENT |
| STONEMASON NAME: | |
| TECHNIQUE OF INSCRIPTION: | INCISED |
| UNDERTAKER: | |
| STONE TOP: | ROUND |
| GRAVE TYPE: | SINGLE |
| HEIGHT: | 193CM |
| WIDTH: | 86CM |
| THICKNESS: | 18CM |

| SURNAME: | CHRISTIAN | ADDRESS | DEATH | AGE |
|---|---|---|---|---|
| MOONEY | PATRICK | | 26 NOV 1834 | 65 |
| | PATRICK | | 26 NOV 1834 | 18 |
| | ALICE | | 17 JUN 1842 | 60 |
| | RICHARD | | 25 JAN 1848 | 60 |
| | CATHERINE | | 20 AUG 1891 | 57 |
| | ROBERT | | 11 APR 1902 | |
| | ALICE | | 16 AUG 1905 | |
| | RICHARD | | 07 DEC 1907 | |
| | ROSE ANNE | | 17 OCT 1908 | 35 |
| MOLLOY | KATIE | | 16 FEB 1913 | 43 |

**INSCRIPTION:**
ERECTED BY ROBERT MOONEY OF DULEEK IN MEMORY OF HIS FATHER PATRICK MOONEY WHO DEPARTE THIS LIFE 26TH NOV.1834 AGED 65YRS AND OF HIS BROTHER PATRICK THE SAME TIME AGED 18 YEARS. AND ALSO OF HIS MOTHER ALICE MOONEY WHO DEPARTED THIS LIFE 17TH OF JUNE 1842 AGED 60 YEARS
ALSO OF HIS BROTHER RICHARD MOONEY WHO DIED 25TH JAN.1898, AGED 80YEARS AND CATHERINE WIFE OF RICHARD WHO DIED 20TH AUG, 1891 AGED 57 YEARS ALSO HIS NEPHEW ROBERT WHO DIED 11TH APRIL 1902. AND HIS NIECE ALICE WHO DIED 16TH AUG.1905
ALSO HIS NEPHEW RICHARD WHO DIED 7TH DEC.1907. AND HIS NIECES ROSE ANNE WHO DIED 17TH OCT.1908 AGED 35 YEARS AND KATIE MOLLOY WHO DIED 16TH FEB.1913, AGED 43 YEARS
*REQUISCANT IN PACE. AMEN*

**SYMBOLS:**
IHS SUNBURST WITH CROSS AND SACRED HEART ABOVE THE H
TWO ANGELS WITH WINGS EACH SIDE OF SUNBURST SCROLL UNDER SUNBURST – MEMENTO MORI (*LATIN MEANS REMEMBER THAT YOU WILL DIE*) IN CENTRE

| | |
|---|---|
| NAME OF RECORDER: | SINEAD AND HELEN FULLAM |
| DATE: | 17 JUNE 2006 |
| PHOTO REFERENCE: | H19 |
| LOCATION/MAP REF: | D1 H19 |

| | |
|---|---|
| GRAVEYARD NAME: | **ST. MARY'S ABBEY OLD GRAVEYARD** |
| GRAVEYARD CODE: | D1 |
| COUNTY: | MEATH |
| MEMORIAL NUMBER: | K22 |
| ERECTED BY: | JOHN MOONEY |
| ORIENTATION: | EAST |
| NUMBER OF COMPONENTS: | 1 |
| NUMBER OF INSCRIBED FACES: | 1 |
| NUMBER OF PEOPLE COMMEMORATED: | 1 |
| MEMORIAL TYPE: | HEADSTONE |
| CONDITION OF MEMORIAL: | SOUND |
| CONDITION OF INSCRIPTION: | LEGIBLE |
| STONEMASON NAME: | |
| TECHNIQUE OF INSCRIPTION: | INCISED |
| UNDERTAKER: | |
| STONE TOP: | ROUND |
| GRAVE TYPE: | SINGLE |
| HEIGHT: | 88CM |
| WIDTH: | 61CM |
| THICKNESS: | 10CM |

| SURNAME: | CHRISTIAN | ADDRESS | DEATH | AGE |
|---|---|---|---|---|
| MOONEY | THOS. | | 07 JULY 1752 | 28 |

**INSCRIPTION:**
THIS BURIAL PLACE
BELONGETH TO JOHN MO
ONEY OF DROGHEDA
AND HIS POSTERITY
HERE LIES THE BODEY OF
THOS. MOONEY SON OF THE
ABOVE JOHN WHO DEPARTED
THIS LIFE THE 7 DAY OF JULY
1752 AGED 28 YERS

**SYMBOLS:**
CROSS

| | |
|---|---|
| NAME OF RECORDER: | PHYLLIS NOONAN |
| DATE: | 24 SEPT 2005 |
| PHOTO REFERENCE: | K22 |
| LOCATION/MAP REF: | D1 K22 |

| | |
|---|---|
| GRAVEYARD NAME: | **ST. MARY'S ABBEY OLD GRAVEYARD** |
| GRAVEYARD CODE: | D1 |
| COUNTY: | MEATH |
| MEMORIAL NUMBER: | C3 |
| ERECTED BY: | CATHERINE AND JANE MOORE |
| ORIENTATION: | EAST |
| NUMBER OF COMPONENTS: | 1 |
| NUMBER OF INSCRIBED FACES: | 1 |
| NUMBER OF PEOPLE COMMEMORATED: | 2 |
| MEMORIAL TYPE: | HEADSTONE |
| CONDITION OF MEMORIAL: | SOUND IN PLACE |
| CONDITION OF INSCRIPTION: | MAINLY DECIPHERABLE |
| STONEMASON NAME: | |
| TECHNIQUE OF INSCRIPTION: | INCISED |
| UNDERTAKER: | |
| STONE TOP: | ROUND |
| GRAVE TYPE: | SINGLE |
| HEIGHT: | 112CM |
| WIDTH: | 69CM |
| THICKNESS: | 17CM |

| SURNAME: | CHRISTIAN | ADDRESS | DEATH | AGE |
|---|---|---|---|---|
| MOORE | BRIDGET | CARNTOWN | 10 FEB 1872 | 70 YEARS |
| | CATHERINE | | 09 MAY 1901 | 67 YEARS |

**INSCRIPTION:**
THIS STONE HAS BEEN
ERECTED BY
CATHERINE & JANE MOORE
TO THE MEMORY
OF THEIR BELOVED MOTHER
BRIDGET MOORE
OF CARNTOWN COUNTY MEATH
WHO DIED 10TH
FEB.1872 AGED 70 YEARS
*MAY SHE REST IN PEACE*
ALSO THEIR DAUGHTER CATHERINE MOORE
WHO DIED MAY 9TH 1901 AGED 67 YEARS

**SYMBOLS:**
CROSS, FLANKED BY CHERUBS

| | |
|---|---|
| NAME OF RECORDER: | PHYLLIS NOONAN AND BEN RYAN |
| DATE: | 2 JULY 2005 |
| PHOTO REFERENCE: | C3 |
| LOCATION/MAP REF: | D1 C3 |

| | |
|---|---|
| GRAVEYARD NAME: | **ST. MARY'S ABBEY OLD GRAVEYARD** |
| GRAVEYARD CODE: | D1 |
| COUNTY: | MEATH |
| MEMORIAL NUMBER: | L28 |
| ERECTED BY: | |
| ORIENTATION: | EAST |
| NUMBER OF COMPONENTS: | 1 |
| NUMBER OF INSCRIBED FACES: | 1 |
| NUMBER OF PEOPLE COMMEMORATED: | 3 |
| MEMORIAL TYPE: | HEADSTONE |
| CONDITION OF MEMORIAL: | SOUND IN PLACE |
| CONDITION OF INSCRIPTION: | LEGIBLE |
| STONEMASON NAME: | |
| TECHNIQUE OF INSCRIPTION: | INCISED |
| UNDERTAKER: | |
| STONE TOP: | DISK TOP |
| GRAVE TYPE: | SINGLE |
| HEIGHT: | 134CM |
| WIDTH: | 66CM |
| THICKNESS: | 12CM |

| SURNAME: | CHRISTIAN | ADDRESS | DEATH | AGE |
|---|---|---|---|---|
| MOORE | JOHN | DULEEK | 21 SEPT 1809 | 55 |
| | JOHN | SON | 15 JAN 1836 | 31 |
| HEENEY | PATRICK | | 17 NOV 1821 | 41 |

**INSCRIPTION:**
TO THE MEMORY OF JOHN MOORE OF DULEEK WHO DIED 21ST SEPT 1809 AGED 55 YEARS. AND OF HIS SON JOHN MOORE WHO DIED 15TH JAN 1836 AGED 31 YRS AND OF PATRICK HEENEY WHO DIED 17TH NOVR 1821. AGED 41 YEARS REQUISCANT IN PACE

**SYMBOLS:**
DISK WITH SUNBURST AND IHS
CROSS WITH HEART

| | |
|---|---|
| NAME OF RECORDER: | LIZ LYNCH AND PHYLLIS NOONAN |
| DATE: | 30 MAY 2006 |
| PHOTO REFERENCE: | L28 |
| LOCATION/MAP REF: | D1 L28 |

| | |
|---|---|
| GRAVEYARD NAME: | **ST. MARY'S ABBEY OLD GRAVEYARD** |
| GRAVEYARD CODE: | D1 |
| COUNTY: | MEATH |
| MEMORIAL NUMBER: | J24 |
| ERECTED BY: | |
| ORIENTATION: | EAST |
| NUMBER OF COMPONENTS: | 1 |
| NUMBER OF INSCRIBED FACES: | 1 |
| NUMBER OF PEOPLE COMMEMORATED: | 5 |
| MEMORIAL TYPE: | HEADSTONE |
| CONDITION OF MEMORIAL: | SOUND IN PLACE |
| CONDITION OF INSCRIPTION: | MAINLY DECIPHERABLE |
| STONEMASON NAME: | |
| TECHNIQUE OF INSCRIPTION: | INCISED |
| UNDERTAKER: | |
| STONE TOP: | STEPPED DISK |
| GRAVE TYPE: | SINGLE |
| HEIGHT: | 70CM |
| WIDTH: | 55CM |
| THICKNESS: | 07CM |

| SURNAME: | CHRISTIAN | ADDRESS | DEATH | AGE |
|---|---|---|---|---|
| MOORE | CHRISTOPHER | | 21 MAY 1788 | 36 |

**INSCRIPTION:**
HERE LIETH YE BODY OF
CHRISTOPHER MOORE WHO
DEPED THIS LIFE YE 21 OF
MAY 1788 AGED 36 YEARS
HERE LIES 4 OF HIS CHILDREN

**SYMBOLS:**
CROSS
IHS

| | |
|---|---|
| NAME OF RECORDER: | LIZ LYNCH AND PHYLLIS NOONAN |
| DATE: | 16 AUG 2005 |
| PHOTO REFERENCE: | J24 |
| LOCATION/MAP REF: | D1 J24 |

| | |
|---|---|
| GRAVEYARD NAME: | **ST. MARY'S ABBEY OLD GRAVEYARD** |
| GRAVEYARD CODE: | D1 |
| COUNTY: | MEATH |
| MEMORIAL NUMBER: | L44 |
| ERECTED BY: | THOMAS MOORE |
| ORIENTATION: | EAST |
| NUMBER OF COMPONENTS: | 1 |
| NUMBER OF INSCRIBED FACES: | 1 |
| NUMBER OF PEOPLE COMMEMORATED: | 2 |
| MEMORIAL TYPE: | HEADSTONE |
| CONDITION OF MEMORIAL: | SOUND IN PLACE |
| CONDITION OF INSCRIPTION: | MAINLY DECIPHERABLE |
| STONEMASON NAME: | |
| TECHNIQUE OF INSCRIPTION: | INCISED |
| UNDERTAKER: | |
| STONE TOP: | ROUND |
| GRAVE TYPE: | SINGLE |
| HEIGHT: | 123CM |
| WIDTH: | 70CM |
| THICKNESS: | 10CM |

| SURNAME: | CHRISTIAN | ADDRESS | DEATH | AGE |
|---|---|---|---|---|
| MOORE | PATRICK | KNOCKISLAND | 12 MAY 1777 | 77 |
| | MARGARET | | 25 MAR 180? | 77 |

**INSCRIPTION:**
THIS STONE WAS ERECTED
BY THOMAS MOORE OF
KNOCKISLAND IN MEMORY
OF HIS FATHER PATRICK MOORE
WHO DEPARTED THIS LIFE THE
12TH MAY 1777 AGED 77
ALSO OF HIS MOTHER
MARGARET MOORE SHE DEP
ARTED THIS LIFE THE 25TH MARCH
180? AGED 77 YEARS

**SYMBOLS:**
IHS IN SUNBURST

| | |
|---|---|
| NAME OF RECORDER: | BEN RYAN, HELEN FULLAM AND JANET LEIGH |
| DATE: | 27 MAY 2006 |
| PHOTO REFERENCE: | L44 |
| LOCATION/MAP REF: | D1 L44 |

| | |
|---|---|
| GRAVEYARD NAME: | **ST. MARY'S ABBEY OLD GRAVEYARD** |
| GRAVEYARD CODE: | D1 |
| COUNTY: | MEATH |
| MEMORIAL NUMBER: | D14 |
| ERECTED BY: | |
| ORIENTATION: | EAST |
| NUMBER OF COMPONENTS: | 5 |
| NUMBER OF INSCRIBED FACES: | 1 |
| NUMBER OF PEOPLE COMMEMORATED: | 6 |
| MEMORIAL TYPE: | ELABORATE CROSS OVER HEADSTONE ON PEDESTAL |
| CONDITION OF MEMORIAL: | SOUND IN PLACE |
| CONDITION OF INSCRIPTION: | CLEAR |
| STONEMASON NAME: | |
| TECHNIQUE OF INSCRIPTION: | INCISED & PAINTED |
| UNDERTAKER: | |
| STONE TOP: | CROSS |
| GRAVE TYPE: | TREBLE |
| HEIGHT: | 265CM |
| WIDTH: | 63CM |
| THICKNESS: | 22CM |

| SURNAME: | CHRISTIAN | ADDRESS | DEATH | AGE |
|---|---|---|---|---|
| MOSS | MICHAEL | DULEEK | 25 FEB 1891 | |
| | ROBERT | | 03 APR 1892 | |
| | THOMAS | | 29 AUG 1929 | |
| | JOSEPHINE | | 28 FEB 1941 | |
| | PETER | | 09 FEB 1990 | |
| | ITA | | 28 SEPT 1998 | |

**INSCRIPTION:**
IN MEMORY OF
MICHAEL MOSS DULEEK
DIED 25 FEB 1891 HIS SONS
ROBERT DIED 3 APRIL 1892
THOMAS DIED 29 AUG 1929
JOSEPHINE WIFE OF THOMAS
DIED 28 FEB 1941
PETER SON OF
THOMAS AND JOSEPHINE
DIED 19 FEB 1990
ITA WIFE OF PETER
DIED 28 SEP 1998
R.I.P

**SYMBOLS:**
ELABORATE HEADSTONE WITH FLEUR DE LIS
CROSS INTERWOVEN IHS

| | |
|---|---|
| NAME OF RECORDER: | LIZ LYNCH |
| DATE: | 13 JULY 2005 |
| PHOTO REFERENCE: | D 14 |
| LOCATION/MAP REF: | D1 D14 |

| | |
|---|---|
| GRAVEYARD NAME: | **ST. MARY'S ABBEY OLD GRAVEYARD** |
| GRAVEYARD CODE: | D1 |
| COUNTY: | MEATH |
| MEMORIAL NUMBER: | D15 A |
| ERECTED BY: | |
| ORIENTATION: | EAST |
| NUMBER OF COMPONENTS: | 3 |
| NUMBER OF INSCRIBED FACES: | 3 |
| NUMBER OF PEOPLE COMMEMORATED: | 3 |
| MEMORIAL TYPE: | CROSS ON PEDESTAL |
| CONDITION OF MEMORIAL: | SOUND IN PLACE |
| CONDITION OF INSCRIPTION: | CLEAR |
| STONEMASON NAME: | |
| TECHNIQUE OF INSCRIPTION: | INCISED |
| UNDERTAKER: | |
| STONE TOP: | CROSS |
| GRAVE TYPE: | DOUBLE |
| HEIGHT: | 254CM |
| WIDTH: | 60CM |
| THICKNESS: | 61CM |

| SURNAME: | CHRISTIAN | ADDRESS | DEATH | AGE |
|---|---|---|---|---|
| MOSS | PATRICK | CUSHINSTOWN | 27 OCT 1882 | 84 |
| | SARAH | | 26 JAN 1879 | |
| | ANNE | | 02 MAY 1884 | 84 |

**INSCRIPTION:**
IN MEMORY OF
PATRICK MOSS
OF CUSHINSTOWN
WHO DIED
OCT 27 1882 AGED 84 YEARS
AND HIS SISTER
SARAH
WHO DIED 26 JAN 1879
ALSO HIS WIFE
ANNE
WHO DIED 2 MAY 1884 AGED 84 EARS
*MAY THEY REST IN PEACE*

**SYMBOLS:**
HIGH CROSS ENTWINED WITH VINE
LEAVES. THREE FACES OF PEDESTAL ENGRAVED
NORTH - AN ANCHOR AND CROSS OVER WAVES
SOUTH - HEART IN FLAMES OVER CROSS

| | |
|---|---|
| NAME OF RECORDER: | PHYLLIS NOONAN |
| DATE: | 14 JULY 2005 |
| PHOTO REFERENCE: | D15 |
| LOCATION/MAP REF: | D1 D15A |

| | |
|---|---|
| GRAVEYARD NAME: | **ST. MARY'S ABBEY OLD GRAVEYARD** |
| GRAVEYARD CODE: | D1 |
| COUNTY: | MEATH |
| MEMORIAL NUMBER: | D15B |
| ERECTED BY: | PETER MOSS |
| ORIENTATION: | EAST |
| NUMBER OF COMPONENTS: | CROSS MISSING |
| NUMBER OF INSCRIBED FACES: | 1 |
| NUMBER OF PEOPLE COMMEMORATED: | 6 |
| MEMORIAL TYPE: | HEADSTONE |
| CONDITION OF MEMORIAL: | SOUND IN PLACE |
| CONDITION OF INSCRIPTION: | CLEAR |
| STONEMASON NAME: | |
| TECHNIQUE OF INSCRIPTION: | INCISED |
| UNDERTAKER: | |
| STONE TOP: | |
| GRAVE TYPE: | SINGLE |
| HEIGHT: | 82CM |
| WIDTH: | 56CM |
| THICKNESS: | 22CM |

| SURNAME: | CHRISTIAN | ADDRESS | DEATH | AGE |
|---|---|---|---|---|
| MOSS | GEORGE | CUSHENSTOWN | 14 MAR 1892 | 60 |
| | CHRISTOPHER | | 26 FEB 1896 | 27 |
| | JULIA | | 22 MAY 1890 | 64 |
| | MICHAEL | | DIED YOUNG | |
| | FRANCIS | | 09 APR 1925 | 55 |
| | PETER | | 03 DEC 1930 | |

**INSCRIPTION:**

ERECTED BY PETER MOSS
IN MEMORY OF HIS FATHER
GEORGE MOSS CUSHENSTOWN
DIED 14 MARCH 1892 AGED 60
HIS SON CHRISTOPHER
DIED 26 FEB 1896 AGED 27
HIS WIFE JULIA (NEE MCKEON)
DIED 12 MAY 1890 AGED 64
THEIR SON MICHAEL DIED YOUNG
THEIR SON FRANCIS
DIED 9 APRIL 1925 AGED 55
THE ABOVE NAMED PETER
WHO DIED 3 DEC 1930
R.I.P.

**SYMBOLS:**

CROSS MISSING ON TOP

| | |
|---|---|
| NAME OF RECORDER: | LIZ LYNCH |
| DATE: | 13 JULY 2005 |
| PHOTO REFERENCE: | D15 |
| LOCATION/MAP REFERENCE: | D1 D 15B |

| | |
|---|---|
| GRAVEYARD NAME: | **ST. MARY'S ABBEY OLD GRAVEYARD** |
| GRAVEYARD CODE: | D1 |
| COUNTY: | MEATH |
| MEMORIAL NUMBER: | F14 A |
| ERECTED BY: | |
| ORIENTATION: | EAST |
| NUMBER OF COMPONENTS: | 2 |
| NUMBER OF INSCRIBED FACES: | 1 |
| NUMBER OF PEOPLE COMMEMORATED: | 2 |
| MEMORIAL TYPE: | HEADSTONE WITH CROSS |
| CONDITION OF MEMORIAL: | COLLAPSED IN SITE |
| CONDITION OF INSCRIPTION: | CLEAR |
| STONEMASON NAME: | |
| TECHNIQUE OF INSCRIPTION: | INCISED |
| UNDERTAKER: | |
| STONE TOP: | CROSS DETACHED |
| GRAVE TYPE: | DOUBLE |
| HEIGHT: | 79CM |
| WIDTH: | 38CM |
| THICKNESS: | 06CM |

| SURNAME: | CHRISTIAN | ADDRESS | DEATH | AGE |
|---|---|---|---|---|
| MURRAY | JOHN | CASTLEMARTIN NAVAN CO. MEATH | 04 MAY 1959 | 76 |
| | CHRISTOPHER | | 07 MAR 1977 | 65 |

**INSCRIPTION:**
IN
LOVING MEMORY
OF
JOHN MURRAY
CASTLEMARTIN NAVAN
DIED 4TH MAY 1959
AGED 76 YRS
HIS SON
CHRISTOPHER
DIED 7TH MARCH 1977
AGED 65 YRS
RIP
KNEEL AND PRAY

**SYMBOLS:**
ORNATE IHS

| | |
|---|---|
| NAME OF RECORDER: | PHYLLIS NOONAN |
| DATE: | 19 JULY 2005 |
| PHOTO REFERENCE: | F14 |
| LOCATION/MAP REF: | D1 F14 |

| | |
|---|---|
| GRAVEYARD NAME: | **ST. MARY'S ABBEY OLD GRAVEYARD** |
| GRAVEYARD CODE: | D1 |
| COUNTY: | MEATH |
| MEMORIAL NUMBER: | F14 B |
| ERECTED BY: | |
| ORIENTATION: | EAST |
| NUMBER OF COMPONENTS: | 1 |
| NUMBER OF INSCRIBED FACES: | 1 |
| NUMBER OF PEOPLE COMMEMORATED: | 3 |
| MEMORIAL TYPE: | HEADSTONE |
| CONDITION OF MEMORIAL: | SOUND IN PLACE |
| CONDITION OF INSCRIPTION: | CLEAR |
| STONEMASON NAME: | T. REID |
| TECHNIQUE OF INSCRIPTION: | INCISED |
| UNDERTAKER: | |
| STONE TOP: | ARCH |
| GRAVE TYPE: | DOUBLE |
| HEIGHT: | 127CM |
| WIDTH: | 53CM |
| THICKNESS: | 05CM |

| SURNAME: | CHRISTIAN | ADDRESS | DEATH | AGE |
|---|---|---|---|---|
| MURRAY | MARGARET | NEWTOWN, DULEEK | 10 AUG 1932 | |
| | CHRISTOPHER | | 12 JUL 1940 | |
| | ELIZABETH | | 27 JUN 1936 | |

**INSCRIPTION:**
IN LOVING MEMORY
OF
MARGARET MURRAY
NEWTOWN
DIED 10 AUG 1932
HER HUSBAND CHRISTOPHER
DIED 12 JULY 1940
THEIR DAUGHTER IN LAW
ELIZABETH
DIED 27 JUNE 1936
*RIP*
KNEEL AND PRAY

**SYMBOLS:**
CROSS WITH VINE LEAVES

| | |
|---|---|
| NAME OF RECORDER: | JANET LEIGH AND PHYLLIS NOONAN |
| DATE: | 19 JULY 2005 |
| PHOTO REFERENCE: | F14 |
| LOCATION/MAP REF: | D1 F14 |

| | |
|---|---|
| GRAVEYARD NAME: | **ST. MARY'S ABBEY OLD GRAVEYARD** |
| GRAVEYARD CODE: | D1 |
| COUNTY: | MEATH |
| MEMORIAL NUMBER: | L10 |
| ERECTED BY: | LUKE MURTAGH |
| ORIENTATION: | EAST |
| NUMBER OF COMPONENTS: | 1 |
| NUMBER OF INSCRIBED FACES: | 1 |
| NUMBER OF PEOPLE COMMEMORATED: | 1 |
| MEMORIAL TYPE: | HEADSTONE |
| CONDITION OF MEMORIAL: | SOUND IN PLACE |
| CONDITION OF INSCRIPTION: | MAINLY DECIPHERABLE |
| STONEMASON NAME: | |
| TECHNIQUE OF INSCRIPTION: | INCISED |
| UNDERTAKER: | |
| STONE TOP: | ROUND |
| GRAVE TYPE: | SINGLE |
| HEIGHT: | 132CM |
| WIDTH: | 80CM |
| THICKNESS: | 14CM |

| SURNAME: | CHRISTIAN | ADDRESS | DEATH | AGE |
|---|---|---|---|---|
| MURTAGH | OWEN | | 12 APR 1799 | 51 |
| | | | | |

**INSCRIPTION:**
ERECTED
BY LUKE MURTAGH IN MEMORY OF
HIS FATHER OWEN MURTAGH WHO
DEPARTED THIS LIFE THE 12TH APRIL
1799 AGED 51 YEARS
REQUIESCANT IN PACE AMEN

**SYMBOLS:**
SMALL CROSS WITH IHS IN
SUNBURST

| | |
|---|---|
| NAME OF RECORDER: | JANET LEIGH AND SINEAD FULLAM |
| DATE: | 20 MAY 2006 |
| PHOTO REFERENCE: | L19 |
| LOCATION/MAP REF: | D1 L10 |

| | |
|---|---|
| GRAVEYARD NAME: | **ST. MARY'S ABBEY OLD GRAVEYARD** |
| GRAVEYARD CODE: | D1 |
| COUNTY: | MEATH |
| MEMORIAL NUMBER: | K12 |
| ERECTED BY: | JOHN NEIL |
| ORIENTATION: | EAST |
| NUMBER OF COMPONENTS: | 1 |
| NUMBER OF INSCRIBED FACES: | 1 |
| NUMBER OF PEOPLE COMMEMORATED: | 3 |
| MEMORIAL TYPE: | HEADSTONE |
| CONDITION OF MEMORIAL: | SOUND IN PLACE |
| CONDITION OF INSCRIPTION: | MAINLY DECIPHERABLE |
| STONEMASON NAME: | |
| TECHNIQUE OF INSCRIPTION: | INCISED |
| UNDERTAKER: | |
| STONE TOP: | STEPPED DISK |
| GRAVE TYPE: | SINGLE |
| HEIGHT: | 135CM |
| WIDTH: | 70CM |
| THICKNESS: | 05CM |

| SURNAME: | CHRISTIAN | ADDRESS | DEATH | AGE |
|---|---|---|---|---|
| NEIL | JOHN | | 09 APR 1834 | 74 |
| | MACELLA | | 03 JAN 1842 | 64 |
| | MARGARET | | 02 JAN | |

**INSCRIPTION:**
ERECTED BY JOHN NEIL OF DULEEK IN MEMORY OF HIS FATHER JOHN NEIL WHO DEPARTED THE 9TH APRIL 1834 AGED 74 YEARS ALSO HIS MOTHER MACELLA THE 3RD OF JANUARY 1842 AGED 64 HIS SISTER MARGARET THE 2ND JANUARY

**SYMBOLS:**
IHS IN SUNBURST ROSETTE

| | |
|---|---|
| NAME OF RECORDER: | JANET LEIGH AND HELEN FULLAM |
| DATE: | 27 AUGUST 2005 |
| PHOTO REFERENCE: | K12 |
| LOCATION/MAP REF: | D1 K12 |

| | |
|---|---|
| GRAVEYARD NAME: | **ST. MARY'S ABBEY OLD GRAVEYARD** |
| GRAVEYARD CODE: | D1 |
| COUNTY: | MEATH |
| MEMORIAL NUMBER: | E6 |
| ERECTED BY: | |
| ORIENTATION: | EAST |
| NUMBER OF COMPONENTS: | 2 |
| NUMBER OF INSCRIBED FACES: | 1 |
| NUMBER OF PEOPLE COMMEMORATED: | 1 |
| MEMORIAL TYPE: | HEADSTONE |
| CONDITION OF MEMORIAL: | SOUND IN PLACE |
| CONDITION OF INSCRIPTION: | CLEAR |
| STONEMASON NAME: | |
| TECHNIQUE OF INSCRIPTION: | INCISED |
| UNDERTAKER: | |
| STONE TOP: | ROUND |
| GRAVE TYPE: | SINGLE |
| HEIGHT: | 190CM |
| WIDTH: | 68CM |
| THICKNESS: | 18CM |

| SURNAME: | CHRISTIAN | ADDRESS | DEATH | AGE |
|---|---|---|---|---|
| NIXON | RICHARD | PLATTEN | 18 SEPT 1897 | 85 |

**INSCRIPTION:**
ERECTED
IN LOVING MEMORY
OF
RICHARD NIXON
PLATTEN
WHO DEPARTED THIS LIFE
SEPTEMBER 18 1897
AGED 85 YEARS
DEATH IS SWALLOWED IN VICTORY
BUT THANKS BE TO GOD
WHICH GIVETH US THE VICTORY
THROUGH OUR LORD JESUS CHRIST
COR:(15 XV CH.) (LIV. LV11) 54 - 57

| | |
|---|---|
| NAME OF RECORDER: | JANET LEIGH AND BEN RYAN |
| DATE: | 16 JULY 2005 |
| PHOTO REFERENCE: | E6 |
| LOCATION/MAP REF: | D1 E6 |

| | |
|---|---|
| GRAVEYARD NAME: | **ST. MARY'S ABBEY OLD GRAVEYARD** |
| GRAVEYARD CODE: | D1 |
| COUNTY: | MEATH |
| MEMORIAL NUMBER: | F26 |
| ERECTED BY: | MARGARET NULTY |
| ORIENTATION: | EAST |
| NUMBER OF COMPONENTS: | 1 |
| NUMBER OF INSCRIBED FACES: | 1 |
| NUMBER OF PEOPLE COMMEMORATED: | 8 |
| MEMORIAL TYPE: | LOW MONUMENT |
| CONDITION OF MEMORIAL: | DISPLACED ON A SLOPE |
| CONDITION OF INSCRIPTION: | MAINLY DECIPHERABLE |
| STONEMASON NAME: | |
| TECHNIQUE OF INSCRIPTION: | INCISED |
| UNDERTAKER: | |
| STONE TOP: | LOW MONUMENT |
| GRAVE TYPE: | TREBLE |
| HEIGHT: | 241 LONG |
| WIDTH: | 121CM |
| THICKNESS: | 13 CM |

| SURNAME: | CHRISTIAN | ADDRESS | DEATH | AGE |
|---|---|---|---|---|
| NULTY | PATRICK | | 1802 | |
| | ELIZABETH | | 09 APR 1835 | |
| | MARY | | 20 OCT 1844 | |
| | DENIS | | 14 SEPT 1864 | |
| | JANE | | 22 SEPT 1868 | |
| | CHRISTOPHER | | 13 MAY 1873 | |
| | MARGARET | ATHLUMNEY | 04 MAY 1877 | |
| | MARY | | 24 MAY 1886 | |

**INSCRIPTION:**
THIS TOMBSTONE WAS ERECTED
BY MARGARET NULTY OF ATHLUMNEY
IN MEMORY OF HER DEAR FATHER PATRICK NULTY
WHO DEPARTED THIS LIFE 1802
ALSO HER DEAR MOTHER ELIZABETH NULTY
WHO DEPARTED THIS LIFE
9 APRIL 1835
ALSO HER SISTER MARY NULTY
WHO DEPARTED THIS LIFE
20 OCTOBER 1844
ALSO HER BROTHER DENIS NULTY
WHO DEPARTED THIS LIFE
14 SEPTEMBER 1864
ALSO HER SISTER JANE NULTY
WHO DEPARTED THIS LIFE
2 DECEMBER 1868
ALSO CHRISTOPHER NULTY
WHO DEPARTED THIS LIFE
THE 13TH MAY 1872
AGED 84 YEARS
ALSO MARGARET NULTY WHO DEPARTED THIS LIFE
ON THE 4 DAY OF MAY 1877
ALSO MARY NULTY WHO DEPARTED THIS LIFE
ON THE 24 MAY 1886

*RESQUISCANT IN PACE*

| | |
|---|---|
| NAME OF RECORDER: | ALFIE WOODS, SINEAD FULLAM AND PHYLLIS NOONAN |
| DATE: | 20 JULY 2005 |
| PHOTO REFERENCE: | F26 |
| LOCATION/MAP REF: | D1 F26 |

| | |
|---|---|
| GRAVEYARD NAME: | **ST. MARY'S ABBEY OLD GRAVEYARD** |
| GRAVEYARD CODE: | D1 |
| COUNTY: | MEATH |
| MEMORIAL NUMBER: | K28 |
| ERECTED BY: | |
| ORIENTATION: | EAST |
| NUMBER OF COMPONENTS: | 4 |
| NUMBER OF INSCRIBED FACES: | 1 |
| NUMBER OF PEOPLE COMMEMORATED: | 1 |
| MEMORIAL TYPE: | TALL CELTIC CROSS ON PEDESTAL |
| CONDITION OF MEMORIAL: | SOUND IN PLACE |
| CONDITION OF INSCRIPTION: | DECIPHERABLE |
| STONEMASON NAME: | T. RIED |
| TECHNIQUE OF INSCRIPTION: | INCISED |
| UNDERTAKER: | |
| STONE TOP: | CELTIC CROSS |
| GRAVE TYPE: | SINGLE |
| HEIGHT: | 94CM |
| WIDTH: | 41CM |
| THICKNESS: | 15CM |

| SURNAME: | CHRISTIAN | ADDRESS | DEATH | AGE |
|---|---|---|---|---|
| O'BRIEN CAMPBELL | GERALDINE ELIZABETH | | 10 MAR 2005 | |

**INSCRIPTION:**
IN LOVING MEMORY
OF
GERALDINE ELIZABETH O'BRIEN
NEE CAMPBELL
A DEVOTED WIFE AND MOTHER
DIED 10TH MARCH 2005

*BEAUTIFUL MEMORIES*
*TREASURED FOREVER OF THE LOVE*
*AND HAPPINESS SHARED TOGETHER*

**SYMBOLS:**
TALL ELABORATE CELTIC CROSS
IHS IN CENTRE

| | |
|---|---|
| NAME OF RECORDER: | LIZ LYNCH AND PHYLLIS NOONAN |
| DATE: | 20 SEPT 2008 |
| PHOTO REFERENCE: | K28 |
| LOCATION/MAP REF: | D1 K28 |

| | |
|---|---|
| GRAVEYARD NAME: | **ST. MARY'S ABBEY OLD GRAVEYARD** |
| GRAVEYARD CODE: | D1 |
| COUNTY: | MEATH |
| MEMORIAL NUMBER: | K54 |
| ERECTED BY: | MICHAEL O'CONNOR |
| ORIENTATION: | EAST |
| NUMBER OF COMPONENTS: | 2 |
| NUMBER OF INSCRIBED FACES: | 1 |
| NUMBER OF PEOPLE COMMEMORATED: | 1 |
| MEMORIAL TYPE: | HEADSTONE CELTIC CROSS |
| CONDITION OF MEMORIAL: | SOUND IN PLACE |
| CONDITION OF INSCRIPTION: | CLEAR |
| STONEMASON NAME: | T. COONEY |
| TECHNIQUE OF INSCRIPTION: | INCISED AND PAINTED |
| UNDERTAKER: | |
| STONE TOP: | CELTIC CROSS |
| GRAVE TYPE: | SINGLE |
| HEIGHT: | 139CM |
| WIDTH: | 55CM |
| THICKNESS: | 05CM |

| SURNAME: | CHRISTIAN | ADDRESS | DEATH | AGE |
|---|---|---|---|---|
| O'CONNOR | THOMAS | THE MOATE DULEEK | 7 JUN 1835 | |

**INSCRIPTION:**
IN LOVING MEMORY
OF
THOMAS O'CONNOR
THE MOATE DULEEK
DIED 7TH JUNE 1935

R.I.P.

| | |
|---|---|
| NAME OF RECORDER: | PHYLLIS NOONAN |
| DATE: | 24 JUNE 2013 |
| PHOTO REFERENCE: | K54 |
| LOCATION/MAP REF: | D1 K54 |

| | |
|---|---|
| GRAVEYARD NAME: | **ST. MARY'S ABBEY OLD GRAVEYARD** |
| GRAVEYARD CODE: | D1 |
| COUNTY: | MEATH |
| MEMORIAL NUMBER: | E5 A |
| ERECTED BY: | |
| ORIENTATION: | EAST |
| NUMBER OF COMPONENTS: | 2 |
| NUMBER OF INSCRIBED FACES: | 1 |
| NUMBER OF PEOPLE COMMEMORATED: | 4 |
| MEMORIAL TYPE: | HEADSTONE WITH CELTIC MOTIFS |
| CONDITION OF MEMORIAL: | SOUND IN PLACE |
| CONDITION OF INSCRIPTION: | CLEAR |
| STONEMASON NAME: | FARRELL & SON, GLASNEVIN |
| TECHNIQUE OF INSCRIPTION: | INCISED |
| UNDERTAKER: | |
| STONE TOP: | CELTIC CROSS |
| GRAVE TYPE: | DOUBLE |
| HEIGHT: | 188CM |
| WIDTH: | 59CM |
| THICKNESS: | 08CM |

| SURNAME: | CHRISTIAN | ADDRESS | OCCUPATION | DEATH | AGE |
|---|---|---|---|---|---|
| O'KEEFFE | WILLIAM JOSEPH | | MD | 16 JAN 1909 | |
| | CATHLEEN | | | 12 JUN 1914 | |
| | JOSEPH RICHARD | | SOLDIER | 04 MAY 1916 | |
| | WILLIAM DESMOND | | | 1916 | |

**INSCRIPTION:**
IN
MEMORY OF
WILLIAM JOSEPH O'KEEFFE MD
DIED 16TH JAN 1909
AND HIS BELOVED WIFE CATHLEEN
DIED 12TH JUNE 1914
ALSO THEIR SONS
JOSEPH RICHARD LT. ROYAL NORTH LANCS.
KILLED IN ACTION IN FRANCE 4TH MAY 1916
WILLIAM DESMOND
KILLED IN SOUTH AMERICA 1916
*MY JESUS MERCY*
R.I.P.

**SYMBOLS:**
CELTIC CROSS WITH INTERWOVEN IHS

**ORNAMENTS:**
CELTIC ORNAMENTATION

| | |
|---|---|
| NAME OF RECORDER: | SHAUN LYNCH |
| DATE: | 16 JULY 2005 |
| PHOTO REFERENCE: | E5 |
| LOCATION/MAP REF: | D1 E5A |

| | |
|---|---|
| GRAVEYARD NAME: | **ST. MARY'S ABBEY OLD GRAVEYARD** |
| GRAVEYARD CODE: | D1 |
| COUNTY: | MEATH |
| MEMORIAL NUMBER: | E5 B |
| ERECTED BY: | |
| ORIENTATION: | EAST |
| NUMBER OF COMPONENTS: | 2 |
| NUMBER OF INSCRIBED FACES: | 1 |
| NUMBER OF PEOPLE COMMEMORATED: | 1 |
| MEMORIAL TYPE: | MARBLE CROSS |
| CONDITION OF MEMORIAL: | SOUND IN PLACE |
| CONDITION OF INSCRIPTION: | CLEAR |
| STONEMASON NAME: | |
| TECHNIQUE OF INSCRIPTION: | INCISED |
| UNDERTAKER: | |
| STONE TOP: | CROSS |
| GRAVE TYPE: | TREBLE |
| HEIGHT: | 40CM |
| WIDTH: | 48CM |
| THICKNESS: | 10CM |

| SURNAME: | CHRISTIAN | ADDRESS | DEATH | AGE |
|---|---|---|---|---|
| O'KEEFFE | CONSTANCE CLARE | | 28 JAN 1895 | 1 YEAR 9 MTHS |

**INSCRIPTION:**
CONSTANCE
CLARE
O'KEEFFE
AGED 1 YEAR
AND 9 MONTHS
DIED JAN 28TH 95

| | |
|---|---|
| NAME OF RECORDER: | PHYLLIS NOONAN |
| DATE: | 16 JULY 2005 |
| PHOTO REFERENCE: | E5 B |
| LOCATION/MAP REF: | D1 E5 B |

| | |
|---|---|
| GRAVEYARD NAME: | **ST. MARY'S ABBEY OLD GRAVEYARD** |
| GRAVEYARD CODE: | D1 |
| COUNTY: | MEATH |
| MEMORIAL NUMBER: | L33 |
| ERECTED BY: | |
| ORIENTATION: | EAST |
| NUMBER OF COMPONENTS: | 1 |
| NUMBER OF INSCRIBED FACES: | MISSING |
| NUMBER OF PEOPLE COMMEMORATED: | |
| MEMORIAL TYPE: | CEMENT CROSS |
| CONDITION OF MEMORIAL: | SOUND IN PLACE |
| CONDITION OF INSCRIPTION: | MISSING |
| STONEMASON NAME: | |
| TECHNIQUE OF INSCRIPTION: | MISSING |
| UNDERTAKER: | |
| STONE TOP: | CROSS |
| GRAVE TYPE: | SINGLE |
| HEIGHT: | 99CM |
| WIDTH: | 86CM |
| THICKNESS: | 14CM |

**INSCRIPTION:**
O'ROURKE
SHEERIN
R.I.P

| | |
|---|---|
| NAME OF RECORDER: | JANET LEIGH AND LIZ LYNCH |
| DATE: | 7 JUNE 2006 |
| PHOTO REFERENCE: | L33 |
| LOCATION/MAP REF | D1 L33 |

| | |
|---|---|
| GRAVEYARD NAME: | **ST. MARY'S ABBEY OLD GRAVEYARD** |
| GRAVEYARD CODE: | D1 |
| COUNTY: | MEATH |
| MEMORIAL NUMBER: | K31 |
| ERECTED BY: | LAURENCE WHITE |
| ORIENTATION: | EAST |
| NUMBER OF COMPONENTS: | 2 |
| NUMBER OF INSCRIBED FACES: | 1 |
| NUMBER OF PEOPLE COMMEMORATED: | 5 |
| MEMORIAL TYPE: | HEADSTONE |
| CONDITION OF MEMORIAL: | SOUND IN PLACE |
| CONDITION OF INSCRIPTION: | CLEAR |
| STONEMASON NAME: | WHYTE CHORD ROAD DROGHEDA |
| TECHNIQUE OF INSCRIPTION: | RELIEF IN LEAD LETTERS |
| UNDERTAKER: | |
| STONE TOP: | ROUND |
| GRAVE TYPE: | SINGLE |
| HEIGHT: | 160CM |
| WIDTH: | 65CM |
| THICKNESS: | 08CM |

| SURNAME: | CHRISTIAN | ADDRESS | DEATH | AGE |
|---|---|---|---|---|
| OSBORNE | MARGARET | | 17 JAN 1887 | 54 |
| WHITE | PETER | | 16 FEB 1904 | 68 |
| | LAURENCE | CARNS | 15 JAN 1908 | 42 |
| | PATRICK | | 03 FEB 1909 | 45 |
| | JANE | | 09 FEB 1912 | 91 |

**INSCRIPTION:**
ERECTED
BY
LAURENCE WHITE
CARNS
IN MEMORY OF HIS AUNT
MARGARET OSBORNE
WHO DIED 17 JAN 1887
AGED 54 YEARS
AND HIS FATHER
PETER WHITE
WHO DIED 16 FEB 1904 AGED 68 YRS
THE ABOVE NAMED
LAURENCE
WHO DIED 15 JAN 1908 AGED 42 YRS
AND HIS BROTHER
PATRICK
WHO DIED 3 FEB 1909 AGED 45 YRS
ALSO HIS MOTHER
JANE
WHO DIED 9 FEB 1912 AGED 91 YRS
R.I.P.

**SYMBOLS:**
ROSES IN SMALL SUNBURST

| | |
|---|---|
| NAME OF RECORDER: | PHYLLIS NOONAN |
| DATE: | 24 APRIL 2006 |
| PHOTO REFERENCE: | K31 |
| LOCATION/MAP REF: | D1 K31 |

| | |
|---|---|
| GRAVEYARD NAME: | **ST. MARY'S ABBEY OLD GRAVEYARD** |
| GRAVEYARD CODE: | D1 |
| COUNTY: | MEATH |
| MEMORIAL NUMBER: | K23 |
| ERECTED BY: | |
| ORIENTATION: | EAST |
| NUMBER OF COMPONENTS: | 1 |
| NUMBER OF INSCRIBED FACES: | 1 |
| NUMBER OF PEOPLE COMMEMORATED: | 2 |
| MEMORIAL TYPE: | HEADSTONE |
| CONDITION OF MEMORIAL: | SOUND |
| CONDITION OF INSCRIPTION: | DECIPHERABLE |
| STONEMASON NAME: | |
| TECHNIQUE OF INSCRIPTION: | INCISED |
| UNDERTAKER: | |
| STONE TOP: | ROUND |
| GRAVE TYPE: | SINGLE |
| HEIGHT: | 112CM |
| WIDTH: | 62CM |
| THICKNESS: | 12CM |

| SURNAME: | CHRISTIAN | ADDRESS | DEATH | AGE |
|---|---|---|---|---|
| OSBURN | RICHARD | | 17 SEPT 1724 | 79 |
| | PATRICK | | 21 APR 1726 | 22 |
| | | | | |

**INSCRIPTION:**
HERE LIES YE BODY OF
RICHARD OSBURN WHO DYED
SEPBR YE 17TH 1724 AGED 79
YEARS
ALSO HIS SON PATRICK WHO
DYED APRL YE 21ST 1726 AGED
22 YEARS

| | |
|---|---|
| NAME OF RECORDER: | SINEAD FULLAM AND HELEN FULLAM |
| DATE: | 08 OCT 2005 |
| PHOTO REFERENCE: | K23 |
| LOCATION/MAP REF: | D1 K23 |

| | |
|---|---|
| GRAVEYARD NAME: | **ST. MARY'S ABBEY OLD GRAVEYARD** |
| GRAVEYARD CODE: | D1 |
| COUNTY: | MEATH |
| MEMORIAL NUMBER: | K33 |
| ERECTED BY: | JOHN OSBURN |
| ORIENTATION: | EAST |
| NUMBER OF COMPONENTS: | 1 |
| NUMBER OF INSCRIBED FACES: | 1 |
| NUMBER OF PEOPLE COMMEMORATED: | 5 |
| MEMORIAL TYPE: | HEADSTONE |
| CONDITION OF MEMORIAL: | SOUND IN PLACE |
| CONDITION OF INSCRIPTION: | MAINLY DECIPHERABLE |
| STONEMASON NAME: | |
| TECHNIQUE OF INSCRIPTION: | INCISED |
| UNDERTAKER: | |
| STONE TOP: | ROUND |
| GRAVE TYPE: | SINGLE |
| HEIGHT: | 79CM |
| WIDTH: | 70CM |
| THICKNESS: | 07CM |

| SURNAME: | CHRISTIAN | ADDRESS | DEATH | AGE |
|---|---|---|---|---|
| OSBURN | JOHN | CITY OF DUBLIN BAKER | | |
| | 4 OF HIS CHILDREN | | | |

**INSCRIPTION:**
THIS STONE AND BURIAL PLACE BELONGETH TO MR JOHN OSBURN BAKER OF THE CITY OF DUBLIN AND HIS POSTERITY 1758 AND ALSO FOUR OF HIS CHILDREN

**SYMBOLS:**
CROSS OVER IHS

| | |
|---|---|
| NAME OF RECORDER: | JANET LEIGH AND PHYLLIS NOONAN |
| DATE: | 22 APRIL 2006 |
| PHOTO REFERENCE: | K33 |
| LOCATION/MAP REF: | D1 K33 |

| | |
|---|---|
| GRAVEYARD NAME: | **ST. MARY'S ABBEY OLD GRAVEYARD** |
| GRAVEYARD CODE: | D1 |
| COUNTY: | MEATH |
| MEMORIAL NUMBER: | A2 |
| ERECTED BY: | |
| ORIENTATION: | EAST |
| NUMBER OF COMPONENTS: | 2 |
| NUMBER OF INSCRIBED FACES: | 1 |
| NUMBER OF PEOPLE COMMEMORATED: | 3 |
| MEMORIAL TYPE: | HEADSTONE |
| CONDITION OF MEMORIAL: | SOUND IN PLACE |
| CONDITION OF INSCRIPTION: | MINT |
| STONEMASON NAME: | CAFFREY |
| TECHNIQUE OF INSCRIPTION: | INCISED PAINTED |
| UNDERTAKER: | |
| STONE TOP: | ROUND |
| GRAVE TYPE: | TREBLE |
| HEIGHT: | 105CM |
| WIDTH: | 68CM |
| THICKNESS: | 07CM |

| SURNAME: | CHRISTIAN | ADDRESS | DEATH | AGE |
|---|---|---|---|---|
| OWENS | JOSEPH (JOE) | DULEEK | 21 DEC 1983 | 86 |
| OWENS | MOLLY | | 03 OCT 1992 | 85 |
| OWENS | MAYPHIL | | 06 MAY 2002 | 71 |

**INSCRIPTION:**
IN LOVING MEMORY
OF
JOSEPH (JOE) OWENS
DULEEK
DIED 21ST DECEMBER 1983
AGED 86 YEARS
HIS WIFE MOLLY
DIED 3RD OCTOBER 1992
AGED 85 YEARS
THEIR DAUGHTER MAYPHIL
DIED 6TH MAY 2002
AGED 71 YEARS:
REST IN PEACE

**SYMBOLS:**
CELTIC CROSS

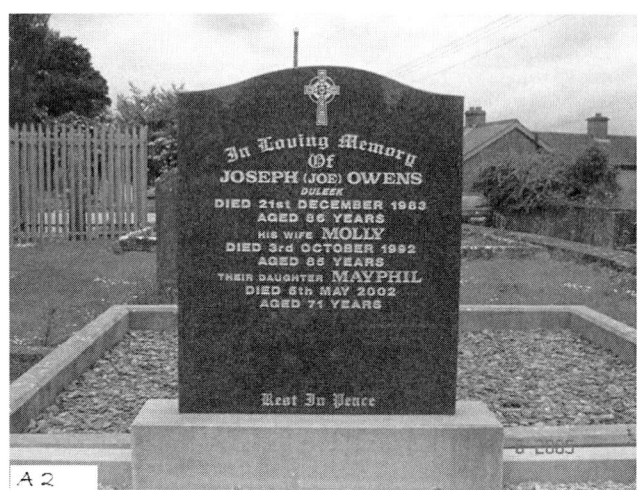

**REMARKS**
LIFETIME HON. SECRETARY
DULEEK COURSING CLUB
REF: ENDA O'BOYLE

| | |
|---|---|
| NAME OF RECORDER: | JANET LEIGH AND HELEN FULLAM |
| DATE: | 18 JUNE 2005 |
| PHOTO REFERENCE: | A2 |
| LOCATION/MAP REF: | D1 A2 |

| | |
|---|---|
| GRAVEYARD NAME: | **ST. MARY'S ABBEY OLD GRAVEYARD** |
| GRAVEYARD CODE: | D1 |
| COUNTY: | MEATH |
| MEMORIAL NUMBER: | E11 |
| ERECTED BY: | |
| ORIENTATION: | EAST |
| NUMBER OF COMPONENTS: | 3 |
| NUMBER OF INSCRIBED FACES: | 1 |
| NUMBER OF PEOPLE COMMEMORATED: | 6 |
| MEMORIAL TYPE: | HEADSTONE CROSS |
| CONDITION OF MEMORIAL: | SOUND IN PLACE |
| CONDITION OF INSCRIPTION: | CLEAR |
| STONEMASON NAME: | J. GIBNEY, DROGHEDA |
| TECHNIQUE OF INSCRIPTION: | INCISED |
| UNDERTAKER: | |
| STONE TOP: | CROSS |
| GRAVE TYPE: | TREBLE |
| HEIGHT: | 250CM |
| WIDTH: | 72CM |
| THICKNESS: | 18CM |

| SURNAME: | CHRISTIAN | ADDRESS | DEATH | AGE |
|---|---|---|---|---|
| PENTONY | WILLIAM | CORBALLIS | 28 NOV 1889 | 90 YEARS |
| | MARY | | 03 JAN 1893 | 90 YEARS |
| | MARGARET | | 30 APR 1927 | 59 YEARS |
| | JOHN | | 19 OCT 1933 | 90 YEARS |
| | ROBERT | | 15 MAR 1966 | 68 YEARS |
| | JOHN | | 21 JAN 1982 | 74 YEARS |

**INSCRIPTION:**
IN FOND AND LOVING MEMORY
OF
WILLIAM PENTONY CORBALLIS
WHO DIED NOV 28TH 1889
AGED 90 YEARS
AND OF HIS WIFE MARY
WHO DIED JAN 3 1893
AGED 90 YEARS
ALSO OF
MRS. MARGARET PENTONY
CORBALLIS WHO DIED APRIL 30TH 1927
AGED 59 YEARS
ALSO HIS SON JOHN PENTONY
WHO DIED OCTOBER 19TH 1933
AGED 90 YEARS
HIS SONS
ROBERT DIED 15TH MARCH 1966 AGED 68
JOHN DIED 21ST JAN 1982 AGED 74
*ON WHOSE SOULS SWEET JESUS
HAVE MERCY AMEN*

**SYMBOLS:**
IHS INTERWOVEN SHAMROCK
FOLIAGE AND BERRIES

**ORNAMENTS:**
CROSS ON TOP FLEUR DE LIS

| | |
|---|---|
| NAME OF RECORDER: | JANET LEIGH AND BEN RYAN |
| DATE: | 16 JULY 2005 |
| PHOTO REFERENCE: | E11 |
| LOCATION/MAP REF: | D1 E11 |

| | |
|---|---|
| GRAVEYARD NAME: | **ST. MARY'S ABBEY OLD GRAVEYARD** |
| GRAVEYARD CODE: | D1 |
| COUNTY: | MEATH |
| MEMORIAL NUMBER: | B5 |
| ERECTED BY: | |
| ORIENTATION: | EAST |
| NUMBER OF COMPONENTS: | 2 |
| NUMBER OF INSCRIBED FACES: | 1 |
| NUMBER OF PEOPLE COMMEMORATED: | 5 |
| MEMORIAL TYPE: | HEADSTONE |
| CONDITION OF MEMORIAL: | SOUND IN PLACE |
| CONDITION OF INSCRIPTION: | MAINLY DECIPHERABLE |
| STONEMASON NAME: | |
| TECHNIQUE OF INSCRIPTION: | INCISED |
| UNDERTAKER: | |
| STONE TOP: | ROUND |
| GRAVE TYPE: | DOUBLE |
| HEIGHT: | 230CM |
| WIDTH: | 80CM |
| THICKNESS: | 10CM |

| SURNAME: | CHRISTIAN | ADDRESS | DEATH | AGE |
|---|---|---|---|---|
| PIERSON | EDWARD | | JAN 1893 | |
| PIERSON | ELIZABETH | | MAY 1895 | |
| PIERSON | JAMES | | MAR 1888 | |
| FENNELL | HANNAH | | DEC 1890 | |
| FENNELL | JAMES | | OCT 1890 | |

**INSCRIPTION:**
IN
LOVING MEMORY OF
EDWARD PIERSON
WHO DIED 1893
HIS WIFE ELIZABETH
WHO DIED MAY 1895
THEIR SON
JAMES
WHO DIED MARCH 1888
ALSO THEIR DAUGHTER
HANNAH FENNELL
WHO DIED DEC 1890
AND HER SON
JAMES
WHO DIED OCT 1890
*THY WILL BE DONE*

| | |
|---|---|
| NAME OF RECORDER: | PHYLLIS NOONAN |
| DATE: | 02 JULY 2005 |
| PHOTO REFERENCE: | B5 |
| LOCATION/MAP REFERENCE: | D1 B5 |

| | |
|---|---|
| GRAVEYARD NAME: | **ST. MARY'S ABBEY OLD GRAVEYARD** |
| GRAVEYARD CODE: | D1 |
| COUNTY: | MEATH |
| MEMORIAL NUMBER: | E4 |
| ERECTED BY: | HIS CHILDREN |
| ORIENTATION: | EAST |
| NUMBER OF COMPONENTS: | 4 |
| NUMBER OF INSCRIBED FACES: | 1 |
| NUMBER OF PEOPLE COMMEMORATED: | 5 |
| MEMORIAL TYPE: | HEADSTONE |
| CONDITION OF MEMORIAL: | SOUND IN PLACE |
| CONDITION OF INSCRIPTION: | GOOD |
| STONEMASON NAME: | T. REID PLATIN |
| TECHNIQUE OF INSCRIPTION: | INCISED |
| UNDERTAKER: | |
| STONE TOP: | CROSS |
| GRAVE TYPE: | DOUBLE |
| HEIGHT: | 219CM |
| WIDTH: | 63CM |
| THICKNESS: | 8CM |

| SURNAME: | CHRISTIAN | ADDRESS | DEATH | AGE |
|---|---|---|---|---|
| POTTER | THOMAS | | 25 DEC 1904 | |
| | CATHERINE | | 12 FEB 1918 | |
| | JOHN | | 07 JUL 1917 | |
| | FRANK | | 01 OCT 1918 | |
| | MATTHEW | | 24 FEB 1963 | |

**INSCRIPTION:**
ERECTED
IN LOVING MEMORY BY THE CHILDREN
OF THOMAS POTTER
WHO DIED DEC 25TH 1904 ALSO THEIR
MOTHER CATHERINE WHO DIED FEB 12TH 1918
ALSO THEIR BROTHER JOHN DIED IN
FRANCE JULY 7TH 1917 AND THEIR
BROTHERS FRANK DIED OCT 1ST 1918
MATTHEW DIED 24TH FEB 1963
R.I.P.

**SYMBOLS:**
CELTIC CROSS IHS ENTWINED
SACRED HEART WITH
SMALL CROSS - 4 RAISED ROSES

| | |
|---|---|
| NAME OF RECORDER: | SHAUN LYNCH |
| DATE: | 16 JULY 2005 |
| PHOTO REFERENCE: | E4 |
| LOCATION/MAP REF: | D1 E4 |

| | |
|---|---|
| GRAVEYARD NAME: | **ST. MARY'S ABBEY OLD GRAVEYARD** |
| GRAVEYARD CODE: | D1 |
| COUNTY: | MEATH |
| MEMORIAL NUMBER: | G6 |
| ERECTED BY: | |
| ORIENTATION: | EAST |
| NUMBER OF COMPONENTS: | 1 |
| NUMBER OF INSCRIBED FACES: | 1 |
| NUMBER OF PEOPLE COMMEMORATED: | 1 |
| MEMORIAL TYPE: | SLAB |
| CONDITION OF MEMORIAL: | SOUND BUT NOT IN PLACE |
| CONDITION OF INSCRIPTION: | MINT |
| STONEMASON NAME: | |
| TECHNIQUE OF INSCRIPTION: | INCISED |
| UNDERTAKER: | |
| STONE TOP: | SQUARE |
| GRAVE TYPE: | |
| HEIGHT: | 124CM |
| WIDTH: | 101CM |
| THICKNESS: | 16CM |

| SURNAME: | CHRISTIAN | | DEATH | AGE |
|---|---|---|---|---|
| PURFIELD | RICHARD | | 16 FEB 1753 | 53 |

**INSCRIPTION:**
THIS STONE AND BURIAL
PLACE BELONGETH TO
RICHARD PURFIELD AND
HIS POSTERITY WHO DEPD
THIS LIFE THE 16 OF FEBRY IN THE YEAR
OF LORD 1753 AGED 53 YEARS

**SYMBOLS:**
COAT OF ARMS
SPES MEAM CRUCE
I HOPE AND BELIEVE

| | |
|---|---|
| NAME OF RECORDER: | LIZ LYNCH AND JANET LEIGH |
| DATE: | 24 JUNE 2006 |
| PHOTO REFERENCE: | G6 |
| LOCATION/MAP REF: | D1—G6 |

| | |
|---|---|
| GRAVEYARD NAME: | **ST. MARY'S ABBEY OLD GRAVEYARD** |
| GRAVEYARD CODE: | D1 |
| COUNTY: | MEATH |
| MEMORIAL NUMBER: | D10 |
| ERECTED BY: | MARTIN RANN |
| ORIENTATION: | EAST |
| NUMBER OF COMPONENTS: | 1 |
| NUMBER OF INSCRIBED FACES: | 1 |
| NUMBER OF PEOPLE COMMEMORATED: | 1 |
| MEMORIAL TYPE: | HEADSTONE |
| CONDITION OF MEMORIAL: | SOUND IN PLACE |
| CONDITION OF INSCRIPTION: | DECIPHERABLE |
| STONEMASON NAME: | |
| TECHNIQUE OF INSCRIPTION: | INCISED |
| UNDERTAKER: | |
| STONE TOP: | FLAT |
| GRAVE TYPE: | SINGLE |
| HEIGHT: | 58 CM |
| WIDTH: | 51 CM |
| THICKNESS: | 10 CM |

| SURNAME: | CHRISTIAN | ADDRESS | DEATH | AGE |
|---|---|---|---|---|
| RANN | WILLIAM | | 01 MAR 1727 | 72 |
| CULLEN | CATHERINE | | 09 MAY 1732 | 67 |

**INSCRIPTION:**

THIS STONE AND BURIAL PLACE BELONGETH
TO MARTIN RANN & HIS POSTERITY
HERE LIETH THE BODY OF HIS FATHER
WILLIAM RANN WHO DEPARTED
THIS LIFE MARCH 1, 1727 AGED 72
YEARS ALSO HIS WIFE CATHRINE CULLEN
WHO DIE MAY THE 9TH 1732 AGED
67 YEARS

**SYMBOLS:**

IHS

| | |
|---|---|
| NAME OF RECORDER: | PHYLLIS NOONAN AND LIZ LYNCH |
| DATE: | 13 JULY 2005 |
| PHOTO REFERENCE: | D 10 |
| LOCATION/MAP REF: | D1 D10 |

| | |
|---|---|
| GRAVEYARD NAME: | **ST. MARY'S ABBEY OLD GRAVEYARD** |
| GRAVEYARD CODE: | D1 |
| COUNTY: | MEATH |
| MEMORIAL NUMBER: | F25 |
| ERECTED BY: | |
| ORIENTATION: | EAST |
| NUMBER OF COMPONENTS: | 1 |
| NUMBER OF INSCRIBED FACES: | 1 |
| NUMBER OF PEOPLE COMMEMORATED: | 2 |
| MEMORIAL TYPE: | HEADSTONE |
| CONDITION OF MEMORIAL: | SOUND IN PLACE |
| CONDITION OF INSCRIPTION: | MAINLY DECIPHERABLE |
| STONEMASON NAME: | |
| TECHNIQUE OF INSCRIPTION: | INCISED |
| UNDERTAKER: | |
| STONE TOP: | ROUND |
| GRAVE TYPE: | SINGLE |
| HEIGHT: | 115CM |
| WIDTH: | 78CM |
| THICKNESS: | 09CM |

| SURNAME: | CHRISTIAN | ADDRESS | DEATH | AGE |
|---|---|---|---|---|
| REILLY | PATRICK | DULEEK | 17 JULY 1803 | 16 |
| CARR | SALLY | | | |

**INSCRIPTION:**
THIS STONE WAS ERECTED
BY PATRICK REILLY DULEEK IN MEMORY OF HIS
SON PATRICK REILLY WHO
BY THE FALL OFF A HORSE
JULY THE 17TH 1887
IN THE 16TH YEAR OF HIS
AGE ALSO OF SALLY CARR
HIS GRANDMOTHER

**SYMBOLS:**
SUNBURST IHS WITH CROSS
SCROLLED EACH SIDE WITH
STONE

| | |
|---|---|
| NAME OF RECORDER: | SINEAD FULLAM AND CATRIONA DILLON |
| DATE: | 20 JULY 2005 |
| PHOTO REFERENCE: | F25 |
| LOCATION/MAP REF: | D1 F25 |

| | |
|---|---|
| GRAVEYARD NAME: | **ST. MARY'S ABBEY OLD GRAVEYARD** |
| GRAVEYARD CODE: | D1 |
| COUNTY: | MEATH |
| MEMORIAL NUMBER: | H21 |
| ERECTED BY: | |
| ORIENTATION: | EAST |
| NUMBER OF COMPONENTS: | 4 |
| NUMBER OF INSCRIBED FACES: | 1 |
| NUMBER OF PEOPLE COMMEMORATED: | 1 |
| MEMORIAL TYPE: | ELABORATE HEADSTONE |
| CONDITION OF MEMORIAL: | SOUND IN PLACE |
| CONDITION OF INSCRIPTION: | CLEAR |
| STONEMASON NAME: | WADE DUBLIN |
| TECHNIQUE OF INSCRIPTION: | INCISED |
| UNDERTAKER: | |
| STONE TOP: | CROSS MISSING |
| GRAVE TYPE: | SINGLE |
| HEIGHT: | 230CM |
| WIDTH: | 55CM |
| THICKNESS: | 38CM |

| SURNAME: | CHRISTIAN | ADDRESS | DEATH | AGE |
|---|---|---|---|---|
| ROGERS | SARAH JANE | RATHRASNEY | 29 APRIL 1863 | 24YRS |

**INSCRIPTION:**
ERECTED
IN MEMORY
SARAH JANE
THE BELOVED AND ONLY
DAUGHTER
OF RICHARD AND MARY
ROGERS
OF RATHRASNEY, DRUMCONRATH
AND GRANDDAUGHTER TO
THE LATE
ROBERT WARREN
OF DRUMMINRATH
DIED APRIL 29TH 1863
AGED 24 YEARS

| | |
|---|---|
| NAME OF RECORDER: | JANET LEIGH AND PHYLLIS NOONAN |
| DATE: | 17 JUNE 2006 |
| PHOTO REFERENCE: | H21 |
| LOCATION/MAP REF: | D1 H21 |

| | |
|---|---|
| GRAVEYARD NAME: | **ST. MARY'S ABBEY OLD GRAVEYARD** |
| GRAVEYARD CODE: | D1 |
| COUNTY: | MEATH |
| MEMORIAL NUMBER: | K48 |
| ERECTED BY: | HUGH RUDDY |
| ORIENTATION: | EAST |
| NUMBER OF COMPONENTS: | 1 |
| NUMBER OF INSCRIBED FACES: | 1 |
| NUMBER OF PEOPLE COMMEMORATED: | 4 |
| MEMORIAL TYPE: | HEADSTONE |
| CONDITION OF MEMORIAL: | SOUND IN PLACE |
| CONDITION OF INSCRIPTION: | MAINLY DECIPHERABLE |
| STONEMASON NAME: | |
| TECHNIQUE OF INSCRIPTION: | INCISED |
| UNDERTAKER: | |
| STONE TOP: | ROUND |
| GRAVE TYPE: | SINGLE |
| HEIGHT: | 167CM |
| WIDTH: | 76CM |
| THICKNESS: | 14CM |

| SURNAME: | CHRISTIAN | ADDRESS | DEATH | AGE |
|---|---|---|---|---|
| RUDDY | PATRICK | NEWLANES | 22 JUN 1800 | 66 |
| | RICHARD | | 02 FEB 1788 | 52 |
| | CATHERINE | | 08 SEPT 1805 | 30 |
| | MARY | | 15 DEC 1805 | 65 |

**INSCRIPTION:**
ERECTED ANNO DOMINI 1802
BY HUGH RUDDY OF NEWLANES
FOR HIM AND HIS POSTERITY
HERE LIETH THE BODY OF HIS
FATHER PATRICK RUDDY WHO
DEPARTED THIS LIFE THE 22ND JUN
1800 IN THE 66 YEAR OF HIS AGE
HERE LIETH THE BODY OF HIS
UNCLE RICHD RUDDY WHO DEP
ARTED THIS LIFE THE 2ND FEBRUAR
1788 IN THE 52ND YEAR OF HIS AGE
HERE LIETH THE BODY OF HIS SISTER
CATHERINE WHO DEPARTED THIS LIFE
THE 8TH OF SEPTR 1805 AGED 30 YRS
HERE ALSO LIETH THE BODY OF HIS
MOTHER MARY RUDDY.....
WHO DEPARTED THIS LIFE THE 15TH
DECEMBER 1805 AGED 65 YEARS
REQUIESCANT IN PACE AMEN

**SYMBOLS:**
JESUS ON CROSS ANGELS FACE EACH SIDE
IHS WITH SUN SYMBOL EACH SIDE

| | |
|---|---|
| NAME OF RECORDER: | SHAUN LYNCH, JANET LEIGH AND SINEAD FULLAM |
| DATE: | 6 MAY 2006 |
| PHOTO REFERENCE: | K48 |
| LOCATION/MAP REF: | D1 K48 |

| | |
|---|---|
| GRAVEYARD NAME: | **ST. MARY'S ABBEY OLD GRAVEYARD** |
| GRAVEYARD CODE: | D1 |
| COUNTY: | MEATH |
| MEMORIAL NUMBER: | H15 |
| ERECTED BY: | JOHN RUSSELL |
| ORIENTATION: | EAST |
| NUMBER OF COMPONENTS: | 1 |
| NUMBER OF INSCRIBED FACES: | 1 |
| NUMBER OF PEOPLE COMMEMORATED: | 4 |
| MEMORIAL TYPE: | HEADSTONE |
| CONDITION OF MEMORIAL: | SOUND IN PLACE |
| CONDITION OF INSCRIPTION: | MAINLY DECIPHERABLE |
| STONEMASON NAME: | |
| TECHNIQUE OF INSCRIPTION: | INCISED |
| UNDERTAKER: | |
| STONE TOP: | ROUND |
| GRAVE TYPE: | SINGLE |
| HEIGHT: | 102CM |
| WIDTH: | 64CM |
| THICKNESS: | 12CM |

| SURNAME: | CHRISTIAN | ADDRESS | DEATH | AGE |
|---|---|---|---|---|
| RUSSELL | MARGARET | BEAUMONT | 18 MAY 1796 | 24 |
| RUSSELL | JOHNS FATHER | | | |
| RUSSELL | JOHNS BROTHER | | | |
| RUSSELL | JOHNS BROTHER | | | |

**INSCRIPTION:**
THIS STONE WAS ERECTED BY JOHN RUSSELL OF BEAUMONT IN MEMORY OF HIS FATHER AND TWO OF HIS BROTHERS, LIKEWISE ONE OF HIS CHILDREN MARGARET RUSSELL WHO DEPARTED THIS LIFE THE 18TH OF MAY 1796 AGED 24 YEARS

| | |
|---|---|
| NAME OF RECORDER: | JANET LEIGH |
| DATE: | 14 JUNE 2006 |
| PHOTO REFERENCE: | H15 |
| LOCATION/MAP REF: | D1 H15 |

| | |
|---|---|
| GRAVEYARD NAME: | **ST. MARY'S ABBEY OLD GRAVEYARD** |
| GRAVEYARD CODE: | D1 |
| COUNTY: | MEATH |
| MEMORIAL NUMBER: | H16 |
| ERECTED BY: | PETER RUSSELL |
| ORIENTATION: | EAST |
| NUMBER OF COMPONENTS: | 1 |
| NUMBER OF INSCRIBED FACES: | 1 |
| NUMBER OF PEOPLE COMMEMORATED: | 3 |
| MEMORIAL TYPE: | HEADSTONE |
| CONDITION OF MEMORIAL: | SOUND IN PLACE |
| CONDITION OF INSCRIPTION: | MAINLY DECIPHERABLE |
| STONEMASON NAME: | |
| TECHNIQUE OF INSCRIPTION: | INCISED |
| UNDERTAKER: | |
| STONE TOP: | DAMAGED |
| GRAVE TYPE: | SINGLE |
| HEIGHT: | 207CM |
| WIDTH: | 97CM |
| THICKNESS: | 10CM |

| SURNAME: | CHRISTIAN | ADDRESS | DEATH | AGE |
|---|---|---|---|---|
| RUSSELL | WILLIAM | KILSHARVAN & BEAUMONT | | |
| RUSSELL | PATRICK | KILSHARVAN & BEAUMONT | | |
| RUSSELL | JOHN | | 18 OCT 1816 | 101 |

**INSCRIPTION:**
ERECTED A.D.1812
BY PETER RUSSELL OF DROGHEDA, MERCHT
IN MEMORY OF WILLIAM AND PATRICK
RUSSELL LATE OF KILSHARVAN AND
BEAUMONT
HERE ALSO LIETH THE REMAINS OF HIS
FATHER JOHN RUSSELL WHO DEPARTED THIS
LIFE 18TH OCT.1816 AGED 101 YEARS

| | |
|---|---|
| NAME OF RECORDER: | JANET LEIGH |
| DATE: | 14 JUNE 2006 |
| PHOTO REFERENCE: | H16 |
| LOCATION/MAP REF: | D1 H16 |

| | |
|---|---|
| GRAVEYARD NAME: | **ST. MARY'S ABBEY OLD GRAVEYARD** |
| GRAVEYARD CODE: | D1 |
| COUNTY: | MEATH |
| MEMORIAL NUMBER: | A3 |
| ERECTED BY: | JOHN AND ELLEN SAMPSON |
| ORIENTATION: | EAST |
| NUMBER OF COMPONENTS: | 2 |
| NUMBER OF INSCRIBED FACES: | 1 |
| NUMBER OF PEOPLE COMMEMORATED: | 2 |
| MEMORIAL TYPE: | ARCHED |
| CONDITION OF MEMORIAL: | SOUND IN PLACE |
| CONDITION OF INSCRIPTION: | MINT |
| STONEMASON NAME: | MOSS |
| TECHNIQUE OF INSCRIPTION: | INCISED PAINTED |
| UNDERTAKER: | |
| STONE TOP: | NONE |
| GRAVE TYPE: | TREBLE |
| HEIGHT: | 138CM |
| WIDTH: | 53CM |
| THICKNESS: | 7CM |

| SURNAME: | CHRISTIAN | ADDRESS | DEATH | AGE |
|---|---|---|---|---|
| SAMPSON | EUGENE | | 1933 | 9 |
| SAMPSON | MAURA | | | INFANT |

**INSCRIPTION:**

ERECTED
BY
JOHN AND ELLEN SAMPSON
DULEEK
IN MEMORY OF THEIR SON
EUGENE
WHO DIED 27TH NOV 1933
AGED 9 YEARS
AND THEIR INFANT CHILD MAURA

RIP

**SYMBOLS:**
IHS CENTRE
IVY EITHER SIDE

| | |
|---|---|
| NAME OF RECORDER: | PHYLLIS NOONAN |
| DATE: | 18 JUNE 2005 |
| PHOTO REFERENCE: | D1 A3 |
| LOCATION/MAP REF: | A3: |

| | |
|---|---|
| GRAVEYARD NAME: | **ST. MARY'S ABBEY OLD GRAVEYARD** |
| GRAVEYARD CODE: | D1 |
| COUNTY: | MEATH |
| MEMORIAL NUMBER: | F24 |
| ERECTED BY: | |
| ORIENTATION: | EAST |
| NUMBER OF COMPONENTS: | 1 |
| NUMBER OF INSCRIBED FACES: | 1 |
| NUMBER OF PEOPLE COMMEMORATED: | 2 |
| MEMORIAL TYPE: | HEADSTONE |
| CONDITION OF MEMORIAL: | SOUND IN PLACE SLIGHTLY LEANING |
| CONDITION OF INSCRIPTION: | DECIPHERABLE |
| STONEMASON NAME: | |
| TECHNIQUE OF INSCRIPTION: | INCISED |
| UNDERTAKER: | |
| STONE TOP: | ARCH |
| GRAVE TYPE: | DOUBLE |
| HEIGHT: | 118CM |
| WIDTH: | 66CM |
| THICKNESS: | 18CM |

| SURNAME: | CHRISTIAN | ADDRESS | DEATH | AGE |
|---|---|---|---|---|
| SAMPSON | THOMAS | STALEEN MOUNT | 01 MAR 1860 | 62 |
| | THOMAS | | 20 JAN 1867 | 25 |

**INSCRIPTION:**
ERECTED
JOHN SAMPSON STALEEN MOUNT
IN MEMORY OF HIS FATHER THOMAS
SAMPSON WHO DIED 1ST MARCH 1860
AGED 62 YRS. HIS BROTHER
THOMAS WHO DIED JAN 20TH 1867 AGED
25 YEARS

RESQUISCANT IN PACE AMEN

**SYMBOLS:**
IHS CROSS IN SUNBURST

| | |
|---|---|
| NAME OF RECORDER: | ALFIE WOODS AND LIZ LYNCH |
| DATE: | 20 JULY 2005 |
| PHOTO REFERENCE: | F24 |
| LOCATION/MAP REF: | D1 F24 |

| | |
|---|---|
| GRAVEYARD NAME: | **ST. MARY'S ABBEY OLD GRAVEYARD** |
| GRAVEYARD CODE: | D1 |
| COUNTY: | MEATH |
| MEMORIAL NUMBER: | H 18 |
| ERECTED BY: | |
| ORIENTATION: | EAST |
| NUMBER OF COMPONENTS: | 5 |
| NUMBER OF INSCRIBED FACES: | 1 |
| NUMBER OF PEOPLE COMMEMORATED: | 6 |
| MEMORIAL TYPE: | CROSS ON PEDESTAL |
| CONDITION OF MEMORIAL: | SOUND |
| CONDITION OF INSCRIPTION: | CLEAR |
| STONEMASON NAME: | J. GIBNEY DROGHEDA |
| TECHNIQUE OF INSCRIPTION: | INCISED |
| UNDERTAKER: | |
| STONE TOP: | ELABORATE FLEUR DE LIS CROSS |
| GRAVE TYPE: | SINGLE |
| HEIGHT: | |
| WIDTH: | 66CM |
| THICKNESS: | 33CM |

| SURNAME: | CHRISTIAN | ADDRESS | DEATH | AGE |
|---|---|---|---|---|
| SAMPSON | MARY | DROGHEDA | 20 NOV 1872 | 42 |
| | ROBERT | | 17 APR 1885 | 30 |
| | JAMES | | 27 JUL 1901 | 49 |
| | ROBERT | | 20 OCT 1902 | 15 |
| | BRIGID AGNES | | 03 SEPT 1921 | |
| | PATRICK | SLANE | 13 APR 1933 | |

**INSCRIPTION:**
OF YOUR CHARITY FOR THE SOUL OF
MRS MARY SAMPSON, DROGHEDA
WHO DIED NOV.20TH 1872
AGED 48 YEARS
ALSO HER SON ROBERT
WHO DIED APRIL 17TH 1885
AGED 30 YEARS
ALSO HER SON
JAMES SAMPSON
WHO DIED 27TH JULY 1901 AGED 49 YEARS
AND HIS SON
ROBERT
WHO DIED 20TH OCT.1902 AGED 15 YEARS
ALSO MRS
BRIGID AGNES SAMPSON
WHO DIED SEP.3RD 1921
PATRICK SAMPSON SLANE
DIED APRIL13TH 1932
R.I.P

**SYMBOLS:**
INTERWOVEN IHS WITH FLEUR DE LIS CROSS
ON TOP – EAST FACE - TEMPLAR SHIELD WITH
CROSS ANCHOR WITH CROSS AND HEART
BEHIND – NORTH FACE

| | |
|---|---|
| NAME OF RECORDER: | SINEAD FULLAM AND JANET LEIGH |
| DATE: | 17 JUNE 2006 |
| PHOTO REFERENCE: | H 18 |
| LOCATION/MAP REF: | D1 H18 |

| | |
|---|---|
| GRAVEYARD NAME: | **ST. MARY'S ABBEY OLD GRAVEYARD** |
| GRAVEYARD CODE: | D1 |
| COUNTY: | MEATH |
| MEMORIAL NUMBER: | B 12 |
| ERECTED BY: | |
| ORIENTATION: | EAST |
| NUMBER OF COMPONENTS: | 4 |
| NUMBER OF INSCRIBED FACES: | 1 |
| NUMBER OF PEOPLE COMMEMORATED: | 3 |
| MEMORIAL TYPE: | HEADSTONE |
| CONDITION OF MEMORIAL: | SOUND IN PLACE |
| CONDITION OF INSCRIPTION: | MAINLY DECIPHERABLE |
| STONEMASON NAME: | REID. PLATTEN |
| TECHNIQUE OF INSCRIPTION: | INCISED |
| UNDERTAKER: | |
| STONE TOP: | ROUND WITH CROSS |
| GRAVE TYPE: | SINGLE |
| HEIGHT: | 212CM |
| WIDTH: | 57CM |
| THICKNESS: | 10CM |

| SURNAME: | CHRISTIAN | ADDRESS | DEATH | AGE |
|---|---|---|---|---|
| SAURIN | MICHAEL ANTHONY | GARBALLAGH HOUSE DULEEK | 01 MAR 1922 | 45 |
| SAURIN | INFANT SON | | | |
| SAURIN | MICHAEL CRISPIN ANTHONY | | JUNE 1976 | |

**INSCRIPTION:**
IN LOVING MEMORY
OF
MICHAEL ANTHONY SAURIN
GARBALLAGH HOUSE DULEEK
WHO DIED MARCH 1ST 1922
AGED 45 YEARS
AND HIS INFANT
WHO DIED YOUNG
MICHAEL CRISPIN ANTHONY SAURIN
DIED JUNE 1976
R.I.P

**SYMBOLS:**
FLEUR DE LIS CROSS
SACRED HEART

**ORNAMENTS:**
LOZANGES - ARCHED

| | |
|---|---|
| NAME OF RECORDER: | JANET LEIGH AND HELEN FULLAM |
| DATE: | 2 JULY 2005 |
| PHOTO REFERENCE: | B12 |
| LOCATION/MAP REF: | D1 B12 |

| | |
|---|---|
| GRAVEYARD NAME: | **ST. MARY'S ABBEY OLD GRAVEYARD** |
| GRAVEYARD CODE: | D1 |
| COUNTY: | MEATH |
| MEMORIAL NUMBER: | K10 |
| ERECTED BY: | JOHN SAVIDGE |
| ORIENTATION: | EAST |
| NUMBER OF COMPONENTS: | 2 |
| NUMBER OF INSCRIBED FACES: | 1 |
| NUMBER OF PEOPLE COMMEMORATED: | 6 |
| MEMORIAL TYPE: | HEADSTONE |
| CONDITION OF MEMORIAL: | SOUND IN PLACE |
| CONDITION OF INSCRIPTION: | CLEAR |
| STONEMASON NAME: | |
| TECHNIQUE OF INSCRIPTION: | INCISED |
| UNDERTAKER: | |
| STONE TOP: | ARCH |
| GRAVE TYPE: | SINGLE |
| HEIGHT: | 148CM |
| WIDTH: | 54CM |
| THICKNESS: | 09CM |

| SURNAME: | CHRISTIAN | ADDRESS | DEATH | AGE |
|---|---|---|---|---|
| SAVIDGE | JOHN GERRARD | INFANT SON | | |
| | ARTHUR JOSEPH | | 25 APR 1924 | 14 |
| | JOHN | DULEEK | 23 JULY 1942 | |
| | MAI | | 25 MAY 1942 | |
| | LIL | | 04 NOV 1943 | |
| | ELIZABETH | | 30 SEPT 1950 | |

**INSCRIPTION:**
ERECTED BY
JOHN SAVIDGE
DULEEK
IN MEMORY OF HIS INFANT CHILD
JOHN GERRARD
ALSO ARTHUR JOSEPH
WHO DIED APRIL 25TH 1924
AGED 14 YEARS
THE ABOVE JOHN DIED
23 JULY 1942
HIS DAUGHTERS
MAI DIED 25 MAY 1942
AND LIL 4 NOV 1943
HIS WIFE ELIZABETH DIED
30 SEPT 1950
RIP

**ORNAMENTS:**
DISK 15CM IN DIAMETER INSERT
MISSING VINE LEAVES EACH SIDE

| | |
|---|---|
| NAME OF RECORDER: | PHYLLIS NOONAN |
| DATE: | 10 SEPT 2005 |
| PHOTO REFERENCE: | K10 |
| LOCATION/MAP REF: | D1 K10 |

| | |
|---|---|
| GRAVEYARD NAME: | **ST. MARY'S ABBEY OLD GRAVEYARD** |
| GRAVEYARD CODE: | D1 |
| COUNTY: | MEATH |
| MEMORIAL NUMBER: | K24 |
| ERECTED BY: | EDWARD SCOTT DULEEK |
| ORIENTATION: | EAST |
| NUMBER OF COMPONENTS: | 1 |
| NUMBER OF INSCRIBED FACES: | 1 |
| NUMBER OF PEOPLE COMMEMORATED: | 2 |
| MEMORIAL TYPE: | HEADSTONE |
| CONDITION OF MEMORIAL: | SOUND |
| CONDITION OF INSCRIPTION: | LEGIBLE |
| STONEMASON NAME: | |
| TECHNIQUE OF INSCRIPTION: | INCISED |
| UNDERTAKER: | |
| STONE TOP: | ROUND |
| GRAVE TYPE: | SINGLE |
| HEIGHT: | 103CM |
| WIDTH: | 83CM |
| THICKNESS: | 15CM |

| SURNAME: | CHRISTIAN | | DEATH | AGE |
|---|---|---|---|---|
| GALLAGHER SCOTT | ANN | MOTHER | 20 DEC 1781 | 66 |
| | | FATHER | | |

**INSCRIPTION:**
+ CROSS
IHS
THIS STONE WAS ERECTED BY
EDWARD SCOTT OF DULEEK IN
MEMORY OF HIS FATHER AND
ALSO OF HIS MOTHER ANN SCOTT
ALIAS GALLAGHER WHO DEPARTED
THIS LIFE THE 20TH OF DEC
1781 AGED 66 YEARS

| | |
|---|---|
| NAME OF RECORDER: | JANET LEIGH AND PHYLLIS NOONAN |
| DATE: | 18 APRIL 2008 |
| PHOTO REFERENCE: | K24 |
| LOCATION/MAP REF: | D1 K24 |

| | |
|---|---|
| GRAVEYARD NAME: | **ST. MARY'S ABBEY OLD GRAVEYARD** |
| GRAVEYARD CODE: | D1 |
| COUNTY: | MEATH |
| MEMORIAL NUMBER: | L27 |
| ERECTED BY: | |
| ORIENTATION: | EAST |
| NUMBER OF COMPONENTS: | 1 |
| NUMBER OF INSCRIBED FACES: | 1 |
| NUMBER OF PEOPLE COMMEMORATED: | 12 |
| MEMORIAL TYPE: | CELTIC CROSS ON HEADSTONE |
| CONDITION OF MEMORIAL: | SOUND IN PLACE |
| CONDITION OF INSCRIPTION: | CLEAR |
| STONEMASON NAME: | MOSS |
| TECHNIQUE OF INSCRIPTION: | INCISED |
| UNDERTAKER: | |
| STONE TOP: | CELTIC CROSS |
| GRAVE TYPE: | DOUBLE |
| HEIGHT: | 170CM |
| WIDTH: | 60CM |
| THICKNESS: | 10CM |

| SURNAME: | CHRISTIAN | ADDRESS | DEATH | AGE |
|---|---|---|---|---|
| SHALVEY | MARY | | 30 DEC 1902 | 53 |
| | CHRISTOPHER | | 1885 | |
| | THOMAS | | 1885 | |
| | JAMES | | 1885 | |
| | JOHN | | 1885 | |
| | ANNE | | 1885 | |
| | PATRICK | | 25 JAN 1932 | 103 |
| | MARY | | 24 FEB 1951 | 82 |
| | BERNARD | | 12 FEB 1960 | 89 |
| | MARY | | 28 AUG 1941 | |
| | SR. MARY GERVASE | | 06 FEB 1981 | |
| CLARKE | MARY | | 28 APRIL 1984 | |

**INSCRIPTION:**
IN LOVING MEMORY OF
MARY
BELOVED WIFE OF
PATRICK SHALVEY
DULEEK
WHO DIED 30 DEC 1902 AGED 53 YEARS
AND THEIR CHILDREN
CHRISTOPHER THOMAS
JAMES JOHN AND ANNE
WHO DIED IN THE YEAR 1885
PATRICK SHALVEY
DIED JAN 25 1932 AGED 103 YEARS
ALSO MARY SHALVEY
DIED 24 FEB 1951 AGED 82 YEARS
BERNARD SHALVEY
DIED 12 FEB 1960
AGED 89 YEARS
HIS WIFE MARY
DIED 28 AUG 1941
AND THEIR DAUGHTER
SR. MARY GERVASE OSF
DIED IN ROME 6 FEB 1981
MARY CLARKE 28 APRIL 1984
RIP

**SYMBOLS:**
CELTIC CROSS WITH VINE LEAVES

| | |
|---|---|
| NAME OF RECORDER: | LIZ LYNCH AND PHYLLIS NOONAN |
| DATE: | 30 MAY 2006 |
| PHOTO REF: | L27 |
| LOCATION /MAP REF: | D1 L27 |

| | |
|---|---|
| Graveyard Name: | **St. Mary's Abbey Old Graveyard** |
| Graveyard Code: | D1 |
| County: | Meath |
| Memorial Number: | A8 |
| Erected By: | Mrs Smith Annesbrook |
| Orientation: | East |
| Number of Components: | 1 |
| Number of Inscribed Faces: | 1 |
| Number of People Commemorated: | 1 |
| Memorial Type: | Headstone |
| Condition of Memorial: | Fair |
| Condition of Inscription: | Poor |
| Stonemason Name: | |
| Technique of Inscription: | Incised |
| Undertaker: | |
| Stone Top: | Disk on Headstone |
| Grave Type: | Single |
| Height: | 190cm |
| Width: | 80cm |
| Thickness: | 18cm |

| Surname: | Christian | Address | Death | Age |
|---|---|---|---|---|
| Shannon | Elizabeth | Annesbrook | 11 Oct 1848 | 67 |

**Inscription:**

Erected
By
Mrs. Smith Annesbrook
To the Memory of
Elizabeth Shannon
Who Departed This Life
The 11th October 1848 aged 67
A Faithful and Trustworthy Servant
Who lived in her Family
For Thirty Years
Her end was Peace

**Symbols:**
Disk on Headstone

| | |
|---|---|
| Name of Recorder: | Phyllis Noonan and Jim Orten |
| Date: | 25 June 2005 |
| Photo Reference: | A8 |
| Location/Map Reference: | D1 A8 |

| | |
|---|---|
| GRAVEYARD NAME: | **ST. MARY'S ABBEY OLD GRAVEYARD** |
| GRAVEYARD CODE: | D1 |
| COUNTY: | MEATH |
| MEMORIAL NUMBER: | L30 |
| ERECTED BY: | THEIR CHILDREN |
| ORIENTATION: | EAST |
| NUMBER OF COMPONENTS: | 3 |
| NUMBER OF INSCRIBED FACES: | 1 |
| NUMBER OF PEOPLE COMMEMORATED: | 6 |
| MEMORIAL TYPE: | FLEUR DE LIS CROSS ON TOP OF HEADSTONE |
| CONDITION OF MEMORIAL: | SOUND IN PLACE |
| CONDITION OF INSCRIPTION: | CLEAR |
| STONEMASON NAME: | |
| TECHNIQUE OF INSCRIPTION: | INCISED |
| UNDERTAKER: | |
| STONE TOP: | ARCHED FLEUR DE LIS CROSS |
| GRAVE TYPE: | DOUBLE |
| HEIGHT: | 160CM |
| WIDTH: | 49CM |
| THICKNESS: | 10CM |

| SURNAME: | CHRISTIAN | ADDRESS | DEATH | AGE |
|---|---|---|---|---|
| SHEERIN | MICHAEL | CARNTOWN DULEEK | 15 MAY 1903 | 50 |
| | MARGARET | | 14 NOV 1908 | 57 |
| | MICHAEL PAUL | | 24 MAR 1942 | 26 |
| | MICHAEL | | 04 JUN 1947 | 67 |
| | JANE | | 15 FEB 1960 | |
| | JOHN JOSEPH | | 16 JUN 2005 | 88 |

**INSCRIPTION:**
IN LOVING MEMORY
OF
MICHAEL SHEERIN
CARNTOWN DULEEK
DIED MAY 15TH 1903 AGED
50 YRS HIS WIFE
MARGARET
WHO DIED NOV 14TH 1908
AGED 57 YRS
AND HIS GRANDSON
MICHAEL PAUL
DIED MARCH 24TH 1942
AGED 26 YRS
ALSO HIS SON MICHAEL
DIED 4TH JUNE 1947
AGED 67 YRS
WHOSE WIFE JANE DIED
15TH FEB 1960
AND THEIR SON
JOHN JOSEPH SHEERIN
DIED 16TH JUNE 2005
AGED 88 YEARS
ERECTED BY THEIR CHILDREN
RIP

**SYMBOLS:**
ELABORATE FLEUR DE LIS CROSS IHS FLANKED BY GRAPES AND VINE

| | |
|---|---|
| NAME OF RECORDER: | LIZ LYNCH AND PHYLLIS NOONAN |
| DATE: | 30 MAY 2006 |
| PHOTO REFERENCE: | L30 |
| LOCATION/MAP REF: | D1 L30 |

| | |
|---|---|
| GRAVEYARD NAME: | **ST. MARY'S ABBEY OLD GRAVEYARD** |
| GRAVEYARD CODE: | D1 |
| COUNTY: | MEATH |
| MEMORIAL NUMBER: | L31 |
| ERECTED BY: | THEIR FAMILY |
| ORIENTATION: | EAST |
| NUMBER OF COMPONENTS: | 2 |
| NUMBER OF INSCRIBED FACES: | 1 |
| NUMBER OF PEOPLE COMMEMORATED: | 2 |
| MEMORIAL TYPE: | HEADSTONE APEX |
| CONDITION OF MEMORIAL: | SOUND IN PLACE |
| CONDITION OF INSCRIPTION: | CLEAR |
| STONEMASON NAME: | |
| TECHNIQUE OF INSCRIPTION: | INCISED AND PAINTED |
| UNDERTAKER: | |
| STONE TOP: | ARCH |
| GRAVE TYPE: | SINGLE |
| HEIGHT: | 102CM |
| WIDTH: | 49CM |
| THICKNESS: | 03CM |

| SURNAME: | CHRISTIAN | ADDRESS | DEATH | AGE |
|---|---|---|---|---|
| SHEERIN | PETER | COMMONS | | |
| | MARY ANN | | | |

**INSCRIPTION:**
LORD HAVE MERCY
ON THE SOULS OF
PETER SHEERIN
COMMONS
AND HIS WIFE
MARY ANN
R.I.P.
ERECTED BY THEIR FAMILY

**SYMBOLS:**
HEART AND CROSS IN FLAMES FLANKED BY ROSES

| | |
|---|---|
| NAME OF RECORDER: | LIZ LYNCH AND PHYLLIS NOONAN |
| DATE: | 30 MAY 2006 |
| PHOTO REFERENCE: | L31 |
| LOCATION/MAP REF: | D1 L31 |

| | |
|---|---|
| GRAVEYARD NAME: | **ST. MARY'S ABBEY OLD GRAVEYARD** |
| GRAVEYARD CODE: | D1 |
| COUNTY: | MEATH |
| MEMORIAL NUMBER: | G11 |
| ERECTED BY: | |
| ORIENTATION: | EAST |
| NUMBER OF COMPONENTS: | 1 |
| NUMBER OF INSCRIBED FACES: | 1 |
| NUMBER OF PEOPLE COMMEMORATED: | 2 |
| MEMORIAL TYPE: | LOW MONUMENT |
| CONDITION OF MEMORIAL: | CRACKED, COVERED IN GRAVEL |
| CONDITION OF INSCRIPTION: | LEGIBLE |
| STONEMASON NAME: | |
| TECHNIQUE OF INSCRIPTION: | WHERE VISIBLE, INCISED |
| UNDERTAKER: | |
| STONE TOP: | LOW MONUMENT |
| GRAVE TYPE: | SINGLE LOW MONUMENT |
| HEIGHT: | |
| WIDTH: | |
| THICKNESS: | |

| SURNAME: | CHRISTIAN | ADDRESS | DEATH | AGE |
|---|---|---|---|---|
| SHERLOCK | JAMES | | 19 APR 1768 | 52 |
| SHERLOCK | ELIZABETH | | | |

**INSCRIPTION:**
HERE LIETH THE BODY OF JAMES SHERLOCK WHO DIED APRIL 19TH 1768 AGED 52 YEARS ALSO HIS MOTHER ELIZABETH SHERLOCK ALIAS MURRAY

**SYMBOLS:**
IHS IN SUNBURST

| | |
|---|---|
| NAME OF RECORDER: | JANET LEIGH |
| DATE: | SEPT 2005 |
| PHOTO REFERENCE: | G11 |
| LOCATION/MAP REF | D1 - G11 |

| | |
|---|---|
| GRAVEYARD NAME: | **ST. MARY'S ABBEY OLD GRAVEYARD** |
| GRAVEYARD CODE: | D1 |
| COUNTY: | MEATH |
| MEMORIAL NUMBER: | K50 |
| ERECTED BY: | WILLIAM SINGLETON |
| ORIENTATION: | EAST |
| NUMBER OF COMPONENTS: | 3 |
| NUMBER OF INSCRIBED FACES: | 1 |
| NUMBER OF PEOPLE COMMEMORATED: | 7 |
| MEMORIAL TYPE: | HEADSTONE |
| CONDITION OF MEMORIAL: | SOUND IN PLACE |
| CONDITION OF INSCRIPTION: | CLEAR |
| STONEMASON NAME: | |
| TECHNIQUE OF INSCRIPTION: | INLAID |
| UNDERTAKER: | |
| STONE TOP: | ARCHED |
| GRAVE TYPE: | DOUBLE |
| HEIGHT: | 187CM |
| WIDTH: | 75CM |
| THICKNESS: | 15CM |

| SURNAME: | CHRISTIAN | ADDRESS | DEATH | AGE |
|---|---|---|---|---|
| SINGLETON | ELIZABETH | | 26 NOV 1860 | 84 |
| | ELIZABETH | | 17 DEC 1858 | 38 |
| HARRIS | SARAH | | 01 FEB 1865 | 66 |
| PENDREY | WILLIAM | | 19 APRIL 1865 | 83 |
| SINGLETON | WILLIAM | | 30 JAN 1872 | |
| SINGLETON HARRIS | ELIZA | | 16 JAN 1881 | |
| HATCH | MARY ANN | | 31 MAY 1930 | |

**INSCRIPTION:**
ERECTED BY WILLIAM SINGLETON
TO THE MEMORY OF
HIS MOTHER ELIZABETH SINGLETON
DIED 26TH NOVR 1860 AGED 84 YEARS
HIS SISTER ELIZABETH SINGLETON
DIED 17TH DECR 1858 AGED 39 YEARS
HIS SISTER SARAH HARRIS
DIED 1ST FEBY 1865 AGED 66 YEARS
HIS UNCLE WILLIAM PENDREY
DIED 19TH APRIL 1865 AGED 83 YEARS
HERE ALSO LIETH
THE ABOVE WILLIAM SINGLETON
WHO DEPARTED THIS LIFE 30TH JAN 1872
I KNOW THAT MY REDEEMER LIVETH
JOB. 13 CH: 25 VR
HERE ALSO LIETH HIS NIECE
ELIZA SINGLETON HARRIS
WHO DEPARTED THIS LIFE ON SUNDAY THE 16TH
JANUARY 1881 ~ ALSO
MARY ANN HATCH
DIED MAY 31ST 1930
BLESSED ARE THE DEAD WHICH DIE
IN THE LORD REV. 14 CH 12 VR

**ORNAMENTS:**
INSCRIPTION FLANKED BY TWO COLUMNS

| | |
|---|---|
| NAME OF RECORDER: | PHYLLIS NOONAN AND JANET LEIGH |
| DATE: | 06 MAY 2006 |
| PHOTO REFERENCE: | K50 |
| LOCATION/MAP REF: | D1 K50 |

| | |
|---|---|
| GRAVEYARD NAME: | **ST. MARY'S ABBEY OLD GRAVEYARD** |
| GRAVEYARD CODE: | D1 |
| COUNTY: | MEATH |
| MEMORIAL NUMBER: | H20 |
| ERECTED BY: | |
| ORIENTATION: | EAST |
| NUMBER OF COMPONENTS: | 2 |
| NUMBER OF INSCRIBED FACES: | 1 |
| NUMBER OF PEOPLE COMMEMORATED: | 1 |
| MEMORIAL TYPE: | PEDESTAL, CROSS MISSING |
| CONDITION OF MEMORIAL: | PEDESTAL IN PLACE CROSS MISSING |
| CONDITION OF INSCRIPTION: | CLEAR |
| STONEMASON NAME: | |
| TECHNIQUE OF INSCRIPTION: | RELIEF LEAD TEXT |
| UNDERTAKER: | |
| STONE TOP: | CROSS MISSING |
| GRAVE TYPE: | SINGLE |
| HEIGHT: | 55CM |
| WIDTH: | 43CM |
| THICKNESS: | 30CM |

| SURNAME: | CHRISTIAN | ADDRESS | DEATH | AGE |
|---|---|---|---|---|
| SKEFFINGTON | FRANCES AMELIA | | 25 FEB 1915 | |

**INSCRIPTION:**
IN LOVING MEMORY
OF
FRANCES AMELIA
WHO ENTERED INTO
HER REST 25TH FEB. 1915

ELDEST DAUGHTER OF THE LATE
HONBLE CHICHESTER
THOMAS SKEFFINGTON

| | |
|---|---|
| NAME OF RECORDER: | PHYLLIS NOONAN AND JANET LEIGH |
| DATE: | 17 JUNE 2006 |
| PHOTO REFERENCE: | H20 |
| LOCATION/MAP REF: | D1 H20 |

| | |
|---|---|
| GRAVEYARD NAME: | **ST. MARY'S ABBEY OLD GRAVEYARD** |
| GRAVEYARD CODE: | D1 |
| COUNTY: | MEATH |
| MEMORIAL NUMBER: | D5 |
| ERECTED BY: | |
| ORIENTATION: | EAST |
| NUMBER OF COMPONENTS: | 1 |
| NUMBER OF INSCRIBED FACES: | 1 |
| NUMBER OF PEOPLE COMMEMORATED: | 1 |
| MEMORIAL TYPE: | HEADSTONE |
| CONDITION OF MEMORIAL: | BROKEN |
| CONDITION OF INSCRIPTION: | MAINLY DECIPHERABLE |
| STONEMASON NAME: | |
| TECHNIQUE OF INSCRIPTION: | INCISED |
| UNDERTAKER: | |
| STONE TOP: | MISSING |
| GRAVE TYPE: | SINGLE |
| HEIGHT: | 85CM |
| WIDTH: | 54CM |
| THICKNESS: | 7CM |

| SURNAME: | CHRISTIAN | ADDRESS | DEATH | AGE |
|---|---|---|---|---|
| SLAVIN | MARY | | 21 DEC 1736 | 4YRS |

**INSCRIPTION:**
HERE LIES THE BODY OF
MARY SLAVIN  HOM
DIED YE 21 OF DISBR 1736
AGED 4 YEARS

| | |
|---|---|
| NAME OF RECORDER: | PHYLLIS NOONAN |
| DATE: | 6 JUNE 2006 |
| PHOTO REFERENCE: | D5 |
| LOCATION/MAP REF: | D1 D5 |

| | |
|---|---|
| GRAVEYARD NAME: | **ST. MARY'S ABBEY OLD GRAVEYARD** |
| GRAVEYARD CODE: | D1 |
| COUNTY: | MEATH |
| MEMORIAL NUMBER: | AA1 |
| ERECTED BY: | WIFE AND FAMILY |
| ORIENTATION: | EAST |
| NUMBER OF COMPONENTS: | 1 |
| NUMBER OF INSCRIBED FACES: | 1 |
| NUMBER OF PEOPLE COMMEMORATED: | 1 |
| MEMORIAL TYPE: | LOW SCROLL |
| CONDITION OF MEMORIAL: | GOOD |
| CONDITION OF INSCRIPTION: | LEGIBLE |
| STONEMASON NAME: | GOGARTY |
| TECHNIQUE OF INSCRIPTION: | INCISED |
| UNDERTAKER: | MICHAEL DUIGNAN |
| STONE TOP: | SCROLL |
| GRAVE TYPE: | DOUBLE |
| HEIGHT: | 30CM |
| WIDTH: | 62CM |
| THICKNESS: | 30CM |

| SURNAME: | CHRISTIAN | ADDRESS | DEATH | AGE |
|---|---|---|---|---|
| SMITH | WILLIAM *LIAM* | | 2006 | 82 |

**INSCRIPTION:**
WILLIAM *LIAM* SMITH
1924 - 2006

REST IN PEACE

**SYMBOLS:**
SCROLL

| | |
|---|---|
| NAME OF RECORDER: | PHYLLIS NOONAN AND JANET LEIGH |
| DATE: | 20 SEPT 2008 |
| PHOTO REFERENCE: | AA1 |
| LOCATION/MAP REF: | D1 AA1 |

| | |
|---|---|
| GRAVEYARD NAME: | **ST. MARY'S ABBEY OLD GRAVEYARD** |
| GRAVEYARD CODE: | D1 |
| COUNTY: | MEATH |
| MEMORIAL NUMBER: | F1 |
| ERECTED BY: | MARGARET BEATY |
| ORIENTATION: | EAST |
| NUMBER OF COMPONENTS: | 1 |
| NUMBER OF INSCRIBED FACES: | 1 |
| NUMBER OF PEOPLE COMMEMORATED: | 2 AND POSTERITY |
| MEMORIAL TYPE: | HEADSTONE |
| CONDITION OF MEMORIAL: | SOUND IN PLACE |
| CONDITION OF INSCRIPTION: | CLEAR |
| STONEMASON NAME: | |
| TECHNIQUE OF INSCRIPTION: | INCISED |
| UNDERTAKER: | |
| STONE TOP: | ROUND SUNBURST DISK |
| GRAVE TYPE: | SINGLE |
| HEIGHT: | 124CM |
| WIDTH: | 73CM |
| THICKNESS: | 15CM |

| SURNAME: | CHRISTIAN | ADDRESS | DEATH | AGE |
|---|---|---|---|---|
| SORAUGHAN | PATRICK | BELLEWSTOWN | 03 JULY 1742 | 57 |
| BEATY | MARGARET | | 21 JULY 1789 | 30 |

**INSCRIPTION:**
HERE LIETH THE BODY OF PATRICK SORAUGHAN OF BELLEWSTOWN AND HIS POSTERITY WHO DEPARTED THIS LIFE THE 3RD DAY OF JULY IN THE YEAR 1742 AGED 57 YEARS ~~ THIS STONE WAS ERECTED BY MARGARET BEATY GRAND DAUGHTER TO THE ABOVE PATRICK WHO DEPARTED THIS LIFE THE 21ST DAY OF JULY 1789 AGED 30 YEARS

**SYMBOLS:**
MALTESE CROSS IHS WITH ANGELS WITH HEART

| | |
|---|---|
| NAME OF RECORDER: | SHAUN AND LIZ LYNCH AND BEN RYAN |
| DATE: | 16 JULY 2005 |
| PHOTO REFERENCE: | F1 |
| LOCATION/MAP REF: | D1 F1 |

| | |
|---|---|
| GRAVEYARD NAME: | **ST. MARY'S ABBEY OLD GRAVEYARD** |
| GRAVEYARD CODE: | D1 |
| COUNTY: | MEATH |
| MEMORIAL NUMBER: | G4 |
| ERECTED BY: | STEPHEN TAAFFE |
| ORIENTATION: | EAST |
| NUMBER OF COMPONENTS: | 1 |
| NUMBER OF INSCRIBED FACES: | 1 |
| NUMBER OF PEOPLE COMMEMORATED: | 5 |
| MEMORIAL TYPE: | HEADSTONE POSITIONED ON WALL |
| CONDITION OF MEMORIAL: | SOUND IN PLACE |
| CONDITION OF INSCRIPTION: | LEGIBLE |
| STONEMASON NAME: | |
| TECHNIQUE OF INSCRIPTION: | INCISED |
| UNDERTAKER: | |
| STONE TOP: | |
| GRAVE TYPE: | TOMB |

| SURNAME: | CHRISTIAN | ADDRESS | DEATH | AGE |
|---|---|---|---|---|
| PLUNCKETT | ALICE | | 06 JUNE 1707 | 36 |
| BARNWELL | MARBELLA | | 1711 | 37 |
| TAFFEE | LAURENCE | | 1709 | |
| BURCK | BRIGID | | 1716 | 27 |
| TAFFEE | STEPHEN | | 15 AUG 1730 | 66 |

**INSCRIPTION:**
IN THE BENEATH TOMB IS BURIED THE BODY OF
STEPHEN TAAFFE ESQR, WITH THAT OF THE HON.
ALICE PLUNCKETT ONE OF THE DAUGHTERS OF YE
RT. HONBLE MATHEW LATE LD OF LOUTH HIS 1ST
WIFE WHO DIED IN THE YEAR 1707 AGED 36 YEARS
& OF THE RT. HONBLE MARBELLA BARNWELL ONE OF
THE DAUGHTERS OF THE RT. HONBLE HENRY LATE LD.
VISCOUNT KINGSLAND & LADY DOWAGER OF LOWTH
HIS 2ND WIFE WHO DIED IN THE YEAR 1711 AGED
37 YEARS & OF HIS FATHER LAURENCE TAAFFE
ESQR WHO DIED IN THE YEAR 1709 & OF BRIGID
BURCK ONE OF THE DAUGHTERS OF ST. JOHN BURCK
BARONETT HIS 3D WIFE WHO DIED IN YE 1716
AGED 27 YEARS. THE SAID STEPHEN BY HIS LAST
WILL APPOINTED THE SAID TOMB TO BE ERECTED IN
HONOUR OF HIS SAID FATHER AND SAID WIVES
AS A BURIAL PLACE FOR HIS POSTERITY HE
DEPARTED THIS LIFE THE 15TH OF AUGUST 1730
AGED 66 YEARS
REQUIESCANT IN PACE

*(UPSIDE DOWN AT THE BOTTOM OF HEADSTONE)*
HERE LYETH THE BODY OF ALICE TAAFFE DAUGHTER
OF MATHEW LORD OF LOWTH AND WIFE TO STEPHEN TAAFFE
OF DOWENSTOWN DIED THE 6 OF JUNE 1707 AGED 36 YEARS.
*NOTE: THERE IS A STORY WHICH HAS COME DOWN IN LOCAL FOLKLORE ABOUT THIS STONE. IT IS SAID THAT ON THE DEATH OF HIS FIRST WIFE STEPHEN TAAFFE NOTED THAT HIS NAME WOULD NOT BE AT THE TOP OF THE TOMBSTONE. HE THEREFORE ORDERED THAT NO FURTHER NAME SHOULD BE INSCRIBED ON IT UNTIL HIS OWN DEATH. ON THE OCCASION OF HIS DEATH THE STONE WAS REVERSED AND THE INSCRIPTION AS SEEN TODAY WAS MADE, WITH THE ORIGINAL INSCRIPTION RECORDING THE DEATH OF ALICE TAAFFE (NEE PLUNCKETT) TO BE UPSIDE DOWN AT THE BOTTOM.*

| | |
|---|---|
| NAME OF RECORDER: | JANET LEIGH AND LIZ LYNCH |
| DATE: | 01 JULY 2006 |
| PHOTO REFERENCE: | G4 |
| LOCATION/MAP REF: | D1 G4 |

| | |
|---|---|
| GRAVEYARD NAME: | **ST. MARY'S ABBEY OLD GRAVEYARD** |
| GRAVEYARD CODE: | D1 |
| COUNTY: | MEATH |
| MEMORIAL NUMBER: | L12 |
| ERECTED BY: | PETER TIERNAN |
| ORIENTATION: | EAST |
| NUMBER OF COMPONENTS: | 1 |
| NUMBER OF INSCRIBED FACES: | 1 |
| NUMBER OF PEOPLE COMMEMORATED: | 2 + |
| MEMORIAL TYPE: | HEADSTONE WITH DISK |
| CONDITION OF MEMORIAL: | SOUND IN PLACE |
| CONDITION OF INSCRIPTION: | MAINLY DECIPHERABLE |
| STONEMASON NAME: | |
| TECHNIQUE OF INSCRIPTION: | INCISED |
| UNDERTAKER: | |
| STONE TOP: | ROUND |
| GRAVE TYPE: | SINGLE |
| HEIGHT: | 120 |
| WIDTH: | 59 |
| THICKNESS: | 14 CM |

| SURNAME: | CHRISTIAN | ADDRESS | DEATH | AGE |
|---|---|---|---|---|
| TIERNAN | PATRICK | RAHILL | | |
| ANDREWS ALIAS | MARGARET | | | |
| | ANCESTORS | | | |

**INSCRIPTION:**
ERECTED IN THIS HIS FAMILYS BURIAL PLACE BY PETER TIERNAN OF RAHILL LIE THE REMAINS OF HIS FATHER PATRICK TIERNAN, HIS MOTHER MARGARET TIERNAN ALIAS ANDREWS WITH THOSE OF THEIR ANCESTORS WAITING FOR A JOYFUL RESURRECTION. ANNO DOMINI 1792

**SYMBOLS:**
CROSS ABOVE IHS

| | |
|---|---|
| NAME OF RECORDER: | BEN RYAN AND HELEN FULLAM |
| DATE: | 20 MAY 2006 |
| PHOTO REFERENCE: | L12 |
| LOCATION/MAP REF: | D1 L12 |

| | |
|---|---|
| GRAVEYARD NAME: | **ST. MARY'S ABBEY OLD GRAVEYARD** |
| GRAVEYARD CODE: | D1 |
| COUNTY: | MEATH |
| MEMORIAL NUMBER: | J11 |
| ERECTED BY: | |
| ORIENTATION: | EAST |
| NUMBER OF COMPONENTS: | 1 |
| NUMBER OF INSCRIBED FACES: | 1 |
| NUMBER OF PEOPLE COMMEMORATED: | 6 |
| MEMORIAL TYPE: | HEADSTONE |
| CONDITION OF MEMORIAL: | GOOD |
| CONDITION OF INSCRIPTION: | LEGIBLE |
| STONEMASON NAME: | |
| TECHNIQUE OF INSCRIPTION: | INCISED |
| UNDERTAKER: | |
| STONE TOP: | CROSS |
| GRAVE TYPE: | SINGLE |
| HEIGHT: | 137CM |
| WIDTH: | 50CM |
| THICKNESS: | 09CM |

| SURNAME: | CHRISTIAN | ADDRESS | DEATH | AGE |
|---|---|---|---|---|
| TIERNAN | BARTW | DULEEK | 25 JAN 1876 | 52 |
| | CATHERINE | | 20 AUG 1863 | 33 |
| | THOMAS | | 18 APR 1851 | 64 |
| | ALICE | | 1838 | |
| | JOHN | | 22 SEPT 1911 | |
| MCKENNA | JAMES | | 05 APR 1947 | 71 |

**INSCRIPTION:**
IN MEMORY OF
BARTHW TIERNAN OF DULEEK DIED JAN 25 1876
AGED 52 YEARS OF HIS SISTER
CATHERINE
WHO DIED AUG 20 1863 AGED 33 YRS
OF HIS FATHER THOMAS DIED APRIL 18 1851 64
YEARS
AND HIS MOTHER ALICE DIED 1838
ALSO JOHN TIERNAN DIED
SEPT 22 1911
JAMES MCKENNA
DIED 5 APRIL 1947 AGED 71
*MAY THEY REST IN PEACE*

**SYMBOLS:**
IHS IN DIAMOND SHAPE

| | |
|---|---|
| NAME OF RECORDER: | BEN RYAN |
| DATE: | 06 AUGUST 2005 |
| PHOTO REFERENCE: | J11 |
| LOCATION/MAP REF: | D1 J11 |

| | |
|---|---|
| GRAVEYARD NAME: | **ST. MARY'S ABBEY OLD GRAVEYARD** |
| GRAVEYARD CODE: | D1 |
| COUNTY: | MEATH |
| MEMORIAL NUMBER: | H6 |
| ERECTED BY: | |
| ORIENTATION: | EAST |
| NUMBER OF COMPONENTS: | |
| NUMBER OF INSCRIBED FACES: | 1 |
| NUMBER OF PEOPLE COMMEMORATED: | 1 |
| MEMORIAL TYPE: | LOW MONUMENT |
| CONDITION OF MEMORIAL: | SOUND IN PLACE |
| CONDITION OF INSCRIPTION: | MAINLY DECIPHERABLE |
| STONEMASON NAME: | |
| TECHNIQUE OF INSCRIPTION: | INCISED |
| UNDERTAKER: | |
| STONE TOP: | SQUARE LOW MONUMENT |
| GRAVE TYPE: | SINGLE LOW MONUMENT |
| HEIGHT: | 224CM |
| WIDTH: | 103CM |
| THICKNESS: | 5CM |

| SURNAME: | CHRISTIAN | ADDRESS | DEATH | AGE |
|---|---|---|---|---|
| TROTTER | THOMAS | DULEEK | 07 NOV 1802 | 69 |

**INSCRIPTION:**
HERE LIETH THE BODY OF THOMAS
TROTTER ESQ LATE OF DULEEK COUNTY
MEATH WHO DEPARTED THIS LIFE ON THE
7TH DAY OF NOVEMBER 1802
IN THE 69TH YEAR OF HIS AGE

| | |
|---|---|
| NAME OF RECORDER: | JANET LEIGH AND LIZ LYNCH |
| DATE: | 07 JUNE 2006 |
| PHOTO REFERENCE: | H6 |
| LOCATION/MAP REF: | D1 H6 |

| | |
|---|---|
| GRAVEYARD NAME: | **ST. MARY'S ABBEY OLD GRAVEYARD** |
| GRAVEYARD CODE: | D1 |
| COUNTY: | MEATH |
| MEMORIAL NUMBER: | J26 |
| ERECTED BY: | |
| ORIENTATION: | EAST |
| NUMBER OF COMPONENTS: | 1 |
| NUMBER OF INSCRIBED FACES: | 1 |
| NUMBER OF PEOPLE COMMEMORATED: | 7 |
| MEMORIAL TYPE: | LOW MONUMENT |
| CONDITION OF MEMORIAL: | SOUND IN PLACE |
| CONDITION OF INSCRIPTION: | MAINLY DECIPHERABLE |
| STONEMASON NAME: | |
| TECHNIQUE OF INSCRIPTION: | INCISED |
| UNDERTAKER: | |
| STONE TOP: | LOW MONUMENT |
| GRAVE TYPE: | DOUBLE |
| HEIGHT: | LENGTH 214 |
| WIDTH: | 109 CM |
| THICKNESS: | |

| SURNAME: | CHRISTIAN | ADDRESS | DEATH | AGE |
|---|---|---|---|---|
| TROTTER | JOHN | | 30 JUL 1833 | 6 |
| | MARY | | 17 MAR 1841 | 42 |
| | STEPHEN | DULEEK | 20 FEB 1851 | 57 |
| | SUSAN | | 20 AUG 1851 | 25 |
| | WILLIAM | | 29 APR 1855 | 34 |
| KNOX | HENRIETTA | | 26 JAN 1860 | 18 MONTHS |
| | MARY | | 18 JAN 1934 | 84 |

**INSCRIPTION:**
ERECTED
TO THE MEMORY OF JOHN TROTTER SON
TO STEPHEN TROTTER OF DULEEK WHO DEPARTED
THIS LIFE 30TH JULY 1833 AGED 6 YEARS
ALSO HIS WIFE MARY TROTTER DAUGHTER TO
NICHOLAS HATCH OF DULEEK WHO DEPARTED
THIS LIFE 17TH MARCH 1841 AGED 42 YEARS
ALSO THE ABOVE NAMED STEPHEN TROTTER
WHO DEPARTED THIS LIFE 20TH FEBRY 1851 AGED 57
YEARS ~~ AND ALSO HIS DAUGHTER
SUSAN
WHO DIED 20TH AUG 1851 AGED 25 YEARS
ALSO HIS SON WILLIAM TROTTER
WHO DEPARTED THIS LIFE THE 29TH APRIL
1855 AGED 34 YEARS

ALSO HIS GRANDDAUGHTER HENRIETTA KNOX
DIED JAN 26TH 1860
AGED 1 YEAR AND 8 MONTHS
AND MARY KNOX DIED JAN 18TH 1934
AGED 84 YEARS

| | |
|---|---|
| NAME OF RECORDER: | LIZ LYNCH AND PHYLLIS NOONAN |
| DATE: | 18 AUG 2005 |
| PHOTO REFERENCE: | J26 |
| LOCATION/MAP REF: | D1 J26 |

| | |
|---|---|
| GRAVEYARD NAME: | **ST. MARY'S ABBEY OLD GRAVEYARD** |
| GRAVEYARD CODE: | D1 |
| COUNTY: | MEATH |
| MEMORIAL NUMBER: | E9 |
| ERECTED BY: | |
| ORIENTATION: | EAST |
| NUMBER OF COMPONENTS: | 2 |
| NUMBER OF INSCRIBED FACES: | |
| NUMBER OF PEOPLE COMMEMORATED: | |
| MEMORIAL TYPE: | HEADSTONE COLLAPSED |
| CONDITION OF MEMORIAL: | |
| CONDITION OF INSCRIPTION: | |
| STONEMASON NAME: | NIXON AND HATCH SHEEPHOUSE QUARRIES |
| TECHNIQUE OF INSCRIPTION: | |
| UNDERTAKER: | |
| STONE TOP: | ARCHED COLLAPSED |
| GRAVE TYPE: | SINGLE |
| HEIGHT: | 200CM COLLAPSED |
| WIDTH: | 63CM COLLAPSED |
| THICKNESS: | 20CM COLLAPSED |

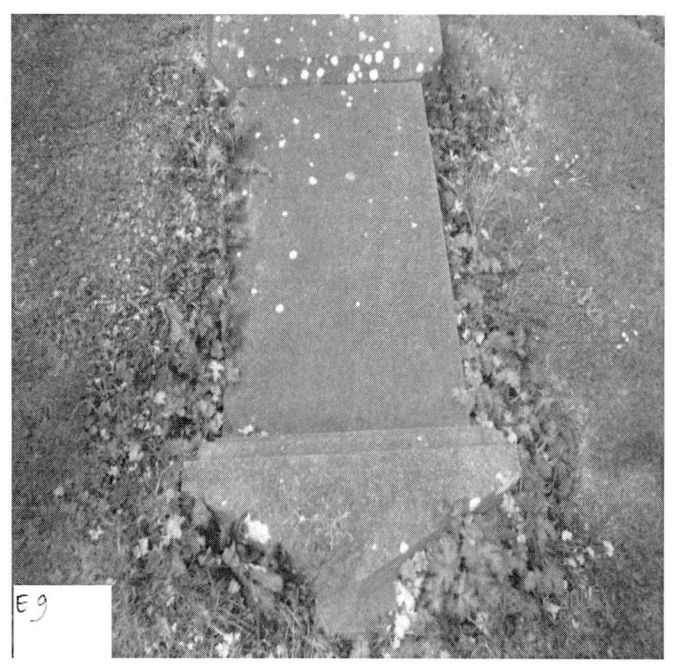

| | |
|---|---|
| NAME OF RECORDER: | JANET LEIGH |
| DATE: | 16 JULY 2005 |
| PHOTO REFERENCE: | E9 |
| LOCATION/MAP REF: | D1 E9 |

| | |
|---|---|
| GRAVEYARD NAME: | **ST. MARY'S ABBEY OLD GRAVEYARD** |
| GRAVEYARD CODE: | D1 |
| COUNTY: | MEATH |
| MEMORIAL NUMBER: | F13 |
| ERECTED BY: | |
| ORIENTATION: | EAST |
| NUMBER OF COMPONENTS: | |
| NUMBER OF INSCRIBED FACES: | |
| NUMBER OF PEOPLE COMMEMORATED: | |
| MEMORIAL TYPE: | UNKNOWN |
| CONDITION OF MEMORIAL: | |
| CONDITION OF INSCRIPTION: | |
| STONEMASON NAME: | |
| TECHNIQUE OF INSCRIPTION: | |
| UNDERTAKER: | |
| STONE TOP: | |
| GRAVE TYPE: | SINGLE |
| HEIGHT: | |
| WIDTH: | |
| THICKNESS: | |

| | |
|---|---|
| NAME OF RECORDER: | JANET LEIGH |
| DATE: | 06 JUNE 2006 |
| PHOTO REFERENCE: | F13 |
| LOCATION/MAP REF: | D1 F13 |

| | |
|---|---|
| GRAVEYARD NAME: | **ST. MARY'S ABBEY OLD GRAVEYARD** |
| GRAVEYARD CODE: | D1 |
| COUNTY: | MEATH |
| MEMORIAL NUMBER: | F28 |
| ERECTED BY: | |
| ORIENTATION: | EAST |
| NUMBER OF COMPONENTS: | |
| NUMBER OF INSCRIBED FACES: | |
| NUMBER OF PEOPLE COMMEMORATED: | |
| MEMORIAL TYPE: | |
| CONDITION OF MEMORIAL: | COLLAPSED UNKNOWN |
| CONDITION OF INSCRIPTION: | |
| STONEMASON NAME: | |
| TECHNIQUE OF INSCRIPTION: | |
| UNDERTAKER: | |
| STONE TOP: | |
| GRAVE TYPE: | SINGLE |
| HEIGHT: | 188CM |
| WIDTH: | 80CM |
| THICKNESS: | 15CM |

| | |
|---|---|
| NAME OF RECORDER: | PHYLLIS NOONAN |
| DATE: | 20 JULY 2005 |
| PHOTO REFERENCE: | F 28 |
| LOCATION/MAP REF: | D1 F28 |

| | |
|---|---|
| GRAVEYARD NAME: | **ST. MARY'S ABBEY OLD GRAVEYARD** |
| GRAVEYARD CODE: | D1 |
| COUNTY: | MEATH |
| MEMORIAL NUMBER: | C2 |
| ERECTED BY: | |
| ORIENTATION: | EAST |
| NUMBER OF COMPONENTS: | 3 |
| NUMBER OF INSCRIBED FACES: | 1 |
| NUMBER OF PEOPLE COMMEMORATED: | CANNOT BE READ |
| MEMORIAL TYPE: | CROSS |
| CONDITION OF MEMORIAL: | OVERGROWN |
| CONDITION OF INSCRIPTION: | MISSING |
| STONEMASON NAME: | |
| TECHNIQUE OF INSCRIPTION: | MISSING |
| UNDERTAKER: | |
| STONE TOP: | CROSS |
| GRAVE TYPE: | SINGLE |
| HEIGHT: | 148CM. |
| WIDTH: | 34CM |
| THICKNESS: | 16CM |

**INSCRIPTION:**

CANNOT BE READ
HOLLY BUSH AND TREE UP AGAINST
THIS HEADSTONE

**SYMBOLS:**

CROSS IHS

| | |
|---|---|
| NAME OF RECORDER: | JANET LEIGH AND HELEN FULLAM |
| DATE: | 02 JULY 2005 |
| PHOTO REFERENCE: | C2 |
| LOCATION/MAP REF: | D1 C2: |

| | |
|---|---|
| GRAVEYARD NAME: | **ST. MARY'S ABBEY OLD GRAVEYARD** |
| GRAVEYARD CODE: | D1 |
| COUNTY: | MEATH |
| MEMORIAL NUMBER: | L29 |
| ERECTED BY: | |
| ORIENTATION: | EAST |
| NUMBER OF COMPONENTS: | 1 |
| NUMBER OF INSCRIBED FACES: | |
| NUMBER OF PEOPLE COMMEMORATED: | |
| MEMORIAL TYPE: | IRON CROSS UNKNOWN |
| CONDITION OF MEMORIAL: | SOUND IN PLACE |
| CONDITION OF INSCRIPTION: | MISSING |
| STONEMASON NAME: | |
| TECHNIQUE OF INSCRIPTION: | MISSING |
| UNDERTAKER: | |
| STONE TOP: | IRON CROSS |
| GRAVE TYPE: | SINGLE |
| HEIGHT: | 107CM |
| WIDTH: | 64CM |
| THICKNESS: | 04CM |

**INSCRIPTION:**
*MISSING*

| | |
|---|---|
| NAME OF RECORDER: | LIZ LYNCH AND JANET LEIGH |
| DATE: | 07 JUNE 2006 |
| PHOTO REFERENCE: | L29 |
| LOCATION/MAP REF: | D1 L29 |

| | |
|---|---|
| GRAVEYARD NAME: | **ST. MARY'S ABBEY OLD GRAVEYARD** |
| GRAVEYARD CODE: | D1 |
| COUNTY: | MEATH |
| MEMORIAL NUMBER: | H1 |
| ERECTED BY: | |
| ORIENTATION: | EAST |
| NUMBER OF COMPONENTS: | 1 |
| NUMBER OF INSCRIBED FACES: | 1 |
| NUMBER OF PEOPLE COMMEMORATED: | 1 |
| MEMORIAL TYPE: | HEADSTONE |
| CONDITION OF MEMORIAL: | SOUND IN PLACE |
| CONDITION OF INSCRIPTION: | CLEAR |
| STONEMASON NAME: | |
| TECHNIQUE OF INSCRIPTION: | INCISED |
| UNDERTAKER: | |
| STONE TOP: | SQUARE |
| GRAVE TYPE: | SINGLE |
| HEIGHT: | 29CM |
| WIDTH: | 35CM |
| THICKNESS: | 10CM |

**INSCRIPTION:**

J+C

| | |
|---|---|
| NAME OF RECORDER: | JANET LEIGH AND LIZ LYNCH |
| DATE: | 07 JUNE 2006 |
| PHOTO REFERENCE: | H1 |
| LOCATION/MAP REF: | D1-H1 |

| | |
|---|---|
| GRAVEYARD NAME: | **ST. MARY'S ABBEY OLD GRAVEYARD** |
| GRAVEYARD CODE: | D1 |
| COUNTY: | MEATH |
| MEMORIAL NUMBER: | L11 |
| ERECTED BY: | |
| ORIENTATION: | EAST |
| NUMBER OF COMPONENTS: | 1 |
| NUMBER OF INSCRIBED FACES: | 1 |
| NUMBER OF PEOPLE COMMEMORATED: | |
| MEMORIAL TYPE: | MARKER STONE |
| CONDITION OF MEMORIAL: | SOUND IN PLACE |
| CONDITION OF INSCRIPTION: | MOST INSCRIPTION MISSING |
| STONEMASON NAME: | |
| TECHNIQUE OF INSCRIPTION: | |
| UNDERTAKER: | |
| STONE TOP: | |
| GRAVE TYPE: | SINGLE |
| HEIGHT: | |
| WIDTH: | |
| THICKNESS: | |

**INSCRIPTION:**

*ONLY INSCRIPTION LEGIBLE*
WIFE AND CHILDREN

| | |
|---|---|
| NAME OF RECORDER: | JANET LEIGH |
| DATE: | 20 JUNE 2006 |
| PHOTO REFERENCE: | L11 |
| LOCATION/MAP REF: | D1 L11 |

| | |
|---|---|
| GRAVEYARD NAME: | **ST. MARY'S ABBEY OLD GRAVEYARD** |
| GRAVEYARD CODE: | D1 |
| COUNTY: | MEATH |
| MEMORIAL NUMBER: | D6 |
| ERECTED BY: | ANNE VERDON DROGHEDA |
| ORIENTATION: | EAST |
| NUMBER OF COMPONENTS: | 1 |
| NUMBER OF INSCRIBED FACES: | 1 |
| NUMBER OF PEOPLE COMMEMORATED: | 6 |
| MEMORIAL TYPE: | HEADSTONE |
| CONDITION OF MEMORIAL: | SOUND IN PLACE |
| CONDITION OF INSCRIPTION: | CLEAR |
| STONEMASON NAME: | |
| TECHNIQUE OF INSCRIPTION: | INCISED |
| UNDERTAKER: | SUNBURST DISK ROUND |
| GRAVE TYPE: | SINGLE |
| HEIGHT: | 153CM |
| WIDTH: | 71CM |
| THICKNESS: | 15CM |

| SURNAME: | CHRISTIAN | ADDRESS | DEATH | AGE |
|---|---|---|---|---|
| VERDON | RICHARD | DROGHEDA | 08 SEPT 1827 | 37 |
| | CHILD | | | |
| | CHILD | | | |
| | CHILD | | | |
| | PATRICK | DULEEK | 30 OCT 1907 | |
| | MARY JANE | DULEEK | 23 SEPT 1919 | |

**INSCRIPTION:**
THIS STONE WAS ERECTED BY
ANNE VERDON OF DROGHEDA
IN MEMORY OF HER BELOVED
HUSBAND RICHARD VERDON
WHO DEPARTED THIS LIFE THE 8TH
OF SEPTR 1827 AGED 37 YEARS
ALSO OF THREE OF THE CHILDREN
WHO DIED YOUNG
ALSO PATK VERDON DULEEK
DIED 30TH OCTOBER 1907
AND HIS WIFE MARY JANE WHO DIED
SEPT.23RD 1919
*RESQUISCANT IN PACE*

**SYMBOLS:**
IHS IN SUNBURST WITH HEART AND
CROSS FLANKED BY CHERUBS WITH
ROSE BENEATH

| | |
|---|---|
| NAME OF RECORDER: | PHYLLIS NOONAN |
| DATE: | 11 JULY 2005 |
| PHOTO REFERENCE: | D6 |
| LOCATION/MAP REF: | D1 D6 |

| | |
|---|---|
| GRAVEYARD NAME: | **ST. MARY'S ABBEY OLD GRAVEYARD** |
| GRAVEYARD CODE: | D1 |
| COUNTY: | MEATH |
| MEMORIAL NUMBER: | B9 |
| ERECTED BY: | |
| ORIENTATION: | EAST |
| NUMBER OF COMPONENTS: | 3 |
| NUMBER OF INSCRIBED FACES: | 1 |
| NUMBER OF PEOPLE COMMEMORATED: | 4 |
| MEMORIAL TYPE: | HEADSTONE |
| CONDITION OF MEMORIAL: | SOUND IN PLACE |
| CONDITION OF INSCRIPTION: | MINT |
| STONEMASON NAME: | |
| TECHNIQUE OF INSCRIPTION: | INCISED |
| UNDERTAKER: | |
| STONE TOP: | ROUND WITH CROSS ON TOP |
| GRAVE TYPE: | TREBLE |
| HEIGHT: | 199CM |
| WIDTH: | 87CM |
| THICKNESS: | 9CM |

| SURNAME: | CHRISTIAN | ADDRESS | DEATH | AGE |
|---|---|---|---|---|
| WALL | ANNE | MAIN STREET DULEEK | 11 NOV 1906 | |
| | JOHN | | 30 JUL 1909 | |
| | ELIZA | | 28 AUG 1913 | |
| | MARY | | 04 OCT 1936 | |

**INSCRIPTION:**
IN LOVING MEMORY
OF
ANNE WALL
MAIN STREET DULEEK
WHO DIED 11 NOV 1906 HER HUSBAND
JOHN WALL
WHO DIED 30 JULY 1909 AND THEIR DAUGHTER
ELIZA
ALSO THEIR DAUGHTER
MARY
WHO DIED OCT 4 1936

R.I.P

**SYMBOLS:**
IHS
CROSS
DOVE
FLOWER

| | |
|---|---|
| NAME OF RECORDER: | HELEN FULLAM AND JANET LEIGH |
| DATE: | 2 JULY 2005 |
| PHOTO REFERENCE: | B9 |
| LOCATION/MAP REF: | D1 B9 |

| | |
|---|---|
| GRAVEYARD NAME: | **ST. MARY'S ABBEY OLD GRAVEYARD** |
| GRAVEYARD CODE: | D1 |
| COUNTY: | MEATH |
| MEMORIAL NUMBER: | K30A |
| ERECTED BY: | CHRISTOPHER WALL |
| ORIENTATION: | EAST |
| NUMBER OF COMPONENTS: | 1 |
| NUMBER OF INSCRIBED FACES: | 1 |
| NUMBER OF PEOPLE COMMEMORATED: | 10 |
| MEMORIAL TYPE: | HEADSTONE |
| CONDITION OF MEMORIAL: | SOUND IN PLACE |
| CONDITION OF INSCRIPTION: | CLEAR |
| STONEMASON NAME: | |
| TECHNIQUE OF INSCRIPTION: | INCISED |
| UNDERTAKER: | |
| STONE TOP: | SUNBURST DISK |
| GRAVE TYPE: | TREBLE |
| HEIGHT: | 162CM |
| WIDTH: | 86CM |
| THICKNESS: | 15CM |

| SURNAME: | CHRISTIAN | ADDRESS | DEATH | AGE |
|---|---|---|---|---|
| WALL | JAMES | MOOR DULEEK | 29 OCT 1781 | 75 |
| | JANE | | 27 MAR 1796 | 78 |
| | EDWARD | | 16 FEB 1810 | 44 |
| | 7 CHILDREN DIED YOUNG | | | |

**INSCRIPTION:**
THIS STONE WAS ERECTED ANNO DOMINI 1811 BY CHRISTOPHER WALL OF THE MOOR PARISH OF DULEEK IN MEMORY OF HIS FA THER JAMES WALL WHO DEPARTD THIS LIFE OCT THE 29TH 1781 AGED 75 YEARS ALSO LIES HERE THE REMAINS OF JANE WALL WIFE TO THE ABOVE JAMES WALL WHO DEPARTED THIS LIFE THE 27TH OF MARCH 1796 AGED 78 YRS ALSO THE REMAINS OF EDWARD WALL HIS SON WHO DEPARTED 16TH FEBRY 1810 AGED 44 YRS ALSO 7 CHILDREN OF THE ABOVE JAMES WALL WHO DIED YOUNG. REQUIESCANT IN PACE AMEN RENEWED BY CHRISTR WALL MOOR IN MEMORY OF HIS FATHER AND MOTHER JAMES & MARY WALL

**SYMBOLS:**
IHS IN SUNBURST WITH WINGED CHERUBS EITHER SIDE

| | |
|---|---|
| NAME OF RECORDER: | PHYLLIS NOONAN |
| DATE: | 21 APRIL 2006 |
| PHOTO REFERENCE: | K30 |
| LOCATION/MAP REF: | D1 K30A |

| | |
|---|---|
| GRAVEYARD NAME: | **ST. MARY'S ABBEY OLD GRAVEYARD** |
| GRAVEYARD CODE: | D1 |
| COUNTY: | MEATH |
| MEMORIAL NUMBER: | K30B |
| ERECTED BY: | JAMES WALL |
| ORIENTATION: | EAST |
| NUMBER OF COMPONENTS: | 2 |
| NUMBER OF INSCRIBED FACES: | 1 |
| NUMBER OF PEOPLE COMMEMORATED: | 5 |
| MEMORIAL TYPE: | HEADSTONE |
| CONDITION OF MEMORIAL: | SOUND IN PLACE |
| CONDITION OF INSCRIPTION: | CLEAR |
| STONEMASON NAME: | WHITE CHORD ROAD DROGHEDA |
| TECHNIQUE OF INSCRIPTION: | INCISED |
| UNDERTAKER: | |
| STONE TOP: | CROSS WITH SACRED HEART |
| GRAVE TYPE: | TREBLE |
| HEIGHT: | 181CM |
| WIDTH: | 70CM |
| THICKNESS: | 10CM |

| SURNAME: | CHRISTIAN | ADDRESS | DEATH | AGE |
|---|---|---|---|---|
| WALL | CHRISTOPHER | MOOR DULEEK | 31 DEC 1888 | 67 |
| | CHRISTOPHER | | 03 JAN 1903 | 45 |
| | BRIDGET | | 10 FEB 1912 | 40 |
| | MARY | | 07 JUNE 1912 | |
| | JAMES | | 14 AUG 1921 | |

**INSCRIPTION:**
ERECTED
BY
JAMES WALL MOOR OF DULEEK
IN MEMORY OF HIS FATHER
CHRISTOPHER WALL
WHO DIED 31ST DEC 1888 AGED 67 YEARS
HIS BROTHER
CHRISTOPHER
WHO DIED 3RD JAN 1903 AGED 45 YEARS
AND HIS WIFE
BRIDGET
WHO DIED 10TH FEB 1912 AGED 40 YEARS
ALSO HIS MOTHER MARY WHO DIED
JUNE 7 1912 AND THE ABOVE
JAMES
WHO DIED AUG 14 1921

R.I.P

**SYMBOLS:**
CROSS WITH SACRED HEART
LAMB ON ALTER IN CIRCLE
UNDER INTERTWINED IHS

| | |
|---|---|
| NAME OF RECORDER: | PHYLLIS NOONAN |
| DATE: | 21 APRIL 2006 |
| PHOTO REFERENCE: | K30 |
| LOCATION/MAP REF: | D1 K30B |

| | |
|---|---|
| GRAVEYARD NAME: | **ST. MARY'S ABBEY OLD GRAVEYARD** |
| GRAVEYARD CODE: | D1 |
| COUNTY: | MEATH |
| MEMORIAL NUMBER: | K30 C |
| ERECTED BY: | CATHERINE WALL |
| ORIENTATION: | EAST |
| NUMBER OF COMPONENTS: | 1 |
| NUMBER OF INSCRIBED FACES: | 1 |
| NUMBER OF PEOPLE COMMEMORATED: | 3 |
| MEMORIAL TYPE: | HEADSTONE |
| CONDITION OF MEMORIAL: | SOUND IN PLACE |
| CONDITION OF INSCRIPTION: | CLEAR |
| STONEMASON NAME: | |
| TECHNIQUE OF INSCRIPTION: | INCISED |
| UNDERTAKER: | |
| STONE TOP: | STEPPED SUNBURST DISK |
| GRAVE TYPE: | TREBLE |
| HEIGHT: | 128CM |
| WIDTH: | 78CM |
| THICKNESS: | 12CM |

| SURNAME: | CHRISTIAN | ADDRESS | DEATH | AGE |
|---|---|---|---|---|
| WALL | PATRICK | | 09 NOV 1789 | 65 |
| | JOSEPH | | 14 AUG 1789 | 6 |
| | MARY | | 28 MARCH 1808 | 24 |

**INSCRIPTION:**
THIS STONE WAS ERECTED
BY MRS CATHERINE WALL OF
THE TOWN OF DROGHEDA IN
MEMORY OF HER HUSBAND PATRICK
WALL WHO DEPARTED THIS LIFE
THE 9TH NOVR 1789 AGED
65 YRS ALSO OF HER SON JOSEPH
WALL WHO DEPARTED THIS LIFE
THE 14TH DAY OF AUG 1789 AGED
6 YRS ALSO OF HER DAUGHTER MARY
WALL WHO DEPARTED THIS LIFE
THE 28TH DAY OF MARCH 1808
AGED 24 YRS

**SYMBOLS:**
IHS IN SUNBURST DISK STEPPED

| | |
|---|---|
| NAME OF RECORDER: | PHYLLIS NOONAN |
| DATE: | 21 APRIL 2006 |
| PHOTO REFERENCE: | K 30 |
| LOCATION/MAP REF: | D1 K30C |

| | |
|---|---|
| GRAVEYARD NAME: | **ST. MARY'S ABBEY OLD GRAVEYARD** |
| GRAVEYARD CODE: | D1 |
| COUNTY: | MEATH |
| MEMORIAL NUMBER: | F29 |
| ERECTED BY: | RICHARD, JOHN AND WILLIAM WALL |
| ORIENTATION: | EAST |
| NUMBER OF COMPONENTS: | 1 |
| NUMBER OF INSCRIBED FACES: | 1 |
| NUMBER OF PEOPLE COMMEMORATED: | 4 |
| MEMORIAL TYPE: | HEADSTONE |
| CONDITION OF MEMORIAL: | SOUND IN PLACE |
| CONDITION OF INSCRIPTION: | MAINLY DECIPHERABLE |
| STONEMASON NAME: | |
| TECHNIQUE OF INSCRIPTION: | INCISED |
| UNDERTAKER: | |
| STONE TOP: | HEADSTONE SUNBURST DISK |
| GRAVE TYPE: | DOUBLE |
| HEIGHT: | 134CM |
| WIDTH: | 80CM |
| THICKNESS: | 13CM |

| SURNAME: | CHRISTIAN | ADDRESS | DEATH | AGE |
|---|---|---|---|---|
| WALL | JOHN | FINNOR | 8 JULY 1797 | |
| | CATHERINE | | 25 SEPT 1826 | |
| | RICHARD | | 13 DEC 1830 | 36 |
| | JOHN | | 17 JULY 1856 | 56 |

**INSCRIPTION:**
ERECTED BY RICHARD
JOHN AND WILLIAM WALL
IN MEMORY OF THEIR
FATHER JOHN WALL WHO DIED
JULY 8 1797 ALSO THEIR MOTHER
CATHERINE WALL WHO DIED
SEPT 25 1826 FINNOR
THE ABOVE RICHARD DIED DECBR 13
1830 AGED 36 YRS THE ABOVE JOHN
DIED JULY 17 1856 AGED 56 YEARS

**SYMBOLS:**
CROSS OVER IHS IN
SUNBURST

| | |
|---|---|
| NAME OF RECORDER: | PHYLLIS NOONAN AND SINEAD FULLAM |
| DATE: | 20 JULY 2005 |
| PHOTO REFERENCE: | F29 |
| LOCATION/MAP REF: | D1 F29 |

| | |
|---|---|
| GRAVEYARD NAME: | **ST. MARY'S ABBEY OLD GRAVEYARD** |
| GRAVEYARD CODE: | D1 |
| COUNTY: | MEATH |
| MEMORIAL NUMBER: | L1 |
| ERECTED BY: | CATHERINE WALL |
| ORIENTATION: | EAST |
| NUMBER OF COMPONENTS: | 3 |
| NUMBER OF INSCRIBED FACES: | 1 |
| NUMBER OF PEOPLE COMMEMORATED: | 1 |
| MEMORIAL TYPE: | CELTIC CROSS |
| CONDITION OF MEMORIAL: | GOOD |
| CONDITION OF INSCRIPTION: | CLEAR |
| STONEMASON NAME: | J. GIBNEY DROGHEDA |
| TECHNIQUE OF INSCRIPTION: | INCISED |
| UNDERTAKER: | |
| STONE TOP: | ELABORATE CELTIC CROSS |
| GRAVE TYPE: | SINGLE |
| HEIGHT: | 235CM |
| WIDTH: | 77CM |
| THICKNESS: | 70CM |

| SURNAME: | CHRISTIAN | ADDRESS | DEATH | AGE |
|---|---|---|---|---|
| WALL | JOHN | | 01 OCT 1908 | 46 |

**INSCRIPTION:**
IN LOVING MEMORY
OF
JOHN WALL
WHO DIED OCT 1 1908 AGED 46 YEARS
R.I.P
ERECTED BY HIS WIFE CATHERINE WALL

**SYMBOLS:**
CELTIC CROSS 4 SYMBOLS ON EACH ARM
INTERTWINED IHS
SCROLLED MY JESUS MERCY INTERTWINED WITH IVY

| | |
|---|---|
| NAME OF RECORDER: | LIZ LYNCH |
| DATE: | 16 MAY 2006 |
| PHOTO REFERENCE: | L1 |
| LOCATION/MAP REF: | D1 L1 |

| | |
|---|---|
| GRAVEYARD NAME: | **ST. MARY'S ABBEY OLD GRAVEYARD** |
| GRAVEYARD CODE: | D1 |
| COUNTY: | MEATH |
| MEMORIAL NUMBER: | F16 |
| ERECTED BY: | RICHARD PRANT |
| ORIENTATION: | EAST |
| NUMBER OF COMPONENTS: | 1 |
| NUMBER OF INSCRIBED FACES: | 1 |
| NUMBER OF PEOPLE COMMEMORATED: | 3 |
| MEMORIAL TYPE: | HEADSTONE |
| CONDITION OF MEMORIAL: | SOUND IN PLACE |
| CONDITION OF INSCRIPTION: | MAINLY DECIPHERABLE |
| STONEMASON NAME: | |
| TECHNIQUE OF INSCRIPTION: | INCISED |
| UNDERTAKER: | |
| STONE TOP: | ROUND |
| GRAVE TYPE: | SINGLE |
| HEIGHT: | 87CM |
| WIDTH: | 55CM |
| THICKNESS: | 10CM |

| SURNAME: | CHRISTIAN | ADDRESS | DEATH | AGE |
|---|---|---|---|---|
| WALSH - PRANT | JANE | | 26 AUG 1760 | 50 |
| PRANT | FATHER | | 1770 | |
| | MOTHER | | 1770 | |

**INSCRIPTION:**
THIS STONE ED.
BY RICHARD PRANT
IN MEMORY OF HIS
FATHER AND MOTHER 1770
HERE LYETH THE BODY
OF JANE WALSH HIS WIF
WHO DIED AUGUS 26
1760 AGED 50 YEARS
GOD REST

**SYMBOLS:**
CROSS WITH IHS UNDER SCROLL
WITH HEART

| | |
|---|---|
| NAME OF RECORDER: | LIZ LYNCH AND JANET LEIGH |
| DATE: | 19 JULY 2005 |
| PHOTO REFERENCE: | F16 |
| LOCATION/MAP REF: | D1 F16 |

| | |
|---|---|
| GRAVEYARD NAME: | **ST. MARY'S ABBEY OLD GRAVEYARD** |
| GRAVEYARD CODE: | D1 |
| COUNTY: | MEATH |
| MEMORIAL NUMBER: | G3 |
| ERECTED BY: | NICHOLAS WALSH |
| ORIENTATION: | EAST |
| NUMBER OF COMPONENTS: | 1 |
| NUMBER OF INSCRIBED FACES: | 1 |
| NUMBER OF PEOPLE COMMEMORATED: | 1 |
| MEMORIAL TYPE: | LOW MONUMENT |
| CONDITION OF MEMORIAL: | SOUND IN PLACE |
| CONDITION OF INSCRIPTION: | GOOD |
| STONEMASON NAME: | |
| TECHNIQUE OF INSCRIPTION: | INCISED |
| UNDERTAKER: | |
| STONE TOP: | ROUND |
| GRAVE TYPE: | SINGLE |
| HEIGHT: | 120CM |
| WIDTH: | 78CM |
| THICKNESS: | NOT ACCESSIBLE LAID IN GROUND OF ABBEY |

| SURNAME: | CHRISTIAN | | DEATH | AGE |
|---|---|---|---|---|
| WALSH | NICHOLAS | DUBLIN LINEN DRAPER | 05 DEC 1768 | 66 |

**INSCRIPTION:**
1766 REQUIESCANT IN PACE THIS STONE AND BURIAL
PLACE BELONG TO NICHOLAS WALSH OF THE CITY OF DUBLIN
LINEN DRAPER AND HIS FAMILY IN THE BENEATH GROUND
LIETH THE BODY OF THE SAID NICHOLAS WALSH WHO DEPARTED
THIS LIFE THE 31TH DAY OF DESEMBER 1768 IN THE 66 YEAR
OF HIS AGE.

| | |
|---|---|
| NAME OF RECORDER: | JANET LEIGH AND PHYLLIS NOONAN |
| DATE: | 6 JUNE 2006 |
| PHOTO REFERENCE: | G3 |
| LOCATION/MAP REF: | D1 G3 |

| | |
|---|---|
| GRAVEYARD NAME: | **ST. MARY'S ABBEY OLD GRAVEYARD** |
| GRAVEYARD CODE: | D1 |
| COUNTY: | MEATH |
| MEMORIAL NUMBER: | G2 |
| ERECTED BY: | ST. GEORGE SMITH |
| ORIENTATION: | EAST |
| NUMBER OF COMPONENTS: | 1 |
| NUMBER OF INSCRIBED FACES: | 1 |
| NUMBER OF PEOPLE COMMEMORATED: | 1 |
| MEMORIAL TYPE: | LOW MONUMENT |
| CONDITION OF MEMORIAL: | SOUND IN PLACE |
| CONDITION OF INSCRIPTION: | CLEAR |
| STONEMASON NAME: | |
| TECHNIQUE OF INSCRIPTION: | INCISED |
| UNDERTAKER: | |
| STONE TOP: | |
| GRAVE TYPE: | SINGLE |
| HEIGHT: | 236CM |
| WIDTH: | 115CM |
| THICKNESS: | |

| SURNAME: | CHRISTIAN | ADDRESS | DEATH | AGE |
|---|---|---|---|---|
| WALSH | PATRICK | GALTRIM, CO. MEATH | APRIL 1838 | 75 |

**INSCRIPTION:**
ERECTED BY ST. GEORGE SMITH OF GREEN
HILL, COUNTY OF LOUTH ESQ, TO THE MEMORY
OF HIS MUCH RESPECTED TENANT MR. PATRICK WALSH
OF BRANGANSTOWN OF GALTRIM COUNTY OF
MEATH WHO DIED  RIL 1838 AGED 75 YEARS

**COMMENTS:**
THIS LOW MONUMENT IS DIVIDED BY A LARGE
HORIZONTAL STONE DEPICTING 2 BISHOPS

| | |
|---|---|
| NAME OF RECORDER: | PHYLLIS NOONE AND JANET LEIGH |
| DATE: | 21 JUNE 06 |
| PHOTO REF: | G2 |
| LOCATION/MAP REF: | D1 G2 |

| | |
|---|---|
| GRAVEYARD NAME: | **ST. MARY'S ABBEY OLD GRAVEYARD** |
| GRAVEYARD CODE: | D1 |
| COUNTY: | MEATH |
| MEMORIAL NUMBER: | D 20 |
| ERECTED BY: | LAURENCE WARREN |
| ORIENTATION: | EAST |
| NUMBER OF COMPONENTS: | 2 |
| NUMBER OF INSCRIBED FACES: | 1 |
| NUMBER OF PEOPLE COMMEMORATED: | 7 |
| MEMORIAL TYPE: | HEADSTONE |
| CONDITION OF MEMORIAL: | SOUND IN PLACE |
| CONDITION OF INSCRIPTION: | MAINLY DECIPHERABLE |
| STONEMASON NAME: | |
| TECHNIQUE OF INSCRIPTION: | INCISED |
| UNDERTAKER: | |
| STONE TOP: | ROUND |
| GRAVE TYPE: | TREBLE |
| HEIGHT: | 170CM |
| WIDTH: | 80CM |
| THICKNESS: | 12CM |

| SURNAME: | CHRISTIAN | ADDRESS | DEATH | AGE |
|---|---|---|---|---|
| WARREN | PATRICK | BELLEWSTOWN | 30 DEC 1821 | 56 |
| | JAMES | | 27 JAN 1831 | 64 |
| | PATRICK | | 18 MAR 1836 | 26 |
| | MARGARET | | 02 JUN 1871 | 92 |
| | SON | | | |

**INSCRIPTION:**
ERECTED
BY LAURENCE WARREN OF BELLEWS
TOWN IN MEMORY OF HIS UNCLE PATK
WARREN WHO DIED 30 DECR 1821
AGED 56 YEARS ALSO HIS FATHER
JAMES WARREN WHO DIED 27 JANY
1831 AGED 64 YRS AND HIS BROTHER
PATK WARREN WHO DIED 18TH MARCH
1836 AGED 26 YEARS ~~
ALSO OF HIS MOTHER MARGARET
WARREN WHO DIED 2ND JUNE 1871 AGED
92 YEARS
ALSO HIS SON DIED YOUNG
ALSO THE ABOVE LAURENCE WARREN
WHO DIED NOV 1894 ALSO HIS SON
JAMES WARREN WHO DIED MAY 24 1916
*MAY THEY REST IN PEACE AMEN*

**SYMBOLS:**
SCROLLED UNDER SUNBURST
CHALICE UNDER SCROLL
FLANKED BY SMALL CROSSES
GRADUATED PEDESTAL

**ORNAMENTS:**
IHS WITH CROSS IN SUN BURST WITH HEART
AND CHALICE

| | |
|---|---|
| NAME OF RECORDER: | PHYLLIS NOONAN |
| DATE: | 15 JULY 2007 |
| PHOTO REFERENCE: | D20 |
| LOCATION/MAP REF: | D1 D20 |

| | |
|---|---|
| GRAVEYARD NAME: | **ST. MARY'S ABBEY OLD GRAVEYARD** |
| GRAVEYARD CODE: | D1 |
| COUNTY: | MEATH |
| MEMORIAL NUMBER: | G18 |
| ERECTED BY: | JOHN WARREN |
| ORIENTATION: | EAST |
| NUMBER OF COMPONENTS: | 1 |
| NUMBER OF INSCRIBED FACES: | 1 |
| NUMBER OF PEOPLE COMMEMORATED: | 9 |
| MEMORIAL TYPE: | HEADSTONE |
| CONDITION OF MEMORIAL: | CLEAR |
| CONDITION OF INSCRIPTION: | CLEAR |
| STONEMASON NAME: | |
| TECHNIQUE OF INSCRIPTION: | INCISED |
| UNDERTAKER: | |
| STONE TOP: | SUNBURST DISK |
| GRAVE TYPE: | SINGLE |
| HEIGHT: | 162CM |
| WIDTH: | 90CM |
| THICKNESS: | 10CM |

| SURNAME: | CHRISTIAN | ADDRESS | DEATH | AGE |
|---|---|---|---|---|
| WARREN | RICHARD | | 21 AUG 1821 | |
| | MARY | | 1810 | |
| | JOSEPH | | 1849 | |
| | JOHN | | | |
| | CATHERINE | | | |
| | MICHAEL | | 28 MAY 1908 | |
| | MARY | | 04 APR 1922 | |
| | MICHAEL | | 03 AUG 1931 | 12 |
| | LILY | | 24 APR 1977 | |

**INSCRIPTION:**
ERECTED
BY JOHN WARREN, MOUNT HANOVER
TO THE MEMORY OF HIS BELOVED
FATHER RICHARD WARREN WHO
DEPARTED THIS LIFE 21 AUGUST 1821 AND
HIS MOTHER MARY WARREN WHO DIED
1810. AND ALSO HIS BROTHER JOSEPH
WARREN WHO DIED 1849.
ALSO THE ABOVE JOHN WARREN AND HIS WIFE
CATHERINE WARREN, ALSO HIS SON
MICHAEL WARREN WHO DIEDMAY28TH1908
ALSO HIS WIFE MARY WHO DIED APRIL 4TH1922
MICHAEL WARREN DIED AUG.3RD1931
AGED 12 YEARS
LILY WARREN DIED APRIL 26TH 1977.

MAY THEY REST IN PEACE AMEN

**SYMBOL:**
LONG CROSS TROUGH IHS IN SUNBURST
CHERUB EACH SIDE

| | |
|---|---|
| NAME OF RECORDER: | PHYLLIS NOONAN AND SINEAD FULLAM |
| DATE: | 01 JULY 2006 |
| PHOTO REFERENCE: | G18 |
| LOCATION/MAP REF: | D1 G18 |

| | |
|---|---|
| GRAVEYARD NAME: | **ST. MARY'S ABBEY OLD GRAVEYARD** |
| GRAVEYARD CODE: | D1 |
| COUNTY: | MEATH |
| MEMORIAL NUMBER: | J2 |
| ERECTED BY: | |
| ORIENTATION: | EAST |
| NUMBER OF COMPONENTS: | 1 |
| NUMBER OF INSCRIBED FACES: | 1 |
| NUMBER OF PEOPLE COMMEMORATED: | 1 |
| MEMORIAL TYPE: | HEADSTONE |
| CONDITION OF MEMORIAL: | SOUND IN PLACE |
| CONDITION OF INSCRIPTION: | MAINLY DECIPHERABLE |
| STONEMASON NAME: | |
| TECHNIQUE OF INSCRIPTION: | INCISED |
| UNDERTAKER: | |
| STONE TOP: | ROUND TOP |
| GRAVE TYPE: | SINGLE |
| HEIGHT: | 68CM |
| WIDTH: | 66CM |
| THICKNESS: | 05CM |

| SURNAME: | CHRISTIAN | ADDRESS | DEATH | AGE |
|---|---|---|---|---|
| WARREN | WILL | GARBALAUGH | 02 FEB 1734 | 60 |

**INSCRIPTION:**
WARREN OF GARBALAUGH
WHO DIED YE 2ND OF FEB
1734 AGED 60 YEARS

| | |
|---|---|
| NAME OF RECORDER: | JANET LEIGH |
| DATE: | 03 AUGUST 2005 |
| PHOTO REFERENCE: | J2 |
| LOCATION/MAP REF: | D1 J2 |

| | |
|---|---|
| GRAVEYARD NAME: | **ST. MARY'S ABBEY OLD GRAVEYARD** |
| GRAVEYARD CODE: | D1 |
| COUNTY: | MEATH |
| MEMORIAL NUMBER: | H17 |
| ERECTED BY: | |
| ORIENTATION: | EAST |
| NUMBER OF COMPONENTS: | 1 |
| NUMBER OF INSCRIBED FACES: | 1 |
| NUMBER OF PEOPLE COMMEMORATED: | 7 |
| MEMORIAL TYPE: | LOW MONUMENT |
| CONDITION OF MEMORIAL: | SOUND IN PLACE |
| CONDITION OF INSCRIPTION: | CLEAR |
| STONEMASON NAME: | |
| TECHNIQUE OF INSCRIPTION: | INCISED |
| UNDERTAKER: | |
| STONE TOP: | LOW MONUMENT |
| GRAVE TYPE: | SINGLE LOW MONUMENT |

| SURNAME: | CHRISTIAN | ADDRESS | DEATH | AGE |
|---|---|---|---|---|
| WARREN | JOHN GRANT | | 08 SEPT 1809 | 76 |
| WARREN | MARY | DRUMMIN | 12 MAR 1810 | |
| WARREN | ROBERT | DRUMMIN | 01 JUN 1830 | 59 |
| WARREN | HENRY | | 05 APR 1869 | 60 |
| WARREN | ANNA EMMELINE | | 01 JUN 1879 | 16 |
| WARREN | HENRY | | 21 FEB 1886 | 24 |
| WARREN | ANNE | | 11 DEC 1905 | 69 |

**INSCRIPTION:**
HERE LYETH THE BODY OF JOHN GRANT
WARREN WHO DEPARTED THIS LIFE THE
8TH DAY OF JULY 1809 AGED 76 YEARS
ALSO
MARY WIFE OF ROBERT WARREN, DRUMMIN
DULEEK WHO DIED MARCH 12TH 1810
ALSO
THE ABOVE NAMED ROBERT WARREN SON
OF JOHN GRANT WARREN WHO DIED JUNE
1830 AGED 59 YEARS
ALSO
HENRY WARREN SON OF ROBERT WARREN
WHO DIED APRIL 5TH 1869 AGED 60 YEARS.
HERE ALSO
ARE INTERRED THE REMAINS OF ANNIE EMMELINE
SECOND DAUGHTER OF HENRY WARREN WHO
FELL ASLEEP JUNE 18TH 1879 AGED 16 YEARS
AND OF
HENRY AE WARREN, L.R.C.S.I.
SECOND SON OF THE ABOVE HENRY WARREN
WHO DIED 21ST FEBRUARY 1886
IN HIS 24TH YEAR, ALSO OF ANNA WIDOW OF THE
ABOVE
NAMED HENRY WARREN WHO DIED ON THE
11TH DECEMBER 1903 AGED 69 YEARS

| | |
|---|---|
| NAME OF RECORDER: | JANET LEIGH |
| DATE: | 6 JUNE 2006 |
| PHOTO REFERENCE: | H17 |
| LOCATION/MAP REF: | D1 H17 |

*East Facing Side*
**Sacred**
**to the Memory of**
**Thomas Warren**
**Leggan Hall**
**Died Decr 10**[TH]
**1826**
**And His Wife Ellen**
**Died Jan 3**[RD] **1846**
**Also Their Son**
**William Warren**
**Died June 11 1874**

*South Facing Side*
**Catherine**
**Warren**
**Died Augst 28**[TH]
**1848**
**Jane Warren**
**Died Jan 3**[RD]
**1866**
**Ellen**
**Warren**
**Died Dec 18**
**1880**

*North Facing Side*
**Nicholas**
**Warren**
**Died March 25**[TH]
**1837**
**Thomas**
**Warren**
**Died Jan 14**
**1861**

| | |
|---|---|
| Graveyard Name: | **St. Mary's Abbey Old Graveyard** |
| Graveyard Code: | D1 |
| County: | Meath |
| Memorial Number: | J3 |
| Erected By: | |
| Orientation: | East |
| Number of Components: | 3 |
| Number of Inscribed Faces: | 3 |
| Number of People Commemorated: | 3 |
| Memorial Type: | Pedestal with Celtic Cross displaced |
| Condition of Memorial: | Sound In Place |
| Condition of Inscription: | Mainly decipherable |
| Stonemason Name: | Warde of Dublin |
| Technique of inscription: | Incised |
| Undertaker: | |
| Stone Top: | Celtic Cross displaced |
| Grave Type: | Single |

| Surname: | Christian | Address | Death | Age |
|---|---|---|---|---|
| *East Facing Side* | | | | |
| Warren | Thomas | Leggan Hall | 10 Dec 1826 | |
| | Ellen | | 03 Jan 1846 | |
| | William | Son | 11 June 1874 | |
| *South Facing Side* | | | | |
| **Surname:** | **Christian** | | **Death** | **Age** |
| Warren | Catherine | | 28 Aug 1848 | |
| | Jane | | 03 Jan 1866 | |
| | Ellen | | 18 Dec 1880 | |
| *North Facing Side* | | | | |
| **Surname:** | **Christian** | | **Death** | **Age** |
| Warren | Nicholas | | 25 Mar 1837 | |
| | Thomas | | 14 Jan 1861 | |

| | |
|---|---|
| Name of Recorder: | Janet Leigh, Liz Lynch and Phyllis Noonan |
| Date: | 3 August 2005 |
| Photo Reference: | **J3 A East     J3 B North          J3 C South** |
| Location/Map Ref: | D1 J3 |

| | |
|---|---|
| GRAVEYARD NAME: | **ST. MARY'S ABBEY OLD GRAVEYARD** |
| GRAVEYARD CODE: | D1 |
| COUNTY: | MEATH |
| MEMORIAL NUMBER: | J27 |
| ERECTED BY: | |
| ORIENTATION: | EAST |
| NUMBER OF COMPONENTS: | 1 |
| NUMBER OF INSCRIBED FACES: | 1 |
| NUMBER OF PEOPLE COMMEMORATED: | 1 |
| MEMORIAL TYPE: | HEADSTONE |
| CONDITION OF MEMORIAL: | SOUND IN PLACE |
| CONDITION OF INSCRIPTION: | MAINLY DECIPHERABLE |
| STONEMASON NAME: | |
| TECHNIQUE OF INSCRIPTION: | INCISED |
| UNDERTAKER: | |
| STONE TOP: | ROUND |
| GRAVE TYPE: | SINGLE |
| HEIGHT: | 196CM |
| WIDTH: | 92CM |
| THICKNESS: | 11CM |

| SURNAME: | CHRISTIAN | ADDRESS | DEATH | AGE |
|---|---|---|---|---|
| WATSON | WILLIAM | LISMULLEN | 28 JAN 1848 | 49 |

**INSCRIPTION:**
SACRED
ERECTED TO THE MEMORY OF
WILLIAM WATSON
OF
LISMULLEN
WHO DEPD. THIS LIFE 28TH JANUARY
1848 AGED 49 YEARS

**SYMBOLS:**
SUNBURST RAYS WITHIN CIRCLE
FLOWERS EACH SIDE

| | |
|---|---|
| NAME OF RECORDER: | LIZ LYNCH AND PHYLLIS NOONAN |
| DATE: | 16 AUG 2005 |
| PHOTO REFERENCE: | J27 |
| LOCATION/MAP REF: | D1 J27 |

| | |
|---|---|
| GRAVEYARD NAME: | **ST. MARY'S ABBEY OLD GRAVEYARD** |
| GRAVEYARD CODE: | D1 |
| COUNTY: | MEATH |
| MEMORIAL NUMBER: | L32 |
| ERECTED BY: | PETER WHEARTY |
| ORIENTATION: | EAST |
| NUMBER OF COMPONENTS: | 3 |
| NUMBER OF INSCRIBED FACES: | 1 |
| NUMBER OF PEOPLE COMMEMORATED: | 7 |
| MEMORIAL TYPE: | FLEUR DE LIS CROSS ON HEADSTONE |
| CONDITION OF MEMORIAL: | SOUND IN PLACE |
| CONDITION OF INSCRIPTION: | CLEAR |
| STONEMASON NAME: | |
| TECHNIQUE OF INSCRIPTION: | INCISED |
| UNDERTAKER: | |
| STONE TOP: | FLEUR DE LIS |
| GRAVE TYPE: | DOUBLE |
| HEIGHT: | 188CM |
| WIDTH: | 53CM |
| THICKNESS: | 08CM |

| SURNAME: | CHRISTIAN | ADDRESS | DEATH | AGE |
|---|---|---|---|---|
| WHEARTY | JOHN | | 12 MAR 1880 | |
| | MARY | | 21 MAY 1910 | |
| | MARGARET | | 10 FEB 1881 | |
| | MARY ANN | | 11 APR 1918 | |
| | JOHN | | 26 JAN 1926 | |
| | MARY | | 07 MAY 1950 | |
| | PETER | | 1956 | |

**INSCRIPTION:**
ERECTED BY
PETER WHEARTY
IN MEMORY OF HIS FATHER
JOHN
WHO DIED 12TH MARCH 1880
HIS MOTHER MARY
DIED 21ST MAY 1910
HIS SISTERS DIED
MARGARET 10TH FEB 1881
MARY ANN 11TH APRIL 1918
HIS BROTHER JOHN
DIED 26TH JAN 1926
AND HIS WIFE MARY DIED
7TH MAY 1950
PETER DIED 1956
R.I.P.

**SYMBOLS:**
FLEUR DE LIS CROSS INTERWOVEN IHS
SURROUNDED BY VINE LEAVES

| | |
|---|---|
| NAME OF RECORDER: | LIZ LYNCH AND PHYLLIS NOONAN |
| DATE: | 30 MAY 2006 |
| PHOTO REFERENCE: | L32 |
| LOCATION/MAP REF: | D1 L32 |

| | |
|---|---|
| GRAVEYARD NAME: | **ST. MARY'S ABBEY OLD GRAVEYARD** |
| GRAVEYARD CODE: | D1 |
| COUNTY: | MEATH |
| MEMORIAL NUMBER: | C6 |
| ERECTED BY: | THEIR CHILDREN |
| ORIENTATION: | EAST |
| NUMBER OF COMPONENTS: | 2 |
| NUMBER OF INSCRIBED FACES: | 1 |
| NUMBER OF PEOPLE COMMEMORATED: | 2 |
| MEMORIAL TYPE: | HEADSTONE |
| CONDITION OF MEMORIAL: | SOUND IN PLACE |
| CONDITION OF INSCRIPTION: | CLEAR |
| STONEMASON NAME: | REID PLATTEN |
| TECHNIQUE OF INSCRIPTION: | INCISED |
| UNDERTAKER: | |
| STONE TOP: | MISSING |
| GRAVE TYPE: | SINGLE |
| HEIGHT: | 146CM |
| WIDTH: | 68CM |
| THICKNESS: | 10CM |

| SURNAME: | CHRISTIAN | ADDRESS | DEATH | AGE |
|---|---|---|---|---|
| WHITE | JAMES | DULEEK | 03 DEC 1887 | |
| WHITE | ANNE | | 03 APR 1913 | |

**INSCRIPTION:**
IN LOVING MEMORY
OF JAMES WHITE DULEEK WHO DIED
DEC.3RD 1887, ALSO HIS WIFE
ANNE
WHO DIED APRIL 30TH 1913

ERECTED BY THEIR CHILDREN
R.I.P

**SYMBOLS:**
IHS

| | |
|---|---|
| NAME OF RECORDER: | PHYLLIS NOONAN AND JIM ORTEN |
| DATE: | 6 JULY 2005 |
| PHOTO REFERENCE: | C6 |
| LOCATION/MAP REF: | D1 C6 |

| | |
|---|---|
| GRAVEYARD NAME: | **ST. MARY'S ABBEY OLD GRAVEYARD** |
| GRAVEYARD CODE: | D1 |
| COUNTY: | MEATH |
| MEMORIAL NUMBER: | L3 |
| ERECTED BY: | |
| ORIENTATION: | EAST |
| NUMBER OF COMPONENTS: | 2 |
| NUMBER OF INSCRIBED FACES: | 1 |
| NUMBER OF PEOPLE COMMEMORATED: | 2 |
| MEMORIAL TYPE: | HEADSTONE |
| CONDITION OF MEMORIAL: | SOUND IN PLACE |
| CONDITION OF INSCRIPTION: | LEGIBLE |
| STONEMASON NAME: | |
| TECHNIQUE OF INSCRIPTION: | INCISED |
| UNDERTAKER: | |
| STONE TOP: | ROUND |
| GRAVE TYPE: | SINGLE |
| HEIGHT: | 94CM |
| WIDTH: | 64CM |
| THICKNESS: | 10CM |

| SURNAME: | CHRISTIAN | ADDRESS | DEATH | AGE |
|---|---|---|---|---|
| WHITE | JULIA | MAIN STREET | 20 FEB 1921 | |
| | JAMES | | 31 JAN 1946 | |

**INSCRIPTION:**
IN LOVING MEMORY
OF
JULIA WHITE
MAIN STREET
WHO DIED 20 FEB 1921
AND HER HUSBAND
JAMES
WHO DIED 31 JAN 1946

**SYMBOLS:**
CROSS ON TOP OF HEADSTONE

| | |
|---|---|
| NAME OF RECORDER: | LIZ LYNCH |
| DATE: | 16 MAY 2006 |
| PHOTO REFERENCE: | L3 |
| LOCATION/MAP REF: | D1 L3 |

| | |
|---|---|
| GRAVEYARD NAME: | **ST. MARY'S ABBEY OLD GRAVEYARD** |
| GRAVEYARD CODE: | D1 |
| COUNTY: | MEATH |
| MEMORIAL NUMBER: | L25 |
| ERECTED BY: | RICHARD WHITE RATHMULLEN |
| ORIENTATION: | EAST |
| NUMBER OF COMPONENTS: | 1 |
| NUMBER OF INSCRIBED FACES: | 1 |
| NUMBER OF PEOPLE COMMEMORATED: | 4 |
| MEMORIAL TYPE: | HEADSTONE |
| CONDITION OF MEMORIAL: | SOUND IN PLACE |
| CONDITION OF INSCRIPTION: | MAINLY DECIPHERABLE |
| STONEMASON NAME: | |
| TECHNIQUE OF INSCRIPTION: | INCISED |
| UNDERTAKER: | |
| STONE TOP: | DISK WITH SUNBURST |
| GRAVE TYPE: | DOUBLE |
| HEIGHT: | 162CM |
| WIDTH: | 66CM |
| THICKNESS: | 13CM |

| SURNAME: | CHRISTIAN | ADRESS | DEATH | AGE |
|---|---|---|---|---|
| WHITE | LUKE | | 24 DEC 1820 | 67 |
| | MARGARET | | 01 NOV 1819 | 66 |
| | PATRICK | | 01 NOV 1834 | 55 |
| | RICHARD | RATHMULLEN | 23 AUG 1845 | 50 |

**INSCRIPTION:**
ERECTED BY RICHARD WHITE OF RATHMULLEN IN MEMORY OF HIS FATHER LUKE WHITE WHO DIED THE 24TH DECR 1820 AGED 67 YEARS ALSO HIS MOTHER MARGT WHITE WHO DIED THE 1ST NOVR 1819 AGED 66 YRS AND OF HIS BROTHER PATK WHITE WHO DIED THE 1ST NOVR 1834 AGED 55 YEARS. AND OF THE ABOVE RICHARD WHITE WHO DIED THE 23RD OF AUGST 1845 AGED 50 YEARS
REQUIESCANT IN PACE AMEN

**SYMBOLS:**
DISK ON TOP WITH IHS CROSS AND HEART IN SUNBURST HORIZONTAL CROSS WITH LAMB AND CHERUBS ON EACH SIDE

| | |
|---|---|
| NAME OF RECORDER: | BEN RYAN AND LIZ LYNCH |
| DATE: | 25 MAY 2006 |
| PHOTO REFERENCE: | L25 |
| LOCATION/MAP REF: | D1 L25 |

| | |
|---|---|
| GRAVEYARD NAME: | **ST. MARY'S ABBEY OLD GRAVEYARD** |
| GRAVEYARD CODE: | D1 |
| COUNTY: | MEATH |
| MEMORIAL NUMBER: | G19 |
| ERECTED BY: | |
| ORIENTATION: | EAST |
| NUMBER OF COMPONENTS: | VANDALISED AND REMOVED FROM ABBEY |
| NUMBER OF INSCRIBED FACES: | VANDALISED AND REMOVED FROM ABBEY |
| NUMBER OF PEOPLE COMMEMORATED: | 6 |
| MEMORIAL TYPE: | |
| CONDITION OF MEMORIAL: | VANDALISED AND REMOVED FROM ABBEY |
| CONDITION OF INSCRIPTION: | VANDALISED AND REMOVED FROM ABBEY |

| SURNAME: | CHRISTIAN | ADDRESS | DEATH | AGE |
|---|---|---|---|---|
| WHYTE | WILLIAM | DULEEK | 06 JUNE 1924 | 72 YEARS |
| | JAMES | FATHER | 18 JULY 1882 | |
| | MARY | MOTHER | 28 SEPT 1898 | |
| | MARY | DAUGHTER | 18 MAY 1919 | 22 YEARS |
| | MARGARET | DAUGHTER | 10 DECEMBER 1919 | 20 YEARS |
| | ELIZABETH | WIFE | 19 NOVEMBER 1944 | |

*HEADSTONE VANDALISED AND REMOVED FROM ABBEY*
*INFORMATION OBTAINED BY MARY MATTHEWS*
*MEMBER OF WILLIAM WHYTE'S FAMILY*

**INSCRIPTION:**

MY DEAREST HUSBAND WILLIAM WHYTE DULEEK
DIED 6TH JUNE 1924 AGED 72 YEARS ALSO OF HIS
FATHER JAMES DIED 18TH JULY 1882 AND HIS
MOTHER MARY DIED 28TH SEPTEMBER 1898 ALSO OF HIS
DAUGHTER MARY WHYTE DIED 18TH MAY 1919 AGED 22
YEARS AND HIS DAUGHTER MARGARET WHYTE
DIED 10TH DECEMBER 1919 AGED 20 YEARS ALSO HIS
WIFE ELIZABETH WHYTE DIED 19TH NOVEMBER 1944

| | |
|---|---|
| NAME OF RECORDER: | JANET LEIGH AND MARY MATTHEWS FAMILY OF WILLIAM WHYTE |
| DATE: | 19 AUGUST 2013 |
| PHOTO REFERENCE: | VANDALISED AND REMOVED FROM ABBEY |
| LOCATION/MAP REF: | D1 G19 |

| | |
|---|---|
| GRAVEYARD NAME: | **ST. MARY'S ABBEY OLD GRAVEYARD** |
| GRAVEYARD CODE: | D1 |
| COUNTY: | MEATH |
| MEMORIAL NUMBER: | D13 |
| ERECTED BY: | FAMILY |
| ORIENTATION: | EAST |
| NUMBER OF COMPONENTS: | 3 |
| NUMBER OF INSCRIBED FACES: | 1 |
| NUMBER OF PEOPLE COMMEMORATED: | FAMILY CLARKE - WOODS |
| MEMORIAL TYPE: | HEADSTONE |
| CONDITION OF MEMORIAL: | SOUND IN PLACE |
| CONDITION OF INSCRIPTION: | CLEAR |
| STONEMASON NAME: | |
| TECHNIQUE OF INSCRIPTION: | INCISED AND PAINTED |
| UNDERTAKER: | |
| STONE TOP: | ROUND ARCH |
| GRAVE TYPE: | MULTIPLE |
| HEIGHT: | 130CM |
| WIDTH: | 82CM |
| THICKNESS: | 21CM |

| SURNAME: | CHRISTIAN | ADDRESS | DEATH | AGE |
|---|---|---|---|---|
| CLARKE | OWEN | | 05 SEPT 1883 | 60 |
| | ANNE | | | |
| | PATRICK | | 1910 | |
| | JOHN | | 1910 | |
| WOODS | MARY | | 28 JAN 1943 | 84 |
| WOODS | PATRICK | | 16 OCT 1932 | 74 |
| | LEO | | 24 SEPT 1902 | 7 |
| | ALFRED | | 18 MAR 1919 | 20 |
| | EDWARD | | 29 DEC 1937 | 53 |
| | FRANCIS | | 27 APR 1946 | 54 |

**INSCRIPTION:**

CLARKE – WOODS
TO THE MEMORY OF
THE CLARKE FAMILY INTERRED HERE SINCE THE 1600'S
OWEN CLARKE
DIED 5TH DEC 1883 AGED 60 YEARS
HIS WIFE ANNE NEE BELLEW
PRE-DECEASED HIM
THEIR SONS PATRICK AND JOHN
DIED CIRCA 1910
THEIR DAUGHTER MARY
DIED 28TH JANUARY 1943 AGED 84 YEARS
HER HUSBAND PATRICK WOODS
DIED 16TH OCTOBER 1932 AGED 74 YEARS
THEIR SONS LEO WOODS
DIED 24TH SEPTEMBER 1902 AGED 7 YEARS
ALFRED WOODS
DIED 18TH MARCH 1919 AGED 20 YEARS
EDWARD WOODS
DIED 29TH DECEMBER 1937 AGED 53 YEARS
FRANCIS WOODS
DIED 27TH APRIL 1946 AGED 54 YEARS REST IN PEACE

**SYMBOL:**

INSET CELTIC CROSS

| | |
|---|---|
| NAME OF RECORDER: | PHYLLIS NOONAN |
| DATE: | JUNE 24 2013 |
| PHOTO REFERENCE: | D 13 |
| LOCATION/MAP REF: | D1 D 13 |

| | |
|---|---|
| GRAVEYARD NAME: | **ST. MARY'S ABBEY OLD GRAVEYARD** |
| GRAVEYARD CODE: | D1 |
| COUNTY: | MEATH |
| MEMORIAL NUMBER: | K36 |
| ERECTED BY: | JOHN WOODS 20/04/02 |
| ORIENTATION: | EAST |
| NUMBER OF COMPONENTS: | 2 |
| NUMBER OF INSCRIBED FACES: | 1 |
| NUMBER OF PEOPLE COMMEMORATED: | 2 |
| MEMORIAL TYPE: | HEADSTONE FLEUR DE LIS CROSS |
| CONDITION OF MEMORIAL: | SOUND IN PLACE |
| CONDITION OF INSCRIPTION: | MAINLY DECIPHERABLE |
| STONEMASON NAME: | F. WHYTE CHORD ROAD DROGHEDA |
| TECHNIQUE OF INSCRIPTION: | LEAD RELIEF LETTERING |
| UNDERTAKER: | |
| STONE TOP: | FLEUR DE LIS CROSS |
| GRAVE TYPE: | SINGLE |
| HEIGHT: | 240CM |
| WIDTH: | 82CM |
| THICKNESS: | 09CM |

| SURNAME: | CHRISTIAN | ADDRESS | DEATH | AGE |
|---|---|---|---|---|
| WOODS | ELLEN | | 27 FEB 1901 | 27 |
| | ELIZABETH | | | 3 DAYS |

**INSCRIPTION:**
ERECTED
BY
JOHN WOODS 20/04/02
IN MEMORY OF HIS WIFE
ELLEN
WHO DIED 27TH FEB 1901 AGED 27 YEARS
ALSO THEIR DAUGHTER
ELIZABETH
AGED 3 DAYS
RIP

**SYMBOLS:**
LAMB ON CROSS IN RESTING POSE

| | |
|---|---|
| NAME OF RECORDER: | JANET LEIGH AND PHYLLIS NOONAN |
| DATE: | 22 APRIL 2006 |
| PHOTO REFERENCE: | K36 |
| LOCATION/MAP REF: | D1 K36 |

| | |
|---|---|
| GRAVEYARD NAME: | **ST. MARY'S ABBEY OLD GRAVEYARD** |
| GRAVEYARD CODE: | D1 |
| COUNTY: | MEATH |
| MEMORIAL NUMBER: | K7 |
| ERECTED BY: | |
| ORIENTATION: | EAST |
| NUMBER OF COMPONENTS: | 3 |
| NUMBER OF INSCRIBED FACES: | 1 |
| NUMBER OF PEOPLE COMMEMORATED: | 1 |
| MEMORIAL TYPE: | CROSS STEPPED |
| CONDITION OF MEMORIAL: | SOUND IN PLACE |
| CONDITION OF INSCRIPTION: | CLEAR |
| STONEMASON NAME: | |
| TECHNIQUE OF INSCRIPTION: | INCISED |
| UNDERTAKER: | |
| STONE TOP: | CROSS |
| GRAVE TYPE: | TREBLE |
| HEIGHT: | 105CM |
| WIDTH: | 60CM |
| THICKNESS: | 10CM |

| SURNAME: | CHRISTIAN | ADDRESS | DEATH | AGE |
|---|---|---|---|---|
| WOODS | MICHAEL | KINGSGATE DULEEK | 24 JAN 1940 | 17 |

**INSCRIPTION:**
IN LOVING MEMORY
OF
MICHAEL WOODS
KINGSGATE DULEEK
WHO DIED ON THE 24TH JANUARY 1940
AGED 17 YEARS
R.I.P

**SYMBOLS:**
SACRED HEART WITH CROSS
IN FLAMES SURROUNDED BY
VINE LEAVES

| | |
|---|---|
| NAME OF RECORDER: | PHYLLIS NOONAN |
| DATE: | 10 SEPT 2005 |
| PHOTO REFERENCE: | K7 |
| LOCATION/MAP REF: | D1 K7 |

## Inscriptions from the Wall Plaques which were in St. Kienan's Church of Ireland Church in Duleek

*Regrettably these plaques do not exist as they have been destroyed during the 1960's and 1970's through repeated acts of vandalism.*

### Faulkner:
To the glory of God and in loving Memory of Matilda, widow of Francis Faulkner Esq. and Daughter of the late Henry Smith Esq. of Annesbrook who died April 3rd 1907 aged 82.
The souls of the righteous are in The Lord God.

### Hammick:
To the glory of God and in loving memory of St. Vincent Charles Farrant Hammick "Derry" only son of Rev. Charles H. W. And Alice Hammick and in recognition of his glad response to his country's call this tablet is erected by his friends in the parish and neighbourhood Born 2nd November 1895 and Died 6th March 1917. He being made perfect in a short time fulfilled in a long time. Wis iv, 13.

### Law:
To the Glory of God and in sacred and loving memory of Michael Augustine Fitzgerald Law J.P. of Beamond who died on 3rd February 1917 aged 56 years. God is my strength and power and He maketh my way perfect. ii Samuel xxii, 3.

### Law:
To the Glory of God and in sacred and loving memory of Mary Melville Law of Queensboro who died 15th August 1939 aged 76 years. Be thou faithful unto death and I will give thee a crown of life

### Smith:
Sacred to the memory of Major Michael Edward Smith of Annesbrook Co Meath of the 64th 78th and 40th Regiments  Son of Henry Jeremiah Smith Esq. J.P. D.L. of Annesbrook, Born November 8th 1814 Died May 19th 1903. Him that cometh to Me I will in my wise cast out. St John iii, 37. This tablet is erected by his widow and his niece Mrs. Walker of Tykillen Co Wexford.

### Smith:
Sacred to the memory of Frederick Augustus Smith late of 1st Royals and 43rd... Died July 23 1887 (1867?) Coates Dublin.

### Smith:
Delectat Amor Patriae
Sacred to the memory St. George W. Smith J.P. of Duleek House 4th Son of Henry J. Smith J.P. and D.L. of Annesbrook. Died 27th Jan 1892 In his tone was the law of kindness Prov. xxxi, 26. This tablet is erected as a token of appreciation by his surviving relatives. Coates Dublin.

### Smith:
To the glory of God and to the beloved memory of Stephen Henry Smith of Annesbrook in this Parish who entered into rest February 5th 1890... This tablet is erected by his wife in the sure and certain hope of his resurrection to eternal life. The God so loved the world that He gave His only begotten son that whosoever believeth in Him should not perish but have everlasting life. Into thine hand I commit my spirit Thou hast redeemed me Lord God of Truth Psalm xxxi, v5.

### Smith:
Sacred to the memory of Elizabeth Smith of Besboro Co Meath and widow of Henry J. Smith Esq. J.P. & D.L. of Annesbrook in the same county died March 5th 1872. This token of respect to the memory of their beloved mother is erected by her surviving sons and daughters.
Delectat Amor Patriae.

**Smith:**
This monument is erected by an effected and bereaved wife and mother to the memory of a beloved husband daughter and son whose mortal remains lie in a vault in the adjoining church yard. Henry Jeremiah Smith of Anns Brook who departed this life February 15th 1857 aged 73 years. Elizabeth his eldest daughter who departed this life September 13th 1822 aged 12 years and Kynaston Walter his youngest son who was accidently shot August 27th 1857 aged 25 years. Also in the same vault lies the mortal remains of Emily their fifth daughter who departed this life April 13th 1864 to the inexpressible grief of her afflicted mother. Delectat Amor Patrae

**Smith:**
In loving memory of Fitzhenry Smith J.P. late of Annesbrook Co Meath who died Sept 6 1930 aged 70. Erected by his loving wife and nephew. An honourable and upright man his soul is at peace.

**Smith:**
In loving memory of Georgina Barbara dearly beloved wife of Lt. Col. Stephen Henry Smith J.P. of Annes Brook and only daughter of Lt. Col. Raymond Pelly CB. 16th Lancers Died June 19th 1854. Come to me all that labour and are heavy laden and I will give you rest.

**Smith:**
The stained glass window in the church bore the following: Sacred to the memory of Stephen Henry Smith this window is erected by his wife and children.

**Warren:**
Dextra Adomini Me Exaltibit
In memory of Henry Warren of Drummin County Meath who died on the 5th April 1869 This tablet has been erected by his bereaved and sorrowing widow. Let me die the death of the righteous and let my last end me like this.

*Members of The Smith Family were interred in the Smith Tomb within the railings to the north of St. Kienan's. The last member of the family to be interred there was Col. Ernest St. George Smith who died in 1946.*

These inscriptions have been recorded by The Late Enda O'Boyle.